12/99

Frank Blair

Frank Blair
Lincoln's
Conservative

William E. Parrish

University of Missouri Press
COLUMBIA AND LONDON

Library of Congress Cataloging-in-Publication Data

Parrish, William Earl, 1931–
 Frank Blair : Lincoln's conservative / William E. Parrish.
  p. cm.—(The Missouri biography series)
 Includes bibliographical references and index.
 ISBN 0-8262-1156-9 (alk. paper)
 1. Blair, Frank P. (Frank Preston), 1821–1875. 2. Legislators—
United States—Biography. 3. United States. Congress. House—
Biography. 4. Generals—United States—Biography. 5. United
States—Politics and government—1861–1865. 6. Missouri—Biography.
7. Missouri—Politics and government—To 1865. 8. Missouri—
Politics and government—1865–1950. I. Title. II. Series.
E467.1.B63P37 1998
973.5'092—dc21
[B]   97-32334
                       CIP

Designer: Mindy Shouse
Typesetter: BOOKCOMP
Printer and Binder: Thomson-Shore, Inc.
Typefaces: Palatino, Willow, Shelley

For HelenSue

Contents

Preface

"Every man in Missouri, whatever his politics, his religion, or his beverage . . . has reason to believe that a braver man than Frank Blair never set foot on Missouri soil or any other soil. No one hereabouts whose hope of eternal life was not well assured, would ever think of drawing a knife or pistol on Frank." Thus spoke an anonymous Missourian to a reporter for the *New York Sun*.[1] Many others echoed similar sentiments during Blair's lifetime as his reputation for fearlessness, both on the political stump and on the battlefield, became legendary.

The youngest son of a politically active family, possibly the nineteenth-century equivalent of the twentieth century's Kennedys, Frank Blair became steeped in politics under the influence of his father, Francis Preston Blair, editor of Andrew Jackson's *Washington Globe* and adviser to presidents from Jackson through Andrew Johnson. A close-knit family, the Blairs maintained a strong personal loyalty to one another throughout their long careers. The senior Blair always harbored the hope that his youngest son might one day become president of the United States and, with Frank's older brother Montgomery, served as his constant mentor and adviser. Frank's sister, Elizabeth Blair Lee ("Lizzie"), adored him and served as his personal unpaid secretary during the various stages of his Washington career. Whether at their country estate in nearby Silver Spring, Maryland, or at their homes across from the White House on Pennsylvania Avenue, Blair family conferences, when Frank was in Washington, could last far into the night and, when apart, produced a voluminous correspondence.

1. Cited in James Neal Primm, *Lion of the Valley: St. Louis, Missouri*, 271–72.

Politics dominated Frank Blair's life, to the dismay of his beloved wife, Apolline, or Apo, who would have much preferred that he pursue the more structured life of a well-to-do lawyer, like his brother Montgomery, keeping politics secondary. But Frank thrived on the give-and-take of the political arena and found himself much in demand as a speaker on both the Missouri and the national circuits. He fought hard for his political causes with a vehemence and a vituperation that few could match. Indeed, one critic remarked that when the Blairs went after someone, they went in for the kill. That was certainly true of Frank. Whether striking a blow for Free-Soilism against what he perceived to be a slave-power conspiracy against free-white labor or in support of conservative fears of a Radical-black alliance after the war, he attacked without quarter. Underlying all his arguments was a strong racial prejudice, typical of most white Americans in the nineteenth century. While maintaining a strong bond with personal and family slaves, Frank, like the others in his family, believed in the racial inferiority of blacks and other nonwhite groups. He consistently worked for the separation of the races through colonization and for the subservience of nonwhites when separation proved unfeasible.

When the Civil War came, Frank Blair carried the same vigor that had characterized his political contests into the military. He played a major role in saving Missouri for the Union, only to have many of his supporters desert him when he failed to move as rapidly and as far on the issue of emancipation as they. Fighting for the Union, he served with valor, not only on the home front in 1861 but throughout the subsequent Vicksburg, Chattanooga, Atlanta, and Carolina campaigns in Sherman's army. He gained the admiration of the officers with whom he served as well as the soldiers who served under him. Simultaneously, Frank did yeoman's work in Congress as chairman of the House Military Affairs Committee at the outset of the war and as Lincoln's conservative counterbalance to the growing power of the Radical Republicans. He defended the president and his policies faithfully and passionately, bringing down the scorn of the Radicals, eventually at the cost of his congressional seat.

In driving himself so incessantly, Frank jeopardized his health. Plagued by neuralgia and painful headaches throughout his life, he seldom allowed these illnesses to interfere with his political activity. His bad habits as an inveterate smoker and a heavy drinker eventually combined with his physical weaknesses to bring him down at the height of his career.

Still, for a period of some twenty-five years in the middle of the nineteenth century, Frank Blair proved himself a major force on the American political scene. George G. Vest, one of his contemporaries, said of Blair, "He had more personal friends than any public man who ever lived in Missouri. He had bitter enemies like all men of positive convictions will always have, but even his enemies never doubted Frank Blair's sincerity, and always respected him because he was open, fair, fearless, honest, and true to his convictions."[2] Strongly loved and admired by many and just as strongly reviled and hated by others, he cut a wide swath across the political firmament, leaving his personal imprint large. As a member of an influential family, a major Civil War politician and soldier, and an exemplar of Reconstruction racism, Frank Blair influenced his times with a driving forcefulness that made him the Missouri legend he became in his own time and that he remains to this day.

2. Cited in H. H. Crittenden, *The Crittenden Memoirs*, 72.

Acknowledgments

This study has benefited from the assistance of numerous individuals and institutions. My friend William E. Foley first suggested that I undertake Frank Blair's story for the Missouri Biography Series several years ago, and he has continued to be supportive as I have pursued this intriguing individual through numerous libraries and volumes. Charles D. Lowery, my department head at Mississippi State University, has supplied research travel money on several occasions. A summer travel grant from the National Endowment for the Humanities made possible a trip to the Princeton University Libraries for my research in the Blair-Lee Family Papers, which are housed in their Manuscripts Division of the Department of Rare Books and Special Collections. There Ann Van Arsdale and Judith Golden were particularly helpful in assisting me with that voluminous collection. My research in this collection was helped further when Virginia Jeans Laas graciously loaned me her microfilm copies of Elizabeth Blair Lee's Civil War correspondence with her husband. I have also appreciated her observations about the Blair family as we have discussed them and her sharing of several pictures. The Princeton University Libraries have kindly given permission for the quotations from the Blair-Lee Family Papers that are found in this study. I am also grateful to the Cincinnati Historical Society, Cincinnati Museum Center, for permission to quote from the "Reminiscences of Andrew Hickenlooper," which are part of the Papers of Andrew Hickenlooper and His Family, MssfH628, in the society.

My colleague John F. Marszalek has been a valuable ally through this campaign, providing me with keen insights into the Blair-Sherman relationship as well as the Civil War in general, assisting me with the various Sherman papers that might be relevant, and reading several portions of the manuscript.

Michael B. Ballard and Christopher Phillips also generously read parts of the manuscript in preparation. My graduate assistants, James Stennett, David Gleeson, and Salli Vargis, and my work-study students, Carl Williams and Bill Randall, provided much needed assistance with tedious library work and other chores. Peggy Bonner and Lonna Reineke, the Mississippi State University History Department secretaries, have made life pleasant by their cheerful assistance in the mundane routine of office management. Martha Irby, Susan Hall, and Lenna Bishop of the Inter-library Loan Service of Mitchell Memorial Library at Mississippi State always handled my requests pleasantly and efficiently.

Richard J. Sommers provided very helpful direction at the U.S. Army Military History Institute, Carlisle Barracks, Pennsylvania, as did Terrence J. Winschel at the Vicksburg National Military Park. Mary Williams was my gracious hostess for a tour of Blair House, Washington, D.C., and provided me with valuable information concerning the Blair family, both past and present. Steven Rowan kindly lent me a manuscript copy of his edited memoir of Henry Boernstein. Richard Reed provided information on the identity and career of Laura C. Redden (Howard Glyndon). Connie Cartledge assisted me on several occasions with my research at the Library of Congress. The staffs of the State Historical Society of Missouri, Columbia, and the Missouri Historical Society, St. Louis, have been generous with their time and assistance as I have visited their archives.

My greatest debt is to my wife, HelenSue, who has been kind enough to share me with Frank Blair these last few years. Her patience and understanding through this project have been invaluable.

Abbreviations

The following list identifies those elements that appear frequently in the notes.

Apo   Apolline Alexander Blair
BLC   Blair Papers, Library of Congress
BLPLC   Breckinridge Long Papers, Library of Congress
B-LP   Blair-Lee Family Papers, Princeton University Libraries
CG   *Congressional Globe*
EB   Eliza Blair
EBL   Elizabeth Blair Lee
FB   Frank Blair Jr.
FPB   Francis Preston Blair Sr.
MB   Montgomery Blair
MHS   Missouri Historical Society, St. Louis
OR   *War of the Rebellion: A Compilation of the Official Records of the Union and Confederate Armies*
SPL   Samuel Phillips Lee
VNMP   Vicksburg National Military Park

Frank Blair

1

Formative Years

Francis Preston Blair Jr., known throughout his lifetime to family and friends simply as Frank, possessed a distinguished heritage. The first American Blairs, Samuel and John, had come to this country in the mid-eighteenth century. Of Scotch-Irish descent, they were Presbyterian ministers, whose evangelistic preaching could stir great zeal. John, the younger of the two brothers, became professor of theology and vice president of Princeton. His son James, Frank's grandfather, one of twelve children, opted for the law at Princeton and then located at Abingdon, Virginia, where he married Elizabeth Smith, descendant of yet another distinguished Scotch-Irish family, the Prestons. There Frank's father, Francis Preston Blair Sr., was born in 1791.

Apparently not too enamored of his choice of professions, James Blair had only minimal success at the practice of law, serving one term in the Virginia assembly. When his wife's parents relocated to Kentucky in the early 1790s, James followed with his wife and young son. Hardly more successful at his legal practice in their new home, James nevertheless managed to maintain a social position befitting his background, though he experienced mounting debts and endless lawsuits. Still, he helped compile the first edition of the laws of Kentucky and served for many years as the state's attorney general.[1]

1. Elbert B. Smith, *Francis Preston Blair*, 1–3. Through various marriages of his grandmother's sisters, Frank would be related to two other notable pioneer Kentucky families, the Marshalls and the Madisons. These connections would prove valuable to him at different times in his career (William E. Smith, *The Francis Preston Blair Family in Politics*, 1:15–16).

On his mother's side Frank had a unique heritage. His great-grandfather, Christopher Gist, had built a strong military reputation in the French and Indian War, as had his son Nathaniel, who also fought with distinction in the American Revolution. Following that conflict, Nathaniel, at the age of fifty, established himself as a Virginia planter with some seventeen thousand acres in land grants from his military service. He married Judith Cary Bell and produced a large family, of which Frank's mother, Eliza Violet, born in 1794, was the seventh child. Nathaniel Gist had roamed extensively throughout the uncharted west and decided to relocate to frontier Kentucky shortly after Eliza's birth. He acquired a four-thousand-acre estate in Bourbon County, which he called "Canewood," only to die three years later. Eliza remembered Canewood, her childhood home, with great fondness. After ten years of widowhood, Judith Gist remarried in 1807. She and her two youngest daughters, Eliza, age 14, and Maria, age 11, accompanied her new husband, General Charles Scott, another Revolutionary hero, to Frankfort the following year when he became Kentucky's governor. There Eliza met and fell in love with the gangling young son of the state's attorney general. Gaining his affections away from Maria, who also felt a romantic attachment, Eliza married Francis Preston Blair in the Kentucky governor's mansion on July 21, 1812. It turned out to be an ideal marriage, destined to last sixty-four years.[2]

Shortly thereafter, Preston Blair began an eighteen-year stint as circuit-court clerk of Franklin County. He also engaged in extensive land speculation and eventually benefited from his wife's share of the Gist family inheritance. He developed a strong friendship with Amos Kendall, publisher of the local *Argus of Western America*, and contributed numerous editorial pieces for that paper. Over nine years Preston and Eliza had six children, two of whom died in infancy. The survivors were Montgomery, born in 1813, Elizabeth (known as "Lizzie") in 1818, James in 1819, and Frank. During her last confinement Eliza was persuaded to spend the winter in nearby Lexington with her sister, Maria, who had recently married Benjamin Gratz, a member of a prominent Philadelphia Jewish family. It was in the Gratz home that Frank first saw the light of day on February 19, 1821. In the years that followed it would become a second home to him as the bond between the Blairs and the Gratzes remained extremely close, even following his Aunt Maria's death in 1841.[3]

2. E. B. Smith, *Francis Preston Blair*, 6–8; Apo, "Reminiscences," 1, BLPLC.
3. E. B. Smith, *Francis Preston Blair*, 8–10, 18–19; Apo, "Reminiscences," 1–2, BLPLC; William Vincent Byars, *B. and M. Gratz, Merchants in Philadelphia, 1754–1798: Papers of Interest to Their Posterity and the Posterity of Their Associates*, 262–63.

Eliza and her new son soon returned to Frankfort, where, over the next decade, Frank grew up in a home filled with warmth and love. Few parents ever doted more on their children than Preston and Eliza Blair; and, in return, their children held them in the highest esteem as long as they lived. As the youngest and his father's namesake, Frank especially found favor and became generally overindulged, growing up as a normal, healthy child with few cares. Frank and his brother Jim, only two years his senior, were constant playmates who loved to hunt, fish, and swim in the nearby woods and streams. One elderly neighbor later recalled watching "Jim & Frank, little barefooted fellows, sometimes hatless and coatless with a pr suspenders between them swimming boats in the gutters, in the pouring rain." His Aunt Maria observed that Frank, in particular, had a somewhat wild streak with a strong sense of adventure.[4]

Little is known of Frank's earliest schooling, but it would presumably have been that of a typical frontier settlement with a schoolmaster offering a subscription school for a few months a year. When Frank was nine years old, all this changed as his father's fortunes took a significant turn. Preston's old friend Amos Kendall had gone to Washington as a prominent adviser to President Andrew Jackson, and in 1830 he persuaded Jackson that the elder Blair was just the man to edit a new administration newspaper, the *Globe*. Once in the national capital, Blair quickly became a Jackson favorite, establishing a close friendship that would have a strong effect on young Frank's subsequent political development.[5]

The Blairs journeyed to Washington in November 1830, leaving Jim and Frank behind with their father's sister Susanna, "Aunt Trigg," to finish their school year. The following spring the two boys made the long journey north alone by boat and stage. The final stagecoach deposited them in Baltimore where they discovered oranges, figs, and other kinds of fruit for the first time. Their father would later regale family and friends with the story of how they marched around the streets of Baltimore all day indulging their newfound tastes.[6]

Frank and Jim were placed in a select school kept by a Yale scholar remembered only as Mr. Smith. Their classmates included Martin and Smith Van Buren, the sons of Jackson's secretary of state. The Blair–Van Buren family

4. Apo, "Reminiscences," 2, BLPLC; Mrs. Benjamin Gratz to Violet Blair, June 10, 1830, BLC.
5. Amos Kendall, *Autobiography*, 370–74.
6. Apo, "Reminiscences," 2–3, BLPLC.

connection remained close throughout their lifetimes. Another classmate, William V. N. Bay, later a prominent St. Louis attorney and for a brief time Frank's law partner, recalled that "Mr. Smith was a strict disciplinarian, and often said Frank gave him more trouble than all the other scholars combined; not that he was deficient in his studies, but he was prone to mischief, and often disposed to *forget* the rules of the school." This bent toward mischievousness would be a marked tendency throughout Frank's educational career. In one incident, Frank outsmarted himself. He and Jim had joined a group of boys on the Chesapeake and Ohio Canal near Washington for a swim. Emerging from the water, Frank picked up the presumed shirt of one of the younger boys and taunted him by throwing it in the canal, only to realize too late that the shirt was his own. Bay remembered Frank as a great favorite with his classmates, however, particularly excelling in athletics. Although he made good marks, "out of school [he] was rarely seen with a book in his hands."[7]

Frank and Jim later attended Ben Hallowell's boarding school in Montgomery County, Maryland. Hallowell's method of discipline was to stand errant scholars against the wall; and Frank later recalled with laughter his teacher's remonstrance, "I will not strike thee, Francis, but I will hold thee exceeding uneasy." At the time, however, he informed his father that if his teacher had ever struck him, he would have returned the blow. Frank's older brother Montgomery noted that Frank and Jim "still seem to be the ruling spirits among a gang of boys, not all the most genteel youths I ever saw." They had also become quite proficient with guns. Each had his own rifle and shotgun, and Frank "already brags of having beaten father & Jim" in some matches. Montgomery reported that he was prudent enough to decline his younger brother's challenge.[8]

Frank was obviously his father's favorite, and the elder Blair early began to harbor political ambitions for his youngest son. Frank loved to spend his spare time at the *Globe* office, where he held long conversations with his father, sometimes causing other callers to cool their heels. The Blairs were frequent guests at the White House; and the president often relaxed from the cares of office in the Blair home. The Blairs spent several summers with Jackson at a resort known as the Rip Raps near Fortress Monroe, Virginia; and Frank,

7. W. V. N. Bay, *Reminiscences of the Bench and Bar of Missouri*, 394; *New York Times*, July 10, 1868. The younger boy in the canal incident later served as a delegate to the Democratic National Convention that nominated Blair for the vice presidency.

8. Apo, "Reminiscences," 3, BLPLC; FB to FPB, February 14, 1835, B-LP; MB to EBL, April 23, 1835, BLC.

here and elsewhere, quickly came under the influence of the president and became his lifelong admirer.[9]

In the fall of 1835, Preston Blair sent Frank to a college preparatory school at Ellington, Connecticut. The younger Blair stayed there for two years. He wrote his sister that, although he liked it very much, he found Ellington to be "a Whig town," where he felt "smothered with Whiggery." He urged Lizzie to have their father send him the *Globe* to counteract the opposition. In a lighter vein, he also asked her to inform all his girlfriends in Washington that "I have not seen one Yankee girl that will hold a light to one of them." Frequent letters followed with numerous other derogatory comparisons of his "Yankee" neighbors to his southern friends. Still, Frank admitted, in mid-December 1836, that these New Englanders had taken good care of him when he had caught a terrible cold, although their care could not replace lying on a sofa with his head in his mother's lap.[10]

Frank now had his mind set on attending Yale in the fall and sought his father's permission to visit New Haven over Christmas. He regretted that he could not come home for president-elect Martin Van Buren's inauguration in March 1837 but feared that such a trip would cost him too much time away from his studies and hurt his chances for Yale. The fall of 1837 found Frank in New Haven, terribly homesick, even though he described the city as "a very pleasant place." He urged Lizzie to have brother Jim come up for a visit. Jim had received an appointment as a naval midshipman in 1835 and was between voyages at the time. Frank reported that he was having a hard time adjusting to the cold weather in New Haven and doubted that he would stay another winter there. He also fretted about the lack of letters from his father and, in typical student fashion, complained that the elder Blair had not sent him the money he had requested earlier.[11]

As it turned out, Frank did not even make it through the first winter at Yale. His father was informed in early January 1838 that the faculty had decided

9. Apo, "Reminiscences," 3–4, BLPLC; FB to Violet Blair, May 22, 1835, MB to FPB, January 8, 1842, B-LP; FPB to Mrs. Benjamin Gratz, August 29, 1831, in Byars, *B. and M. Gratz*, 300; W. E. Smith, *Blair Family in Politics*, 1:102; Wheaton J. Lane and Nelson R. Burr, "Francis Preston Blair, Jr.: Border Statesman," in Willard Thorp, ed., *The Lives of Eighteen from Princeton*, 246; FPB to Andrew Jackson, August 26, 1841, BLC; FPB to Andrew Jackson, August 4, 1844, in *Correspondence of Andrew Jackson*, 6:311.

10. FB to EBL, August 31, September 7, 15, 20, 22, November 17, 22, December 2, 16, 1836, BLC.

11. FB to EBL, December 16, 1836, October 9, 25, November 23, 1837, BLC; FB to EBL, October 18, November 5, 1837, B-LP; Apo, "Reminiscences," 3–4, BLPLC.

that Frank "would probably do better at some other institution than here." He had complained earlier to his sister that he could enjoy Yale better "if the faculty didn't glance at me every time I pass one of them as if they thought I was a little bashful about showing the Silver." Frank's tendency toward mischievousness, which had plagued him at every school he attended, had obviously caught up with him at Yale, for his letter of dismissal indicated that the faculty believed he had run with the wrong crowd and on one occasion even broken the windows of one of the college tutors.[12]

Undaunted, Frank transferred to the University of North Carolina, beginning classes there at the end of January. He wrote his father: "I feel more comfortable here than amongst the Yankees, not being obliged to look upon every other fellow student as a tale bearer, and although I don't boast of being too good yet I am confident that not even the best like to have their conduct too tightly scrutinized." He promised to rid himself of the vice of gambling, one of the apparent reasons for his downfall at Yale, and hoped that his father would think better of him "when my next report comes home."[13]

After a few weeks Frank noted that "the fellows here are not such book worms as those at Yale." They liked to spend their spare time hunting, "and I am very much afraid lest the Silver Diana will seduce me to partake of her rural sports, of which it is needless to tell you I am a passionate admirer." He also indicated that he had acquired another habit, one that would plague him throughout his life, and one that, family members later believed, contributed to his final illness and demise. He had just chewed a big piece off the end of his "segar" and experienced bad heartburn as a result. Still, he assured Lizzie, "if I can only study a little and go regular to prayers and recitations I can very easily stand first or second."[14]

When the university made its first report to his father the following April, Frank appeared to be having difficulty in maintaining his resolve; he had been absent from chapel fourteen times and recitations thirteen times. Nevertheless, the faculty reported him doing "quite well in languages and mathematics." He continued his erring ways when he returned to Chapel Hill in the fall of 1838, however, and by early November his father received a letter suggesting that he be withdrawn from yet another university. Frank assured the faculty of better behavior and expressed his desire to graduate, so, by

12. J. L. Kingsley to FPB, January 5, 1838, FB to EBL, October 18, 1837, B-LP.
13. FB to FPB, January 27, 1838, BLC.
14. FB to EBL, February 14, 1838, BLC.

mutual agreement, they allowed him to remain. The university bursar made the point with the senior Blair that parental pressure from home would be desirable: "Advice on the score of industry, punctuality and good morals coming from that quarter is the more effective as it is free from all suspicion of interested motives."[15]

Although his father did lecture him about his seeming lack of seriousness and undue extravagance, Frank remained unrepentant. By the end of January 1839 he had tired of Chapel Hill and wrote Lizzie that he wished "to leave after this session and go to Princeton." His mischievousness remained unchecked. He had just had all his red hair shaved and was now wearing a wig to the amusement of his companions. In March, he wanted to go to dancing school as "I am told that the cultivation of this art . . . lends grace to one's every movement & confidence to his step." Once he had acquired this new ability, he expected his sister to introduce him to "some wealthy heiress" of her acquaintance.[16]

The one thing Frank took seriously was politics. Indeed, it would become the consuming passion of his life. He constantly remonstrated with Lizzie to have their father send him Democratic papers so that he could keep himself properly informed on political happenings. The campus had a reputation for being under the sway of Presbyterianism and the newly emerging Whig party, which dominated North Carolina politics. The university's new president, David Lowry Swain, was trying to erase that image, but Frank felt uncomfortable within the constraints of both compulsory chapel and a strong Whig bias among faculty and students. It showed in his behavior. A final report from the university in June indicated that Frank had thirty-seven absences from chapel and thirty-two from recitations over the past three months. He had been recorded three times for "irreverence at prayers" and fifteen times for other improprieties. The faculty had voted not to readmit him the following fall.[17]

In the fall of 1839, Frank migrated to Princeton. The university had gone through some difficult times financially during the 1830s but had established a strong reputation for research as well as teaching, attracting an excellent faculty, including Joseph Henry, one of the foremost scientists of the era. A

15. University of North Carolina Report, May 2, 1838, E. Mitchell to FPB, November 13, 1838, May 30, 1839, B-LP.
16. FB to EBL, January 2, 31, March (n.d.), 1839, BLC.
17. William D. Snider, *Light on the Hill: A History of the University of North Carolina at Chapel Hill*, 54–59; FB to EBL, January 31, 1839, BLC; E. Mitchell to FPB, May 30, 1839, University of North Carolina Report, June 20, 1839, FB to EBL, June (n.d.), 1839, B-LP.

scholar of renown, Henry also took a keen interest in his students, who gave him their "unbounded admiration and affection."[18]

Things began well for Frank at Princeton. He wrote Lizzie shortly after his arrival: "Tell father & mother that I am better pleased with Princeton than I expected. I have regular hours allotted, I might say consecrated, for I permit nothing to interrupt me." He finally seemed to have adopted a calm acceptance of the need to complete his education. As had been true at his two previous universities, Frank found the Princeton curriculum heavily weighted in the classical mode with an admixture of mathematics, surveying, history, philosophy, "evidences of Christianity," and natural theology. He and the other students faced a tiresome round of classroom recitations, essays, and examinations, which the faculty did little to enliven.[19]

To help relieve the tedium, Frank joined the Cliosophic Literary Society, asking Lizzie to have his father send a small sum for his initiation fee. He assumed his father would approve of the move, for "he knows the nature of such associations tends to improve a person in writing, speaking & debating." One of his professors had told him that the societies "were better suited to expand & develop the faculties of the mind & to fit a person for the everyday business of the world than even our textbooks." In the Cliosophic Society, Frank had the opportunity to begin honing the oratorical skills that he would later put to good use in endless political campaigns.[20]

Frank's biggest complaints as the year wore on were the cold weather, to which he never adjusted, and the constant interruptions of his fellow students. He was living in Nassau Hall but wanted to move off campus his senior year, not only to get away from intrusive fellow students, but also because he had been warned that in summer the college dormitories swarmed with bedbugs, of which he had a deadly fear.[21]

At the end of his first year at Princeton, Frank wrote his father that "altho I cannot boast of having conducted myself this session in a faultless manner I yet hope it will be considered an improvement on my past life and an earnest of better things." He continued in a retrospective vein a few weeks later in a letter to his sister, "The phantoms of my neglected studies rise up in judgement

18. Thomas Jefferson Wertenbaker, *Princeton: 1746–1896*, 218–23.

19. FB to EBL, October 15, December 20, 1839, BLC; FB to EBL, November 10, 1839, B-LP; Wertenbaker, *Princeton: 1746–1896*, 234.

20. FB to EBL, January 5, 1840, B-LP. Frank was later suspended from the Cliosophic Society for nonpayment of fines (Lane and Burr, "Francis Preston Blair, Jr.," in Thorp, *Lives of Eighteen*, 247).

21. FB to EBL, November 26, 1839, B-LP; Wertenbaker, *Princeton: 1746–1896*, 250–52.

against me." He compared himself unfavorably to his brother Jim, "our noble little sailor," and was particularly concerned that he had disappointed his parents.[22]

That fall Lizzie, never strong physically, had to seek a warmer climate for the winter. She went to Havana with her father as companion. On the day they left New York, November 5, 1840, Frank wrote her from Washington, where he was temporarily keeping his mother company. Apologizing for not having written earlier, he explained that Eliza had kept him busy "writing *squibs* for the Globe." He reported that he did not find editorializing to his taste—a sentiment that would not prove lasting.[23]

As he entered his final semester at Princeton, Frank informed Lizzie that the place had become "dull & dreary." While preparing his senior speech, he began "to experience those peculiar & disagreeable sensations incident to such a momentous occasion." He was distracted by the thought of a grand ball on the evening following his required oration, "where I expect to figure in the mazy dance," as well as by "an 'angels visit' from a beautiful young lady with fair locks and large blue eyes with whom I have well nigh fallen in love." The girl must have turned out to be a passing fancy because, by July 1841, he again complained that "Princeton is devilish dull" and that he could hardly wait for graduation in a few weeks. After final examinations in August, he stood forty-first in a class of fifty-six.[24]

Princeton turned out to be a little more lively than anticipated. On the eve of commencement, Frank got into a barroom brawl and severely wounded another student. By his own account, he had come to the aid of a freshman, who was being mistreated by one of the seniors, and thus acted in self-defense. The faculty refused him graduation, however, but later relented at the instigation of Professor Henry. As a result, his diploma was dated 1842—one year later.[25]

Frank spent the next two winters in Lexington, living with relatives and studying law at Transylvania University, probably the foremost law school in the west, where his brother Montgomery had studied earlier. From every indication Frank took his studies seriously as he began to settle down to

22. FB to FPB, July 8, 1840, FB to EBL, July 23, 1840, B-LP.

23. FB to EBL, November 5, 1840, B-LP.

24. FB to EBL, February 12, July 22, 1841, BLC; Varnum Lansing Collins [Registrar] to Walter H. Ryle, October 28, 1924, B-LP.

25. E. B. Smith, *Francis Preston Blair*, 96; Apo, "Reminiscences," 6, BLPLC; Lane and Burr, "Francis Preston Blair, Jr.," in Thorp, *Lives of Eighteen*, 247; Collins to Ryle, October 28, 1924, B-LP.

the realization of preparing for a career. He enjoyed being back in the region where he had grown up. He would return there frequently throughout his life and always with great fondness. He wrote his father on December 13, 1841, "I have visited all my old haunts and stomping grounds & have given the light of my countenance and the weight of my company to each and everyone of our relatives." He also reported hearing lots of tales of his father's youth from his aunts.[26]

During that first winter of 1841–1842 Frank began to notice one cousin in particular, Agatha Apolline Alexander, or "Apo." She was the daughter of Andrew Jonathan and Mira Madison Alexander, who maintained a family estate at Sherwood in nearby Woodford County. Descended on her father's side from a distinguished English family, she had close family connections with the Biddles of Philadelphia, where she spent one or two winters attending school. Her maternal grandfather, George Madison, was the nephew of President James Madison and had served briefly as governor of Kentucky before his untimely death in 1816. Preston Blair's favorite uncle, Madison, had helped finance the elder Blair's own Transylvania education; the two families had always been close. Still, Apo was a young girl of thirteen, and how soon Frank's notice of her began to ripen into love is unclear.[27]

In April 1842, Frank went to St. Louis to spend the summer with his brother Montgomery, who had gone there five years earlier to practice law under the watchful eye of Sen. Thomas Hart Benton, an old family friend and distant relative. Montgomery had since established his own practice and had only recently been appointed U.S. attorney for Missouri. In addition, he had just been elected mayor of St. Louis. He welcomed the opportunity to provide his younger brother with additional legal training while also having his services to assist with a busy schedule. Within a week of Frank's arrival, Montgomery wrote their father: "[Frank] is exceedingly able indeed and I think will make a pretty keen lawyer some day. He is ambitious too & when he gets the wise

26. W. W. Jennings, *Transylvania: Pioneer University of the West*, 256; FB to FPB, December 13, 1841, MB to FPB, January 8, 1842, FB to EBL, February 20, 1842, B-LP; FB to Apo, May 9, 1842, BLPLC; Apo, "Reminiscences," 7, BLPLC.

27. Apo, "Reminiscences," 8, BLPLC; James Harrison Wilson, *The Life and Services of Brevet Brigadier-General Andrew Jonathan Alexander, United States Army*, 12–15; William E. Railey, *History of Woodford County (Kentucky)*, 207–8; Benjamin Gratz to Henry Howard Gratz, October 28, 1844, in Byars, *B. and M. Gratz;* Apo to Apolline Hankey, n.d., FB to Apo, May 9, 1842, Mira Alexander to Apolline Hankey, July 8, October 25, 1845, BLPLC; E. B. Smith, *Francis Preston Blair*, 6, 189.

edge off his conceit of which he has a little too much for the West he will be a proper fellow enough."[28]

Frank quickly became enamored of St. Louis. He told his sister that he found St. Louis "quite a Kentucky colony" and that he was "content to make this my 'continuing city.' " His newfound home was rapidly changing, however. St. Louis's population in 1840 had stood at 16,439, but it was growing. Its population doubled by 1845 and then doubled again by the end of the decade as its boundaries grew from .75 to 4.78 square miles. St. Louis found itself increasingly attracting large numbers of Irish and German immigrants. The latter would become particularly important for Frank's later political career. As he took his first walks around the city, the would-be lawyer-politician could scarcely imagine the opportunities that St. Louis would provide him over the next thirty years.[29]

Arriving simultaneously, and possibly on the same boat from Louisville, came Charles Dickens on his first American tour. St. Louis welcomed him lavishly. During his brief visit, he made an overnight trip to the Illinois prairie; and Frank went along as part of his escort, obviously thrilled at the opportunity of "eating and riding & talking with Mr. Boz," who shared many of young Blair's emerging democratic feelings. No doubt, Frank also attended the soiree honoring the distinguished writer at the Planters House on the evening of their return.[30]

Frank attended many parties, as he wrote Apo, but planned to avoid the "Presbyterian kind," as they had no dancing, only eating; and he grew tired of "praising each lady's faded bouquet without having the privilege of touching a fair lady's hand." Not overly impressed with the women of St. Louis anyway, he told his sister that they were "not the prettiest I ever blinked at," an unfortunate "calamity." Their only redeeming quality was that "most of them have money which I admit makes some amends for the lack of good looks."[31]

Frank quickly settled down to his legal studies. St. Louis proved unbearably hot in the summer; and many of its citizens, if they could afford to do so,

28. W. E. Smith, *Blair Family in Politics*, 1:158, 380–81; MB to FPB, April 22, 1842, B-LP.

29. Primm, *Lion of the Valley*, 147–54; FB to EBL, April 10, 1842, BLC; FB to EBL, May 9, 1842, B-LP.

30. FB to EBL, May 9, 1842, B-LP; FB to Apo, May 9, 1842, BLPLC; *St. Louis Missouri Republican*, April 11, 12, 13, and 15, 1842. For Dickens's reaction to his St. Louis visit, see Charles Dickens, *American Notes and Pictures from Italy*, 172–86, and *The Letters of Charles Dickens*, 3:192–202.

31. FB to Apo, May 9, 1842, BLPLC; FB to EBL, May 9, 1842, B-LP.

fled to the outlying areas, putting aside any socializing until cooler weather returned. By mid-June Frank had determined to return to Lexington and Transylvania in the fall to continue his legal studies. "This thing of serving an apprenticeship in a law shop is all *humbug*," he informed Lizzie. "There are always sufficient persons in the office to divert a person's attention from reading . . . and Gum [Montgomery] has enough trouble with his own cases, without talking them over to me." He begged his sister to come west for a visit to break the monotony and urged her to bring brother Jim along.[32]

The only respite Frank had that summer was an excursion up the Illinois River in late July to help escort former president Martin Van Buren down to St. Louis. Frank reported, in his own inimicable way, that Van Buren, an old family friend, "was quite affable to me & took such condescending notice of me, that I began to suspect that he foresaw with his usual sagacity that I fully intended to be a great man in these 'diggins' & wished to conciliate and preengage my support."[33] Little did he realize at the time that one of his first major political battles in Missouri would entail Van Buren's Free-Soil campaign for the presidency four years later.

When Frank returned to Lexington that fall he stayed at the home of his uncle Benjamin Gratz. His Aunt Maria had died in November 1841, leaving her husband with four sons: Michael Barnard, age twenty-one; Henry Howard, age nineteen; Hyman Cecil, age sixteen; and Cary Gist, age fourteen. In July 1843, Benjamin Gratz married Anna Maria Shelby, a young widow with a twelve-year-old son, Joseph Orville ("Jo"). The careers of Howard and Cary Gratz and Jo Shelby would become strongly intertwined with that of Blair after all of them moved to Missouri. Frank wrote his sister in December, "Tell the old gentleman I am studying very hard & if he believes you, his faith is very great & needs only a little cultivation to entitle him to the rewards." He reported that he had been trying to save some money but to no effect.[34]

Lizzie had her own problems that winter as her four-year courtship with Samuel Phillips Lee, a grandson of Richard Henry Lee, was coming to a head. She had met Phil, as he became known within the family, through her brother Jim, with whom he shared a naval career. Theirs had been love

32. J. D. Blair to FPB, June 2, 1842, BLC; FB to EBL, June 9, July 29, 1842, B-LP.
33. FB to EBL, July 29, 1842, B-LP.
34. Apo, "Reminiscences," 7–8, BLPLC; Byars, *B. and M. Gratz*, 263; FB to EBL, December 14, 1842, B-LP; Daniel O'Flaherty, *General Jo Shelby: Undefeated Rebel*, 13–17. Anna Maria Shelby was the daughter of an older sister of Eliza Gist Blair, Frank's mother, and Maria Gist Gratz, Ben's first wife. E. B. Smith, *Francis Preston Blair*, 190; Robert Peter, *History of Fayette County, Kentucky*, 612–14.

at first sight, and Phil quickly proposed. Preston Blair opposed a marriage, as did Montgomery, because of Lizzie's fragile health and an overly paternal attitude. The courtship continued over the next few years on those occasions when Lieutenant Lee had leave from his naval duty. One of the reasons for Lizzie's winter in Havana in 1840–1841, in addition to the concern for her health, had been her father's hope that this would cool the romance. It did not, and finally, in late 1841, Lizzie agreed to spring nuptials if Montgomery would give his approval. Although her older brother declined to do so, Frank gave her his full support. Theirs had been a close relationship throughout, as evidenced by the many letters between them during his school years and after. At last, Lizzie and Phil were married on April 27, 1843, at the Blair home, opposite the White House, much to Frank's delight and with him present. It turned out to be a loving and lasting marriage.[35]

Frank spent that spring in Washington, helping out at the *Globe* while his father took a vacation pilgrimage to visit Montgomery and family in St. Louis and Andrew Jackson at the Hermitage. The young maverick outfitted himself in style, purchasing a green coat with brass buttons and a pair of very loud plaid trousers, which remained a family joke for years thereafter. Displaying his emerging Jacksonian tendencies, he wrote some fiery editorials in his father's absence, beginning with a scathing attack on President Tyler and his "mongrel cabinet." "Finding themselves rejected by the Democrats with contempt and scorn," he raged, "they have boldly come forth and denounced the old Jeffersonian phalanx of Democracy as radicals and ultras, turned them out of house and home, and taken possession of their name and honors." Frank took particular delight in attacking Secy. of State Daniel Webster, who had just completed a significant treaty with England resolving the long-standing issue of the boundary between Maine and Canada, among others. In a fit of Anglophobia, Frank argued that Webster had given away too much territory in the bargain, having been duped by the map chicanery of the British.[36]

Not content with attacks on the secretary, who resigned shortly after the treaty's ratification, Frank struck at young Fletcher Webster, whose father had appointed him secretary of the China legation as one of his last acts.

35. FB to EBL, February 8, 26, 1843, B-LP; E. B. Smith, *Francis Preston Blair*, 143–44, 179–81; Dudley Taylor Cornish and Virginia Jeans Laas, *Lincoln's Lee: The Life of Samuel Phillips Lee, United States Navy, 1812–1897*, 51–52.
36. E. B. Smith, *Francis Preston Blair*, 147–48; *Washington Globe*, April 20, 27, May 12, 23, 1843.

Frank denounced the younger Webster, who had a rakish reputation, as a "frequenter of 'hells'" with "nothing but his father's vices to qualify him for this situation." Continuing in a vitriolic vein that would become a later characteristic of many of his political speeches, Frank asserted, "Young as he is, he has given a deeper dye of infamy to his already polluted name." Webster's friends threatened a lawsuit but backed off when Frank asserted that the *Globe* had more than enough evidence to support its charges. Years later he boasted to Apo that the New York papers, apparently not aware of his father's absence, reported that "Old Blair had either gone mad or was in his dotage."[37]

Frank's brief stint at the *Globe* completed his educational experiences. His work there revealed something that would dominate his political rhetoric in later life: a tendency toward unrestrained vituperation against those with whom he disagreed. His strong ties to his family and their close associations with Andrew Jackson had made him into a thoroughgoing Jacksonian. He was now ready to join Montgomery in the practice of law in St. Louis. He had taken a keen interest in politics, wherever he had been, from boarding school and Yale in Connecticut to North Carolina to Princeton to Kentucky and St. Louis, and it would quickly become evident that he had politics in his blood. This would lure him into one political fray after another to the neglect of his legal practice and bring both high moments of exhilaration and low valleys of despair. Through it all, however, Frank would maintain an unburnished zeal and a certain equanimity of purpose for the causes in which he believed.

37. *Washington Globe*, May 1, 4, 18, 1843; Apo, "Reminiscences," 6–7, BLPLC.

2

New Mexico Adventure

On October 8, 1843, Montgomery Blair wrote his father that he hoped Frank would soon make his appearance in St. Louis. He had erected a new office building at the corner of Third and Chestnut, only a block from the courthouse, keeping his office on the second floor while renting out the ground quarters. He had a room on the third floor waiting for Frank. The younger Blair had spent the last part of the summer into early fall in his beloved Kentucky, visiting relatives with particular attention being paid to his cousin Apolline Alexander. Upon his arrival in St. Louis, Frank found Montgomery and his wife, Caroline, excitedly expecting their second child. The joy turned to sadness, however, when Caroline died in childbirth on January 11, 1844. The infant daughter survived but tragically succumbed to whooping cough later that summer.[1]

Montgomery quickly resigned as district attorney and relinquished his private law practice to accept a judgeship on the court of common pleas. He told his father that he felt the need to get away from the conflicts of the bar in the wake of his wife's death. Frank now found himself in the unenviable position of having to establish his own legal practice and reputation apart from his brother. He wrote his sister, "I have stepped into his shoes, they are considerably oversized for me, but who knows but one day I may dance in them." He probably could not have managed had he not been able to draw on his father for loans during the following year.[2]

1. MB to FPB, November 7, 1842, October 8, 1843, B-LP; E. B. Smith, *Francis Preston Blair,* 155–56.
2. MB to FPB, February 4, 1844, FB to EBL, February 3, 1844, FB to FPB, July 26, 1844, B-LP.

Shortly thereafter, Montgomery left for Washington with his older daughter, Betty, and her infant sister to visit his parents. He took his slave, Nancy, with him, which caused Frank to complain, as she really kept things neat in their rooms. He told Lizzie, "It is indispensable to comfort to have a neat servant, particularly in this region of dirt and coal dust." His mother had earlier promised him the slave Ned to act as his body servant but had then backed away from it. He now asked his sister to remind her of the promise.[3]

Frank's arrival back in St. Louis coincided with a political maelstrom in state Democratic politics that had been brewing for more than a year. The Blair family's close friend and Montgomery's legal mentor, Sen. Thomas Hart Benton, found himself increasingly at odds with certain party leaders who had long been his allies and champions. Initially, the divisions centered around the issue of soft versus hard money, with "Old Bullion" Benton a staunch advocate of the latter. The leadership of the Softs came generally from St. Louis business interests and the Whig Party, who wanted more liberalized banking laws and less stringent currency regulation. Beneath the surface, however, lay a growing concern by many Democrats that Benton had dominated the state's politics too long and had begun to take Missouri for granted as his personal fiefdom.[4]

The situation became further complicated in the winter of 1843–1844 with the approach of presidential and state elections. Preston Blair at the *Globe* supported his old friend Martin Van Buren for the Democratic presidential nomination at Baltimore in May, but the former president proved unable to garner the necessary two-thirds votes to secure the bid. A deadlocked convention stampeded to James Knox Polk of Tennessee on the tenth ballot. In a strong expansionist mood, it also endorsed "the re-annexation of Texas," something the senior Blair and Benton feared could lead to possible war with Mexico. Benton successfully led a fight in the Senate the following month to defeat a treaty of annexation proposed by the Tyler administration, a move that placed him in opposition to most Missourians. The *Globe* and Benton supported Polk's candidacy, but they continued to oppose Texas annexation. That Benton would be up for reelection the following winter further complicated an already divisive campaign.[5]

3. FB to EBL, n.d., B-LP. Frank's mother finally agreed to send Ned to St. Louis the following year (FB to EBL, April 19, 1845, BLC).
4. William E. Parrish, *David Rice Atchison of Missouri: Border Politician*, 31–32; William Nisbet Chambers, *Old Bullion Benton: Senator from the New West*, 260–63, 266–67.
5. E. B. Smith, *Francis Preston Blair*, 150–60; Chambers, *Old Bullion Benton*, 273–87.

Benton had helped underwrite a new Democratic paper in St. Louis, the *Missourian,* under the editorship of V. P. Van Antwerp, after his previous journalistic organ, the *Reporter,* had drifted into the camp of the Softs. By the summer of 1844 Van Antwerp ran into financial difficulties. With Montgomery in the East, Frank took the lead in securing the necessary funds to maintain the *Missourian,* including more than five hundred dollars of his own money. He also contributed several editorials to the paper. It marked his introduction to Missouri politics, and he relished it.[6]

Once the state contests had been completed in early August, with Democrat John C. Edwards elected governor and a presumably safe Democratic majority in the legislature, Frank headed east to Nashville. The ostensible purpose was to attend a Democratic convention called to rally support behind the Polk ticket; but, in reality, Frank wished "more particularly to see Old Hickory," his boyhood idol, anticipating that it might be his last opportunity. Preston Blair wrote Jackson, assuring the former president that Frank "entertains for you a feeling of affectionate reverence that would carry him to the ends of the earth to see and serve you." Frank would carry fondly the memory of this final meeting with Jackson the rest of his life. After the Nashville visit, he went on to Kentucky, where he stayed until mid-October.[7]

It was becoming obvious that Frank's Kentucky interests went deeper than merely his love for his native state and visiting relatives. Although Apolline Alexander had been studying in Philadelphia for the past year, she had visited the Blairs in Washington on occasion, where she had made a favorable impression. The two families had long been close, as noted previously. Frank had maintained a regular correspondence with Apo while she was in Philadelphia, and infatuation had slowly ripened into love. In February 1845, he wrote his brother-in-law Phil Lee, noting that one of his Gratz cousins "will certainly strike a bargain [for an engagement] & I rather think [I will also] from some indications I saw last summer."[8]

By April, Frank's "bargain" had been struck. He wrote Lizzie, "I presume you have heard from home all about my engagement to Apo Alexander." His

6. Chambers, *Old Bullion Benton,* 268–69; FB to MB, July (n.d.), July 27, 1844, MB to FPB, November 16, 1844, FB to FPB, February 19, 1845, B-LP.

7. FB to MB, July (n.d.), 1844, MB to FPB, October 16, 1844, B-LP; FPB to Jackson, August 4, 1844, in *Correspondence of Andrew Jackson,* 6:311; Benjamin Gratz to Henry Howard Gratz, October 28, 1844, in Byars, *B. and M. Gratz,* 311.

8. FB to SPL, February 3, 1845, B-LP; Agatha Marshall to Apo, March 9, 1841, Apo to Apolline Hankey, August 30, October 30, 1844, July (n.d.), 1845, Mira Alexander to Apolline Hankey, July 8, October 25, 1845, BLPLC.

parents "appear to be pleased, and I don't concern myself much about the rest of you," although Frank hoped his sister would be happy for him. He asked her to write Apo "a kind letter" because she believed "that you have taken an unfavorable impression of her." Frank added, "I, of course, think she is a very charming person." Lizzie quickly came around so that Frank could tell her two weeks later, "I am glad that you are pleased with Apo."[9]

Frank's biggest problem at this time seemed to be a somewhat reluctant mother-in-law-to-be. Mira Alexander sent two letters to her sister and Apo's namesake, Apolline Hankey, in England that summer and fall, outlining her concerns about the match. While "this young friend [Frank] was very dear to me," Mrs. Alexander wrote, she had long considered it far too soon for her daughter to be seriously attracted to someone seven years her senior. She had hoped that time and Apo's absence at school in Philadelphia would have cooled the relationship, but such had not been the case. Now she had accepted the engagement, feeling that Frank had established himself professionally in St. Louis and that Apo at seventeen had gained maturity during her two winters in Philadelphia. Regarding marriage, however, "it shall be postponed as long as I can." Recalling that she herself had married at eighteen and suffered difficulties with her new responsibilities, Mrs. Alexander saw no reason for Apo to rush into such an arrangement. But, she continued, "I find Frank as near being all that I could desire in a son-in-law as I can hope to meet with."[10]

Frank spent two months in Kentucky that summer and must have discovered Mira Alexander's feelings concerning a hasty marriage. He also feared that his family did not accept Apo quite as readily as they did Montgomery's new fiancée, Mary Elizabeth (Minna) Woodbury. Frank had not been in good health for some time, his weight having dropped to 125 pounds. He had injured his foot somehow the previous winter, and it had taken time to heal. In addition, he had suffered some kind of physical setback while in Kentucky, from which he had been slow in recovering. Undoubtedly, this, and his apprehensions about the two families' acceptance of his engagement, began to take their toll.[11]

The seriousness of Frank's physical problems is not entirely clear. It appears that the immaturity, which had led him from one college to another, plagued him again at this critical juncture of his relationship with Apo.

9. FB to EBL, April 19, 1845, BLC; FB to EBL, May 4, 1845, B-LP.

10. Mira Alexander to Apolline Hankey, July 8, October 25, 1845, BLPLC.

11. MB and FB to FPB, December 1, 1844, FB to EB, September 5, 1845, B-LP; Apo to MB, October (n.d.), 1845, BLC.

Later correspondence indicated his need to get away and put everything in perspective. Whatever the case, Frank determined by early September 1845 to go on "a buffalo hunt on the far western prairies," convinced that "a short time in the open air & on horseback" would restore his vitality. His legal practice since Montgomery's elevation to the bench had been minimal so there really was little keeping him in St. Louis. He told neither family nor Apo until the last minute, lest they try to dissuade him. While the family was skeptical about the adventure, it left Apo devastated. She feared that something that had occurred in Kentucky that summer, perhaps her mother's overprotectiveness, had caused Frank to rethink their engagement. She wrote him, desperately trying to straighten out any misunderstandings, but the letter arrived after he had already gone.[12]

Frank left St. Louis in late September, going by way of Boonville to visit his father's youngest sister, Eliza Jane. By October 2, he was in Westport, where he joined an expedition of fifteen wagons and some thirty individuals, which he assured his brother would be large enough to see them safely across the plains. His companions included Charles Bent, a distant cousin and a veteran of the western prairies. Bent and his brothers had built a trading post, known as Bent's Fort, during the late 1820s on the upper Arkansas River, just north of Raton Pass, and it had become a major outpost on the Santa Fe Trail. This was the caravan's initial destination.[13]

The trip apparently went without incident and probably took about three weeks. Another visitor to Bent's Fort during this period left the following description:

> The establishment is constructed of . . . *adobes*—a sun dried brick. . . . The fort is oblong, the wall about twenty feet in height, and sufficiently thick to resist all attempts with small arms. At the angles are round towers, commanding the outside of the walls. . . . The area enclosed within the walls would probably comprise over an acre, which is subdivided by high walls; so, in case of siege, all the mules, cattle, wagons, etc. can be secured and protected inside the walls. Round the inside of the wall of the fort *proper*, are the

12. FB to EB, September 5, 1845, FB to MB, October 2, 1845, MB to EBL, October 12, 1845, B-LP; Apo to MB, October (n.d.), 1845, MB to EBL, October 15, 1845, BLC. Montgomery wrote his mother that he thought Frank might have made the trip a year earlier except that the Mackenzie party, in which he was interested, had left before he returned to St. Louis (MB to EB, October 12, 1845, B-LP).

13. FB to MB, October 2, 1845, B-LP; David Lavender, *Bent's Fort*, 132–35. Frank went alone, leaving his slave, Ned, in Montgomery's care to be leased to a barber to learn that trade, as was Ned's wish (MB to EBL, October 12, 1845, B-LP).

storehouses, shops for blacksmith, gunsmith and carpenters, men's quarters, private rooms for gentlemen, dining room, kitchen, etc.[14]

Within the comfortable confines of Bent's Fort and during long rides across the countryside, Frank's health rapidly improved. The fort served as home that winter to a wide variety of idle trappers and traders including Indians, Mexicans, and French Canadians. Frank proved a genial companion and frequently entertained the fort's other occupants with his banjo playing. The group also occupied its time with hunting and playing cards, pool, or checkers. They often stayed in the dining room for rowdy taffy pulls with candy boiled from New Orleans molasses. At Christmas the fort became the scene of an all-night ball, at which some of the consorts and wives of the traders provided lively entertainment with backwoods American dances to the amazement of the Mexican and Indian women present.[15]

Frank became particularly close friends with George Bent, Charles's younger brother. In early March 1846, he and George set out for Taos across Raton Pass to visit his new friend's wife and children. They made it in six days, but it was a bitterly cold ride with temperatures dropping below zero for most of the trip. Frank held up well, but one of their traveling companions, riding next to him, froze to death and fell from his saddle.

Hearing of a party about to leave Taos for Missouri, Frank penned a hasty note to Montgomery on March 25, reporting that he was in excellent health and "getting fat fast." He had spent much of his time on horseback and had ridden up the Arkansas as far as "the Canon" (known today as the Royal Gorge) and over much of the New Mexican countryside east of the Rio Grande. Frank reported that he had acquired a little aptitude for Spanish and enough "knowledge of these people and countries to keep me away from them in all future time." Displaying his strong Anglo-Saxon bias, he told his brother, "I confess that I am getting tired of Indians & Mexicans, especially the latter, such a lying, thieving, treacherous, cowardly, bragging & depraved race of people it has never been my lot to see." Generally bored, he had become "restless and discontented." Lacking adventure, he anticipated starting home

14. George Rutledge Gibson, *Journal of a Soldier under Kearny and Doniphan, 1846–1847,* 167 n. For another interesting description, see Susan Shelby Magoffin, *Down the Santa Fe Trail and into Mexico,* 59–62.

15. George Bird Grinnell, "Bent's Old Fort and Its Builders," 55–56; Lavender, *Bent's Fort,* 248; W. E. Smith, *Blair Family in Politics,* 1:207; Charles Bent to Manuel Alvarez, December 17, 1845, in Benjamin M. Read Collection; FB to MB, March 25, 1846, B-LP.

in May or June. Things were about to change, however, and the events of the next few months would bring more action and excitement than he could imagine.[16]

From Taos Frank and George Bent continued on to Santa Fe where they stayed several weeks. Frank wrote his father from there, elaborating on his disdain for the country and its people. He particularly complained about the local populace's subservience to Catholicism and its "fat priests." He decried their lack of resistance to the various Indian tribes, who were raiding the frontier. Rather than fight back, they "only recite a few prayers to the virgin Guadalupe and the saints for their interference & protection." He remained in Santa Fe during the Easter weekend, while the people conducted elaborate reenactments of the Crucifixion events in the streets. All of this pageantry left him even more bitter and cynical at what he considered the Mexicans' naïveté.[17]

By April 13, Frank and George had returned to Taos. They found the atmosphere charged with tension because of continuing quarrels between Charles Bent and the local priest, Padre Antonio Martinez, whose mutual enmity for each other stretched back many years. Martinez had accused Charles of aiding hostile Ute Indians in their raids on nearby ranches, a charge Bent strongly denied. The matter spilled over into local politics, with each man having his own candidate for the district's superior judgeship, a post that went to Martinez's brother Pasqual in what Charles considered an unfair election.[18]

Shortly after Frank's return, Charles Bent's stepdaughter married, with appropriate postceremony festivities. Frank apparently had too much to drink, and it became necessary for George to help him home the following morning, Sunday, May 3. As they crossed the plaza, they encountered a crowd of Mexicans idling in front of one of the stores. Among them were the new justice, Pasqual Martinez, and another one of his brothers. What happened next is unclear. Perhaps the drunken Frank made a disparaging remark or gesture. Suddenly, the Mexicans attacked the two men, and Frank was badly beaten. George managed to hold off the mob until friends arrived to get the two bruised and bloody Americans back to the Bent home. Charles, who had

16. Charles Bent to Alvarez, March 19, 1846, Read Collection; FB to MB, March 25, May 29, 1846, B-LP.

17. FB to FPB, April 10, 1846, B-LP.

18. Lavender, *Bent's Fort*, 204–5, 249–50.

been at a nearby ranch, quickly returned to town and sought redress at the hands of Justice Martinez, who replied that he could take no action because it was Sunday. That evening a mob gathered outside the Bent home, drunk, waving torches, and making threats. Charles now appealed to the governor, who ordered the prefect of the district to arrest the attackers. Several were jailed, only to gain their release through further mob action. Charles blamed Padre Martinez and his brothers for instigating the whole affair, but nothing more apparently came of it. All of this further strengthened Frank's disdain for the Mexicans.[19]

In early June, Charles left Taos en route back to Missouri. Frank had originally intended to go with him but then changed his mind. Word of the recent U.S. declaration of war against Mexico had not yet reached them, for Frank indicated in a letter to Montgomery on May 29 that if no war broke out he would return that fall by way of Mexico City and Vera Cruz. He sent home a little pacing horse and Spanish bridle with the Bent party and asked Montgomery to forward them to Apo. Should she refuse the gifts, he wanted them sent to his sister. He also informed his brother that he had borrowed one thousand dollars to cover additional expenses and needed him to reimburse the donor, who would be traveling east. He asked Montgomery to send the rest of his clothes and his double-barreled shotgun with Bent when he returned in the fall as well as a "fast horse," as the latter "could take a man safely out of a bad scrape and thus serve him in his need."[20]

Montgomery wrote Lizzie that he did not understand Frank's reasons for remaining in New Mexico. Since Frank had written regularly to Apo, Montgomery believed that his lingering obviously had nothing to do with any estrangement there. His brother's staying, he concluded, "is therefore like his going, only a freak." He hoped only that his brother did not plan on a military career. He had little fear for Frank's safety, as the Bents had many powerful friends among the Mexican officialdom, so "there is not the least danger of him coming to any harm from the Mexicans."[21]

The Charles Bent party learned of the war with Mexico four days out of Bent's Fort when they encountered George Thomas Howard. He had been sent by Secy. of War William L. Marcy to hurry down the Santa Fe Trail, warning caravans and then going into the New Mexico capital, hoping to alert

19. Ibid., 250–51; Charles Bent to Alvarez, April 14, May 3 (three letters), May 10, June 1, 1846, Read Collection.
20. FB to MB, May 29, 1846, B-LP.
21. MB to EBL, July 5, 13, 1846, BLC.

Americans there before Mexican governor Manuel Armijo, Charles Bent's good friend, heard the news. Undoubtedly, Frank and George Bent learned about the war's outbreak from Howard shortly thereafter. The Charles Bent party hurried on to Westport, arriving there June 27, and then headed north to Fort Leavenworth where Col. (later Brig. Gen.) Stephen Watts Kearny was preparing a military expedition to march overland to Santa Fe. Upon learning that Frank still remained in New Mexico, Kearny indicated to friends that he hoped to add him to his staff in some capacity.[22]

Frank returned with George to Bent's Fort to await Kearny's army. The first troops began to arrive during the final week of July, and the fort became an extremely busy place. On August 1, Kearny wrote to Governor Armijo, informing him that the United States was annexing all of New Mexico east of the Rio Grande and warning him not to resist the approaching American army. The next day he sought out William Bent with the request that he put together a scouting party to precede the army through the Raton Pass. Bent selected his brother George and Frank among the half dozen men to accompany him. They quickly reconnoitered and sent back word that no enemy forces awaited in the pass. They captured five Mexican scouts, however, and then met more Mexicans carrying copies of an order from the Taos prefect drafting all males between ages fifteen and fifty. In spite of continuing rumors that Governor Armijo was mounting opposition with the help of Indians, William Bent and his scouts could find no such activity. On August 18, Kearny's Army of the West entered Santa Fe, having met no opposition. They were welcomed by Lt. Gov. Juan Batista Vigil as Governor Armijo had fled south. One of those accompanying the expedition found the town's appearance "shabby, without either taste or a show of wealth—no gardens that deserved the name, the fields all unenclosed, the people poor and beggarly, and nothing to pay us for our long march."[23]

Kearny quickly established American authority. He asked Frank to assist Alexander Doniphan and others in drafting a constitution and code of laws for the new territory. They retained as much of the Mexican law as they could,

22. Lavender, *Bent's Fort*, 253–55; *Niles Register*, July 11, 1846; W. M. Tompkins to MB, July 2, 1846, BLC.

23. Lavender, *Bent's Fort*, 258–63; William H. Emory, *Notes of a Military Reconnaissance from Fort Leavenworth in Missouri to San Diego in California*, 6–7; Ralph Emerson Twitchell, *The History of the Military Occupation of the Territory of New Mexico from 1846 to 1851 by the Government of the United States*, 45–72; John Taylor Hughes, *Doniphan's Expedition and the Conquest of New Mexico and California*, 34–42. The quote is from Gibson, *Journal of a Soldier*, 205–6.

modifying it with borrowed sections of the Missouri code. Finding a small printing press left by the departing Mexican government, they soon turned out copies of their work in both English and Spanish, with the two versions placed in juxtaposition in double columns on each page.[24]

Charles Bent returned to Bent's Fort from Missouri the day before Kearny occupied Santa Fe and hastened on to the New Mexico capital by way of Taos. Given his extensive knowledge of the region and its people, Kearny quickly put him to work as chief adviser to the code makers. Meanwhile, the general, with a body of men, toured the surrounding countryside to placate the priests and other Mexican leaders and to negotiate with the various Indian tribes. Things generally went peacefully. Learning that Sterling Price was marching with reinforcements via the Cimarron Cutoff, Kearny determined that he could safely leave Santa Fe and the surrounding area in the hands of Price and the Bent group while he pushed on to California.[25]

Before leaving, on September 22, Kearny named a set of civil officials to govern the region with the help of Price's military. He appointed Charles Bent governor and obviously accepted his advice with regard to the rest. Donaciano Vigil, a relative of Charles's wife and the only holdover from the Armijo regime, became territorial secretary and lieutenant governor. Frank, as the only civilian with legal training, assumed the post of prosecuting attorney. The three judges with whom he would work were all friends of Bent's.[26]

The following evening, the Santa Fe merchants entertained Kearny and his staff with a fandango at the governor's palace, prior to their departure for California. Susan Magoffin, the young wife of an American trader, who was present, reported that the Mexican women wore "large sleeves, short waists, ruffled skirts, and no bustles," while old and young alike "smoked cigarittos." Apparently, Gertrudes Barcelo, best known as La Tules, the notorious one-time mistress of Governor Armijo, whom Susan described as "the old woman with false hair and teeth," set the pace. La Tules ran a gambling salon on the outskirts of Santa Fe and had numerous American connections. Susan herself wore "a scarlet Canton crape [*sic*] shawl . . . to be in trim with the Natives." Charles Bent and his new staff were, of course, present. By this time Frank

24. Hughes, *Doniphan's Expedition,* 64.
25. Lavender, *Bent's Fort,* 263–64; Hughes, *Doniphan's Expedition,* 54–63; Twitchell, *Military Occupation,* 84–86.
26. Lavender, *Bent's Fort,* 164; Twitchell, *Military Occupation,* 84; Charles Bent to Secy. of State James Buchanan, September 24, 1846, Charles Bent to Thomas Hart Benton, September 24, 1846, in Record Group 393.

had undoubtedly attended enough of these dances to be hardly shocked by anything.[27]

Kearny left Bent and the others with few resources. Two days after his appointment, Charles wrote to Secy. of State James Buchanan and Sen. Thomas Hart Benton informing them of the new government. Fearing any precipitate attempt to tax the local populace, he asked for salary money from the U.S. Treasury, including authorization for the appointment of a Spanish translator to assist Frank and the judges in the courts until things got settled. He also requested American law books, as none were available in the territory. He reported that he believed it would be necessary to maintain a military force in the region for several years to assist the civil authorities in the administration of justice. Charles further sought assistance from the Bureau of Indian Affairs, sending the commissioner a complete description of all the Native American groups in the area, giving the numbers of their lodges and population. At the end of November, he wrote Benton once again, urging a prompt response to his previous request and seeking appropriations to erect public buildings to house the government offices and courts. He expressed particular concern that they had no secure jails.[28]

The new administration had its hands full. Several groups of Native Americans began once again to raid outlying settlements. Sterling Price's recently arrived troops, performing garrison duty in Santa Fe, caused problems of their own as they took a conqueror's attitude toward the local populace with little respect for the rights of the Santa Fe citizenry. Rumors abounded of Mexican activity to the south. Col. Alexander Doniphan, who had been left in charge of the remaining military by General Kearny, worked to bolster the city's defenses while also requiring twice-daily drills for Price's men. He then took some of this force and began a sweep of the surrounding countryside to deal with the marauding natives.[29]

Meanwhile, Charles and Frank and their associates tackled the daily routine of administration. In mid-December, with Doniphan having been ordered to march directly south after his Indian forays, a plot against Bent's government became public. Led by a group of prominent New Mexicans, the plotters planned an uprising on Christmas Eve when Price's troops would presumably

27. Gibson, *Journal of a Soldier,* 243; Magoffin, *Down the Santa Fe Trail,* 142–45; Lavender, *Bent's Fort,* 266–67.

28. Charles Bent to Buchanan, September 24, 1846, Bent to Benton, September 24, November 30, 1846, Bent to Commissioner of Indian Affairs, November 13, 1846, Record Group 393.

29. Lavender, *Bent's Fort,* 273–75.

be indulging themselves in celebration. Bent and Price were to be kidnapped; and the other American officials, including Frank, and their collaborators killed. Word of the conspiracy leaked out; one report indicated that a mulatto wife of one of the rebels went to La Tules for advice and the salon keeper reported it to Lieutenant Governor Vigil, who quickly informed Charles. Although the military seized seven "secondary" plotters, the ringleaders escaped. They would continue to hatch their plans and strike again more tragically a month later.[30]

An unsuspecting Frank dispatched a letter to Montgomery from Taos on December 18 with the notation, "There is nothing in the way of news worth telling." He planned to leave for Santa Fe the next day and after Christmas would spend time exploring along the Gila River in extreme southwestern New Mexico. He anticipated returning home later in the spring. His failure to get mail irritated him. He had had only one letter from Montgomery since arriving in New Mexico. His thoughts turned increasingly to Apo. He told his brother that he wanted to hear from him "about my own little lady love, if I thought it was all right in that quarter I would return home with a light heart and get married and promise not to run off again." Frank continued, "You must not think that I left home for any want of affection for her to whom I have pledged my love," and he asked Montgomery to reassure Apo in that regard. "If I know anything about myself," he wrote, "I can say with perfect sincerity that I love her as well as I ever did, that I cannot love anyone better than I do her & never did love anybody half as well."[31]

Frank returned to Santa Fe to learn of the plot uncovered in his absence. He found the capital more relaxed and joined in Charles Bent's elaborate Christmas gala on December 26, at which there was food and champagne in abundance. The Americans' fears further subsided when the new year brought word that Doniphan had delivered a crushing blow to Mexican forces near El Paso. Concluding that this would weaken whatever hope the escaped plotters might have for outside Mexican assistance, Charles released additional artillery to join Doniphan in the south. On January 5, 1847, Bent officially proclaimed Doniphan's victory and the thwarting of the planned rebellion. He urged the local citizenry to disregard any rumors of continued resistance.[32]

30. Ibid., 276–78; Twitchell, *Military Occupation*, 122–23.

31. FB to MB, December 18, 1846, BLPLC. Montgomery undoubtedly forwarded this letter to Apo for it appears in a collection passed down to her granddaughter, Christine Long, which is included in the papers of that individual's husband, Breckinridge Long.

32. Lavender, *Bent's Fort*, 298–99; Twitchell, *Military Occupation*, 124–25.

However, unrest still smoldered in Taos, the scene of the attack on Frank and George Bent some eight months earlier. Several officials came down to Santa Fe in early January expressing their uneasiness. Against the advice of others, Charles Bent agreed to return with them, refusing to take a military escort lest it betray a lack of confidence. Taos, after all, was his home.[33]

It took the governor's small party four days to reach Taos through a heavy snow, arriving there on January 18. A group of hostile Pueblo Indians met them on the outskirts of town, demanding the release of their tribesmen being held for theft. Charles patiently told them that the cases would be handled through the normal legal processes, and then he and the rest of the party separated to go to their respective homes. Later that evening, Bent received warnings that a mob had gathered on the outskirts of town. Gunfire could be heard in the streets. His family and friends urged Charles to flee, but he refused.[34]

The attack came with dawn on January 19. Although there is no evidence of the involvement of Charles Bent's old enemy, Padre Martinez, many of his friends later expressed this belief. The ringleaders were Pablo Montoya, who styled himself the Santa Anna of the north, and a Taos Indian named Tomasito. The latter quickly led his Indian followers to the Bent home where they confronted Charles through the closed door. Bent's offers of conciliation and consultation came to naught. Firing through the door, the mob wounded him in the chin and stomach. As they crashed into the home through the door and a hole in the ceiling, Charles took arrows to the face and chest. His family hid in the back of the house, while the mob seized the staggering governor, scalped him, and hacked his head from his body. Then they tacked his scalp to a board and went off after additional victims, leaving Charles's wife and children alone in the shattered home. Before they finished in Taos, the insurgents had killed at least three other officials in equally bloody fashion. The rioting spread to other communities throughout the territory with numerous Americans killed.[35]

When word reached Sterling Price in Santa Fe of the Taos uprising, he quickly put together a force of some three hundred men and headed north. Confronting a large group of Mexicans near the present village of Santa Cruz,

33. Lavender, *Bent's Fort*, 279; Twitchell, *Military Occupation*, 125.
34. Lavender, *Bent's Fort*, 280–81.
35. Acting Gov. Donaciano Vigil to Secy. of State James Buchanan, February 26, 1847, *House Executive Documents No. 70*, 19–20; Grinnell, "Bent's Old Fort," 76–78; Lavender, *Bent's Fort*, 281–85; Twitchell, *Military Occupation*, 125–28, 133.

he dispersed them and then pursued them all the way to Taos. There a fierce battle ensued before Price finally routed the insurrectionists and captured and imprisoned Pablo Montoya and Tomasito. Tomasito escaped a drumhead court when a recruit named Fitzgerald shot him.[36]

Frank had left Santa Fe for the Gila River area shortly after New Year's Day and hence was not in the capital at the time of the attack. He hastened back to Santa Fe and took charge of judicial proceedings against those involved in the insurrection. At the next term of court in Santa Fe, Frank secured four indictments for treason from a hastily called grand jury. Only one of these resulted in conviction, but that individual appealed, claiming that the newly established territorial courts lacked jurisdiction for such a charge since the defendants were Mexican citizens.[37]

Frank reported the proceedings to Atty. Gen. John Y. Mason on April 1 with the additional news that fifty others were confined to the Taos jail awaiting trial within a few days. With the others also claiming that they could not be tried for treason against the United States as Mexican citizens, Frank sought Mason's opinion as to the correctness of the indictments. Long after Frank's departure for Missouri, Sterling Price received a reply from Secretary of War Marcy that, although the inhabitants of New Mexico were not citizens of the United States, they were bound by the laws that "a temporary civil government in a conquered country" might adopt. Those involved in the recent insurrection could be tried for murder in either civil or military courts, but "it is not the proper use of the technical term to say that their offense was treason committed against the United States," as it could not be said that they owed that government allegiance.[38]

Frank had proceeded, meanwhile, to try the remaining cases, including Montoya's, in the U.S. District Court in Taos with Judges Carlos Beaubien and Joab Houghton presiding. The former jurist, a French Canadian, had had a son murdered during the insurrection and had participated in the Price expedition

36. Lavender, *Bent's Fort*, 289–93; Twitchell, *Military Occupation*, 128–33.

37. Minna Blair to EBL, March 21, 1847, BLC; FPB to Martin Van Buren, July 7, 1847, Martin Van Buren Papers; FB to Atty. Gen. John Y. Mason, April 1, 1847, *House Executive Documents No. 70*, 26–27; Twitchell, *Military Occupation*, 139–42; Lavender, *Bent's Fort*, 411.

38. FB to Mason, April 1, 1847, Marcy to Price, June 11, 26, 1847, *House Executive Documents No. 70*, 26–27, 31–33. Thomas C. Reynolds, who would serve as lieutenant governor in the pro-Confederate Claiborne Jackson administration during the Civil War, mentioned in his post–Civil War memoir, *Gen. Sterling Price and the Confederacy*, that Price had arrested Blair during this period for some unspecified disagreement, which caused Frank to hold a lifelong enmity against Price (Thomas C. Reynolds Papers). This author has found nothing to support this, however.

against Taos. The latter, a native of New York, had been a close friend of Charles Bent and owed his judicial appointment to the late governor. George Bent served as foreman of the grand jury, made up of nineteen men, of whom four were Americans. They brought in seventeen indictments for murder. At the trials that followed, Frank handled the prosecution while the defendants were represented by Theodore D. Wheaton, a volunteer private, on furlough for the occasion. Ceran St. Vrain, a Bent partner, served as interpreter. The juries consisted primarily of trappers and Bent employees, although many of them were Mexican. The trials hardly constituted impartial proceedings, but it would have been difficult to find any neutral jury in Taos.[39]

The witnesses included Ignacia Bent, the late governor's widow. Lewis Garrard, an adventurer who happened upon the proceedings, wryly observed, "When the witnesses (Mexican) touched their lips to the Bible, on taking the oath, it was with such a reverential awe for the book, and fear of *los Americanos,* that I could not repress a smile." He described Frank Blair as "slight formed, young, and agreeable in his manners, and, to judge from his labors in the courtroom, possessed of some legal talent and adroitness."[40]

Justice was quickly served. The court met for fifteen working days with the juries finding fifteen of the seventeen men indicted for murder guilty. Most of the juries remained out for only a few moments before they rendered their decisions. As Judge Beaubien pronounced the words "muerto, muerto, muerto, dead, dead, dead" after each verdict, a painful silence fell over the courtroom. The prisoners were taken to the nearby jail and quickly hanged. Soldiers and armed trappers formed a hollow within which the gallows stood. Two howitzers, one on the roof of the jail, were conveniently placed nearby to help prevent any further disturbance. The condemned men were seated on a single plank on the back of a government wagon drawn by mules. Once the nooses had been firmly placed, a driver whipped the mules, completing the execution.[41]

At the end of the court term, Frank resigned his post as prosecuting attorney and began preparations for his long-anticipated return home. He joined a

39. Francis T. Cheetham, "The First Term of the American Court in Taos, New Mexico," includes the indictments and trial records. For a vivid description of the courtroom and the trials by one of those present, see Lewis H. Garrard, *Wah-To-Yah and the Taos Trail,* 238–39. In addition to those indicted for murder, there were seventeen indicted for larceny with six convicted, three found not guilty, seven discharged by a nolle prosequi, and one apparently held over to the next term.

40. Garrard, *Wah-To-Yah,* 239, 247, 249.

41. Ibid., 251–70, contains a vivid description of the entire proceedings.

party headed by Ceran St. Vrain, which left Santa Fe in early May and arrived back in St. Louis on June 13. Frank had had far more adventure than he had anticipated when he fled west twenty months earlier. His experiences in New Mexico marked a turning point in his maturing process, leaving him strengthened both physically and emotionally. He had regained his health, and his love for Apo had been reinforced by the long absence. He had also had his first taste of public service and had acquitted himself well. He now stood ready for marriage and whatever avenues down which a career in law and politics might take him.[42]

42. Ibid., 351–52; Lavender, *Bent's Fort*, 298–99; FB to FPB, June 15, 1847, B-LP. Shortly after Frank left New Mexico, his good friend George Bent became critically ill and died in late October 1847. Recalling a promise that Frank had made before leaving, George, on his deathbed, requested that his friend serve as guardian for his son, Elfego, and provide for his education in St. Louis. This Frank did, assuming care for the boy until his education was completed in 1854 (Dorcas Carr to Silas Bent, December 26, 1848, William C. Carr Papers; Lavender, *Bent's Fort*, 303–4, 417).

3

Marriage and Politics

Within a few weeks of his arrival in St. Louis, Frank headed to Kentucky to mend his fences with Apo. Whatever concerns he might have had about their engagement had been resolved during his stay in New Mexico. Indeed, he had asked Montgomery in his December 18 letter to reassure Apo that he had never ceased loving her. Now he sought to reiterate that sentiment personally. It did not take long for the two to make up "our squabble." Apo wrote a friend, "You know the old adage, 'Amantium irae, etc.,'" adding, "I never felt happier in my life." The two were married on September 6, 1847, at Sherwood and quickly left on a honeymoon by way of Cincinnati and the Great Lakes to Philadelphia, where they stayed with the Biddles before going on to Washington to see the senior Blairs. Apo's and Frank's families had long been close, and his father had written Frank on the eve of the marriage, "Tell Apolline that she is the last of my victories, so to her credit I shall account her 'my crowning mercy,' and I have no doubt I shall have more joy in the future [that] she will bring me of domestic love."[1]

The marriage of Frank and Apolline Blair proved to be a long and generally happy one. While not beautiful, Apo possessed a strong intelligence and personality that made her the ideal mate for her energetic husband. Although she often regretted Frank's obsession with politics, Apo supported him devotedly throughout his tumultuous political career, his often disastrous

1. Woodford County, Kentucky, Marriage Records, 1788–1851, 3; FB to MB, December 18, 1846, BLPLC; FB to FPB, August 21, 1847, B-LP; Apo to Abram Ward, August 27, 1847, FPB to FB, August 30, 1847, FB to EBL, November 30, 1847, BLC.

financial ventures, and his mercurial moods. Frank, in return, remained faithful throughout their marriage, writing Apo long letters during their frequent absences from one another. In her "Reminiscences," which Apolline wrote for her son James in the 1890s, she noted,

> For three short years we had great happiness in our domestic life but your father's taste for politics was born in him & nurtured in him. Political life puts an end to domestic happiness & after that we were much separated but your father was always most considerate to me & had perfect confidence in my judgment & so left all family matters to me & so my children were my consolation & his great joy for no one could have been fonder or more tender to all his children.[2]

Apo's relationship with her in-laws was a close one, but she did not allow herself to be dominated by them. Frank accepted her family as his own. Indeed, Mrs. Alexander and her other three children moved to St. Louis in the late 1840s, on occasion living with the Blairs under the same roof. The youngest daughter, Mira, known as "Midge," married Frank's close associate Franklin A. Dick in the early 1850s, and their two families grew up together.

By mid-November 1847, Frank and Apo had returned to St. Louis, where they took a room at the Planters House, adjacent to the quarters of Montgomery and Minna, with whom they shared a parlor. Frank reported that the two women got along admirably, a relationship that would continue unabated in the years to come. "They are together almost all the time," he told his mother, "and when the Judge [Montgomery] is not on the bench & I return from my office we make quite a family party." Apo wrote her namesake aunt in England that she liked what she saw of St. Louis. She and Frank had a "pleasant cheerful room." They breakfasted at eight after which Frank went to the office until two-thirty when he came home for a late lunch. She spent her mornings reading and studying Spanish at Frank's insistence, and they often took a walk in the evening before dinner. After dinner the four usually gathered in the parlor, where either Frank or Montgomery read aloud, the current interest being Prescott's *The Conquest of Mexico*.[3]

Frank told his mother that he already had plans underway to build a small house with a five-thousand-dollar inheritance left to Apo by one of her uncles. They could not move into it before the following fall, however, and it would

2. Apo, "Reminiscences," 8–9, BLPLC. Apo's best expression of her concern about Frank's political career to her husband may be found in Apo to FB, December 16, 1857, BLC.
3. FB to EB, November 23, 1847, FB to EBL, November 30, 1847, BLC; Apo to Apolline Hundley, December 5, 1847, BLPLC.

then require furniture for which he asked his mother to advance them the money. This request proved to be the beginning of a periodic reliance on his parents for financial support, which they usually supplied, although Apo did her best to manage within their resources and keep their dependence at a minimum. Preston Blair wrote his son a few years later, "If, as you say, you *don't charge & don't collect;* it is not hard to see how you become straitened."

For the most part, however, Frank did well financially during the 1850s. Even with his political interests, he built a good law practice. He also engaged extensively in real estate speculations in rapidly growing St. Louis, not only for himself but also for his father, his brother Jim, and his brother-in-law Phil Lee. After Montgomery moved back east in 1853, Frank looked after his brother's considerable real estate holdings as well, with the help of Samuel Simmons, the senior Blair's agent. By 1853, Frank had prospered sufficiently to acquire a home in west St. Louis County, which he and Apo named "Rose Bank." They initially used this as a summer retreat while continuing their residence in the city. Apo loved it in the country, however, especially after more children arrived, and increasingly spent more of her time there with Frank coming out on weekends.[4]

Blair soon became enmeshed in what would become the consuming passion of his life—politics. The election of 1848 proved a pivotal turning point in Frank's career, marked, as it was, by the volatile issue of the extension of slavery into the territories acquired from Mexico and the impact it would have on the reelection prospects of Sen. Thomas Hart Benton, whose political interests would become closely linked with Frank's throughout much of the following decade.

Frank had played only a peripheral role in Benton's last reelection campaign in 1844, when the senator's relations with certain elements of the Missouri Democracy had become strained over the money issue and the annexation of Texas. Frank now took the lead in trying to ensure "Old Bullion" yet another term. The campaign got under way at the annual Jackson Day celebration on January 8 when St. Louis Democrats chose their delegates to the state convention. The *Missouri Republican* indicated that the old divisions

4. FB to EB, November 23, 1847, FB to FPB, November 25, 1847, September 13, 1848, FB to EBL, April 8, 1848, MB to EBL, October 4, 1848, FPB to FB, April 20, 1851, BLC; Apo to FPB, November 16, 1847, n.d., and November 22, 1848, MB to FPB, January 5, 1848, FB to FPB, December 17, 1848, B-LP. BLC contains numerous deeds and receipts from sales of property in the early 1850s. Frank and Apo's first home was located at 54 South Fourth Street (*Green's St. Louis Directory for 1851*, 54).

between the Hards and Softs within the Democracy remained as strong as ever. To prevent a split, Frank maneuvered himself into the chairmanship of the resolutions committee and brought in a strong set endorsing Benton, thus forcing the Softs to support him for the sake of party unity. Although the delegation elected to the state convention was divided between the two groups, Blair also secured instructions of support for former governor M. M. Marmaduke, known to be a staunch Hard and Benton supporter. Montgomery wrote his father that Frank "made quite a figure . . . and bore himself so manfully and coolly throughout the controversy as to win great applause from his friends."[5]

At the end of March, Frank took a boat to Jefferson City to be sure that the state convention followed the lead of the St. Louis meeting. Apo confided to her father-in-law, "My only fear at present is that Frank's mind will become so interested & engrossed in politics that the law will suffer." She asked Preston for his opinion on the matter, while assuring him that she did not want to attempt to influence Frank one way or the other. There is no record of the senior Blair's reply, but there can be little doubt that he harbored strong political ambitions for his youngest son. Only half in jest, Apo reported, "I laugh & tell him that he thinks the whole conduct of the assembly devolves upon his broad shoulders & that nothing would go at all right without him. Of course, he does not believe a word of this, so he has gone off in fine spirits & I tell him full of conceit & dignity."[6]

Apo had hit upon one of Frank's strengths that could also be considered a weakness. He frequently acted as if whatever cause he championed depended on his leadership alone, and thus he poured everything he had into it. This intensity gained him the respect of his contemporaries, one of whom noted:

> After entering upon a political campaign, Mr. Blair was tireless in his efforts for success. . . . He knew the value of organization, and superintended every detail of the work required. He was everywhere. I have known him in the hot month of August (formerly the time when Congressional elections occurred) to deliver short speeches in every ward of the City, expounding party principles and cheering and encouraging his followers. No obstacles, no discouragements, deterred him from fighting his utmost to the end. He attended every

5. John J. Lowry to M. M. Marmaduke, December 25, 1847, M. M. Marmaduke Papers; *Missouri Republican,* January 10, 1848; Thomas Gray to Marmaduke, January 9, February 14, 1848, George Penn to Marmaduke, January 11, 1848, John Sappington Papers; MB to FPB, January 15, 1848, B-LP.
6. Apo to FPB, March 23, 1848, B-LP; Apo, "Reminiscences," 8–9, BLPLC.

caucus and every ward meeting where he thought his presence would
add to the chances of success. On election day he rode from poll to poll
to consult with friends and see that all needed work was being done.[7]

Yet that same intensity undoubtedly contributed to his frequent attacks of
neuralgia headaches, which could plague him for days on end. The tug
of politics, which took her husband away from his concentration on his
law practice, as well as his bouts of ill health, would give Apo concern
throughout her husband's career and cast a shadow over their otherwise
happy relationship.

Frank had his work cut out for him in Jefferson City because of the number
of gubernatorial rivals from each camp seeking the top spot on the ticket. In
addition to Marmaduke, the chief candidates included Austin A. King, a noted
Soft from the western part of the state, who had remained generally aloof from
the recent factional quarrel; James M. Hughes, a close friend of Sen. David R.
Atchison and the choice of the St. Louis Softs; and Claiborne Fox Jackson,
a prominent Hard from central Missouri, who had split with Benton over
the question of Texas annexation and who apparently had strong ambitions
to replace Old Bullion in the Senate. After twenty ballots, the convention
gave the nomination to King over Jackson, Hughes and Marmaduke having
withdrawn earlier. The *Missouri Republican*, the St. Louis Whig organ, tried
to stir up difficulty by reporting that Frank had maneuvered the nomination
of King. If that was the case, he must have done so only after realizing that,
having failed to secure the spot for Marmaduke, King represented less of a
threat to Benton.[8]

Although not totally pleased with the King nomination, the Hards determined to maintain party unity. Frank's real concern was the state party
platform. He managed to secure the post of chairman of the resolutions committee at the state meeting and brought in a strong endorsement of Benton.
It "was well thought of by our friends generally," he wrote his sister, after his
return; and he felt "very satisfactory" about the convention as a result.[9]

The state's delegation to the Democratic National Convention at Baltimore,
which included Montgomery, went uninstructed as to a presidential preference, although Frank's brother favored Minna's father, Judge Levi Woodbury

7. Charles P. Johnson, "Personal Recollections of Some of Missouri's Eminent Statesmen
and Lawyers," 12.
8. Clarence Henry McClure, *Opposition in Missouri to Thomas Hart Benton*, 149–50.
9. John J. Lowry to M. M. Marmaduke, April 9, 1848, Sappington Papers; FB to EBL,
April 8, 1848, BLC.

of New Hampshire. Montgomery had asked Frank to nominate Woodbury at the state convention, but he had declined. Frank had hoped to persuade Benton to be a presidential candidate. When Old Bullion emphatically refused, Frank supported their old family friend Martin Van Buren, with whom his father maintained a brisk correspondence. Van Buren was known to favor the Wilmot Proviso, which would bar slavery from the newly acquired territories, and both Frank and his father leaned strongly in that direction. Preston also went to the national convention as a delegate from Maryland; since Van Buren had proved a reluctant candidate, the senior Blair sought to promote his old friend Gen. William O. Butler of Kentucky as a counterweight to the anticipated Whig choice of Gen. Zachary Taylor.[10]

The Democrats at Baltimore found themselves even more fractious than the Missouri party had been at Jefferson City. The biggest split had occurred in New York, which sent rival delegations: the Barnburners, who favored Free-Soilism and Van Buren; and the Hunkers, led by Secy. of War William L. Marcy, who supported the prosouthern policies of President Polk. The infighting in New York had cost the Democrats the gubernatorial election of 1846 and led to the death, so Van Buren and Preston Blair believed, of their good friend Silas Wright, the defeated Democratic candidate. At Baltimore, the remaining delegates sought to appease both factions by giving each delegate from both sides a half-vote. This so angered the Barnburners that they withdrew. The convention eventually nominated Lewis Cass of Michigan for president. Cass advocated the middle-ground doctrine of popular sovereignty, namely, let the people in the territories make the decision for or against slavery. William O. Butler received the vice presidential nomination.[11]

Preston Blair had been simmering over disagreements with the Polk administration ever since the president had forced him out of the editorship of the *Globe*. Increasingly attracted to Free-Soilism, Blair found it hard to swallow Cass. Although Benton was willing to accept Cass as a nonsouthern candidate and to ensure party unity, the senior Blair and Van Buren refused to do so. Blair now began pushing an independent Free-Soil candidacy on Van Buren.[12]

Frank was not yet ready to go that far. On June 7, he wrote Montgomery, "I am quite satisfied with the nomination of Cass because I feel convinced that he

10. FB to EBL, February 19, April 8, 1848, FB to FPB, April 5, 1848, B-LP; FB to FPB, April 22, 1848, Van Buren Papers.
11. W. E. Smith, *Blair Family in Politics*, 1:230–31.
12. Thomas Hart Benton to Van Buren, May 29, 1848, FPB to Van Buren, June 2, 26, 1848, Van Buren Papers.

will be beat and our party will be purified by the fires of adversity." He did not believe that anybody could wish the Democrats success when their "worst men are put forward to carry out [the party's] principles." A Cass victory would simply mean that "all the factions & corrupt politicians . . . will be cherished by him." Defeat would give the Barnburners the opportunity to gear up for the next election when, they hoped, they could gain control of the party.[13]

The previous day, however, a large gathering of Barnburners had met in New York City, where they heard John Van Buren, the former president's son, deliver a blistering attack on slavery and the Slave Power. They issued a call for a convention to be held at Utica, New York, on June 22 to take further action. Out of the Utica convention came the nomination of Martin Van Buren as the Free-Soil candidate for president. Six weeks later some four hundred delegates, including Frank, part of a mass meeting of ten thousand, came together at Buffalo to create a national Free-Soil ticket headed by Van Buren and Charles Francis Adams, son of former president John Quincy Adams. The Free-Soilers included disgruntled Whigs, who found their party's candidate, Zachary Taylor, a Kentucky slaveholder, hard to swallow, as well as disillusioned Democrats, dismayed by what they considered Cass's and their party's compromise with the southern wing at Baltimore. Amid cheers of "Free Soil, Free Speech, Free Labor, and Free Men," the group went forth to do battle against Democrats and Whigs alike.[14]

An enthusiastic Frank returned to St. Louis and began "getting up the Barnburner spirit." He induced the proprietors of a local paper, the *Democratic Flag*, which had already been producing pro–Van Buren editorials, "to consent to wheel into line & issue a daily paper" to be called the *Barnburner*. Frank had high hopes that they could attract the German and perhaps a portion of the Irish vote, which, when combined with a great many "Yankee Whigs" and the Benton Hards, would make a strong showing for Free-Soilism in Missouri.[15]

The Blairs' endorsement of the Free-Soil ticket placed Senator Benton in an awkward position. He sympathized with the principles of the Free-Soilers; but, confronted with the probability of a tough reelection campaign of his own two years hence, he endorsed Cass and the regular ticket as the only means of holding the Missouri Democracy together. The defection of his key

13. FB to MB, June 7, 1848, B-LP.
14. W. E. Smith, *Blair Family in Politics*, 1:233–38; *Missouri Republican*, August 2, 1848.
15. *Missouri Republican*, July 12, 1848; Henry F. Watson to Van Buren, August 17, 1848, Van Buren Papers; FB to EBL, August 30, 1848, B-LP.

St. Louis supporters, however, raised serious questions about his own loyalty among the vast majority of proslavery Missouri Democrats. Many believed that Benton could have headed off Van Buren's defection with a personal visit to his old friend. The state's major Democratic paper, the *St. Louis Union*, edited by Samuel Treat, the secretary of the Democratic National Committee, sought to downplay reports from its Whig rival, the *Missouri Republican*, that Benton would join the defection. Treat's efforts to secure a direct statement from the senator came to naught, however, and caused the editor considerable disillusionment. Benton remained in the East and kept his silence throughout the campaign, while Frank and Montgomery, through their *Barnburner* editorials, implied his support.[16]

For all his enthusiasm, Frank, in mid-September, confided to his father, "Benton's course, in endorsing Cass, has shut us out from all hope of carrying the state for Van Buren, but I find it easy to convince people of the rectitude of [Benton's] course & such is the kindness which the stouthearted Democracy bear him that I would not despair of the state if we had time & able men to defend his course." Montgomery had been won over to the cause and had written some articles for the *Barnburner*, much to the dismay of his father-in-law, Levi Woodbury, who, like Benton, stayed with the regular ticket. For all their enthusiasm, however, Frank and Montgomery found minimal support. Although the *Barnburner* created a considerable sensation, it failed to attract sufficient subscriptions or capital to maintain itself beyond the election. Nor did it create the vote for Van Buren that the brothers had hoped. The Free-Soil defection siphoned off enough votes from the Democratic ticket in New York to throw the national election to Taylor and the Whigs. In Missouri, the Van Buren ticket attracted only a few thousand votes.[17]

Strongly influenced by his father and Van Buren, Frank emerged from this election fully committed to the Free-Soil doctrine. Part of the Blair family's concern centered around their enmity with John C. Calhoun. Preston's and Jackson's antagonist from the early days of Old Hickory's administration, Calhoun strongly advocated the extension of slavery into the territories recently acquired from Mexico as the slaveholder's right. Beyond that, however, the Blairs believed that the proslavery leaders constituted a "privileged class"

16. James B. Bowlin to Andrew Jackson Donelson, May 5, 1851, Andrew Jackson Donelson Papers; Chambers, *Old Bullion Benton*, 334–37; C. H. McClure, *Opposition in Missouri*, 138–40; Parrish, *David Rice Atchison*, 71.

17. FB to FPB, September 13, 1848, MB to EBL, October 4, 1848, BLC; W. E. Smith, *Blair Family in Politics*, 1:242–43.

who threatened free institutions and the rights of free white men to enter and control the territories without fear of competition from black slaves, whom the Blairs, like many of their contemporaries, held as innately inferior.[18]

Simultaneously with his political pursuits, Frank kept busy on the domestic scene during this time. He hoped to finish his new house before Apo returned from Kentucky, where she had spent the summer of 1848. Apo was apprehensive about the senior Blair's willingness to furnish the house lest her husband spend more than intended, but Frank assured his father that this could be done comfortably for one thousand dollars. Apo wrote her father-in-law from Kentucky thanking him for his generosity and reporting that her Biddle relatives in Philadelphia had agreed to provide their silver. She was anxious to move into their new home, in part no doubt, because of the arrival of their first child, Andrew, who was born in Kentucky on September 20. Frank made a hurried trip the following month to bring mother and son back to St. Louis. Minna reported to Lizzie by mid-December that the new baby was "fat and healthy." Apo's mother and younger sister, Midge, had come to St. Louis for the winter to help. Anticipating their return to Kentucky in the spring, Frank wrote his father in January, asking that the slave Joanna be dispatched from the Silver Spring homestead to help care for the baby if his parents could spare her.[19]

Politics were never far from Frank's mind, however. The *Missouri Republican* reported shortly after the 1848 election that "an effort will be made at the coming session of the legislature to instruct Col. Benton out of his seat in the Senate" through the use of the slavery question. Both Frank and Montgomery informed their father that they anticipated the General Assembly would require Old Bullion to vote against the Wilmot Proviso and Free-Soilism. If that should happen, Frank thought that the senator ought to either resign or make an outright appeal to the people over the heads of the legislature.[20]

There had been growing dissatisfaction with Old Bullion for some time over various issues. Several Missouri Democratic leaders, including Samuel Treat, the editor of the *St. Louis Union*, had made contact with John C. Calhoun,

---

18. E. B. Smith, *Francis Preston Blair*, 194–200.

19. FB to FPB, September 13, 1848, MB to EBL, October 4, 1848, Minna Blair to EBL, December 15, 1848, BLC; Apo to FPB, n.d. and November 22, 1848, FB to FPB, January 3, 1849, B-LP. The senior Blairs had acquired their Silver Spring, Maryland, estate outside Washington in the early 1840s. Frank's growing family would enjoy its rural pleasures during their many summer sojourns there (E. B. Smith, *Francis Preston Blair*, 172–73).

20. *Missouri Republican*, November 7, 1848; FPB to Van Buren, January 6, 27, 1849, Van Buren Papers.

the leader of the southern ultras in Congress and Benton's longtime foe. Benton's fellow senator from Missouri, David R. Atchison, moved strongly into the Calhoun camp that winter as one of the signers of the Southern Address, drafted by the South Carolinian and adopted by a caucus of southern congressmen to protest what they considered northern aggression against southern interests. Atchison would assume a major role in the anti-Benton movement in the months to come.[21]

During January 1849 Frank wrote a series of articles for the *Missouri Republican,* under the pseudonym "Radical," castigating those whom he claimed were working to bring Benton down. In the first of these titled "The Wolf Is on His Walk Again," Frank accused Atchison of plotting to replace Benton with Claiborne Jackson, one of the leaders of the "Central Clique" and an ardent proslavery man.[22]

In yet another article, Frank charged Loring Pickering, who edited the *Union* while Treat wintered in Cuba, with having anti-Benton sentiments. Pickering demanded of the *Republican* the name of the writer, and upon learning that it was Blair, responded with a blistering editorial, which concluded, "It is to know the coward, the slanderer, the liar, to despise him, and we hereafter dismiss the imbecile creature from present consideration." Frank quickly challenged Pickering to a duel in defense of his honor, which the latter declined. In a subsequent encounter near the *Union* office, the two got into a fight, with Frank attacking Pickering with his umbrella and the *Union* editor retaliating by drawing a bowie knife. When Blair threatened to shoot him on the spot if he used it, Pickering left the scene, rubbing an eye that Frank had struck with his umbrella.[23]

About a week later, as he left a meeting at the courthouse, Frank became suspicious of a shadowy character following him. Apparently the fellow was a lookout for Pickering, who approached him, "wrapped up in a cloak," and fired three shots with a revolver. Unhurt, Frank responded with his double-barreled pistol. He struck his assailant in the thigh and elbow before the latter fled into the darkness. A grand jury subsequently indicted both Pickering and his accomplice for assault, but they were acquitted. Frank was indicted for

21. C. H. McClure, *Opposition in Missouri,* 136–45; Chambers, *Old Bullion Benton,* 340–43; Parrish, *David Rice Atchison,* 70–80, 92–93.

22. *Missouri Republican,* January 13, 18, 24, 28, 1849. The article cited is January 13. A copy may be found in the Thomas Hart Benton Papers.

23. FB to SPL, March 19, 1849, with clipping enclosures from *Missouri Republican,* January 27, 1849, and *St. Louis Daily Union,* February 2, 1849, MB to FPB, March 23, 1849, B-LP.

challenging Pickering to a duel, which was against Missouri law. He pleaded guilty, received a sentence of one minute in jail, and paid a one-dollar fine.[24]

The encounter with Pickering would not be the last time Frank faced such danger. Subsequent political campaigns frequently brought even more direct confrontations. Contemporary newspapers and the reminiscences of his political associates frequently mention such encounters. Realizing that his political views were frequently unpopular with large segments of the voters, Blair met the opposition head-on and usually carried a small pistol for protection. "We never knew a man less amenable to the charge of fear than General Blair," recalled W. V. N. Bay. "We have seen him tried under circumstances well calculated to unnerve the stoutest heart." Regardless of their feelings about his political opinions, most of his contemporaries admired his courage.[25]

Meanwhile, Benton's enemies in the Missouri legislature moved forward with their plan to replace him. Governor King took a strong proslavery stand in his inaugural address, and the legislature promptly reelected Atchison to the Senate by an overwhelming vote. On January 15, 1849, Claiborne Jackson introduced resolutions in the House that denied Congress's authority to legislate against slavery in the territories and proclaimed the right of all citizens to emigrate there with whatever property they chose to take, including slaves. The Jackson Resolutions "instructed" Missouri's senators and congressmen to act in accordance with these sentiments. They carried by large majorities in both houses and, during the decade that followed, served as the focal point of the controversy dividing the Missouri Democracy.[26]

Senator Benton immediately responded to the challenge. He wrote Montgomery on January 29, "I have been perfectly aware of the plot against myself & friends. It was all directed from this place [Washington] and is only a new form of an old work. . . . I shall be out among them as soon as Congress adjourns & drive them out to open war." The Blair brothers, with thirty-six other Benton supporters, quickly issued an "address to the Democracy," attacking the southern conspiracy and proclaiming that Congress had

---

24. Walter B. Stevens, ed., *St. Louis, the Fourth City*, 1:211–12; *Missouri Republican*, April 24, 1849; FB to SPL, March 19, 1849, MB to FPB, March 23, 1849, Apo to FPB, April 18, 1849, B-LP. Pickering subsequently sold his interest in the *Union* to Richard Phillips, who tended to be pro-Benton, and left the area (MB to FPB, June 4, 1849, FB to SPL, June 7, 1849, B-LP).
25. Bay, *Reminiscences*, 398–99; Daniel Grissom, "Personal Recollections of Distinguished Missourians."
26. C. H. McClure, *Opposition in Missouri*, 151–59; Parrish, *David Rice Atchison*, 86–87; Chambers, *Old Bullion Benton*, 341–42.

the absolute right to govern territories, including their policies concerning slavery. Montgomery wrote Van Buren that he could have procured more signatures but he had wanted to get the address out during the spring canvass for municipal elections. "I have no doubt but that we can sustain Col. Benton in the doctrines here ascribed to him," he argued, "and at this moment the [Free-Soil] doctrine will not more need his help, than he does the help of the doctrine for his enemies are in the ascendant now in this State & it requires something potent to physic them with."[27]

Benton returned to Missouri in early May after an absence of two years. On May 9, he issued a blunt manifesto denouncing the Jackson Resolutions and appealing to the people to sustain him. He then went on a statewide speaking tour, blasting Calhoun as "the prime mover and head contriver" of a new slavery conspiracy that could threaten the Union and accusing Atchison and Claiborne Jackson of being his minions. Preston Blair informed Van Buren, "Benton has you see begun in earnest. He writes to his family that he was never better received by his constituents." Indeed, Old Bullion did seem to be making headway as he attracted large and generally receptive audiences across Missouri.[28]

Frank, meanwhile, became concerned with getting his family out of St. Louis for the summer because of the fear of a cholera epidemic that had struck New Orleans and might be headed upriver. Before they could leave, Apo's mother, who had been visiting for the winter, came down with an attack, although she recovered quickly. A worried Apo wrote her father-in-law that Frank was worn out from overwork with his law practice and politics and badly needed a rest. She, too, had had a hard winter following the birth of young Andrew. She complained to Preston that the whole affair with Pickering had caused her more unhappiness than she could express. Her hope to get away to Kentucky by mid-April was negated by the necessity for Frank's testimony at the Pickering trial, but by mid-May they were safely ensconced at Sherwood.[29]

27. MB to M. M. Marmaduke, February 22, 1849, Sappington Papers, enclosing Benton's letter; MB to Van Buren, March 12, 1849, Van Buren Papers. Benton and the Blairs were convinced that Calhoun was directing the Missouri effort from Washington, although there is no proof of this (Chambers, *Old Bullion Benton*, 340–49; Parrish, *David Rice Atchison*, 87).

28. *Jefferson Inquirer*, May 19, 1849; FPB to Van Buren, June 10, 1849, Van Buren Papers; Chambers, *Old Bullion Benton*, 344–52.

29. FB to FPB, January 3, 1849, Apo to FPB, April 18, 1849, B-LP; Apo to FPB, April 10, 1849, BLC; Apo to Apolline Hundley, May 28, 1849, BLPLC.

The time away from St. Louis did Frank a great deal of good. He wrote his father in early June that he had been able to relax and felt physically transformed since his arrival in Kentucky. Never completely divorced from politics, Frank had several visits with Henry Clay at his Lexington home and was gratified to hear that the Great Compromiser had put past animosities aside and favored the reelection of Benton. With cholera continuing to ravage St. Louis (the city would lose 10 percent of its population in the epidemic), the Blair family decided to spend the entire summer in Kentucky with Frank maintaining his legal affairs through correspondence.[30]

Frank returned to St. Louis in mid-September in time for the reopening of the courts, concerned with attending to the needs of his law practice, leaving Apo and young Andrew at Sherwood. A devastating fire had struck the city shortly after their departure, and Frank anticipated that there would be a need for considerable capital in rebuilding. St. Louis was growing rapidly as new immigration poured in from Europe and the East. Frank urged his father to invest in St. Louis real estate and invited him and Eliza to visit later in the fall. His parents declined the invitation, but when Montgomery returned from his summer sojourn in the East, he and Frank decided to resume a joint law practice. Montgomery reported that their prospects looked quite favorable and that they had agreed to stay out of politics for the time being, at least in terms of running for office, although they might write an occasional political article. He further informed his father that Frank seemed to be prospering with his investments as land values increased. In addition to his home, Frank owned a store on Fourth Street and numerous houses and lots around town. Montgomery estimated Frank's worth at thirty thousand dollars, with his only liability a four-thousand-dollar note to the George Bent estate. "In fact," Montgomery told his father, "I think his judgment excellent & tho he seems lazy he rarely neglects anything. . . . Another good point is that he is grown more considerate of expenses, & does not waste his money as he formerly did." This latter change could be attributed, no doubt, to Apo's influence and concern for financial independence.[31]

---

30. FB to FPB, June 7, July 2, 18, August 19, 1849, Apo to EBL, August 5, 1849, FB to SPL, January 7, 1850, B-LP; Apo to Apolline Hundley, May 28, 1849, BLPLC.

31. Primm, *Lion of the Valley*, 174–75, 188–89; FB to FPB, September 20, 1849, MB to FPB, October 11, 1849, B-LP. For Frank's view of the new partnership, see FB to FPB, November 5, December 15, 1849, BLC. The 1850 census revealed that Frank's net worth was twenty-five thousand dollars. Apo's mother, her son George, age twenty-four, and her daughter, Mira,

Apo returned early in November, bringing her brother George with her. Frank found employment for him in the commission house of James E. Yeatman. Also accompanying Apo was one of Frank's cousins, B. Gratz Brown, with whom her husband's political career would be closely entwined over the next twenty-five years. Gratz was the son of Mason and Judith Bledsoe Brown, his mother being a niece of Frank's mother, Eliza. Born in 1826 in Lexington, in the same house where Frank had first seen the light of day five years earlier, Brown was named for their beloved uncle. He and Frank had become close friends when Gratz attended Transylvania University while Frank was in law school there and both lived in their uncle's Lexington home. Montgomery and Frank took the fledgling lawyer under their wing as an associate and quickly converted him to the political support of Benton as well.[32]

Frank watched closely the unfolding events in Congress that winter as that badly divided body wrestled with the questions of California and the other issues arising from the Mexican War. He deplored any effort at compromise with the southerners over allowing slavery to enter the territories. By June 1850, he seemed reassured that "Calhounism is doomed to a most disgraceful defeat," as Henry Clay's Omnibus Bill worked its way through the Senate. Apo continued to worry about the effect of his work habits on his health, complaining to her father-in-law that her husband refused to exercise.[33]

Except for two weeks during July spent in Kentucky, Frank remained in St. Louis, tending to the law business while Montgomery vacationed in the East. He also worked hard for the pro-Benton ticket in the August state elections. Shortly before leaving St. Louis, he wrote his brother that Benton's "prospects appear to be brightening very much and our friends are taking heart and courage." Yet, it became increasingly evident as the Democracy fragmented that the Whigs would hold the balance of power in the next

---

age seventeen, were living with the Blairs temporarily in their new home. Frank owned three slaves: a couple, ages thirty-five and thirty, and their daughter, age eight. George Alexander had two male slaves, ages twenty-two and twenty (1850 Missouri Census, St. Louis City, in U.S. Bureau of the Census, 386). Apo had written Preston Blair in October 1849 that her mother planned to move to St. Louis, with Frank intending to have her build a house on one of his town lots (Apo to FPB, October 11, 1849, B-LP).

32. Norma Lois Peterson, *Freedom and Franchise: The Political Career of B. Gratz Brown*, 3–5, 13–16; Apo to FPB, October 11, 1849, B-LP; FB to FPB, November 5, 1849, December 2, 1850, BLC; B. Gratz Brown to Orlando Brown, May 31, June 1, 1850, Orlando Brown Papers.

33. FB to SPL, January 7, 1850, Apo to FPB, February 9, 1850, B-LP; FB to MB, June 15, 1850, BLC.

assembly. And Benton did little to endear himself to Whigs as he attacked the compromise efforts of their great hero, Henry Clay, in Congress.[34]

When the state election finally took place, it became obvious that a badly divided legislature would decide Benton's fate. The Benton men held sixty-two seats in both houses, while the anti-Benton forces had only thirty-five, but the Whigs controlled sixty-four and immediately became the object of conciliation efforts by both Democratic factions. Frank believed the Benton men had a good chance for success and outlined several plans to accomplish it. When the General Assembly convened in December 1850, Frank traveled to Jefferson City to try to effect them. His efforts proved futile, however, as the Antis and the Whigs coalesced behind a proslavery Whig, Henry S. Geyer, on the fortieth ballot to send Thomas Hart Benton down to defeat.[35]

In the wake of this setback, Frank confided to his father, "The result of the senatorial election, altho expected gave me a sharp pang." Undaunted and convinced that it did not have to mark the end of Benton's political career, he projected a comeback for Old Bullion as a candidate for the House seat from the St. Louis district while hoping to persuade him to be a candidate for the presidency in 1852. When the senior Blair approached Benton, Old Bullion proved amenable to the idea of running for the House seat but eschewed any presidential ambitions. In the meantime, Benton planned to devote himself to writing his memoirs.[36]

During 1851 Frank settled down to the practice of law and the management of his increasing real estate holdings. He suffered "severely" from rheumatism that spring, his first attack in two years. Montgomery reported to his father, "For your comfort I can tell you that Frank is a pretty good charger and collector, & in no ways awkward in asking & having what is his."[37]

A contemporary, John Hume, left a vivid description of Frank during this period:

> Blair was a man not only of strong ambition but of arbitrary temperament. He could not tolerate the idea of a newcomer pre-empting what he had considered his premises. If he could not rule he was ready

34. FB to MB, June 15, 1850, BLC; C. H. McClure, *Opposition in Missouri*, 203–11.
35. FB to FPB, August 17, 1850, February 3, 1851, B-LP; FB to FPB, December 2, 1850, BLC; C. H. McClure, *Opposition in Missouri*, 211–16; Chambers, *Old Bullion Benton*, 369–77.
36. FB to FPB, February 3, 1851, B-LP; FPB to Van Buren, February 6, 1851, Van Buren Papers.
37. FB to FPB, March 12, 1851, B-LP; MB to FPB, May 5, 1851, BLC.

to ruin. That disposition accorded with both his mental and physical makeup. Bodily he was a bundle of bones and nerves without a particle of surplus flesh. His hair was red, his complexion was sandy, and his eyes, when he was excited and angry, had a baleful expression that led some one in my presence on a certain occasion to speak of them as "brush-heaps afire."

He was not an eloquent man, although a ready and frequent public speaker. His voice was not musical. His strong forte was invective. He was nearly always denouncing somebody. Apparently, he was never so happy as when making another miserable. . . . That he was not almost all the time in personal difficulties was due to the fact that he was known to be a man of exceptional courage. He was a born fighter. Physically I think he was the bravest man I ever knew.[38]

In the early months of 1852, both Frank and Montgomery, together with their father, became enamored with another dashing figure whom they considered a "born fighter." Louis Kossuth, the leader of an aborted Hungarian revolution against the Austrian Empire, arrived in the United States to seek support for his beleaguered cause. Americans welcomed him enthusiastically as the embodiment of their own principles in eastern Europe. The senior Blair helped arrange his appearance at the annual Democratic dinner in Washington celebrating the battle of New Orleans, while Frank and Montgomery were instrumental in extending him an invitation to visit St. Louis. He swept into that city in March as part of a nationwide tour. Frank reported that he had met with Kossuth privately several times during his visit and was active in "collecting material aid for his cause."[39]

The national Kossuth enthusiasm proved short-lived, however, as Americans increasingly turned their attention to the upcoming national elections. While keeping politics on the back burner, Frank, nevertheless, quizzed his father about various Democratic presidential prospects. He had earlier expressed dismay that Benton would consider the conservative Levi Woodbury for the position, declaring that Old Bullion "ought now to stand by the Radical Democrats who have upheld him for 30 years and allow us to make him President." His father tended to agree with Benton, however, seeing in Woodbury a compromise candidate who could help restore some unity to the Democracy.[40]

38. John F. Hume, *The Abolitionists, Together with Personal Memories of the Struggle for Human Rights,* 189.

39. FPB to Martin Van Buren, January 2, 9, 11, 18, 1852, Van Buren Papers; EBL to SPL, January 2, 29, 30, 1852, B-LP; MB to FPB, January 26, 1852, FB to FPB, March 17, 1852, BLC.

40. FB to FPB, March 12, 1851, B-LP; FB to James Blair, September 4, 1851, BLC.

Whatever chances Woodbury, Minna Blair's father, had were cut short, however, by his sudden death in September 1851. Minna, in confinement in St. Louis with her second child, took the news hard, and it was feared for a time that she might follow her father. The situation became sufficiently serious for Preston Blair to travel to St. Louis to check on his two sons and their spouses. Minna recovered, giving birth to a healthy baby boy whom she and Montgomery named for her father.

The visit of the senior Blair allowed plenty of time for political discussions. The Blairs now began to focus their attention on Preston's old friend, Gen. William O. Butler of Kentucky, the party's vice presidential candidate in 1848, as the best hope for the Democratic presidential nomination. Their enthusiasm for Butler proved short-lived, however, when he publicly approved a set of proslavery resolutions in the Kentucky legislature in January 1852. When the Democratic National Convention finally nominated Franklin Pierce of New Hampshire, who had avoided taking a stand on the controversial issues of the day, as a compromise candidate, the Blairs supported him enthusiastically.[41]

Frank took the next logical step to expand his political base that spring by announcing his candidacy for one of the ten St. Louis seats in the Missouri House of Representatives. He had decided that this offered the best way to have a hand in promoting both his own and Benton's political fortunes, participating in the actual give-and-take of the legislature, rather than trying to operate from the outside. He made it quite clear that he stood on a Free-Soil platform. His cousin B. Gratz Brown also announced his intention to run, and the two campaigned vigorously throughout the St. Louis area. They were joined in the political fray by Thomas Hart Benton, when a rally of his followers nominated him to run for the national House of Representatives from Missouri's First District, which extended from St. Louis south to the Arkansas border.[42]

Only one cloud marred the Blair-Benton Missouri political horizon that summer, the state convention's choice of Sterling Price as the Missouri Democracy's gubernatorial candidate. Price, who owed his Mexican War career to Benton's patronage, had since deserted Old Bullion over the slavery-expansion question, although some believed the split came because of

41. FB to FPB, October 10, December 9, 1851, B-LP; FPB to Van Buren, November 24, 1851, Van Buren Papers; E. B. Smith, *Francis Preston Blair,* 209–10.

42. FB to FPB, April 21, 1852, FB to MB, May 21, 1852, B-LP; Benjamin C. Merkel, "The Slavery Issue and the Political Decline of Thomas Hart Benton, 1846–1856," 399–402; Peterson, *Freedom and Franchise,* 17–18; Chambers, *Old Bullion Benton,* 384–87.

Benton's closeness with the Blairs. Benton had favored another Price, Thomas L. (no relation to Sterling), for the governorship; and Montgomery had nominated that Price at the state convention. At one point in the balloting Frank challenged the pro–Sterling Price delegate votes from Pulaski County with a strong denunciation of the Mexican War hero. This drew a heated response; and he later backed down, proposing former governor M. M. Marmaduke as a compromise candidate. The Sterling Price backers had gained enough support in the meantime to carry the day, however. Both sides then agreed on a compromise platform, and the Missouri Democracy went into the fall campaign united.[43]

The Blairs, together with Benton and Brown, determined that they needed a new journalistic organ to support their campaigns. Frank's previous attempt at running a newspaper, the *Barnburner,* had proved short-lived, expiring after the 1848 election. Now he and Brown, backed by a group of influential Free-Soil friends, acquired the *Morning Signal,* a paper begun by a group of New England printers the previous January. Renaming it the *Missouri Democrat,* the new owners published their first issue on July 1, 1852, a month before the August election. One of twenty-one newspapers in St. Louis at the time, the *Missouri Democrat* proved to be one of the longest lasting, ultimately consolidating with the *Globe* in 1875.[44]

Both Blair and Brown wrote hard-hitting editorials for the new organ, and Benton contributed several of his own. These especially appealed to the German and Irish immigrants. The Germans, particularly, would become a key element in the political success of Frank and Gratz in the decade that followed. Strongly antislavery and receptive to the free-labor theme of the Free-Soil movement, the Germans admired the fiery rhetoric of Frank and his cousin. The result was victory for all three men. Benton won handily over two opponents, while Brown ran fourth and Blair eighth in an open field of twenty for the ten St. Louis legislative seats.[45]

While the campaign raged, the Blair family also found itself occupied with two events of a personal nature. Apo's younger sister, Midge, became engaged to Franklin A. Dick, a young attorney from Philadelphia who had an office

43. *St. Joseph (Mo.) Gazette,* April 14, 1852; FB to Martin Van Buren, April 30, 1852, Van Buren Papers; Robert E. Shalhope, *Sterling Price: Portrait of a Southerner,* 94–96.

44. Stevens, *St. Louis, the Fourth City,* 1:212; Jim Allee Hart, *A History of the "St. Louis Globe-Democrat,"* 2–4, 117–18.

45. Peterson, *Freedom and Franchise,* 17; Chambers, *Old Bullion Benton,* 369; Steven Rowan, ed., *Germans for a Free Missouri: Translations from the St. Louis Radical Press, 1857–1862,* 6–7; Abstract of Election Returns, St. Louis County, August 2, 1852.

in the same building as Frank and Montgomery. Montgomery pronounced Dick "a fine fellow & every way worthy of her," although Mrs. Alexander questioned his Philadelphia family connections since they were not on the Biddles' "visiting list." The Dicks' marriage proved to be a long and happy one, however, and the Dick and Frank Blair families remained very close in the years that followed. The other event was the arrival of Frank and Apo's second child, a healthy eleven-pound baby girl, on April 5, 1852, whom they named Christine after Apo's Biddle relative in Philadelphia. The proud father described her at great length to his parents.[46]

It had been an exciting and tumultuous five years for Frank since his return from New Mexico. He had launched four careers simultaneously: marital, legal, property entrepreneur, and political. It would quickly become evident in the next decade that the latter occupied his primary interest as he plunged from one political contest to another. An individual of unbounded ambition and energy, Frank drove himself unceasingly, often at the expense of his health and frequently to the despair of his wife, to accomplish his political goals. Having committed himself to the Free-Soil doctrine, he would, nevertheless, reveal a strong antipathy for the slaves as he championed the cause of free-white labor.

46. MB to FPB, September 18, 1851, BLC; FB to FPB, April 5, 1852, B-LP.

4

Reputation Established

On December 29, 1852, Apo wrote her mother-in-law that Frank had gone to Jefferson City for the reconvening of the legislature. "He took up plenty of books to keep him reading all the winter," she reported. "He & Gratz [Brown] are to have two rooms (a sitting room & bedroom) together. Frank takes bedding and a servant so that I think they will be pretty comfortable. Not so much so as if I had gone with him I suppose but Jefferson is a miserable place at best. Frank is very well & in good spirits."[1]

Frank found one of his pleasures greatly restricted early in the session when the House voted to ban the smoking of cigars. To get even with those who thus curtailed one of his favorite pastimes, Blair quickly amended the motion to read "and pipes." The January session was but a continuation of one called the previous fall to deal with the distribution of public lands for the construction of railroads within the state. While the legislature had resolved that matter, the railroad question had become overshadowed by the division of both parties over the 1849 Jackson Resolutions. Frank quickly found himself the storm center of controversy when he moved to repeal the resolutions, a major goal of the pro-Benton party as it began its campaign to return Old Bullion to the Senate when David R. Atchison's term expired in 1855.[2]

Frank launched his attack on February 1, 1853, in a speech whose themes he would reiterate time after time in the decade that followed. He argued for

1. Apo to EB, December 29, 1852, BLC.
2. Peterson, *Freedom and Franchise*, 20; *Journal of the House of Representatives of the State of Missouri*, extra session of the 17th General Assembly, 250.

repeal of the Jackson Resolutions, not over the issue of slavery, but because, he contended, they represented a plot by nullifiers who sought to destroy the Union by undoing the work of Congress as exemplified by the Northwest Ordinance of 1787 and the Missouri Compromise of 1820. He invoked the image of the Founding Fathers in vitriolic language, asking who best represented the interests of the country: "the men who achieved the independence of our country, and framed the government under which we live," or "the small beer politicians of the present day who have lately endangered the very existence of the Union of the States." Benton, he reminded his listeners, had always supported southern interests but only within the context of a strong Union. Those who had thrust the Jackson Resolutions upon the people were the disciples of John C. Calhoun, who had "always prescribed nullification and disunion." In closing, Frank pointed out that Benton supported a central route, which would assist Missouri and unite the country, for the proposed transcontinental railroad then being debated before Congress. The southerners urged a sectional route beginning at Memphis, which would have the opposite effect. In sum, the Jackson Resolutions undermined the strong nationalism for which Benton and Blair's cherished model, Andrew Jackson, had stood for so long.[3]

The House spent several days in strenuous debate over Frank's proposal. A. S. Mitchell, editor of the pro-Whig *St. Louis Evening News*, wrote Abiel Leonard, "We have got the Demmies into a fight at last. . . . Blair and Claib Jackson had it hip and thigh. . . . Jackson was, in the judgment of the House, clearly floored." The Benton men had been carefully cultivating the moderate Whigs in an effort to secure enough votes for passage. However, when the issue came to a head on February 14, the House tabled it seventy-two to forty-nine, with many Whigs favoring this move to avoid its divisive effect on their own party. In the waning days of the session, a committee headed by Gratz Brown drew up an address calling on all true Democrats to work for the election of a pro-Benton majority to the next legislature. Writing his father a few days after he returned home, Frank expressed satisfaction with his initial efforts and predicted Benton's ultimate triumph.[4]

3. Blair's remarks are printed in full in the *Jefferson Inquirer*, March 5, 1853. An excellent analysis of Blair's ideas, as reflected in his speeches, can be found in Leonard B. Wurthman Jr., "Frank Blair of Missouri: Jacksonian Orator of the Civil War Era."

4. FB to MB, February 11, 1853, FB to FPB, March 5, April 7, 1853, BLC; *Jefferson Inquirer*, February 17, 24, 1853; FB to James S. Rollins, July 1, 1853, James S. Rollins Papers; John Vollmer Mering, *The Whig Party in Missouri*, 194–95; Frederic A. Culmer, "Abiel Leonard," 37.

A new concern now clouded the horizon, however. In mid-February, a rumor circulated that Claiborne Jackson had gone to Washington to assist Senator Atchison with Missouri patronage matters in the new Pierce administration. Frank warned his father to keep an eye on Jackson and to relay any information to Benton. The latter had recommended Montgomery to the new president for attorney general, and numerous letters had been forwarded from Missouri on his behalf. Initially, it appeared that Pierce would seek to appease both factions of the Missouri Democracy in his appointments; but, by the end of April, following Benton's departure from Washington to Missouri, the president capitulated completely to Atchison and the southern ultras, who warned that they had the votes in the Senate to block any appointment not to their liking. There would be no cabinet appointment for Montgomery; and most of the Missouri appointments, including the postmastership in St. Louis, went to anti-Benton Democrats.[5]

Benton launched an all-out campaign for a return to the Senate that spring. He published a long letter strongly endorsing the construction of a "central national road" to the Pacific, claiming that Atchison and the southern ultras were conspiring with Pierce for a more southerly route, which could not benefit Missouri. Frank attended a commercial convention in Memphis that summer as one of twenty-nine Missouri delegates out of some five hundred from throughout the Mississippi valley region seeking common ground to offset the trade disparity between their area and the Northeast. Assisted by young John Kasson, later governor of Iowa, Frank worked assiduously in support of Benton's central route. While everyone agreed on the need for a Pacific railroad, they could not coalesce on a location. The delegates sought to avoid sectional strains of a political nature, however, with all agreeing on the need for improving economic and commercial relations throughout the region and along its north-south corridor.[6]

Meanwhile, the *Missouri Democrat* and other pro-Benton papers took up the cause as Benton headed for the western border to dispatch an exploring party to investigate the feasibility of the central avenue for the transcontinental railroad. Atchison and the anti-Benton press responded in kind, claiming that they had no objection to the central route if the Nebraska territory to

5. Minna Blair to General Peaslee, February 3, 1853, Benton to FPB, April 30, 1853, BLC. The BLC contains numerous letters to Pierce endorsing Montgomery. For a thorough discussion of the patronage question, see Parrish, *David Rice Atchison*, 132–38.

6. Thomas H. Benton to "Dear Sir," March 12, 1853, BLC; Edward Younger, *John A. Kasson: Politics and Diplomacy from Lincoln to McKinley*, 66–67.

the west of Missouri could be organized in such a way as to allow Missouri slaveholders to emigrate there, something currently barred by the Missouri Compromise of 1820. In the midst of this struggle, Gov. Sterling Price did little to endear himself to Benton or the Blairs when he removed the state printing contract from the pro-Benton *Jefferson Inquirer* and gave it to the anti-Benton *Missouri Examiner.*[7]

Still, Frank wrote his father that things seemed to be going well for Benton politically, and he denounced Atchison as "a damned intriguer and a tool of the nullifiers." Frank took added hope because the St. Louis city elections had gone for the Benton Democrats that spring. He was recovering from rheumatism in his foot, which had hampered his activity earlier. He had also been giving a great deal of attention to the development of his new country home, "Rose Bank," which the family would use as a summer residence to escape the crowded city. Interestingly, Frank made no mention in any of his letters of another event that would affect his legal career: the decision of his brother Montgomery to leave St. Louis that summer and move with his family back to Washington.[8]

Later that fall Frank took Apo and the children on an extended trip east to visit his family at Silver Spring and the Biddles at Philadelphia. Shortly after their return to St. Louis, word came that his brother Jim had died unexpectedly in California of a ruptured aorta. Frank openly mourned the loss of his brother, who had been his close playmate in childhood years but who had spent most of his adult life in the navy. He felt grateful for the last visit the two had enjoyed when he had accompanied Jim to New Orleans the previous May to see him off to California. When Apo gave birth to their third child the following April 1854, they named him James. Frank volunteered to go to California to help straighten out his brother's affairs, if necessary. His father decided that Montgomery could better undertake that mission, however, as Frank needed to concentrate on his law practice with his brother-in-law Franklin A. Dick, who had joined him in the office.[9]

Concerned for his parents in his brother's absence, Frank made a quick trip to Washington at the end of February 1854. Finding them well, he hastened

7. Chambers, *Old Bullion Benton*, 397–98; Parrish, *David Rice Atchison*, 125–29; Peterson, *Freedom and Franchise*, 25–26.

8. FB to FPB, March 5, April 7, May 10, July 12, 1853, BLC; FB to FPB, May 27, 1853, B-LP.

9. FB to FPB, May 27, November 14, 1853, April 2, 1854, B-LP; Samuel Simmons to MB, October 15, 1853, FB to FPB, December 3, 1853, January 20, 23, 1854, BLC; *St. Louis Directory for the Years 1854–1855*, 15, 45.

back to St. Louis, anticipating a run for Benton's congressional seat inasmuch as Old Bullion had indicated he would not seek reelection to the House, preferring to concentrate on the Senate race. By late April, as a result of the passage by Congress of the Kansas-Nebraska Act, which Benton opposed, that decision had been reversed; and Frank now agreed to seek reelection to the legislature, where he could help engineer Old Bullion's Senate race against Atchison.[10]

The Kansas-Nebraska Act, which repealed the Missouri Compromise of 1820 and opened the newly created Kansas Territory to the possibility of proslavery settlement, quickly became the focal point of the 1854 congressional and legislative elections in Missouri as elsewhere. With free-soil and antislavery Democrats and Whigs alike feeling betrayed by this measure, the political scene became very unsettled. Throughout the Midwest, a variety of local organizations sprang up that would coalesce to form the Republican Party. The development within Whig ranks of the Know-Nothing movement further complicated the situation.

Frank worked hard to take advantage of this new atmosphere to ensure Benton's return to the Senate through a coalition of free-soil Whigs and Benton Democrats in the forthcoming legislature. He solicited candidates throughout the state, and in one case offered to support the reelection of a Whig congressional incumbent in central Missouri if the Whigs, in turn, would help elect a pro-Benton man to the legislature. In April, he installed Gratz Brown as the regular editor of the *Missouri Democrat*, telling his father that Gratz had the advantage of being better known throughout the state because of his legislative experience and his having no "Barnburner antecedents." He also "is a better writer & thinker and has more energy & industry." Such hard work would be badly needed in the upcoming campaign.[11]

The congressional and legislative returns in August produced mixed results. Frank and Gratz Brown returned to the legislature, placing tenth and twelfth, respectively, in the field of thirty-nine candidates for thirteen seats from St. Louis. Benton, however, went down to defeat by not quite one thousand votes at the hands of Luther M. Kennett, a former St. Louis mayor

10. FB to MB, March 2, 1854, FB to FPB, April 23, 1854, BLC; Chambers, *Old Bullion Benton*, 406–7.

11. FB to M. M. Marmaduke, February 5, 1854, Sappington Papers; James O. Broadhead to James S. Rollins, March 12, 1854, Rollins Papers; FB to FPB, April 18, 1854, B-LP; FPB to MB, July 17, 1854, BLC; FB to Abiel Leonard, July 18, 1854, Leonard to FB, July 21, 1854, Abiel Leonard Papers.

who had secured Whig and Know-Nothing votes with nativist speeches. The anti-Benton faction utilized the German paper, the *Anzeiger des Westens,* to stir up trouble among the immigrant groups, which caused them to desert Benton in sufficient numbers to throw the balance to Kennett. Violence marked election day in St. Louis as an election judge sought to examine the naturalization papers of Irish voters a bit too carefully. The new Missouri House would have forty-eight Whigs, forty-five anti-Benton men, and thirty-four Bentonites. The Senate's makeup showed the Whigs and anti-Benton men with twelve each to counterbalance nine Benton supporters.[12]

With the Whigs holding the balance of power between the two wings of the Democratic Party, their leaders maneuvered to secure support for one of their own, as they had done with Henry S. Geyer four years earlier. Frank, Gratz Brown, and the Benton men in the House swung their support successfully to the Whig candidate for speaker and then divided the remaining offices in the House between their two groups. The Senate Whigs, however, formed a coalition with the Atchison forces. The Whigs were similarly divided on a senatorial candidate of their own. Although the Whig legislators finally rallied behind Alexander W. Doniphan, a former law partner of Atchison's, this action brought criticism from some of the party leaders outside their ranks. It also failed to gain Democratic support.[13]

Tempers flared as the joint session went through endless ballots with little change among the three candidates. At one point, Gratz Brown became offended by some remarks made against Benton and his supporters by Sen. Robert M. Stewart of St. Joseph and challenged the senator to a duel. Brown arrived at the dueling grounds ready to defend his side's honor only to discover that Stewart had withdrawn the offensive remarks. On the twenty-fourth ballot, the anti-Benton men temporarily abandoned Atchison in favor of Sterling Price, which led Frank to denounce the governor as a traitor after all that Benton had done in promoting him during the Mexican War. "He has betrayed every party with which he acted," Blair claimed, "and his present position was obtained by perfidy." Price was withdrawn after two additional ballots yielded no change in the results. In the end, the legislature gave up

12. Abstract of Election Returns, St. Louis County, August 7, 1854; *Missouri Statesman,* September 1, 1854; Chambers, *Old Bullion Benton,* 406–8; Peterson, *Freedom and Franchise,* 31; Primm, *Lion of the Valley,* 177–79.

13. A. S. Mitchell to James S. Rollins, November 25, 1854, Rollins Papers; Jo Davis to Abiel Leonard, December 27, 1854, January 1, 1855, Leonard Papers; *Journal of the House,* 18th General Assembly, 1st sess., 1–20; *Journal of the Senate of the State of Missouri,* 1st sess., 1–12.

the contest after forty-one ballots and agreed to leave the seat vacant for two years until after the next legislative election. Frank had maneuvered Atchison out of the Senate, but he had failed to secure the election of Benton.[14]

Blair's supporters exulted in young Frank's role during the legislative proceedings. Gratz Brown wrote his uncle Orlando that Frank had "justly earned the soubriquet of the Randolph of the West," while Samuel Simmons, the Blair solicitor in St. Louis, informed Montgomery that "Frank has this winter proved himself a man of marked legislative ability. Every person whom I've heard speak of him say unhesitatingly that he is the first man in the legislature." Blair had also performed yeoman's service as a member of the committee on elections to save Gratz's seat in the House against a challenge from John A. Goodlett, who had received only twelve less votes than Brown and claimed errors in the returns.[15]

Apo wrote her father-in-law that she was proud of the accolades she had heard about Frank's course that winter even though she worried about his health. Although he had been bothered by intense neuralgia headaches throughout the session, Blair felt good about what he had accomplished. In spite of their political differences, he had made a number of firm friendships among his Whig colleagues. One of these, James S. Rollins of Columbia, would become one of his closest friends and allies in the years to follow. "I must tell you," Frank boasted to his father on February 15, "that notwithstanding the outbursts of mine I have managed to press through so much of the session without a single quarrel with any member of the House & I have the best reasons for believing that I have been as much if not more influence than any member of the House."[16]

Preston particularly commended his son's speech on the need to people Kansas with free labor, believing it would go far in defeating Atchison's crusade to make Kansas a slaveholding state. In that speech, Frank had developed a theme that his father had urged upon him earlier in the session: "the great source of commercial advantages which a thriving free population to the West of [Missouri] by its enterprises would create in our Western regions."

14. B. Gratz Brown to Orlando Brown, February 9, 1855, Brown Papers; *Jefferson Inquirer,* January 13, 1855; *Journal of the Senate,* 1st sess., 189; *Journal of the House,* 18th General Assembly, 1st sess., 350.
15. B. Gratz Brown to Orlando Brown, February 9, 1855, Brown Papers; Samuel Simmons to MB, March 6, 1855, BLC.
16. FPB to FB, January 11, 1855, Blair Family Papers, MHS; Apo to FPB, February 1, 1855, FB to FPB, February 15, 1855, BLC.

The 1850s brought a strong infusion of New England businessmen into the St. Louis area. Many of these shared Free-Soil views similar to those espoused by the Blairs. They also saw the need for state support for railroad development and other economic benefits to complement the existing river system. Franklin Dick reflected their concerns when he wrote Montgomery that Frank had been instrumental in reviving a 10 percent interest rate that would help St. Louis remove "the barriers against the flow of money from the East."[17]

Frank continued to be bothered by his neuralgia headaches when he returned home from Jefferson City in early March 1855. Apo wrote her father-in-law that she hoped time and rest would help. The senior Blair had an important mission for his son, however: enlisting his aid in rescuing Andrew Jackson's home, the Hermitage, from the creditors of his adopted son and heir, Andrew Jackson Jr. When his father asked him to go to Nashville and assist William B. Lewis with the project, Frank quickly agreed, pleased to try to help preserve the home of his boyhood hero. He left for Nashville in early April and, with Lewis, arranged a settlement whereby the state of Tennessee acquired the property as a permanent shrine for its favorite son.[18]

The Missouri political scene, meanwhile, continued very much in flux. Both Whigs and Benton men sought to accommodate themselves to the changes being wrought by the Kansas-Nebraska Act and the struggle between proslavery forces led by Atchison and Free-Soil elements from New England and the Ohio valley for control of Kansas. The Know-Nothing movement attracted many Whigs, who saw it as a middle ground. In a letter to James M. Stone sometime in 1855, Frank acknowledged that the group represented "the deep seated dissatisfaction which exists in both parties" but asserted that the "Know Nothings are by no means as formidable as would appear from their recent victories."[19]

17. Primm, *Lion of the Valley*, 236–38; Jeffrey S. Adler, "Yankee Colonizers and the Making of Antebellum St. Louis"; FPB to FB, February 21, 1855, Dick to MB, March 2, 1855, BLC.

18. FPB to W. B. Lewis, March 20, 1855, Blair Family Papers, MHS; Apo to FPB, March 11, 1855, FPB to FB, April 4, 1855, W. B. Lewis to FB, April 28, 1855, G. M. Fagg to FB, May 12, 1855, BLC; FB to FPB, April 1, 1855, B-LP; FPB to W. B. Lewis, March 20, 1855, FB to Blair and Rives, April 9, 16, 1855, Andrew Jackson Jr. to John Rives, February 11, 27, 1856, W. B. Lewis to John Rives, March 2, 1856, Blair-Rives Papers.

19. FB to James M. Stone, n.d., 1855, Blair Family Papers, MHS. The known origins of the Know-Nothing movement in Missouri are discussed briefly in Walter Harrington Ryle, "Slavery and Party Realignment in Missouri in the State Election of 1856," 323–24.

Frank sought increasingly to shore up his ties with Whig leaders around the state, especially James Rollins. He wrote Rollins on May 27 that he noticed the "nullifiers" planned a rally in Boone County to endorse the course of Atchison and the proslavery element in Kansas. He hoped his Whig friend could get out a good crowd to oppose them. Later that summer Gratz Brown transmitted to Rollins his observations about a proslavery convention at Lexington called to support Atchison's efforts in Kansas. Brown pronounced it "a decided failure" and argued forcibly for the Whigs to dissociate themselves from those in their ranks who would support the "nullifiers." Rollins, in turn, argued for a coalition with the Benton forces in the forthcoming legislative session in the hope of electing two senators, Benton and a Whig.[20]

Throughout the summer Brown also kept up a steady editorial drumbeat against the Atchison forces. He assured the readers of the *Missouri Democrat* that the Benton party had no desire to interfere with slave property where it existed in Missouri. In an effort to undermine the Know-Nothing movement, Brown sought to associate it with the extremist elements of both sections. He claimed that the Know-Nothing abolitionists were intolerant of slavery, on the one hand, while, for the benefit of immigrant and business readers, he argued that the "nullification" newspapers in the state preached the Know-Nothing line against foreigners, Catholics, and Yankees. By such editorials Brown hoped to appeal to moderate Whigs to make common cause with the Benton men in counteracting those forces that he and Blair believed would destroy the Union.[21]

Frank wrote his father in late October that Atchison had been secretly initiated into the Know-Nothing Party during a stopover in St. Louis; and he and Brown used this with effect when the adjourned session of the legislature convened that fall. No agreement could be reached on an election for filling the senatorial vacancy, however, and so Missouri continued with one senator for another year. James S. Green, an anti-Benton man who would eventually succeed Atchison in the Senate, wrote Abel R. Corbin on December 5 that "Our old friend Atchison is losing his popularity with the party for various reasons, one of which is his adhesion to the K. N.'s. If we can't succeed with him, we must look for others."[22]

    20. FB to James S. Rollins, May 27, 1855, B. Gratz Brown to Rollins, July 20, 22, 1855, Rollins Papers; Rollins to Abiel Leonard, November 19, 1855, Leonard Papers.
    21. Peterson, *Freedom and Franchise*, 45–47; Parrish, *David Rice Atchison*, 183–84.
    22. FB to FPB, October 23, November 13, December 17, 1855, B-LP; *Missouri Democrat*, November 13, 23, 1855; James S. Green to Abel R. Corbin, December 5, 1855, Rutgers

Preston Blair had written his son on October 28 to stir up the railroad issue in the forthcoming legislature. In particular, he suggested showing how Illinois and Chicago would benefit, at the expense of St. Louis, from another route through Iowa as a means of persuading the Missourians to take action. Frank did just that. He joined Gratz Brown and George R. Smith, a prominent Whig from Pettis County, in sponsoring a program for $10 million in state-bond guarantees for several railroad companies. This had the dual effect of pleasing the St. Louis business interests while also strengthening the movement toward a Benton-Whig coalition, looking to the 1856 elections. Although a joint committee investigating state railroads issued a report indicating mismanagement, in part because of inexperience by many railroad board members, the bill passed over Governor Price's veto to the great joy of both Benton men and Whigs. A subsequent challenge before the Missouri Supreme Court came to naught.[23]

Frank returned from Jefferson City at the end of the adjourned session elated with its accomplishments. He wrote his father that Price's actions in relation to the railroad bill had permanently alienated the Whigs from the anti-Benton Democrats. He believed this augured well for their hoped-for support of Benton men in the 1856 elections. In this regard, he had been quietly pushing the candidacy of John C. Fremont for president. Fremont, Benton's son-in-law, popularly known as "the Pathfinder," had gained a strong reputation from his explorations in the West and his subsequent career in California and was a well-known Free-Soiler.[24]

James Rollins wrote his fellow Whig George R. Smith on January 30, 1856, that he had met with Frank, who proposed a coalition of their two groups behind a Benton candidate for governor. When Rollins doubted that he could bring the Whigs into line behind such a scheme, Frank indicated that he could go for either Rollins or Smith from the Whig ranks. His major concern was to avoid a Know-Nothing candidate for fear of alienating the Irish and German vote in St. Louis. Frank quickly found his efforts at coalition politics stymied on two unanticipated fronts, however, in the persons of Thomas Hart Benton

College Papers. Atchison denied any connection with the Know-Nothing movement, and this author found no specific evidence to link him to it (Parrish, *David Rice Atchison*, 245 n).

23. FPB to FB, October 28, 1855, BLC; FB to Apo, November 20, 1855, B-LP; *Journal of the House*, 18th General Assembly, adjourned sess., 3–125; Samuel Bannister Harding, *Life of George R. Smith: Founder of Sedalia, Missouri*, 197–209; John W. Million, *State Aid to Railways in Missouri*, 99–102.

24. FB to FPB, December 17, 1855, B-LP.

and his father. Early in 1856, Benton indicated his desire to run for governor on his own ticket. Preston Blair, meanwhile, had become involved in the national organization of the fledgling Republican Party, presiding over its convention at Pittsburgh in late February.[25]

While "well satisfied" with the Republicans' free-soil stand, Frank was "astonished" that his father had allowed them to name him as a member of the executive committee. He told Phil Lee that such a move, done without his consent, placed him in an extremely embarrassing position in relation to both the Whigs and the Missouri Democracy. Anticipating running for Congress in the fall, Frank could ill afford to alienate his local supporters by openly joining the new party. He had hoped that his father might come to St. Louis from Pittsburgh so that he could discuss matters with him face-to-face, but the senior Blair had returned to Silver Spring. Given the circumstances, Frank felt he had no recourse but to resign from the Republican National Committee. He issued a statement through the *Missouri Democrat* to that effect on March 4. Claiming no prior knowledge of the move to put him on the committee, he assured his friends that he remained "a Democrat of the Jackson and Benton school and I do not intend to abandon that faith, or surrender that proud title."[26]

This accomplished, Frank turned his attention to the Benton ticket for the spring city elections. At a mass meeting on March 17 at the courthouse, announced as a "Democrat Anti–Know Nothing" rally, he engineered the nomination of John How for mayor. How had previously served two terms (1853–1854) and, with Irish and German support, easily defeated the Know-Nothing incumbent by twenty-five hundred votes.[27]

Frank next went to work on the state ticket. The anti-Benton Democrats had called a state convention for April 21 in Jefferson City. Frank countered with a meeting of his own forces at the same time and place. The two groups met at opposite ends of the state capitol: the anti-Bentonites in the House chamber and the Benton men in the Senate. One hundred twenty delegates from thirty counties appeared for the Benton meeting. Frank and the Benton leadership brushed aside attempts by former governor Austin A.

25. James S. Rollins to George R. Smith, January 30, 1856, George R. Smith Papers, also in Harding, *George R. Smith*, 243–45; W. E. Smith, *Blair Family in Politics*, 1:325–36.

26. FB to SPL, February 27, March 3, 1856, B-LP; FB to FPB, March 4, 1856, BLC; *Missouri Democrat*, March 4, 1856; Henry Boernstein, *Memoirs of a Nobody: The Missouri Years of Henry Boernstein (1849–1866)*, 235–36.

27. *Missouri Democrat*, March 7, 18, April 8, 1856; FB to FPB, March 9, 1856, BLC.

King to secure a compromise between the two groups based on acceptance of the Kansas-Nebraska Act, whereupon their convention selected a slate of candidates headed by Old Bullion for governor. The anti-Benton forces nominated Trusten Polk of St. Louis and chose Claiborne Jackson as party chairman. All hope of reconciliation vanished. Both groups named delegates to the Democratic National Convention. In late May, the Benton Democracy held its St. Louis County convention and nominated Frank for Congress and Gratz Brown for another term in the General Assembly.[28]

With plans for a coalition evaporating and their national party seemingly disintegrating, most of Missouri's Whigs sought refuge in the American (Know-Nothing) Party. That group had held its national convention in Philadelphia at the end of February and nominated former president Millard Fillmore and Andrew Jackson Donelson, the nephew and adopted son of "Old Hickory," as its ticket. This proved acceptable to Missouri's Whig leaders, who now called a state convention in St. Louis under the American banner for mid-April. On the eve of that convention, Frank met secretly with several of the group's leaders in one of their hotel rooms, hoping to secure the gubernatorial nomination for Rollins. Exactly how this strategy fit in with what he planned for his own Benton Democracy convention a few days later is not clear. Regardless, Rollins failed to get the nomination, which went to Robert C. Ewing of Lafayette County. Obviously disappointed, Rollins wrote George R. Smith that if elected the Ewing ticket would represent "precisely the same combinations of political elements that we had to contend with last winter," seemingly referring to the proslavery element within the old Whig Party.[29] It was becoming clear that the Democrats were not alone in their divisions.

The situation became even more complicated following the Democratic and Republican National Conventions. The Democrats met at Cincinnati in early June to find two competing Missouri delegations seeking recognition. The Benton group, led by Gratz Brown, arrived after their rivals and thus found them occupying the delegation's seats within the convention hall. An angry Brown provoked a confrontation, but, in the end, the convention voted to seat the anti-Benton group. Repudiating Franklin Pierce, who had become too controversial in light of the Kansas difficulties, the Democrats turned to James Buchanan as their candidate for president. Buchanan, who had a long

28. *Missouri Democrat*, April 22, 24, May 20, 1856; Ryle, "Slavery and Party Realignment," 329–31.

29. Harding, *George R. Smith*, 247–51; James Madison Wood Jr., "James Sidney Rollins of Missouri: A Political Biography," 128–29; Ryle, "Slavery and Party Realignment," 327–28.

political career dating back to Jackson's time, had been out of the country the past four years serving as minister to England and thus had avoided much of the controversy surrounding the struggles in Kansas. The party's platform stood by the Kansas-Nebraska Act as "the only sound and safe solution to the slavery question."[30]

The Republicans convened in Philadelphia with Preston Blair in attendance. They easily nominated Benton's son-in-law John Charles Fremont as their presidential candidate to the satisfaction of the senior Blair, who had a warm regard for the Pathfinder. Indeed, he had become angry with Frank because his son had not attended the Democratic convention in Cincinnati where he might have gained some support for Fremont among disaffected Democrats. The Republican platform called for opposition to "those twin relics of barbarism—polygamy and slavery in the territories," the former a reference to the Mormons in Utah.[31]

To the dismay of Preston Blair, who personally solicited his support for Fremont, Benton refused to endorse his son-in-law. Old Bullion feared that the Republicans represented a sectional party whose triumph would lead to difficulties for the South and a possible disruption of the Union. Instead, he announced his support for Buchanan, for whom he had worked ardently at the Cincinnati convention, as "the safest chance for preserving the peace of the country, now gravely endangered." The aging statesman arrived in St. Louis on June 19 to an enthusiastic reception, addressing an overflow rally of some ten thousand people two days later in Washington Square. While denouncing the Democratic platform for its acceptance of the Kansas-Nebraska Act, Benton preached national harmony and then launched an extensive tour of the state, where he continued to reiterate that theme.[32]

Frank wrote Montgomery on June 12, shortly before Benton's arrival, that Old Bullion had placed them in a "very embarrassing" position. He "did not conceive it possible that Benton would support the Cincinnati nominee"; but, given that circumstance, Frank assumed that both wings of the Missouri Democracy would do the same. Indeed, the *Missouri Democrat* had already raised Buchanan's name to its masthead as it was "a *question of meat & bread with them.*" Frank feared that this would deliver Missouri into the hands of the

30. Peterson, *Freedom and Franchise*, 60–61.
31. E. B. Smith, *Francis Preston Blair*, 228–30.
32. Chambers, *Old Bullion Benton*, 421–23; W. E. Smith, *Blair Family in Politics*, 1:343.

anti-Benton wing of the party and anticipated that if so "they will inaugurate in Missouri the same reign of terror which exists in Kansas." He reported that he would concentrate on his own congressional race and the state contest. "Shall we make a useless effort for the 'Wild Turkey' [Fremont] or shall we make an effort which may be effective to save the State from the Nullifiers?" he asked. "I have made up my mind to fight for the state & let those in more fortunate circumstances fight the great battle of the nation."[33]

Frank reiterated these views in a lengthy letter to his father the day after Benton's Washington Square address. He regretted that his stance embarrassed his father while seeking to make him understand his predicament. Although he strongly preferred Fremont over Buchanan and hoped that his father would convey that to the Pathfinder, he could not desert Benton after having nominated him for governor. He had never dreamed that Old Bullion would take the stand that he did. To come out publicly for Fremont now would undoubtedly hinder his own election chances and that of the state ticket, to which his father finally agreed.[34]

Because the state and congressional elections took place in August prior to the national contest in November, it became possible for Frank to focus his attention locally; and for the next month and a half he did just that. In spite of their outward loyalty to the national Democracy and Buchanan, Frank and Gratz Brown, with their supporters, were regularly branded as "Black Republicans" by the anti-Benton press. Two days before the state election, someone sneaked into the office of the *Missouri Democrat* and changed the masthead of the morning edition to read "Black Republican ticket" at the head of the list of Benton Democratic candidates. The paper offered a reward for any information as to the culprit, but he was never caught.[35]

Election day, August 4, brought the desired results in St. Louis. Frank easily secured election to Congress over American and anti-Benton candidates, while Gratz Brown returned to the Missouri legislature. Benton ran substantially ahead of his opponents in St. Louis, but the outstate vote went quite differently. There, the anti-Benton Trusten Polk placed first with almost forty-seven thousand votes, some six thousand ahead of the American Robert Ewing and nineteen thousand ahead of Benton. While the combined opposition had polled 59.1 percent of the total votes cast, its division had allowed the

---

33. FB to MB, June 12, 1856, BLC.
34. FB to FPB, June 22, 1856, B-LP; FPB to FB, July 1, 1856, BLC.
35. *Missouri Examiner,* February 9, March 1, 1856; *Missouri Democrat,* August 3, 1856; FB to FPB, October 6, 1856, B-LP.

anti-Bentonites to retain control of the governor's mansion.[36] It was Benton's
last hurrah. He died a year and a half later.

Exulting in his own triumph, Frank wrote his father that many of the
Know-Nothings had voted for him. "My idea is now to consolidate the two
parties here," he confided, "& I think with proper management it can be
accomplished." For all his careful maneuvering during the campaign, most
of his supporters in Missouri and many observers elsewhere realized that his
election to Congress as essentially a Free-Soil Democrat signaled a change in
Missouri politics. The radical *National Era,* based in Washington, predicted
that it marked the beginning of a strong Republican movement that would
soon be sweeping the border states. Sen. William H. Seward of New York, who
was moving into the forefront of national Republican leadership, proclaimed
Frank "the man of the West, of the age," and many others agreed.[37]

Although Apo was having a difficult confinement with their fourth child,
Frank made a hurried trip east in late August to visit his parents at Silver
Spring and confer with Fremont at his campaign headquarters in New York.
He returned full of enthusiasm for the Pathfinder's success. He wrote Rollins
a few days later that should Fremont win the election, "I think it is likely
there will be an attempt to dissolve the Union." He urged Rollins to ready his
friends for such a possibility and concluded, "You know that both of us have
long foreseen the state of things which have now come to pass and discussed
the propriety of forming a Union Party." The time had arrived to move ahead
with such a program at the forthcoming session of the legislature.[38]

The national election did not go as Frank had hoped. Buchanan managed
to put together sufficient pluralities in key states, north and south, to gain a
majority in the electoral college: 174 to 114 for Fremont and 8 for Fillmore,
who carried only New Jersey. In the popular balloting, Buchanan outdistanced
Fremont by some 500,000 votes and Fillmore by another 500,000. He carried
Missouri by 10,000 votes. Most surprising, Fillmore led in St. Louis County,
indicating that many of the Blair-Brown-Benton supporters found it difficult
to accept Fremont as an alternative to Buchanan. While disappointed, Frank
told his father that he had found many Fillmore men there and in St. Louis who

36. Abstract of Election Returns, St. Louis County, August 4, 1856; Chambers, *Old Bullion
Benton,* 424; Ryle, "Slavery and Party Realignment," 331.

37. FB to FPB, n.d. (but obviously 1856), B-LP; John A. Kasson to FB, August 6, 1856,
BLC; Eric Foner, *Free Soil, Free Labor, Free Men: The Ideology of the Republican Party before the
Civil War,* 121.

38. FB to Apo, September 4, 1856, BLPLC; FB to James S. Rollins, September 15, November 24, 1856, Rollins Papers; FB to FPB, October 6, 1856, B-LP.

wished they had done differently and gone for Fremont. He urged that the Republicans stick with the Pathfinder, who he believed could win in 1860.[39]

When the new Missouri General Assembly convened at the end of December, it quickly became evident that the anti-Benton Democrats had full control. Although no longer a member because of his elevation to Congress, Frank went to Jefferson City to assist Gratz Brown and observe the trend of the senatorial elections. Little hope existed of securing Benton's election to the Senate, but Frank tried to arrange an appointment with the Bank of Missouri for his cousin, Cary Gratz. To that end, he even brought in Gratz's stepbrother, Jo Shelby, who had moved to western Missouri in the early 1850s and had become an active Border Ruffian in the Kansas troubles, to assist him, but to no avail.[40]

Apo reported to her father-in-law that Frank was in as good health as he had been for some time. He had been studying German with a tutor to assist him with that element of the electorate. Together with Gratz, he had recently taken a pledge to abstain from liquor, which pleased Apo greatly, as "it is not taken too soon." The pledge proved of short duration. Frank had developed a reputation as a heavy drinker, and he would continue this pattern to the end of his active career. A genial companion, his contemporaries frequently commented on his tendency to occasionally overindulge. One of these, Henry Boernstein, noted, however, "Blair was a powerful nature, he could bear a great deal, and he never lost his judgement; he thereby was able to reduce the burdens of his position, particularly popular toasting, to a minimum." There is no evidence of habitual drunkenness nor any indication that this habit diminished his work ethic. Gideon Welles, in later comparing Frank with Ulysses S. Grant, noted in his diary, "Grant loves drink for the sake of drink. He is not like Blair, convivial, social and given to a spree."[41]

---

39. FB to FPB, July 25, 1856, B-LP; *Missouri Democrat*, November 6, 1856; FB to FPB, November 11, 1856, BLC.

40. Apo to FPB, January 14, 1857, BLC. Cary Gratz was the youngest son of Frank's Uncle Ben. He had come to St. Louis from Kentucky sometime in the 1850s, and Frank had helped establish him as a commission merchant. Jo Shelby, who would gain fame as a Confederate cavalry commander, was the son of Benjamin Gratz's second wife. He had followed his cousin Gratz Brown to St. Louis in 1849 and eventually settled in Waverly, Missouri, where he and his stepbrother, Howard Gratz, operated a hemp factory. Although Jo Shelby and Frank disagreed strongly on the slavery issue, they had long been close friends and would remain so throughout the Civil War and postwar period (O'Flaherty, *General Jo Shelby*, 2–16, 22–25; Byars, *B. and M. Gratz*, 268).

41. Apo to FPB, January 14, 1857, BLC; Boernstein, *Memoirs*, 242; Gideon Welles diary, cited in Charles H. Coleman, *The Election of 1868: The Democratic Effort to Regain Control*, 97.

With Benton having endorsed Buchanan in the presidential race, many of his former supporters now consolidated their positions within the Missouri Democratic Party, lest they lose out on the anticipated national patronage. Most of the Benton men outside St. Louis had little sympathy with the Free-Soil proclivities of the Blairs, seeing this as an attempt by Frank to win German support in St. Louis. With two U.S. Senate seats to fill, the newly united Democrats moved quickly. They named James S. Green, a former Atchison lieutenant from northeast Missouri, to the seat that had been vacant for two years. Then the party played directly into the hands of the opposition by electing its new governor, Trusten Polk, to replace the Whig Henry S. Geyer, whose term had expired. This necessitated a special election to fill the governor's chair, and Frank predicted that this, together with the elimination of Benton as a force in Missouri politics, would help consolidate the opposition forces on a new basis.[42]

Things came together quickly. Frank helped organize a caucus of Benton men, Know-Nothings, and old-line Whigs at Jefferson City on February 26, who agreed to support James Rollins for governor on an "Opposition" ticket. Blair wrote Rollins a few days later urging him to accept and promising a five-thousand majority from St. Louis. He told Rollins that he would need to make a vigorous canvass, not raising any new issues but sticking to the one that had made his reputation as a moderate Free-Soiler. Further encouragement came from other quarters, including the election of John Wimer, the emancipation Democratic candidate for mayor in St. Louis. In late April, Rollins made his announcement. To oppose him the Democrats chose Robert M. Stewart, a state senator from Buchanan County.[43]

B. Gratz Brown sought to set a tone for the campaign in a speech before the Missouri House on February 12. Taking a cue from the speech Frank had made three years earlier in the same chamber advocating the importance of freeing

---

A later political rival and congressional colleague, Albert G. Riddle of Indiana, reported in his memoirs that, during the 37th Congress, Frank and Abram B. Olin of New York would spend three or four hours during the middle of the day away from the House and return "none the better for it" (Albert Gallatin Riddle, *Recollections of War Times: Reminiscences of Men and Events in Washington, 1861–1865*, 200). The daily record of the *Congressional Globe* fails to sustain this charge, however, and Frank's energetic leadership as chair of the Military Affairs Committee also belies it.

42. H. T. Blow to Minerva Blow, December 31, 1856, Blow Family Papers; FB to FPB, January 14, 19, 1857, BLC.

43. William F. Switzler to James S. Rollins, February 27, 1857, FB to Rollins, February 28, March 17, 1857, Rollins Papers; B. Gratz Brown to George R. Smith, March 3, 1857, Rollins to Smith, April 23, 1857, Smith Papers; *Missouri Democrat*, April 7, 1857.

white labor from the competition of slavery in Kansas, Gratz now focused that theme on Missouri and raised for the first time that decade the question of emancipation. He argued for a gradual compensated emancipation, not from any humanitarian concern for the slave, he said, but to "emancipate the white man from the yoke of competition with the Negro. I aim to relieve the free man from conflict with the slave." Missouri must increasingly tie itself economically to the industrial East and upper Midwest toward which its commerce was already leading it. "She is a central state," he argued, "at present the advanced leader of the Western states."[44]

Temperate in its approach, Brown's speech reflected a growing sentiment among northern Free-Soilers. Yet, in Missouri, it seemed to confirm what the anti-Benton Democrats had been saying all along, that the Blair-Brown crowd were really abolitionists in disguise. Benton himself did not help matters by denouncing his former allies in a letter that found its way into the proslavery press. "For persons [Blair and Brown] calling themselves my friends," he wrote, "to attack the whole policy of my life, which was to keep slavery agitation out of the State, and get my support in the canvass by keeping me ignorant of what they intended to do, is the GREATEST OUTRAGE I have ever experienced."[45]

In spite of this, Benton endorsed Rollins's bid for governor, while admonishing him to avoid the emancipation issue. Once committed to the race and warned by Frank that he could not "stick to the rivers," Rollins made a vigorous campaign throughout the state. He urged the unity of those opposed to the ruling Democracy and stressed his previous support for railroad improvements and a strong educational system. One of the largest slaveholders in Boone County, he declared himself no abolitionist and pointed out his southern birth, contrasting it with that of his opponent, Stewart, a native of New York. Increasingly, he tuned his message to his audience, assuring those in the St. Louis area of his great admiration for Thomas Hart Benton while arguing elsewhere his opposition to agitation of the slavery question, something he accused the Democrats of exploiting endlessly.[46]

44. Peterson, *Freedom and Franchise*, 71–74.

45. Foner, *Free Soil*, 11–39; Eugene H. Berwanger, *The Frontier against Slavery: Western Anti-Negro Prejudice and the Slavery Extension Controversy*, 129–31; Thomas Hart Benton to J. B. Brant, February 23, 1857, quoted in *Missouri Examiner*, April 18, 1857.

46. FB to Rollins, March 17, 1857, Thomas L. Price to Rollins, May 6, 1857, Rollins Papers; Rollins to George R. Smith, April 23, June 29, 1857, Smith Papers; Wood, "James Sidney Rollins," 149–64.

Initially, Rollins found receptive audiences, as Gratz Brown and the *Missouri Democrat* kept up a steady stream of editorial support. Denying that it stood for abolition, the paper strongly condemned the extension of slavery into the territories while maintaining "The Union must be preserved." Concerned, the Democratic press worked hard to rally support for its party, arguing that Missouri had never been out of the Democratic fold since its inception. Stewart also campaigned vigorously. Indeed, the two candidates met head-on in several debates. By late June, Rollins began complaining of apathy on the part of some supporters. He was encouraged, however, by Benton's endorsement and wrote George R. Smith that he thought this could be used to advantage if widely circulated in the right places.[47]

Election day, August 3, 1857, found Rollins 334 votes short of victory. It was the closest call the Democrats experienced in the entire pre–Civil War era. Rollins accepted his defeat philosophically while urging the continuation of efforts to unite the opposition forces. It would take some accommodation by both the Benton men and the Know-Nothing/former Whigs, he argued. They should advocate a platform that included a free system of common schools and economy in public works and the encouragement of immigration with the protection of free labor while avoiding agitation of the "nigger question." Frank agreed. Mortified at Rollins's close defeat, he blamed the shortfall of his predicted St. Louis margin (Rollins carried St. Louis County by only eighteen hundred votes) on a last-minute defection of proslavery Know-Nothings. He nevertheless assured Rollins, "you have made a party," which he predicted would find success in the future.[48]

Frank had not been concentrating solely on the Missouri election during 1857. In February, he traveled to Springfield, Illinois, to confer with Abraham Lincoln and other Republican leaders, who were making plans to confront Sen. Stephen A. Douglas, the prime mover of the Kansas-Nebraska Act, when he came up for reelection the following year. When they asked Frank his opinion about a platform, he reiterated the theme that he and Gratz Brown were now preaching: "I told them to drop the Negro and go the whole hog for the white man. . . . [T]he territories should be reserved for free white men or surrendered to the slaves & their masters." They asked him to draw up a resolution to this effect, which he did. Frank assured Lincoln and the others

47. *Missouri Democrat*, passim, February–August 1857; Rollins to Smith, June 29, 1857, Smith Papers.
48. Rollins to FB, August 15, 1857, FB to Rollins, September 9, 1857, Rollins Papers; Wood, "James Sidney Rollins," 166.

that the *Missouri Democrat* would fall into line for the Republican cause in 1860, and he anticipated that the *Louisville (Ky.) Journal* would follow.[49]

In late April, Frank went east to confer with his father at Silver Spring. He also visited the Fremonts in New York. The Buchanan administration had been installed in Washington; and things were heating up on the Kansas front in the wake of the Supreme Court's decision in the Dred Scott case, which had seen Montgomery serving as one of Scott's attorneys. The Court's verdict that Congress did not have the right to control slavery in the territories merely gave added impetus to the Republican cause.[50]

Frank and his father had been corresponding since early in the year about something the two of them saw as a potential solution to the slavery problem, namely, the colonization of freed blacks in Central America. Frank began to see this as the only "safety valve" to save the nation from the evils of slavery. He had studied the British penal colonies in that region and believed they "afford[ed] the best examples to illustrate the advantage." Certainly not a new scheme, the idea of colonization could be traced back to Jefferson, Madison, and others of the Founding Fathers. The American Colonization Society had been organized by border-state men in 1817 to facilitate sending free blacks back to Africa. By late March, Frank had outlined an elaborate scheme to his father. He hoped to induce Congress to grant Missouri all of the remaining public lands within the state, amounting to some 15 million acres, with the understanding that they would be sold and the proceeds used to purchase the state's slaves and transport them to Central American colonies. Undoubtedly, this dominated their conversations at Silver Spring, as it did continuing correspondence after Frank's return to St. Louis.[51]

That summer and fall, Frank read every book about Central America he could acquire to better enable himself to define his colonization proposals. Nathaniel Banks invited him to speak at Faneuil Hall in Boston in October, but his father advised against it. Preston argued that his son did not need to intrude himself into Massachusetts's Republican factionalism at this particular moment, and Frank admitted to Montgomery that he had heard from some of the anti-Banks men urging him to stay away. He decided to refrain

49. FB to FPB, February 18, 22, 1857, BLC; W. H. Herndon to Parker, April 8, 1857, cited in Joseph Fort Newton, *Lincoln and Herndon*, 113–14.

50. Jessie Benton Fremont to EBL, late April 1857, in *The Letters of Jessie Benton Fremont*, 154; W. E. Smith, *Blair Family in Politics*, 1:380–97.

51. FB to FPB, February 12, 1857, FPB to FB, March 19, 1857, Blair Family Papers, MHS; FB to FPB, February 22, 1857, BLC; FB to FPB, March 25, 1857, B-LP.

from speeches until he got to Washington in order that he could make the most of his debut there. Meanwhile, he sought his brother's help in finding suitable rooms in the capital where he could entertain his supporters when they visited him. Given "some of my *rough* constituents," the rooms should be in a house whose other occupants did not mind a lot of coming and going. He had also concluded to bring his slave, Louis, whom he had acquired earlier that year from his mother-in-law, with him, which would necessitate extra accommodations.[52]

Frank departed for Washington in mid-November. While Apo hated to have him absent for so long, she had reconciled herself to his political ambition by this time. They had obviously discussed this shortly before he left, for she now wrote,

> I am sorry that you should for a moment suppose that I do not sympathize with you in your political career. It is true that at first I felt such unhappiness at your choosing this life that I could not rejoice in your success but that is over now my dear husband & I can now rejoice in all that gives you pleasure even tho it lead you away from me & from the home I did hope to enjoy with you. I was wrong to be so selfish . . . & no one could be more thoroughly convinced of the purity of your motives than I am.

A lonely Frank soon asked his wife to join him, but various illnesses among the children prevented her going until late March. Her letters throughout this period reflect a strong sense of reluctance at having to continually postpone the journey.[53]

Frank, meanwhile, lost little time in promoting his constituents' interests. The first bill he introduced on January 4, 1858, would authorize the contractors for the California overland mail to select their own route for its delivery. He followed this a few days later with a resolution requesting information concerning the possibility of railroad construction through South Pass. All of this occurred against the backdrop of a volatile debate over the Lecompton Constitution, which had been forwarded to Congress by the proslavery element in Kansas under highly questionable circumstances. Drafted by a convention in whose election the Free State Party had declined to participate, it provided for Kansas's admission as a slave state. Almost

52. FB to FPB, September 2, 21, 29, 1857, FB to MB, October 13, 1857, FB to SPL, November 21, 1857, B-LP; FPB to FB, September 29, 1857, BLC.

53. Apo to FB, November 28, December 16, 26, 1857, January 7, 14, 16, 27, 30, February 1, 6, 10, 12, 21, 23, March 4, 7, 11, 14, 24, 25, 29, 1858, BLC.

simultaneously with its drafting, however, all Kansans participated in an election for a new territorial legislature, which resulted in a slight Free State majority. This body now sought the constitution's rejection, claiming it a fraud. President Buchanan, however, endorsed the Lecompton Constitution and urged its acceptance by Congress as a means of ending the slavery controversy in Kansas. This inflamed not only the Free-Soil Republicans but Sen. Stephen A. Douglas of Illinois, chief sponsor of the Kansas-Nebraska Act, as well.[54]

Into this mix Frank threw his own bombshell. On January 14, he proposed that a select committee be appointed to examine the expediency of securing territory in Central or South America where free blacks and liberated slaves might be colonized. In strident tones, Frank appealed to the racist sentiments of many northerners while reinforcing his previously stated concerns against black competition for free-white labor. "Freed blacks hold a place in this country which cannot be maintained," he argued. "Those who have fled to the North are most unwelcome visitors. The strong repugnance of the free white laborer to be yoked with the negro refugee, breeds an enmity between races, which must end in the expulsion of the latter."

Drawing on Thomas Jefferson and John Randolph to support his arguments, Frank stated that previous attempts at African colonization had been a failure. Then, citing the reading that he had done over the previous summer, he argued that Central America was ripe for such an experiment. It already had a predominantly mixed-blood population who had been ruled for decades by mestizo dictators. The region was marked by poverty and insurrection. Great Britain had designs on certain areas. Indeed, a similar proposal was being discussed in British circles to send free Jamaicans to help develop Belize. To counter all this, Frank offered strong overtones of Manifest Destiny, which had dominated much of American thinking for the past decade and a half. Not only would the freed slaves benefit by such a move, but the people of Central America could profit by the presence within their midst of blacks "bred and educated within civilized communities, who speak our language, are listeners at our canvasses [*sic*], lookers-on at the elections, worshippers in our churches." Such an infusion would enable the Central Americans to break the yoke of tyranny that suppressed them and help move them more rapidly toward stability and wealth.

54. *CG*, 35:1:183; James A. Rawley, *Race and Politics: "Bleeding Kansas" and the Coming of the Civil War*, 213–17.

As for the freed slaves, Frank declared that "one would think [them] quite as capable of being disciplined in colonies" as the Indians of the West, who had been given reservations in that region to allow them to develop their own civilizations in a similarly segregated society. Even as the federal government had assisted in colonizing the Indians, it ought also to aid "such portions of the unfortunate race born to slavery, but who, having attained freedom, find it renders them a burden to those among whom they live." Frank thus supported a policy of racial separation for both blacks and Native Americans.[55]

Frank's speech exploded into an already volatile setting. Southerners had been seeking throughout the decade to expand slavery into the Caribbean. Indeed, Frank had accused the Buchanan administration of trying to support that expansion in Honduras, even as the president appeared to be assisting it in Kansas with his endorsement of the Lecompton Constitution. Cong. Lucius J. Gartrell of Georgia responded for the embattled South on January 25 by declaring, "Slavery has been written on the brow of Africans" and that those areas of the Caribbean that had freed their slaves had suffered economic decline. Frank quickly shot back that U.S. exports to the free-black Republic of Haiti exceeded those to Mexico, with its "eight millions population," by $350,000, which had to say something for the industry of Haiti's people.[56]

Frank's resolution never came to a vote; but, in the continuing debate on Lecompton, he made two more appearances on the floor. On March 16, he added fuel to his earlier fire by moving that the Judiciary Committee be instructed to bring in a bill "to prohibit the importation or immigration of free persons from Africa under indentures of apprenticeship or stipulations for service." One week later, on the eve of the final vote on Lecompton in the Senate, he delivered a long speech denouncing Buchanan for trying to saddle Kansas with slavery when the majority of its citizens had indicated their sentiments to the contrary. Later that day, March 23, the Senate voted 33 to 25 to admit Kansas under the Lecompton Constitution. On April 1, however, the House, by a 120 to 112 margin, voted to send it back to the people of Kansas for a referendum. The Senate accepted, and the Kansans then proceeded to reject it overwhelmingly.[57]

Frank hurried home when Congress adjourned in mid-June to face a tight race for reelection. Gratz Brown supported him vigorously in the editorial columns of the *Missouri Democrat,* and he found additional support from the longtime pro-Benton paper in central Missouri, the *Jefferson Inquirer.* As early as December 16, 1857, Frank had urged George R. Smith to work for a full slate of opposition candidates in 1858. The following April he wrote to James O. Broadhead, a convert from Whiggery, "Shall we in Missouri after having begun the battle so gloriously be recreant? It must not be. . . . I feel perfectly that all that is requisite is to make a vigorous canvass and lay the matter fairly and squarely before the people." The biggest difficulty lay with labels. In the changing milieu of national and state politics, opposition candidates were not certain what to call themselves. Frank and Gratz Brown, who was seeking a fourth term in the legislature, simply ran as "Free Democrats," hoping to attract the broad spectrum that had supported them in the past. Frank addressed an enthusiastic mass meeting, which the *Missouri Democrat* estimated at ten thousand, in Washington Square at the end of July and followed this with a long parade through downtown St. Louis.[58]

Election day, August 3, proved disappointing for both Blair and Brown. The *Missouri Democrat* cried fraud and ran long stories of various irregularities at the polls, especially in the Eighth and Ninth Wards, where "a ring of Irish bullies" kept many Blair-Brown supporters away from the polls. Whatever the case, Frank lost in a three-man race. He polled 6,631 votes to 7,057 for Richard Barrett, his National Democratic opponent. Samuel Breckinridge, running as a Know-Nothing, polled 5,668, splitting off considerable votes that might otherwise have gone to Frank. Gratz ran fifteenth in a field of thirty-seven for St. Louis's twelve seats in the Missouri House.[59]

Washington officialdom, led by President Buchanan, rejoiced over Frank's defeat. Apo told her father-in-law that the fraud was blatantly obvious, yet she also admitted, "There was great mismanagement among Frank's friends. They were so confident he would have an overwhelming majority that they were not near as vigilant as they have been." She reported from Rose Bank that Frank was spending most of his time in town preparing to contest the election. Montgomery arrived at the end of August to assist with this process.

58. *Missouri Democrat,* January 22, February 19, May 28, June 11, August 1, 1858; *Jefferson Inquirer,* April 3, June 19, 1858; FB to George R. Smith, December 16, 1857, Smith Papers; FB to James O. Broadhead, April 19, 1858, James S. Rollins to Broadhead, July 11, 1858, James O. Broadhead Papers.

59. Abstract of Election Returns, St. Louis County, August 3, 1858; *Missouri Democrat,* August 4, 5, 1858.

While chagrined by his brother's setback, he still believed that "Frank has the points in him to maintain himself through an extended career and to deepen the impression in the public mind he has made as each new occasion offers itself to bring his character & powers before the people."[60]

The contest involved taking countless depositions amid numerous threats by the opposition forces. Frank and his friends went armed on their rounds throughout the city. Montgomery reported one encounter with a man named Davis, who had been charged by Frank with participation in the fraud. Davis had been drinking and haranguing a crowd when Frank appeared on the scene. As Davis approached him with oaths and threats, Frank went for his pistol. He assured Davis that he would prove his charges at the proper time but would not hesitate "to kill him on the spot" if he wanted to start a fight here. Montgomery concluded, "This was said in a manner so convincing that the fellow . . . cooled down instantly & it ended by Frank's treating him to a glass of whisky instead of to an ounce of lead."[61]

In spite of his electoral setback, Frank's strong stand against the Lecompton Constitution and his advocacy of colonization had gained him new recognition within Republican ranks across the North. Invitations to speak poured in; and Frank responded vigorously, preaching his doctrine of colonization wherever he went. Frank took time out from his contest in October for an extended tour of Wisconsin, Indiana, and Illinois, where state elections were held in November, to assist with various campaigns. In Illinois he made several appearances to assist Abraham Lincoln in his challenge against Douglas for that state's Senate seat.[62]

Frank had found himself on the horns of a potentially embarrassing dilemma earlier in the year where the Douglas-Lincoln contest was concerned. Frank and Douglas had been on the same side in the struggle to reject the Lecompton Constitution. Both men had fallen out of favor with the Buchanan administration because of their stand. Many Free-Soil Republicans now urged that Douglas be sent back to the Senate from Illinois without opposition. Sometime during the congressional session, Schuyler Colfax arranged a meeting between Frank and Douglas, at the latter's request, in which the Illinois

60. Apo to FPB, August 6, 9, 1858, FB to FPB, n.d. and August 13, 22, 1858, MB to FPB, August 27, 1858, B-LP; MB to FPB, August 5, 6, 1858, BLC; *Missouri Democrat*, September 1, 10, 12, 1858.

61. MB to FPB, August 27, September 3, 1858, B-LP.

62. Walter B. Stevens, "Lincoln and Missouri," 68; FB to FPB, n.d. [late October 1858], B-LP; Alexander M. Black to Jane Black, October 14, 1858, Hagaman Family Papers; *Liberty (Mo.) Tribune*, October 22, 1858.

senator sought to have Blair muffle the attacks being made against him by the *Missouri Democrat*. Apparently, Douglas even hinted during their discussions that he might consider switching to the Republican Party in 1860. Frank wrote Gratz Brown about the conversation, and word of the letter leaked out. Isaac Sturgeon, a staunch proslavery Democrat from St. Louis, reported to President Buchanan in May that he had seen the letter and warned him to beware of his enemies. After Frank declared for Lincoln and actively campaigned for him, Douglas maligned Frank heavily, which led Blair to write Sturgeon detailing the original conversation in bitter tones.[63]

Frank returned to Washington in December, accompanied by Apo and the children, for the lame-duck session of Congress, determined to press his case there for the right to another term. He had accepted an invitation to give a major address before the Mercantile Library Association of Boston on January 26, 1859, and he and his father now worked carefully on the final draft. Titled "The Destiny of the Races of This Continent," it developed at greater length the arguments Frank had made for colonization in his maiden congressional speech a year earlier. Before an audience that included Ralph Waldo Emerson, Gov. Nathaniel Banks, and other noted New Englanders, Frank urged federal and state cooperation in the colonization effort. Generally well received, this speech further enhanced his national reputation and led to additional speaking invitations, which kept him busy on the lecture circuit later that fall.[64]

With the completion of the lame-duck session in early March, Frank and Apo hurried home to St. Louis. The children had been sick much of time they were in the East, but the home atmosphere seemed to restore them. Frank found numerous problems awaiting him, and he attacked them with his usual vigor. With the city elections only a month away, he discovered everything in confusion with "our people ready to give up . . . in despair and fighting against each other like cats & dogs." He wrote Montgomery that he

63. FB to James O. Broadhead, April 19, 1858, Broadhead Papers; FB to Isaac Sturgeon, October 25, 1858, in *Jefferson Inquirer*, October 30, 1858; W. E. Smith, *Blair Family in Politics*, 1:418–21; Robert W. Johannsen, *Stephen A. Douglas*, 626. Cf. Sturgeon to John F. Snyder, May 5, 1860, C. J. Corwin to Snyder, July 8, 1860, John F. Snyder Collection.

64. Frank P. Blair Jr., "The Destiny of the Races of This Continent" (pamphlet, MHS); FB to FPB, September 10, n.d. [late October], 1858, October 6, 25, November 2, 1859, EBL to SPL, January 29, February 1, 4, 1859, B-LP; *Missouri Democrat*, December 21, 1858; FB to Willard Nye, January 8, 1859, Blair Family Papers, MHS; FB to FPB, n.d. [1859], FB to MB, October 15, 20, 1859, BLC; FB to James R. Doolittle, October 15, November 3, 1859, in James R. Doolittle Papers. For a discussion of Republican reactions to the colonization idea, see Foner, *Free Soil*, 268–80.

felt "compelled to devote myself night & day to the task of infusing confidence into the leaders and making reconciliation among them."[65]

Frank also found matters in disarray at the *Missouri Democrat,* where things had not gone well for some time. During Frank's frequent absences Gratz had apparently neglected the business end of the paper in favor of editorializing. The thirty-two-year-old Brown had recently married Mary Hansome Gunn, the seventeen-year-old daughter of a former St. Louis mayor, and they were expecting their first child. Frank complained, "His young wife has occupied his time too much and made him inefficient instead of inspiring him with the ambition to push ahead." In addition, Frank told his brother, Gratz "assumes the dictator and makes everybody mad at him." Shortly after the city elections, which the Republicans carried handily, Brown announced his resignation as editor. Apo complained that Frank would now have to spend more time at the paper "and without any of the profits." Peter Foy replaced Brown as editor. He had previously been the paper's legislative correspondent in Jefferson City and Washington and would become one of Frank's staunchest supporters in the years ahead.[66]

Brown's departure from the *Missouri Democrat* marked the beginning of a significant break in the relationship between the two cousins. Political allies for the past decade, they would continue that same allegiance; but, as Blair shifted increasingly to the political right in the 1860s, Brown would move to the political left, causing a bitter division. Yet, by the end of the decade, their political paths would merge once again for expediency's sake as they battled the forces of Radical reconstruction, each from his own perspective. In the interim, although Brown left the *Democrat* with some bitterness, he remained close to the Blair family in Washington and always found a welcome in their homes during his later service in the capital.[67]

Frank's personal problems did not end at the paper. With the lame-duck session ended and his new term in doubt, he lost his congressional salary. His law practice stood in disarray because of his long absences from the city.

65. EBL to SPL, January 29, February 8, 14, 1859, B-LP; FB to MB, March 17, 1859, BLC.

66. Apo to FPB, January 14, 1857, FB to MB, n.d. [1857] and March 17, 1859, BLC; Apo to EB, March 13, 1859, Apo to FPB, April 7, 1859, FB to FPB, April 16, 1859, B-LP; *Missouri Democrat,* April 15, 1859; Hart, "*St. Louis Globe-Democrat,*" 39. Brown's biographer claims that Gratz's increasing political popularity, especially among the workingmen of St. Louis, had also irritated Frank, "who found the competition with Brown for popularity and political honors intolerable" (Peterson, *Freedom and Franchise,* 88).

67. Peterson, *Freedom and Franchise,* 90; EBL to SPL, January 12, 22, June 8, 1864, February 21, 1865, B-LP.

He had invested heavily in St. Louis real estate during the 1850s, incurring heavy mortgages. The panic of 1857 had hit St. Louis hard and caught Frank in a cash-flow problem as his rents declined. Much to Apo's dismay, in the spring of 1859, he determined to lease Rose Bank, the country home that had become their permanent residence, and acquire a house in town. He also began to sell other properties to meet his debts. His father offered to help, but Frank declined, declaring that he had already taken too much from the senior Blair.[68]

Then, in late May, a new disaster hit. Cary Gratz and Andrew Alexander, Frank's cousin and brother-in-law, respectively, failed in the commission business. Frank had underwritten several of their notes and now had to sell additional real estate to cover these losses. Dismayed by this misadventure, he wrote Montgomery, "I am done with endorsements and making myself liable for others." Unfortunately for Frank, his financial affairs continued to worsen. The hemp factory in Waverly, which his cousin Howard Gratz owned with Jo Shelby, collapsed financially in February 1860. Again, Blair bore the brunt of the loss because of notes he had underwritten. He had no recourse but to fall back on his father, who agreed to sell sufficient securities to meet Frank's various payments as they fell due. In return, Frank assigned to the senior Blair the rents generated by his various properties, which amounted to thirty-two hundred dollars annually, except for the twelve-hundred-dollar rental he was receiving for Rose Bank. Preston apparently helped Frank willingly, concerned to maintain him in his political career, which the senior Blair hoped might inevitably lead to high office; but it proved a bitter pill for Frank and Apo to swallow.[69]

The son wrote his father on December 23, 1860, that he was mortified to have to appeal to him for relief and did so only because he knew Preston was on safe ground financially while Apo and the children would be in jeopardy if anything happened to him. His total indebtedness to his father now rose to one hundred thousand dollars, which Frank labored to pay off as he could. He resumed the active practice of law with W. V. N. Bay, his old classmate of

68. EBL to SPL, February 10, 1859, Apo to EB, March 13, 1859, FB to FPB, April 16, May 2, 1859, B-LP.

69. FB to MB, June 14, 1859, FB to Apo, June 21, 1860, BLPLC; FB to MB, June 3, 1859, Samuel Simmons to MB, June 16, July 12, September 29, November 2, 22, December 9, 1859, January 10, February 4, 13, April 10, 19, 1860, F. A. Dick to FPB, June 20, October 31, November 1, 27, December 14, 1860, BLC; EBL to SPL, December 25, 1860, B-LP; O'Flaherty, *General Jo Shelby*, 50–51; W. E. Smith, *Blair Family in Politics*, 1:460–61; E. B. Smith, *Francis Preston Blair*, 289–90.

earlier days, with the assurance from Montgomery, "Your political reputation will not in the least interfere with it. On the contrary the judges of any court you choose to go into will feel themselves flattered and defer to you."[70]

The past decade had been a time of both triumph and tragedy for Frank Blair. Having tied his political fortunes to those of Thomas Hart Benton, he found himself increasingly on the horns of a dilemma as he and Old Bullion went separate ways over the free-soil question. Concerned to build a new political alliance out of the shambles of the party disarray of the 1850s, Frank worked unceasingly to that end, not only in St. Louis but also throughout the state. While managing personal triumphs in his elections to the state legislature and Congress, his efforts statewide bore less fruit because of the factionalism that continued to tear Missouri politics asunder. By the end of the decade, his own congressional career stood endangered even as he moved increasingly to the forefront of those embracing the new Republican faith. His zest for politics had placed a strain on both his marriage and his law practice. It also had made him increasingly dependent upon his father financially. Yet his political star appeared to be rising nationally as he found himself much in demand on the Republican lecture circuit. He faced the new decade determined to rebuild both his local political base and his financial security. Yet, that decade would take him down new pathways that even he could not foresee.

70. FB to FPB, December 23, 1860, MB to FB, December 27, 1860, BLC.

5

Missouri for the Union

With the election of 1860 rapidly approaching, Frank was far from idle during the fall of 1859. The family spent August on the New Jersey shore to help Apo regain her health after the birth of George, their fifth child, named for Apo's brother. Although he enjoyed fishing while at the seashore, Frank also made side trips to New York and Boston for political conferences with Free-Soil leaders and editors. Then, he stopped by Silver Spring to confer with his father before setting out on an extensive speaking tour, during which he gave ten speeches in as many days across Minnesota. While there he encountered Carl Schurz, engaged in a similar mission, when their two buggies met on a dusty country road. Frank introduced himself and invited the noted German to an improvised roadside lunch of sandwiches and claret, much to Schurz's delight.[1] Not all their encounters would be so congenial in the years that followed.

Frank devoted most of his speeches to the colonization scheme and found a good reception. He received a request from Gov. Samuel Kirkwood of Iowa for copies with the hope that he could persuade his legislature to endorse the proposition. Both Frank and Montgomery, meanwhile, sought to enlist the aid of Sen. James R. Doolittle of Wisconsin in stirring up the support of the other governors of the northwestern states.[2]

1. FB to FPB, August 14, October 6, 1859, B-LP; FB to James R. Doolittle, October 15, 1859, Doolittle Papers; Carl Schurz, *Reminiscences*, 2:147–48.

2. FB to FPB, October 6, 25, November 2, 1859, B-LP; FB to MB, October 20, 1859, BLC; FB to Doolittle, November 3, 1859, MB to Doolittle, November 11, 1859, Doolittle Papers.

At the end of November, Frank took his cause to Cincinnati and then climaxed his touring on January 25, 1860, with an address at Cooper Institute in New York City. Concerned about the impact of John Brown's raid on Harper's Ferry, Virginia, the previous October, he assured his New York listeners that the fiery abolitionist had no Republican support. "The Republicans propose to open new avenues of commerce, especially advantageous to the Southern States," he told his audience, "by making colonies of the class obnoxious to them, as well as to the Northern States, by their presence, but, by their removal to the tropics, converting them to usefulness to their native States and the nation." Frank brushed aside arguments that colonization was not feasible by responding "that it was the only solution to the Negro question." As to talk that the South might take up arms to defend slavery, he predicted that would make it "responsible for a contest which, if swayed by the opinions of this enlightened age, will probably be the last it will wage." Mistakenly, he did not believe such a war would occur because "cemented by the capital involved in their institution, [southerners] are not inclined to stake it all on a war against free institutions." Frank failed to realize that the election of a Republican president would hardly reassure the South of the safety of its slave property.[3]

Even as he urged colonization for other freedmen, Frank moved to free his own slaves. When C. W. Waite, in September 1858, sent him an article claiming that Blair owned thirty slaves, Frank replied, "I am the proprietor of some few slaves, of whom the most were purchased to prevent the separation of families and the number of those to whom I have given their freedom is greater than that of those I now possess." The following year he went into St. Louis Circuit Court to free Sarah Dupé and her three daughters, having previously freed the husband and father, Henry Dupé. The 1860 census revealed that Frank no longer had any slaves, but had three live-in women servants, one German and two Irish.[4]

Frank had been casting about for a Republican presidential candidate who might help accomplish his goals. He thought he had found him in his own backyard in the person of Edward Bates, a conservative Whig attorney who

3. *Speech of Hon. F. P. Blair, Jr., of Missouri, at the Cooper Institute, New York City, Wednesday, January 25, 1860* (pamphlet, MHS); *New York Times,* January 26, 1860; W. E. Smith, *Blair Family in Politics,* 1:450–51; E. B. Smith, *Francis Preston Blair,* 252–55.

4. *Missouri Republican,* October 4, 1858; Stevens, "Lincoln and Missouri," 67; *Anzeiger des Westens,* August 16, 1860, in Rowan, *Germans for a Free Missouri,* 125; 1860 Missouri Census, St. Louis City, in U.S. Bureau of the Census, St. Louis County, 406.

had long been one of the leading forces in Missouri and national Whig-gery. Hailing from a border state and being only moderately antislavery, Bates had a consistent record favoring the national development of internal improvements. Blair believed Bates could appeal to a broad spectrum of voters needed to coalesce Missouri's opposition elements and secure the necessary support for the success of a national Republican ticket.[5]

As early as April 27, 1859, Frank had invited Schuyler Colfax to help him evaluate Bates. The three men had a frank discussion in St. Louis during which all concerned laid out their respective agendas. The sixty-five-year-old Bates, who had had his share of political disappointments, agreed to consider a candidacy through the summer. By the time Frank returned from his Minnesota tour in early October, he could report, "I find that the mania has bitten old Bates very severely and I think he will play out more boldly for it than he has heretofore done. The plan his friends have is to hold an opposition convention this fall and recommend him for the Republican nomination."[6]

Frank immediately wrote to James Rollins, urging an early convention to allow Bates to get his views before the country quickly; but things did not proceed quite as smoothly as Bates or Blair would have liked. The Opposition Party's convention did not occur until February 29, 1860, when Gratz Brown, as chair of the state central committee, called it to order in Jefferson City. Frank had already gone to Washington for the opening of the new Congress and thus could not play much of a role. It quickly became evident that while all supported Bates for president, considerable disagreement existed regarding a platform. The one finally adopted said much about the preservation of the Union and little about slavery. Still, Charles Gibson, who served as Bates's liaison, reported to Frank that the convention "was in every respect a successful movement & is an event in the political history of Missouri." The convention endorsed Bates while leaving the selection of delegates to the Republican National Convention at Chicago to the Republican state convention scheduled for March 10 at the St. Louis Mercantile Library.[7]

5. FB to MB, October 15, 1859, BLC; W. E. Smith, *Blair Family in Politics*, 1:461–62; Marvin R. Cain, *Lincoln's Attorney General: Edward Bates of Missouri*, 90–92.

6. Edward Bates, *The Diary of Edward Bates, 1859–1866*, 11–12; FB to FPB, October 6, 1859, B-LP.

7. FB to Rollins, November 10, 1859, George C. Bingham to Rollins, December 16, 1859, Broadhead to Rollins, January 29, February 5, 1860, Edward Bates to Rollins, February 7, 1860, Rollins Papers; James O. Broadhead to William Newland, December 6, 1859, James S. Rollins to Broadhead, February 1, 17, 1860, Broadhead Papers; Bates, *Diary of Bates*, 106–7; *Missouri Statesman*, March 9, 1860. The day following the Opposition meeting, those who

This second gathering was small and not altogether harmonious. After agreeing unanimously to resolutions calling for the colonization of freed blacks, a homestead bill, a central route for the Pacific railroad, equal rights for naturalized citizens, and continuation of the current naturalization laws, the delegates argued over the endorsement of Bates. Many of the Germans held reservations because of his support for Fillmore and the Know-Nothing ticket in 1856. They also questioned his enthusiasm for Free-Soilism. In the end, however, Frank prevailed, and the delegates endorsed Bates; but the furor prompted several of the Germans to walk out. The convention chose eighteen delegates to go to Chicago, including Frank, Gratz Brown, and Peter Foy, the new editor of the *Missouri Democrat*.[8]

Concerned by the possibility of a serious German defection, Frank now employed a device previously suggested by Gibson. On March 12, he convinced Foy, together with Charles L. Bernays, editor of the *Anzeiger des Westens*, and nine other Republican leaders to address a questionnaire to Bates to ascertain his views on issues of critical concern to the Germans, including the extension and constitutionality of slavery, colonization, free homesteads, the Pacific railroad, and statehood for Kansas. The prospective candidate worked carefully on his responses. He opposed the extension of slavery and called the Dred Scott decision a mistake, while endorsing the other issues with only slight reservations.[9]

Frank believed that this statement should satisfy the opposition and became angry when he learned that Gratz Brown still might be trying to sow discord. Apparently disturbed by Bates's lack of endorsement for his gradual emancipation scheme, Brown wanted a stronger enhancement of free-white labor at the expense of slavery. When Rollins wondered what the national convention's outcome would be, Frank responded, "After Bates I say I don't care a d—n. . . . Bates could certainly be elected & make a good President & therefore I consider his chances best." Although Rollins gave Bates his wholehearted endorsement, other old-line Whigs and Know-Nothings in Missouri and elsewhere expressed dismay at his apparent sellout to the Republicans.

---

supported Bates but disliked the idea of jumping into the Republican Party met in the same location and selected delegates to the Constitutional Union convention at Baltimore with the intention of pushing Bates's candidacy there (*Missouri Statesman*, March 9, 1860).

8. *Missouri Republican*, March 11, 1860; *Missouri Democrat*, March 12, 1860.

9. *Missouri Democrat*, March 21, 1860; Bates, *Diary of Bates*, 111–14, 117–18. For reactions of the German press, see Rowan, *Germans for a Free Missouri*, 101–2, 105–6.

Still, Bates attracted considerable support in the other border states. Preston and Montgomery managed to control the Maryland state convention for him while also helping to sway votes in the Delaware and Kentucky delegations.[10]

Frank, meanwhile, had other concerns. He had gone to Washington in early 1860 to contest for his congressional seat before the House Committee on Elections. Lizzie wrote Phil that he was staying at their home on Pennsylvania Avenue across from the White House and working hard on his presentation. He had sent for Apo and the children, and they arrived in mid-April, after an exhausting two-day train ride, to stay at the senior Blairs' Silver Spring estate. The House finally made its decision in Frank's case on June 8 when it voted to seat him over Richard Barrett by the narrow margin of ninety-three to ninety-one. Within the Missouri delegation, only Thomas L. Anderson supported him. A Know-Nothing, Anderson had received Frank's endorsement for reelection in 1858 as a member of the Opposition Party and now proved himself worthy of that support. Although gratified by all the congratulations he received, Frank impetuously determined to resign at the end of the session and make his case directly with the electorate in the fall. To that end, he sent the *Missouri Democrat* a long letter explaining his reasons for the move.[11]

The Republican National Convention opened in Chicago on May 16 with all the Blairs in attendance. Frank led the Missouri delegation, while his father and brother served as delegates from Maryland. Frank immediately began pushing the Bates candidacy in a field crowded with numerous favorite sons, including Abraham Lincoln. Aided by Horace Greeley, the editor of the *New York Tribune*, and others, Frank circulated a paper extolling Bates's attributes, including his conservative appeal to all sections and consequently his ability to weaken the support for John Bell, the Constitutional Union candidate, in the border states. The Lincoln men countered with arguments that Bates was unacceptable to the critical German vote because of his past Know-Nothing associations. Indeed, they argued, he could not even carry his own state. In addition, they noted his advanced age. Shrewdly, Lincoln's supporters also packed the galleries of the Wigwam, the site of the convention, even as the

10. FB to Rollins, April 7, 1860, Rollins Papers; Peterson, *Freedom and Franchise,* 94–95; Reinhard H. Luthin, "Organizing the Republican Party in the 'Border State' Regions: Edward Bates's Presidential Candidacy in 1860," 151–57.

11. EBL to SPL, March 27, April 1, 4, 8, 18, 1860, B-LP; FB to Apo, June 13, 1860, BLPLC; Bates, *Diary of Bates,* 137; CG, 36:1:2678–81, 2761–73.

supporters of Sen. William H. Seward of New York, considered the leading contender coming into the convention, paraded through the streets.[12]

In the end, the Lincoln strategists carried the day, nominating their candidate on the third ballot. Bates remained among the also-rans throughout. The Missouri delegation loyally supported him through all three ballots; but, when it became evident that the tide had turned to Lincoln, Gratz Brown rose and loudly proclaimed, "I am instructed to cast the entire vote of Missouri—18 votes—for that gallant son of the West, Abraham Lincoln!" to which the convention responded with "great enthusiasm." The Blairs had no qualms about the decision. Frank had campaigned for Lincoln in 1858, and the two had kept in touch over the past two years. Although a moderate, the prairie lawyer from Illinois shared many of the family's views, including colonization.[13]

Bates took his defeat philosophically. He realized that, as a latecomer to Republican ranks, he could not expect the enthusiastic support of many Republicans. Still, he believed that he offered the only hope for a truly national candidacy, which might help deter the "black Republican" image in the border states and parts of the South. Although he had some misgivings and refrained from active campaigning, Bates agreed to support Lincoln.[14]

Frank, on the other hand, entered the campaign enthusiastically. He joined Carl Schurz and others on the official notification committee, which traveled to Springfield to convey the news of the nomination directly to the candidate. Then he hastened to St. Louis to prepare for his and Lincoln's campaigns. The Illinoisan's nomination had shattered any hope of a united effort in Missouri. Many former Missouri Whigs and Know-Nothings now fell into line behind the Constitutional Unionist John Bell. These included Frank's friend James Rollins, who reluctantly agreed to run for Congress on the Bell ticket. Rollins rightly concluded that his candidacy as a Republican in central Missouri would simply ensure another defeat.[15]

12. Gustave Koerner, *Memoirs*, 2:87–89; Luthin, "Organizing the Republican Party," 157–60; W. E. Smith, *Blair Family in Politics*, 1:475–78; Peterson, *Freedom and Franchise*, 96–97; Cain, *Lincoln's Attorney General*, 107–12.

13. W. E. Smith, *Blair Family in Politics*, 1:482–83; Peterson, *Freedom and Franchise*, 96–97; Cain, *Lincoln's Attorney General*, 112–13. Many years later Montgomery would claim that Seward had offered Frank the vice presidential nomination in return for their support, but Preston Blair refused to drop Bates (MB to Cassius Clay, December 31, 1881, BLC).

14. Bates, *Diary of Bates*, 129–33; *Missouri Republican*, June 19, 1860; Cain, *Lincoln's Attorney General*, 113–17.

15. W. E. Smith, *Blair Family in Politics*, 1:484–85; *Missouri Statesman*, May 25, 1860; Rollins to James O. Broadhead, June 5, 1860, Rollins to Edward Bates, June 6, 1860, Rollins Papers; MB to Minna Blair, July 21, 1860, BLC; Koerner, *Memoirs*, 2:98–99.

The statewide canvass became even more complicated after the Democrats split permanently at Baltimore in late June. The Democrats had initially divided at Charleston in February over the issue of slavery extension and later failed in their attempts at unity when they held separate conventions at Baltimore. Stephen A. Douglas became the candidate of the regular Democrats, endorsing their traditional stand of popular sovereignty, while Vice President John C. Breckinridge led the breakaway group, which stood by the Dred Scott decision. This resulted in four statewide tickets in Missouri as well, with two Democratic candidates for governor: Claiborne F. Jackson, Frank's old nemesis, as the regular Democratic candidate, and former governor Hancock Jackson representing the Breckinridge group. The Constitutional Unionists nominated Sample Orr from southwest Missouri as their gubernatorial candidate, while the Republicans ran James B. Gardenhire of Cole County. Although Gardenhire made a statewide tour, he met with little enthusiasm. Frank quickly realized the need to concentrate his energies on St. Louis and his own campaign for reelection.[16]

Even before Frank's return to St. Louis, the Young Republicans organized a grand rally at Mercantile Library with a ringing endorsement of Lincoln. The St. Louis Republicans convened on July 9 and unanimously nominated Frank for reelection from the First District. Because of his resignation at the end of the session, he ran to complete the current term during the lame-duck session as well as the new term beginning March 4, 1861. His opponent was again Richard Barrett. Taking nothing for granted, Frank campaigned vigorously. It proved to be a raucous campaign. During one of his early rallies, Blair and the other Republican speakers found themselves being constantly heckled and even stoned by opposition thugs. Fights broke out between the two groups, and the meeting ended in tumultuous fashion. This incident led Frank to organize his followers into the St. Louis Wide Awakes. This group now formed the vanguard at every meeting, with the intention of preventing a further repetition of such violence.[17]

Campaign rhetoric filled the air as both parties rallied incessantly. The Wide Awakes and Blair Rangers regularly marched en masse to the site of Frank's speaking, while the Constitutional Guards and Broom Rangers, their Democratic equivalents, did likewise for their rallies. The latter group got

---

16. Walter Harrington Ryle, *Missouri: Union or Secession,* 134–35, 152–53.

17. W. E. Smith, *Blair Family in Politics,* 1:489–91; James Peckham, *General Nathaniel Lyon and Missouri in 1861,* xi–xiii.

their name from hickory brooms, which they carried to symbolize the clean sweep that they hoped to accomplish in the election. Blair challenged Barrett to a series of four no-holds-barred debates in different parts of the county, when both groups came together in mass demonstrations for their respective candidates. In addition, he imported several noted Republicans to speak on his behalf, including Sen. Lyman Trumbull of Illinois and Carl Schurz from Wisconsin. The German press, particularly the *Anzeiger des Westens* and the *Westliche Post,* also gave Frank its support.[18]

Election day, August 6, brought a strange mixture of results. In the race for the rest of the current term, Barrett defeated Frank by 150 votes in a two-way contest and would thus return to Washington for the lame-duck session. For the new term, however, Frank won by 1,500 over Barrett and Albert Todd, the Constitutional Union candidate, who had stayed out of the short-term contest. James Peckham, one of Frank's key lieutenants, attributed the short-term defeat to the Constitutional Unionist support of Barrett and the circulation of a bogus ballot, which indicated Blair "for Congress" but did not designate "to fill vacancy," with the result that enough ballots were thrown out to swing that contest. Frank wrote Montgomery, "Old Bates was absent and his friends did nothing to assist me." In a public letter to the *Missouri Democrat,* he asserted that his election made St. Louis a Republican city, claiming that he had lost in 1858 and for the short-term only because of fraud and the fusion of the opposition elements.[19]

Statewide, Missourians elected Claiborne Jackson governor in a tight contest with Sample Orr, while Hancock Jackson and James B. Gardenhire ran far behind. James Rollins secured his congressional seat, but the remainder of the state's places went to Democrats, three of them incumbents. Although Claiborne Jackson strongly sympathized with the dissident proslavery element of his party, he realized the necessity of endorsing Douglas for president in order to have any hope of success. This strategy paid off. Following the election of Lincoln, however, the new governor began to show his true colors.[20]

18. Peckham, *Lyon and Missouri,* xii–xiv; W. E. Smith, *Blair Family in Politics,* 1:489–95; Peterson, *Freedom and Franchise,* 98; Rowan, *Germans for a Free Missouri,* 114–20; Galusha Anderson, *A Border City during the Civil War,* 16–18; *Missouri Republican,* August 4, 5, 1860; Jane Magill to Ellen Magill, August 1, 1860, Ellen Magill Papers.

19. Abstract of Election Returns, St. Louis County, August 6, 1860; Peckham, *Lyon and Missouri,* xiv–xv; FB to MB, August 7, 15, 1860, BLC; *Missouri Democrat,* August 14, 1860.

20. William E. Parrish, *Turbulent Partnership: Missouri and the Union, 1861–1865,* 4–5; Wood, "James Sidney Rollins," 196; *Biographical Directory of the American Congress, 1774–1989,* 169, 173.

Frank's reelection as the only Republican from a border state further enhanced his popularity in national Republican circles. He spent the remainder of August trying to straighten out his financial difficulties and making two forays to outstate Missouri to help the Republican cause. At one speech in Ironton, some three hundred Wide Awakes accompanied him on a special train to provide protection. W. V. N. Bay, who was present, later reported,

> It was proclaimed in advance that if he attempted [to speak] he would be mobbed. At his request we accompanied him, and on reaching Ironton learned that an armed crowd had assembled at the courthouse to resist him. When he rose to address the meeting, the few friends he had became greatly alarmed for his safety; but their fears were soon dissipated when they saw how calm and collected he was, and heard him boldly declare that any man who came armed to the meeting, with the intention to use violence against him, was too great a coward to attempt it.

Frank spoke for nearly two hours without interruption "and on leaving the stand received the congratulations of many who differed with him on the slavery question." He was not as fortunate when he went to Hannibal at the invitation of Samuel T. Glover, who would become a close wartime associate. With no Wide Awakes to protect him, Frank found himself effectively interrupted by the opposition. He made no further attempts to go out into the state.[21]

Although his father urged him to bring the family to Silver Spring for a respite, Frank declined, claiming "the expense of traveling [is] so great with a large family and my finances so straightened [*sic*] by my unfortunate endorsements that we think it better to remain quietly at home and at as small expense as possible until I can retrieve myself a little." While Apo and the children stayed in St. Louis, however, Frank embarked on an extensive campaign tour for the national ticket and local Republican candidates, which took him to Indiana, Ohio, and Pennsylvania, with a stopover in Springfield to confer with Lincoln.[22]

In late September, Montgomery and his father traveled to Harrisburg to hear Frank speak and to confer with Schurz, Preston King, and the Pennsylvania Republican boss, Simon Cameron. Frank had spoken six times within

21. FB to MB, August 15, 1860, BLC; James Peckham to John L. Bittinger, August 28, 1860, St. Louis History Collection; Peckham, *Lyon and Missouri*, xvi–xvii; Bay, *Reminiscences*, 394.
22. EBL to SPL, August 14, 16, 21, 24, September 1, 1860, FB to FPB, August 24, 1860, B-LP; W. E. Smith, *Blair Family in Politics*, 1:496.

the last thirty-six hours. Many of these speeches lasted up to two hours and attracted large crowds. Speaker and audience did not have the modern-day advantage of a public-address system, and Frank's voice suffered. L. E. Chittenden, who was frequently with Frank on the Pennsylvania circuit, described the experience: "In the afternoons Col. Blair and myself usually addressed the same mass-meeting. As soon as one had concluded he was hurried away to a distant town or city, to be in time for the evening meeting. The other made his speech, and was rushed off in the opposite direction. . . . Such sleep as we got was on the cars." After the Harrisburg rally, Frank retreated to Silver Spring for the weekend, where Lizzie found him "quite worn out, hoarse & fagged out with travel & mental labor." The following day, however, she reported that "a good long sleep has revived him & he has [been] working all day nearly on two speeches he is to make in Philadelphia."[23]

By mid-October, Frank was back in Missouri, accompanied by his brother-in-law Phil Lee, who came to help straighten out the troubled finances. Frank stayed home only briefly, however, before heading for Illinois to aid Lyman Trumbull's reelection efforts for the Senate in return for that individual's previous assistance in his own campaign. Election day found Trumbull successful and Lincoln chosen president, though by only a plurality of the popular vote. In Missouri, Lincoln garnered only seventeen thousand votes, mainly in St. Louis and in the German-dominated counties immediately west of it, yet that was ten thousand more than Gardenhire had polled three months earlier. Douglas won the state by a narrow margin over Bell, polling fifteen thousand fewer votes than Claiborne Jackson in the earlier race. It was evident from both elections that most Missourians wanted to avoid taking an extreme position.[24]

In the aftermath of the election, the Blairs turned their attention to the makeup of the new Lincoln cabinet. Frank wrote his father on November 8 that he had gone to Alton to confer with Trumbull and to give him Preston's letters. He reported that the senator favored Montgomery for the cabinet and would pursue the matter with the president-elect. Frank told the senior Blair to let him know if he wanted him to go to Springfield to press Montgomery's case in person. He had reason to know that Lincoln had been well pleased with his efforts in Illinois and elsewhere during the campaign. Two weeks later, Frank wrote that he planned to stop in Springfield en route to a family rest in

23. EBL to SPL, September 22, 26, 28, 29, 1860, B-LP; Chittenden quote in W. E. Smith, *Blair Family in Politics*, 1:498–99.

24. F. A. Dick to MB, October 20, 1860, BLC; W. E. Smith, *Blair Family in Politics*, 1:506–7; Peckham, *Lyon and Missouri*, xviii.

Kentucky with Apo and the children. He had heard nothing from Trumbull or anyone else, but it appeared that Lincoln was "very close" when it came to revealing the direction of his thinking. Frank urged his father to come west in the hope that it might lead to a Springfield meeting, but Montgomery and Lizzie discouraged such a trip. Instead the senior Blair conveyed his concerns in letters to Frank, which the son passed on to Lincoln.

The Blairs initially sought the attorney generalship for Montgomery, but Lincoln informed Frank that he had decided to offer that post to Bates and asked him to gain his fellow Missourian's acceptance. Frank then suggested that his brother should go for the War Department appointment. In all of this, he also saw an opportunity to promote his own interests, reporting to his father, "I have thought also that I should probably be able to get elected to the Speakership of the next House of Representatives, if the Judge gets into the Cabinet." In the end, after much political maneuvering by all sides, Lincoln offered Montgomery the postmaster generalship, which he accepted.[25]

In addition, Frank concerned himself with patronage positions for his local lieutenants. Chief among these was the St. Louis post office, which went to Peter Foy, who had worked hard for Lincoln's election at the *Missouri Democrat.* The president called this "the best office in my gift within Missouri." Frank also secured the post of U.S. consul in Bremen for Henry Boernstein, the editor of the *Anzeiger des Westens.* Lesser posts went to other supporters.[26]

As the secession crisis deepened nationally, Missourians debated how to respond to it. In the ensuing struggle, Frank played a pivotal role. Governor Jackson made his sentiments clear in his inaugural address on January 4, 1861, when he asserted, "The destiny of the slave-holding States of this Union is one and the same. . . . Missouri, then, will in my opinion best consult her own interest, and the interest of the whole country, by a timely declaration of her determination to stand by her sister slave-holding States, in whose wrongs she participates, and with whose institutions and people she sympathizes."[27]

Frank wrote Montgomery on the twelfth that he had recently returned from Jefferson City, where he found secession sentiment rife among the Democrats. He had little faith in his old antagonist, Claiborne Jackson, with

25. FB to FPB, November 8, December 23, 1860, FB to MB, December 14, 1860, January 24, 1861, February 12, 16, 1861, BLC; FB to MB, November 23, n.d. [December 13,] 1860, B-LP; Bates, *Diary of Bates,* 156, 164–65; E. B. Smith, *Francis Preston Blair,* 269–72; Earl Schenck Miers, ed., *Lincoln Day by Day: A Chronology, 1809–1865,* 2:301, 3:7.

26. Harry J. Carman and Reinhard H. Luthin, *Lincoln and the Patronage,* 74, 194, 198–99.

27. *Messages and Proclamations of the Governors of the State of Missouri,* 3:33–37.

whom he had tangled eight years earlier in their House debates over the Jackson Resolutions. Frank had believed him the tool of the southern ultras then, and the governor's inaugural address seemed to reveal that he had not changed his colors. The Breckinridge Democrats dominated the legislature with sixty-two members in the House and Senate, compared with forty-six Douglas Democrats, forty-four Constitutional Unionists, and thirteen Republicans. The new speaker of the House, John McAfee of Shelby County, was decidedly proslavery, while there presided over the Senate one of the staunchest secession sympathizers in Missouri, Lt. Gov. Thomas C. Reynolds, with whom Frank had crossed political swords numerous times in the 1850s.[28]

Frank reported that Reynolds had already gone to Washington to consult with the secessionists there. On the morning of Jackson's inaugural, the lieutenant governor conferred with a number of his supporters, both in and out of the legislature, to determine a course of action. All agreed that control of St. Louis was critical to their cause, especially since the U.S. arsenal there contained some sixty thousand stand of arms, two hundred or more barrels of powder, and other implements of war. On the afternoon of January 8, Reynolds addressed a large sympathetic audience in St. Louis, proclaiming the need for cooperation with the other southern states, whatever course that might take. The secessionists, meanwhile, organized a paramilitary group known as the "Minute Men" and began to drill secretly at various locations in anticipation of seizing the arsenal when the right moment arrived.[29]

To counteract this movement, Frank reorganized his Wide Awakes in a similar fashion, taking the name of Union Home Guards. Primarily made up of Germans, the guards also drilled secretly at night in the various Turner halls around St. Louis. James Peckham later recalled that "the floors of these houses were thickly strewn with saw-dust to avoid noise in drilling." Another participant remembered that Frank "was incessantly engaged in the great work," making the rounds of the various meetings to encourage the men in their activities. To add to whatever arms the guards themselves had, their leaders devised a clever scheme. They held an art exhibition, which included a number of items from the East. Concealed among these materials,

---

28. FB to MB, January 12, 1861, B-LP; Parrish, *Turbulent Partnership*, 6.
29. FB to MB, January 12, 1861, B-LP; FB to MB, January 18, 1861, BLC; Peckham, *Lyon and Missouri*, 27–30; Thomas L. Snead, *The Fight for Missouri from the Election of Lincoln to the Death of Lyon*, 105–10; Robert J. Rombauer, *The Union Cause in St. Louis in 1861*, 193–94; James O. Broadhead, "St. Louis during the War," Broadhead Papers, 21; Basil W. Duke, *Reminiscences of General Basil W. Duke, CSA*, 37–42.

marked plaster casts, were munitions, forwarded by friends. In addition, numerous monetary contributions flowed in from the East to assist the cause. Frank also recommended the establishment of a Union Committee of Safety, which included James O. Broadhead and Samuel T. Glover, both prominent attorneys; J. J. Witzig; Mayor O. D. Filley; and former mayor John How, all of whom had been actively involved with Frank politically. This group's task was to mobilize resistance during his frequent absences.[30]

As tensions mounted, threats against Frank and his family became common. One evening, as Blair sat writing in the back room of his home at 1129 Washington Avenue, someone fired through the window, narrowly missing him. Indeed, Frank later said that had he not leaned forward to pick up a paper at that moment, the shot would have killed him. Samuel Simmons, who had studied law in Frank's office in the 1850s and had played a major role in helping straighten out his tangled finances, had appointed himself a bodyguard and rushed into the yard to chase the assailant down. On other occasions, Simmons would take it upon himself to go into the street in front of the house when a disturbance occurred to try to prevent further trouble.

One of the Blair sons later recalled that during Frank's absences from the city Simmons would sleep at the Blair home, constituting himself "the family guardian." One afternoon the younger Blair went to the neighborhood bakery for some bread. A southern man, the baker "set his son upon me and he gave me a sound thrashing." On hearing of it, Simmons immediately left the house and dealt with the baker in a similar fashion. On another occasion, when Frank was absent, Simmons, anticipating an attack on the house, "bundled up the whole family and took us down to Jefferson Barracks." It proved a good move when a mob appeared on Washington Avenue that evening.[31]

Against this background the General Assembly proceeded to deal with Governor Jackson's legislative agenda. On January 18, it passed a bill calling for a state convention on March 4, the same day as Lincoln's inauguration, to consider Missouri's relationship with the Union. To ensure against precipitate action, the moderates in the assembly attached a proviso requiring

30. Broadhead, "St. Louis during the War," Broadhead Papers, 27–28; Snead, *Fight for Missouri*, 104; James F. How, "Frank P. Blair in 1861," 385; Anderson, *Border City*, 21–22; Franklin A. Dick, "Memorandum of Matters in Missouri in 1861," Franklin A. Dick Papers, 7. Peckham, *Lyon and Missouri*, provides a detailed list of contributors (30–41).

31. Military Order of the Loyal Legion of the United States, *In Memoriam: Samuel Simmons* (pamphlet, MHS).

a popular referendum on any ordinance of secession the convention might pass. Although Jackson had recommended sending delegates to the gathering of the Confederate States at Montgomery, the legislature instead appointed five men to go to Washington to attend a conference called by Virginia in the hope of working out some method of conciliation.[32]

The legislature also postponed consideration of a proposed reorganization of the state militia, which would have given the governor nearly absolute power. It did pass a Jackson-sponsored bill removing the control of the Republican-dominated St. Louis City Council over its police force and substituting a board of four commissioners appointed by the governor, with the mayor serving ex officio as the fifth member. The new board would have control over the St. Louis volunteer militia, the sheriff, and "all conservators of the peace." In the days that followed, this proved a force with which the Union men had to reckon.[33]

Missourians elected delegates to the state convention on February 18, the same day the Confederacy inaugurated Jefferson Davis as its new president. Although some of his supporters had wanted to run a straight Republican slate from St. Louis, Frank secured a coalition ticket of the various conservative pro-Union elements. When someone protested, "I don't believe in breaking up the Republican party, just to please these tender footed Unionists—I believe in sticking to the party," Frank responded, "Let us have a country first and then we can talk about parties." He had tried to play the coalition game, with mixed success, for the last few years and wisely saw it now as the best way to carry the day against the secessionists. The coalition ticket, made up of one-third Douglas men, one-third Bell men, and one-third Republicans, all of them pro-Union, proved successful. Thomas L. Snead, the editor of the *St. Louis Bulletin* and a leading secessionist, later attributed the ticket's success to "the courage, moderation, and tact of Francis P. Blair." Statewide, Missourians expressed their concern for conciliation by refusing to elect any of the states' rights candidates, much to the dismay of Governor Jackson and his associates.[34]

32. William E. Parrish, *A History of Missouri: Volume III, 1860 to 1875*, 6.
33. Samuel T. Glover to MB, February 1861, BLC; Peckham, *Lyon and Missouri*, 25; Snead, *Fight for Missouri*, 30–33; Duke, *Reminiscences*, 42–43.
34. *Missouri Democrat*, January 12, 1861; EBL to SPL, February 12*, 14*, 1861, B-LP; Broadhead, "St. Louis during the Civil War," Broadhead Papers, 18; Peckham, *Lyon and Missouri*, 49–50, 83–86; Thomas L. Snead, "The First Year of the War in Missouri," in *Battles and Leaders of the Civil War*, ed. Robert Underwood Johnson and Clarence Clough Buel, 1:263; Ryle, *Missouri: Union or Secession*, 201–10. Those letters in the Blair-Lee Family Papers

After convening in Jefferson City, the group quickly adjourned to St. Louis. Although Frank's old foe, former governor Sterling Price, presided over the convention, conservative Unionist Hamilton R. Gamble of St. Louis, a former Whig and former Missouri Supreme Court justice, dominated the proceedings. As chairman of the Federal Relations Committee, Gamble reported resolutions against secession while urging a conciliatory policy to avoid conflict. Its work completed, the convention adjourned, subject to call should conditions change.[35]

In the midst of this political maneuvering, an important new arrival reached the St. Louis scene on February 6. Capt. Nathaniel Lyon would play a major role in keeping Missouri in the Union in the critical days ahead. A native of Connecticut and an ardent antislavery Unionist, Lyon had been stationed at Fort Riley, in the Kansas Territory, for the last several years. There he had seen firsthand the efforts of the proslavery men in the border warfare. Lyon and his eighty-man company had been transferred to St. Louis at Frank's instigation. Concerned by the Minute Men's preparations, Frank and the Union Committee of Safety suspected the disloyalty of Maj. William H. Bell, who had commanded the St. Louis arsenal since 1858 with only a forty-man contingent. Bell, a native of North Carolina and an 1820 West Point graduate, had been wavering for some time. On January 24, he met with Daniel M. Frost, who served as Governor Jackson's liaison. Frost convinced Bell that Missouri could lay claim to the arsenal under state sovereignty, whereupon the major agreed not to resist any attempt at state seizure should it come nor to remove any of the arsenal's armaments without first notifying state authorities.[36]

Working through Lincoln and his brother Montgomery, Frank urged not only the reinforcements Lyon and his men provided but also the removal of Bell as an added precaution. General-in-Chief Winfield Scott agreed and replaced Bell with Bvt. Maj. Peter V. Hagner, a native of Maryland and an 1836 West Point graduate, transferred from Fort Leavenworth. The arrival of Lyon a week later produced an intense rivalry between the two officers. Lyon was dismayed to find himself and his company under the control of Hagner, whose permanent captaincy postdated his and whom he began to suspect of

hereafter designated with an * may also be found in *Wartime Washington: The Civil War Letters of Elizabeth Blair Lee.*

35. Parrish, *Turbulent Partnership*, 10–13.

36. Ashbel Woodward, *Life of General Nathaniel Lyon*, 236; FB to MB, January 18, 24, 1861, BLC; D. M. Frost to C. F. Jackson, January 24, 1861, in Rombauer, *Union Cause*, 142–43, and Peckham, *Lyon and Missouri*, 43–45.

disloyalty. He also became aware of the activities of the Minute Men, who had begun to parade openly through the streets. Lyon demanded additional security at the arsenal, which Hagner deemed unnecessary. Appealing his case to Maj. Gen. William S. Harney, who commanded the Department of the West from Jefferson Barracks, Lyon got nowhere. Harney did not take the activities of the Minute Men seriously.[37]

Shortly after his arrival, Lyon met with Frank and the Union Committee of Safety. He found in Blair an ardent and willing compatriot, and the two worked closely together beyond this point. Concerned by Harney's seeming complacency, Frank realized that in Lyon he had someone he could trust to work with his Union Home Guards if crisis came. Indeed, he got the captain's unofficial agreement to assist the guards in their drills and organization behind the scenes in return for which Frank would press Lyon's case against Hagner in Washington with the incoming Lincoln administration.[38]

Frank left St. Louis on February 21 to attend Lincoln's inauguration and confer with the new president on Missouri affairs. He had established a good rapport with Lincoln over the last several years and quickly persuaded him of the need to have Lyon in command of the arsenal. The War Department forwarded orders to that effect to General Harney on March 13. Irritated by the persistence of Lyon and concerned with maintaining control of what he saw as an increasingly threatening situation, Harney chose to enforce the new orders narrowly. He acknowledged Lyon's command of the arsenal's defenses but left Hagner in charge of the arsenal's ordnance. Lyon could not secure any supplies without Harney's prior approval. The general also arranged a court of inquiry at Fort Leavenworth to examine charges against Lyon stemming from an incident while he was in Kansas, which required the captain to leave St. Louis at this critical moment.[39]

37. FB to MB, January 18, 24, 1861, BLC; Peckham, *Lyon and Missouri*, 58–59, 65–68; Christopher Phillips, *Damned Yankee: The Life of General Nathaniel Lyon*, 142–46.
38. Dick, "Memorandum," Dick Papers, 9–10; Peckham, *Lyon and Missouri*, 75; Phillips, *Damned Yankee*, 147–48; Stephen D. Engle, *Yankee Dutchman: The Life of Franz Sigel*, 50–51.
39. EBL to SPL, February 14*, 1861, B-LP; *OR*, 1:1:658–59. Harney found himself in a difficult situation. He had been transferred to St. Louis the previous November at his own request because of his wife's connection with the aristocratic Mullanphy family, who were avowed secessionists. A native Tennessean, Harney was undoubtedly loyal to the Union, which he had served for the past forty-two years. He tried to tread lightly between the contending forces in St. Louis in 1861, hoping that this would maintain the peace there. He knew Lyon from service in Florida, Mexico, and Kansas, and realized his stubborn determination to have his way in things (Phillips, *Damned Yankee*, 124, 150).

Lyon immediately appealed to Frank, who was still in Washington. Franklin Dick and others wrote also, sending the additional bad news that the city elections had gone against the Republicans. In a surprising upset, Constitutional Unionist Daniel G. Taylor had defeated John How for mayor, thus ending several years of coalition control of St. Louis politics. Frank managed to rescind Lyon's court of inquiry; and Harney began to sense the political drift. Further alarmed by the increasingly open activity of the Minute Men, who had recently raised a secession flag over their headquarters at the Berthold Mansion and had attempted to do so over the courthouse, Harney now gave Lyon the authority to proceed with the strengthening of the arsenal's defenses.[40]

The situation exploded nationally on April 12 with the Confederate firing on Fort Sumter, South Carolina. President Lincoln promptly issued a call for seventy-five thousand volunteers for ninety days' service to put down the insurrection, assigning each state a quota. Secy. of War Simon Cameron informed Governor Jackson that Missouri's share would be four thousand men, but the state's chief executive refused to honor the order on the ground that these forces would be used to "make war" on the people of the seceded states. Jackson termed Lincoln's request "illegal, unconstitutional, and revolutionary; in its objects inhuman and diabolical."[41]

Frank returned to St. Louis the same day that Jackson issued his stinging refusal. He brought with him a War Department order giving Lyon five thousand stand of arms from the arsenal, to be used in arming loyal citizens. The captain informed Blair, however, that General Harney had refused to muster any of the Union Home Guards who had volunteered for service, fearful that such action would further exacerbate the increasing tension within the city. The pro-Jackson police board had demanded the withdrawal of Lyon's patrols, which had been keeping watch on the streets around the arsenal, so Harney now withheld his consent to Frank's order and sent a request to the adjutant general asking that Lyon be replaced.[42]

An angry Frank quickly informed Harney that he planned to seek his transfer from the command of the Western Department. Although Harney

---

40. Nathaniel Lyon to FB, April 6, 1861, in Peckham, *Lyon and Missouri*, 69–71, 93–95; F. A. Dick to FB, April 2, 1861, Henry T. Blow to FB, April 3, 1861, O. D. Filley to FB, April 4, 1861, BLC; Duke, *Reminiscences*, 37–42; Phillips, *Damned Yankee*, 153–54.

41. *OR*, 3:1:67–69, 82–83.

42. *OR*, 1:1:666–70, 56:489; L. U. Reavis, *The Life and Military Services of General William Selby Harney*, 354.

realized Blair's political influence, he refused to be intimidated. Frank wrote Montgomery on April 19 that the Western Department needed a new commander who would not obstruct the government's orders, and he urged his brother to move War Department officialdom to recall Harney. He also telegraphed Secretary of War Cameron asking for authority to muster the Union Home Guards into military service to meet Missouri's quota. Within twenty-four hours he had permission to proceed.

Still, Lyon feared to move without a direct personal order. Lt. John M. Schofield, on army leave while teaching at Washington University, had been contacted by the War Department to muster Missouri troops, but Blair and Lyon questioned his credentials to muster the Home Guards. A visit to Harney again proved fruitless. Increasingly frustrated by these complications, Frank telegraphed Cameron once again, using Pennsylvania governor Andrew G. Curtin as an intermediary to relay the urgency of the situation. As it turned out, Maj. FitzJohn Porter, assistant adjutant general, was in Harrisburg on a recruiting mission and took it upon himself to send a telegram of authorization to Harney, Lyon, and Blair.[43]

Frank now made the rounds of his supporters at the various German beer gardens, Turner halls, and elsewhere, informing them that the muster would take place in secrecy that evening at the arsenal. Those designated to enlist arrived throughout the evening, and the muster proceeded smoothly. While it was taking place, a telegram arrived from Adj. Gen. Lorenzo Thomas confirming Porter's authorization and bringing the additional news that General Harney had been relieved of his command and ordered to Washington. This left Lyon completely in charge.[44]

The mustering process continued throughout the week, eventually reaching twenty-five hundred; and Frank proudly assured Washington that Missouri's quota would soon be filled. As more men enlisted, it became impossible to house all of them at the arsenal. Lyon and Frank simply told many to remain in their homes, to be ready for action at a moment's notice, should the need arise. Gov. Richard Yates had previously been detailed to send Illinois troops to guard the arsenal, but the War Department now ordered these kept east of the Mississippi. On April 24, Yates sent Capt. James H. Stokes to requisition ten thousand muskets from the arsenal to arm these

43. FB to Simon Cameron, April 18, 1861, FB to MB, April 19, 1861, FB to Andrew G. Curtin, April 21, 1861, BLC; *OR*, 1:53:350; Peckham, *Lyon and Missouri*, 102–12; Broadhead, "St. Louis during the War," Broadhead Papers, 41–43.
44. *OR*, 1:1:669, 63:350; Rombauer, *Union Cause*, 211; *Missouri Democrat*, April 24, 26, 1861.

men. Realizing that the Minute Men might try to prevent such a transfer, Lyon diverted them by a ruse and then secretly transferred the arms by steamboat the following midnight across the river.[45]

News of all this activity quickly spread throughout St. Louis. Unionists rejoiced, while the Minute Men and other secession sympathizers increased their threats of violence against Blair, whom they considered their principal protagonist. To ensure the safety of Frank's family, Franklin Dick secreted Apo and the children, together with his own family, out of the city for the duration of the crisis, taking them to Philadelphia, where Apo stayed with the Biddles and Midge with her in-laws. Apo and the children split their time thereafter between Philadelphia and Silver Spring until Frank returned east for the opening of Congress in July.[46]

As the mustering continued, the First Regiment, Missouri Volunteers, elected Frank as its colonel. According to Albert D. Richardson, the *New York Tribune's* reporter, Blair's regiment consisted of three companies of German Turners, "sinewy, muscular fellows, with deep chests and well knit frames," and two companies "from the Far West—old trappers and hunters, who have smelt gunpowder in Indian warfare." The latter undoubtedly included acquaintances from Frank's days in New Mexico.[47]

Following the departure of General Harney on April 23, Frank summoned to his home an individual with whom his subsequent military career would become inextricably bound. William T. Sherman, a West Point graduate and member of a distinguished political family, had recently moved to St. Louis from Alexandria, Louisiana, where he had served as superintendent of the Louisiana Military Academy (now Louisiana State University), to become president of the St. Louis Railroad Company. He had earlier sought a U.S. Treasury job in St. Louis through his brother, Sen. John Sherman of Ohio, only to be told that Frank controlled all Missouri patronage jobs. When his brother suggested that he cultivate Blair, Sherman wrote back: "I would starve and see my family want, rather than ask Frank Blair or any of the Blairs whom I know to be a selfish and unscrupulous set of ——." Montgomery, in conjunction with Secy. of the Treasury Salmon Chase, had offered Sherman

45. *Missouri Democrat*, April 26, 30, 1861; Anderson, *Border City*, 76–80; F. A. Dick to Benson J. Lossing, July 6, 1865, Dick Papers; Peckham, *Lyon and Missouri*, 138; Rombauer, *Union Cause*, 221.

46. F. A. Dick to MB, April 23, 1861, BLC; EBL to SPL, June 19, 1861, B-LP.

47. Albert D. Richardson, *The Secret Service, the Field, the Dungeon, and the Escape,* 139. The complete roster of the First Missouri Regiment will be found in Rombauer, *Union Cause,* 351–66.

the chief clerkship in the War Department with the promise that they would work for his elevation to assistant secretary when Congress convened, but Sherman had turned that down to stay in St. Louis.[48]

Sherman later recalled that Frank told him that, with Harney's removal, "he held it in his power to appoint a brigadier-general, and put him in command of the department, and he offered me the place." Sherman declined, writing his brother angrily, "He wants to make use of me. In Washington I was not a citizen of St. Louis and not entitled to be thought of for any office that would support me, but now I am good enough to be consulted." The appointment then went to Lyon, who had just been elected brigadier general of the newly enlisted Missouri volunteers. Secretary of War Cameron authorized Lyon to enlist as many as ten thousand men into Union service under Lincoln's ninety-day plan and to proclaim martial law in St. Louis should he and the Union Committee of Safety deem it necessary. General-in-Chief Winfield Scott appended this endorsement: "It is revolutionary times, and therefore I do not object to the irregularity of this."[49]

Aside from the munitions available for the support of these men, they needed other equipment. Frank now sought assistance from quartermasters in the East through Cameron as well as other friends and supporters. He asked the secretary to authorize one hundred thousand dollars to the local quartermaster for this purpose. Cameron replied that such a sum was out of the question but that "camp and garrison equipage have already been ordered to be furnished." It would be impossible to send clothing promptly, he told Frank, informing him that "[i]n New York and Pennsylvania their troops have either furnished themselves or been furnished, relying for reimbursement of the expenditure hereafter by the General Government." The Blairs and others thereupon made a concerted effort to raise outside funds for equipment and clothing for the new recruits. By June 8, more than fourteen thousand dollars had been received, of which six thousand dollars came from New York City.[50]

48. William T. Sherman, *Memoirs*, 1:188–89; Lloyd Lewis, *Sherman: Fighting Prophet*, 148–54.

49. Sherman, *Memoirs*, 1:188–89; Lewis, *Sherman*, 156–57; Peckham, *Lyon and Missouri*, 119–20; *OR*, 1:1:675; Phillips, *Damned Yankee*, 165.

50. *OR*, 1:1:679–81; Broadside, "Appeal in Behalf of the Missouri Union Volunteers," May 6, 1861, with endorsement by a Massachusetts committee, May 14, 1861, Isaac Sherman to FPB, May 27, 1861, BLC; George Winston Smith, "New England Business Interests in Missouri during the Civil War," 5; Irving Katz, *August Belmont: A Political Biography*, 90; Phillips, *Damned Yankee*, 210–11.

Governor Jackson had not been idle in the midst of all this Union activity. He found considerable support from the state's conservative press for his refusal to furnish the United States with troops. He met with leading secessionists at St. Louis, the most prominent being Major General Frost, the commander of the St. Louis militia district. Frost outlined a rather audacious plan for a militia encampment overlooking the arsenal, from which he could make preparations for its capture. Because he lacked sufficient artillery to accomplish his purpose, Frost suggested that Jackson seek aid from the Confederacy at Montgomery. With the others in agreement, the governor dispatched two agents to Jefferson Davis, requesting siege guns and mortars for an assault on the arsenal. He sent a similar request to Virginia, which had just seceded. Five days later, the governor ordered the state militia to assemble within its respective districts on May 6 for six days of instruction and drill. He also called the General Assembly into special session "to place the State in a proper attitude of defense."[51]

Prompt assurances of support came from the Confederacy. Jefferson Davis wrote Governor Jackson on April 23 that "our power to supply you with ordnance is far short of the will to serve you." He agreed to forward two twelve-pound howitzers and two thirty-two-pound guns to Frost for use in taking the arsenal. "We look anxiously and hopefully for the day when the star of Missouri shall be added to the constellation of the Confederate States of America," Davis proclaimed, while requesting a Missouri regiment for service in Virginia, something that Jackson had to decline for the moment. "We are using every means to arm our people," the governor asserted, "and, until we are better prepared, must move cautiously." State militia had already seized, without authorization, the small federal arsenal at Liberty on the western border, taking four brass guns and fifteen hundred stand of arms. Allen P. Richardson wrote James Broadhead from Jefferson City on April 30, "The arrival of near ten thousand kegs of powder has made large men of small material."[52]

Lyon's disposal of the arms from the arsenal removed the purpose for the militia encampment at St. Louis, but Frost went ahead with his plans.

51. Arthur Roy Kirkpatrick, "Missouri in the Early Months of the Civil War," 236–37; Anderson, *Border City*, 87–88; Snead, *Fight for Missouri*, 148–49; Duke, *Reminiscences*, 43–44; *Messages and Proclamations*, 3:384; C. F. Jackson to J. W. Tucker, April 28, 1861, Broadhead Papers.

52. *OR*, 1:1:689–90; Allen P. Richardson to James O. Broadhead, April 30, 1861, Broadhead Papers.

He established Camp Jackson, named in honor of the governor, on Monday, May 6, in a wooded valley known as Lindell Grove, just west of Grand Avenue. The hills overlooking the arsenal, where he had intended to camp originally, had long since been occupied by Lyon. Realizing that this effectively prevented the launching of any surprise attack, the secessionists, through their St. Louis police board, formally demanded that Lyon withdraw his forces from the area outside the arsenal on the ground that this was a usurpation of state territory. Lyon refused, with the result that he rendered Camp Jackson virtually harmless so far as its accomplishing its original purpose.[53]

Lyon, however, did not see things that way. Various observers brought reports that small secessionist flags flew from many of the encampment's tent poles and that some handmade street signs had been placed at corners designating "Davis" and "Beauregard" avenues. Early on Thursday morning, May 9, the steamboat *J. C. Swon* pulled up to the St. Louis docks with several boxes of various sizes marked "marble Tamaroa." Militia officers met the boat and delivered the boxes to Camp Jackson, some six miles distant, where they remained unopened. They contained two twelve-pound howitzers, two thirty-two-pound siege guns, five hundred muskets, and a large amount of ammunition, all taken from the Baton Rouge arsenal and sent to Missouri under the instructions of Jefferson Davis. Word of this transfer reached Lyon from loyal deckhands, who strongly suspected the real contents.[54]

Lyon now determined to scout the camp for himself. In looking for an inconspicuous way to do that, he received assistance from Franklin Dick, who borrowed a dress, shawl, and bonnet from his and Frank's mother-in-law, Mira Alexander, with which to disguise the general. Mrs. Alexander was well known as being blind, so Lyon could thereby arouse no suspicion in that disguise. That afternoon, he drove through Camp Jackson, accompanied by J. J. Witzig, one of the Union committee members. Returning to the arsenal, the disguised Lyon found Frank and Samuel Simmons sitting on one of the porches. Frank rose to assist his mother-in-law from the carriage, only to discover "when the bombazine gown was slightly raised, a pair of stout cavalry boots." He and Simmons exchanged a sly look but said nothing. Thus, Lyon saw for himself what his scouts had been reporting all week.[55]

53. Snead, *Fight for Missouri,* 162–63.
54. Peckham, *Lyon and Missouri,* 136; Snead, *Fight for Missouri,* 167–68; Duke, *Reminiscences,* 45–50.
55. Dick, "Memorandum," Dick Papers, 3; Charles D. Drake to B. J. Lossing, December 23, 1864, Civil War Papers; Peckham, *Lyon and Missouri,* 139–40; Anderson, *Border City,* 92.

Upon his return to the arsenal, Lyon received further bad news. General Harney had been reinstated to his command and would be arriving in two days. The general had been captured by Confederates at Harper's Ferry, Virginia, on his way east and taken to Richmond under military escort in the hope of persuading him to join their cause. When he declined in dramatic fashion, the Confederates released him. Harney continued to Washington, where he persuaded General Scott, a close personal friend, and the War Department that his firm but conciliatory policy would keep Missouri in the Union.[56]

Lyon now determined that he must demand the surrender of Camp Jackson before Harney's return made it impossible to punish the suspect secessionists. He called a meeting of the Union Committee of Safety for that evening, reporting to them his findings of the afternoon. Although he realized that he was treading on shaky ground, Lyon sought the committee's agreement to take the camp the following day. Four of the six members, including Frank, readily agreed. John How and Samuel T. Glover held back. Glover argued effectively that the camp had been legally called and that it flew the U.S. flag at its staff. It was due to break up of its own accord on Saturday, May 11. When Lyon raised the matter of the stolen armaments from the Baton Rouge arsenal, Glover suggested getting a writ of replevin for government property and letting a U.S. marshal deliver it to Frost. The men argued through the evening as a strong storm raged outside. Finally, when told of Harney's scheduled return, Glover acquiesced, but with the understanding that a U.S. marshal would be at the head of the column to make the demand for the return of the Baton Rouge munitions. He hurried to his office to prepare a writ.[57]

Lyon was not interested in writs. He "resolved to act as a soldier, and not as a lawyer." After the departure of the other committee members, he and Frank proceeded with orders to bring the Union Home Guards together the next morning for a march against Camp Jackson. Blair then returned to Jefferson Barracks to prepare his men. The next morning the untrained Home Guards straggled in as muddy roads from the previous night's rain made the going difficult. Frank's regiment, in particular, had difficulty covering the twelve miles from Jefferson Barracks. As the guards began to gather, it quickly became evident to the alarmed secessionists in St. Louis that Lyon intended

56. Reavis, *Life of Harney*, 355–56; W. S. Harney to John O'Fallon, May 1, 1861, Rollins Papers.
57. Peckham, *Lyon and Missouri*, 140–42; Broadhead, "St. Louis during the War," Broadhead Papers, 60–61.

some kind of action. Although forewarned of all this, Frost, who had been Lyon's classmate at West Point, hesitated to believe that the Union commander would do anything rash. He finally sent Lyon a note in late morning, asking his intentions in the hope that the rumors he had heard were unfounded.[58]

Lyon refused to receive Frost's message, which arrived just as he prepared to march at the head of his column. He then moved out the six miles to Camp Jackson, where he demanded Frost's surrender. With no viable alternative, the militia commander quickly complied, although not without protest. While some militia escaped before Lyon could completely surround the camp, the bulk of the encampment was taken prisoner and marched out in the direction of the arsenal to await parole. A crowd quickly gathered along the route, and the procedure soon became unmanageable. People began throwing rocks and brickbats, amid cries of "Damn the Dutch" and "Hurrah for Jeff Davis." A friend later wrote Frank that he had been informed by a "gentleman of high standing" that "a very rich influential man drew and cocked his pistol to shoot you . . . and was only prevented by his wife who was in the carriage with him."[59]

William Tecumseh Sherman was among those who hurried to the scene of action, accompanied by one of his sons. He arrived in time to see Frank's regiment lined up on either side of Grand Avenue with ranks open and the militia prisoners between them. He stayed long enough to see an altercation between a drunk trying to cross the lines and a Home Guard. The drunk whipped out a pistol and fired toward the raw troops, who then loosed a volley over the heads of the crowd. In the melee that followed, twenty-eight persons were killed and many others wounded before Lyon and Frank restored order and the march continued.[60]

The move against Camp Jackson was a colossal blunder, for which Frank, as well as Lyon, must be held accountable. While it forced many Missourians to get off the fence and make immediate personal choices, the means used proved far too drastic. Frost could not have moved against the arsenal with

58. Peckham, *Lyon and Missouri*, 142–43; Ray W. Irwin, ed., "Missouri in Crisis: The Journal of Captain Albert Tracy, 1861," 152; Dick, "Memorandum," Dick Papers, 2–3.

59. *OR*, 1:3:4–9; Peckham, *Lyon and Missouri*, 149–53; Anderson, *Border City*, 96–108; Dick, "Memorandum," Dick Papers, 3–4; I. C. Spaulding to FB, May 13, 1861, BLC. Sometime during this period, Frank wired his cousin Jo Shelby to come to St. Louis to discuss a possible commission. Shelby came, but being fully committed to the Southern cause, declined, and eventually ended up in the Missouri State Guard and subsequently in Confederate service, where he fought with great distinction (O'Flaherty, *General Jo Shelby*, 51–52).

60. Sherman, *Memoirs*, 1:190–92.

only seven hundred men against Lyon's ten thousand. As Lyon himself admitted in his official report, many of the muskets later found at the camp stood in pieces, "all separate, and apparently without ever having been put together." Furthermore, neither Arkansas nor Tennessee had yet seceded, while Union forces in Iowa, Kansas, and Illinois could have been readily brought into Missouri if needed to keep the peace. The St. Louis Unionists felt a strong sense of relief, however. James O. Broadhead wrote a friend in Pike County that the Camp Jackson incident had "operated like a poultice, the inflammation has been drawn out of a great number of men who were heretofore rampant secessionists."[61]

The General Assembly, which had convened on May 2, had been at a standstill on the governor's request for greater military power because of the obstructionist tactics of the more adamant Union members. But, when word of Camp Jackson was flashed to Jefferson City on the evening of the tenth, the legislature rushed through the military bill. Amid later rumors from St. Louis indicating that Frank might be on his way there with three regiments of Germans, real panic set in; but these reports were soon proved false. The *Missouri Democrat*, whose offices had been attacked by a mob the night before, only to be protected by a squad of thirty policemen, headlined the next day: "The name of Colonel F. P. Blair seems to strike terror to all—the Governor, the officers, and the Assembly." Certainly, many saw Frank as a major instigator in what had happened.[62]

General Harney returned the next day to a panic-stricken city. That afternoon he met with a number of leading St. Louis moderates, who sought the removal of Lyon as a first step to restoring order. Although he did not approve of the rioting that had been going on in the aftermath of Camp Jackson, Harney refused to take action against his subordinate. He did promise his visitors, however, that he would either disband the Home Guards or remove them to Jefferson Barracks.[63]

The following morning Harney met with Frank and informed him of the previous day's conversation. Frank countered with the president's order of April 30, which authorized him to enlist the Home Guards under Lyon's command for defense of the city and to impose martial law if necessary. After

61. *OR*, 1:3:4–7; James O. Broadhead to Edwin Draper, May 21, 1861, Broadhead Papers.
62. Snead, *Fight for Missouri*, 172–74; Allen P. Richardson to James O. Broadhead, May 11, 1861, Broadhead Papers; Broadhead, "St. Louis during the War," Broadhead Papers, 54–55; *Missouri Democrat*, May 11, 1861.
63. Reavis, *Life of Harney*, 361–62, 385–86.

a lengthy discussion, Harney realized that his options were limited. He had learned the power of the Blairs during his recent stay in Washington, and he had no desire to oppose them further. The next day, May 13, he issued a proclamation approving the capture of Camp Jackson while denouncing the military bill just passed by the legislature. Without proclaiming martial law, he nevertheless authorized the U.S. marshal, armed with federal warrants and supported by regular troops, to search out and seize all illegal arms caches in the city. Although enlistments continued, Harney, with Frank's support, sought to broaden them to include at least one Irish regiment as a counterbalance to the Germans.[64]

Meanwhile, Governor Jackson moved forward with the organization of the new Missouri State Guard, authorized by the military bill. At the persuasion of Lieutenant Governor Reynolds, Jackson offered its command to Frank's old enemy, former governor Sterling Price, who promptly accepted. Orders went out across the state urging men to enroll in its defense and be properly mustered in their respective districts. More than one thousand men poured into Jefferson City, where they received supplies gathered earlier at St. Louis and the arms taken from the Liberty arsenal.[65]

As matters seemed to be rapidly getting out of hand, the St. Louis moderates decided to make a direct appeal to President Lincoln. They sent James E. Yeatman, joined by Hamilton R. Gamble, then in the East, to Washington. The two men secured an interview with Lincoln through the auspices of Attorney General Bates and pleaded with the president to call a board of inquiry into the rioting that had followed Camp Jackson. They also requested that regular troops, rather than the German Home Guards, be used for control within the city. While Lincoln agreed to take these matters under advisement, Yeatman and Gamble soon learned that he placed greater credence in the Blairs.[66]

Frank had not waited to see what action Harney might take. After their conversation of May 12, he dispatched Franklin Dick to Washington to press for the general's removal a second time. Dick arrived before Yeatman and Gamble and immediately went to the White House with Montgomery, where they found Secretary of War Cameron with the president. He argued that

64. FB to MB, May 20, 1861, BLC; Reavis, *Life of Harney*, 386; Peckham, *Lyon and Missouri*, 184–87; *OR*, 1:3:373–74.

65. Snead, *Fight for Missouri*, 181–85; Allen P. Richardson to James O. Broadhead, May 20, 1861, Broadhead Papers; Reynolds, "Price and the Confederacy," Reynolds Papers, 28; James B. Gardenhire to MB, May 16, 1861, BLC.

66. Gamble and Yeatman to Lincoln, May 15, 1861, Abraham Lincoln Papers; Rombauer, *Union Cause*, 246; Peckham, *Lyon and Missouri*, 191–94.

Harney's southern background made him questionable in the present circum-stances and hinted that a number of his St. Louis relatives had become avowed secessionists. He also requested a brigadier general's commission for Lyon to confirm his election by the recently mustered troops. At the urging of Attorney General Bates, Lincoln demurred until he could hear from Yeatman and Gamble. Dick proved the more persuasive, however, and the president and Cameron finally agreed, with some reservations, to go along with the Blairs.[67]

The War Department drew up orders authorizing the removal of Harney a second time and Lyon's appointment as brigadier general. These documents were given to Montgomery for forwarding to Frank with instructions that he hold the first of them in abeyance for the present. Frank should deliver it to Harney only if he considered it imperative. To reinforce this, the president personally wrote Frank two days later that the more he pondered the affair, the more he feared the administration might be accused of vacillation, given Harney's recent return. He closed by stating, however, "Still if, in your judgment it is *indispensable* let it be so."[68]

Frank received the president's letter on May 20, the same day that a special messenger arrived with the order for Harney's removal and a cover letter from Montgomery. The latter communications had been held up to await the drafting of the order appointing Lyon brigadier general of volunteers. Simultaneously, Harney met in St. Louis with Sterling Price, commander of the Missouri State Guard, at Governor Jackson's request, in the hope of effecting some kind of truce between state and federal forces. The Harney-Price Agreement resulted, by which the former pledged (in effect) that the federal government would respect the neutrality of the state with both gov-ernments helping to maintain peace: Harney in the St. Louis area and Price in the state's interior. Harney now called upon the people "to observe good order, and respect the rights of their fellow-citizens, and give them assurance of protection and security in the most ample manner." Three days later, Price ordered all troops at Jefferson City to return home to be organized by the commanders of their respective districts. Only one company remained on duty at the capital.[69]

67. F. A. Dick to Ben Farrar, May 16 (two letters), 17, 1861, MB to FB or Ben Farrar, May 17, 1861, BLC; James O. Broadhead to MB, May 22, 1861, Broadhead Papers. For a neutral observer's opinion of St. Louis at this moment, see Lyman Trumbull to Abraham Lincoln, May 15, 1861, Lincoln Papers.

68. *OR*, 1:3:9; MB to FB or Ben Farrar, May 17, 1861, BLC; Lincoln to FB, May 18, 1861, in *The Collected Works of Abraham Lincoln*, 4:372–73.

69. Peckham, *Lyon and Missouri*, 209–10; *OR*, 1:3:374–75; Snead, *Fight for Missouri*, 186–88.

The Harney-Price Agreement aroused considerable alarm among the members of the Union Committee of Safety, including Frank. Lyon had already dispersed two groups of secessionists who were harassing Unionists in the lead-producing region southwest of St. Louis. While Blair and Lyon adopted a wait-and-see attitude, the former made it clear, in a message to Cameron, that the agreement "gives me great disgust and dissatisfaction to the Union men; but I am in hopes that we can get along with it, and think that Harney will insist on its execution to the fullest extent, in which case it will be satisfactory." He wrote in a similar vein to Montgomery, who also received complaints from other Unionist leaders. Yet, respecting the president's wishes, Frank tried to give Harney the benefit of the doubt.[70]

In the days that followed, reports began pouring into St. Louis from all corners of the state complaining of mistreatment at the hands of secessionists and of military preparation and organization being carried on by the state government. Thomas W. Knox, the *New York Herald's* correspondent, who would become one of Frank's confidants, visited Jefferson City on May 26 and came away convinced that the state authorities were merely playing for time. He reported that the Confederate flag flew over Camp Frost, the Missouri State Guards' headquarters, as well as from the staff in front of the governor's mansion, and elsewhere in town. All of this news found its way to Washington, where President Lincoln became alarmed. He directed the adjutant general to remind Harney that such outrages must be stopped, regardless of whether they continued from the inability or from the indisposition of the state government to prevent them. Harney wired Price about these concerns and received assurances from the State Guard commander that they were false rumors. The general accepted this at face value and so informed Frank.[71]

In the face of what appeared to be overwhelming evidence to the contrary, Blair decided that he could withhold the order for Harney's removal no longer. He delivered it on May 30 and promptly informed the president of his reasons

70. Phillips, *Damned Yankee*, 204; Peckham, *Lyon and Missouri*, 210; *OR*, 1:3:9–11, 376; Thomas T. Gantt to MB, May 21, 1861, FB to MB, May 25, 1861, BLC; James O. Broadhead to MB, May 22, 1861, Broadhead Papers.

71. Peckham, *Lyon and Missouri*, 211–19, cites excerpts from many of these letters that have since been lost; Thomas T. Gantt to MB, May 21, 1861, BLC; Allen P. Richardson to James O. Broadhead, May 24, 1861, Richard C. Vaughn to Broadhead, May 30, June 11, 1861, James O. Henderson to Broadhead, June 10, 1861, Broadhead Papers; *OR*, 1:3:376–81; Samuel T. Glover to Abraham Lincoln, May 24, 1861, Lincoln Papers; Thomas W. Knox, *Camp Fire and Cotton Field: Southern Adventure in Time of War*, 33–35.

for doing so. Harney at first resisted, understanding, through other sources, that the order of the sixteenth had been rescinded. When he found, to his "bitter mortification," that such was not the case, he grew angry and protested to Washington to no avail. He then requested transfer to California, but instead was placed on inactive duty for the remainder of the war.[72]

Montgomery informed Frank on June 4 that Washington officialdom acquiesced in his action, with only Attorney General Bates "satisfied to let things remain as they are." Given the circumstances, Bates recommended that Missouri be placed under the authority of Maj. Gen. George B. McClellan, the commander of the Department of Ohio, then campaigning in West Virginia. Montgomery objected to this and sought Secretary of the Treasury Chase's intervention with General Scott to prevent it. But, after Lyon took the field, the change was accomplished. It proved short-lived, however, as the Blairs quickly put another plan in motion.[73]

Lyon, meanwhile, assumed temporary command of the Department of the West and relinquished command of the arsenal to Frank as colonel of the First Missouri Regiment. Lyon's total strength rose to 10,730, as he quickly mustered in those troops whose enlistment Harney had turned down. Assistance in outfitting these men continued to pour in from the East as the Blairs' friends rallied to the cause. In addition, Lyon wrote the War Department asking that troops from Kansas, Iowa, and Illinois be held in reserve in case they should be needed. Price, meanwhile, assumed that the removal of Harney ended their agreement, and he instructed his district commanders to hasten their enrollments in anticipation of an invasion of the state from St. Louis.[74]

Unwilling to resign themselves to open conflict within Missouri's borders, if they could prevent it, moderates sought Harney's reinstatement. Failing that, they tried to work out a new compromise between Lyon and Price. Through the auspices of Blair and Thomas T. Gantt, they arranged for Governor Jackson and General Price to come to St. Louis on June 11 for a conference with Lyon and Blair. Jackson initially expressed reluctance to schedule the

---

72. Peckham, *Lyon and Missouri,* 221–25; Thomas T. Gantt to MB, May 31, 1861, FB to MB, June (n.d.), 1861, BLC; *OR,* 1:3:381–83.

73. MB to FB, June 4, 1861, BLC, reprinted in Peckham, *Lyon and Missouri,* 225–27; MB to Edward Bates, June 19, 1861, BLC.

74. *OR,* 1:3:381–2; Phillips, *Damned Yankee,* 210–11; Katz, *August Belmont,* 90; Snead, *Fight for Missouri,* 196–97.

meeting for fear of arrest for treason, as Bates had already instructed James O. Broadhead, the U.S. attorney, to draw up such a warrant. Lyon, however, guaranteed both men safe conduct through the evening of June 12.[75]

Jackson and Price, accompanied by the governor's secretary, Thomas L. Snead, reached St. Louis on Sunday evening, June 10, and registered at the Planters House. They sent word of their arrival to Lyon the following morning. Although he wanted the meeting to take place at the arsenal, Lyon acquiesced in the governor's refusal to come there. Accompanied by Frank and an aide, Maj. Horace Conant, Lyon met Jackson, Price, and Snead at the Planters House at eleven o'clock on June 11. Initially, Lyon indicated that Frank would serve as the principal spokesman for the Union. As Jackson and Price made clear that they wished the disbanding of the Home Guard regiments in return for their dispersing the State Guard, however, Lyon entered more actively into the exchange.

The four men argued for several hours until the impetuous Lyon rose and emphatically ended the discussion. Assuring the governor that he had done all that he could to maintain the peace while finding little cooperation from the state officials, Lyon informed Jackson, "Better, sir, far better, that the blood of every man, woman, and child within the limits of the State should flow, than that she should defy the federal government. *This means war.* In one hour one of my officers will call for you and conduct you out of my lines." Turning on his heel, he strode from the room, leaving Frank, Conant, and the state officials in shock. Frank and Conant quickly shook hands with their counterparts and followed Lyon back to the arsenal.[76]

Although Frank had not anticipated quite this dramatic a climax, he undoubtedly realized that it was inevitable. His distrust of the state authorities and his subsequent actions had certainly helped to precipitate such a showdown. While it seems strange that the usually domineering Blair would have allowed Lyon to call the shots at this critical stage of their deliberations, the events of the past several weeks had indicated an increasing tendency for Frank to yield to the strident Yankee in military matters.

75. James S. Rollins to Edward Bates, June 1, 1861, Rollins Papers; John S. Phelps to Abraham Lincoln, June 3, 1861, Lincoln Papers; *OR*, 1:3:381–83; Snead, *Fight for Missouri*, 197–98; John McElroy, *The Struggle for Missouri*, 109.

76. There are several versions of Lyon's final remarks. The one used here appeared in the *Missouri Democrat*, July 2, 1861. See also Snead, *Fight for Missouri*, 199–200; Peckham, *Lyon and Missouri*, 243–48.

Not waiting for Lyon's escort, the state officials hurried to the railroad yards, where they secured a locomotive to speed them to Jefferson City. En route, they decided that the governor should issue a proclamation calling the state's citizens to arms in the state's defense, with General Price commanding whatever troops he could muster to resist any advance by Lyon. In the meantime, Price ordered the railroad bridges over the Gasconade and Osage Rivers destroyed to impede movements along that line. The next morning, Jackson asked for fifty thousand volunteers to fill the ranks of the State Guard with a detailed report of his disastrous interview with Lyon and Blair. He quickly made plans to evacuate the capital and retreat up the Missouri River to Boonville. Price had directed the removal of the state armory there immediately after Harney's removal on the ground that it constituted more friendly territory.[77]

As soon as he learned of the governor's proclamation, Lyon called Frank and his other advisers together to draw up a plan of attack. Moving quickly, they determined on a two-pronged offensive. Lyon moved upriver to Jefferson City, taking with him a light-artillery battery, two companies of regulars, Frank's First Missouri Volunteers, and nine companies of the Second Missouri Volunteer Regiment, while Col. Franz Sigel took additional troops by rail to secure the southern branch of the Pacific Railroad, which extended to Rolla. Wasting no time, Lyon left St. Louis on Wednesday afternoon, June 13, with some two thousand men, just as Governor Jackson and his supporters evacuated the capital to head upriver to Boonville.[78]

Moving slowly up the Missouri River, Lyon, Frank, and the Home Guards met little resistance. Thomas W. Knox, who accompanied the expedition, recalled cheering crowds at various points along the riverbank, which was not too surprising given the large number of Germans in those counties. An enthusiastic group of local Germans met them at the Jefferson City docks when they arrived on the afternoon of the fifteenth. Finding the capitol deserted and learning of Governor Jackson's retreat, Lyon detailed a small contingent under Col. Henry Boernstein to occupy the city while he and the bulk of the troops pressed on toward Boonville the following day. General Price, meanwhile, had left only some five hundred men encamped south

77. *OR*, 1:53:697; *Missouri Democrat*, June 12–14, 1861; Snead, *Fight for Missouri*, 200–207; Peckham, *Lyon and Missouri*, 248–52.

78. Phillips, *Damned Yankee*, 215–17; *OR*, 1:3:12–13; Peckham, *Lyon and Missouri*, 253–55; *Missouri Democrat*, June 14–17, 1861; Knox, *Camp Fire and Cotton Field*, 43–44.

of Boonville under the general direction of Governor Jackson and Col. John Marmaduke. Learning that federal troops from Kansas threatened Lexington to the west, Price hastened there to prepare its defenses.[79]

En route to Boonville, Lyon stayed in his cabin, conferring only with Frank. Slowed by low water, the Union forces disembarked eight miles below the town on the morning of the seventeenth. Part of Frank's First Missouri Regiment joined in the advance. They met only brief resistance from the hastily assembled and ill-equipped State Guard just east of the town. Union artillery under Capt. James Totten proved effective in scattering the enemy, who fled toward Boonville and kept going. The Union forces captured some sixty prisoners, together with considerable materials left behind in the State Guard camp. Lyon and Frank soon encountered a group of local officials coming out under a flag of truce and assured them that "if no resistance was made to their entrance, that no harm need be feared."[80]

The action at Boonville amounted to little more than a skirmish, but it sent Governor Jackson and the remainder of his State Guard in full retreat into the southwest corner of the state. Knox and other newspaper correspondents filed glowing reports, which played heavily on the vigor with which Lyon had routed the state government from its capital and the field of battle. Frank exulted in the triumph. He remained close to Lyon's side in the days that followed. Iowa troops, who joined the Missouri forces at Boonville a few days later, noted that Frank and Lyon met them upon arrival, the former "dressed in citizen's clothes with an army cap." Frank particularly interested them as he had summoned them into the state with a message to the Iowa adjutant general. As they docked, Frank "stooped and dipped a long black bottle into the raging Missouri. While he churned the bottle up and down, he watched us and turned up his face ever and anon to talk with Lyon." One of the Iowans, observing this, recalled later that he wondered what Frank had in the bottle, but he never found out.[81]

Frank did not tarry in Boonville long. He was anxious to check on his family and concerned with the forthcoming special session of Congress, which President Lincoln had called. He hastened back to St. Louis and then on to

---

79. *OR*, 1:3:11–14; Knox, *Camp Fire and Cotton Field*, 43–44; Snead, *Fight for Missouri*, 208–9, 212–14.

80. *OR*, 1:3:11–14; Peckham, *Lyon and Missouri*, 269–73; Knox, *Camp Fire and Cotton Field*, 45–52.

81. Emmet Crozier, *Yankee Reporters, 1861–1865*, 72–75; Eugene F. Ware, *The Lyon Campaign in Missouri, Being a History of the First Iowa Infantry*, 128; EBL to SPL, June 23, 1861, B-LP.

Washington via New York, where Apo and the children were vacationing on Long Island. With his usual vigor and uncompromising mind-set, he had fought energetically to keep Missouri in the Union in the face of what he considered a serious secessionist threat. In the midst of the struggle, he had found a new and trusted ally and friend in Nathaniel Lyon, in whom he had come to repose his strongest confidence. While many questioned the forceful tactics Blair had used in carrying out his campaign, few, be they friends or enemies, doubted his zeal for the Union cause. Under the influence of Attorney General Bates and General Scott, the War Department extended the jurisdiction of General McClellan to include Missouri. As Frank headed for Washington, he was determined that this not interfere with Lyon's plans to complete the rout of the state forces and the occupation of Missouri. In the weeks ahead, Frank would work energetically to secure support for Lyon's forces even as he helped organize, as chairman of the House Military Affairs Committee, the nation's resources for the larger struggle.[82]

82. Knox, *Camp Fire and Cotton Field*, 52; EBL to SPL, June 25*, 26*, 27, 1861, B-LP; *OR*, 1:3:12.

6

The Fremont Controversy

Frank arrived at Silver Spring on June 30, 1861, bringing Apo and the children with him. The family made arrangements for them to stay at "No. 4," the Blair home across from the White House.[1] Frank's recent exploits in Missouri, coupled with his extensive participation on the national political circuit during the election, had made him a household name. He had had strong encouragement from numerous individuals to stand for Speaker of the new House, and his father worked vigorously to promote that end. Lengthy dinners and conversations followed at Silver Spring with various House supporters and other leaders. Lizzie wrote Phil that "our people talk confidently." The guests included John Charles Fremont, recently returned from Europe, whom the Blairs began to push as the military commander of a new Department of the West to be created in an effort to move Missouri out from under the wing of General McClellan and provide Lyon with more direct support.[2]

1. Blair House, as it is known today, originally consisted of two residences. No. 4 belonged to the senior Blairs, who spent most of their time at their country home in Silver Spring, Maryland. Their daughter, Lizzie, her husband, Phil Lee, and their son Blair stayed at No. 4 when in Washington. Next door at No. 6 lived the Montgomery Blair family. Considerable enmity existed between the Lees and the Montgomery Blairs for a variety of reasons, and Lizzie and her mother were barely on speaking terms with her sister-in-law Minna, Montgomery's wife. Apo, who had become good friends with Minna during their early St. Louis days together, usually stayed at No. 4 with the children, although they would alternate that domicile with the Silver Spring estate when in Washington, and she was always a welcome guest at No. 6 (EBL to SPL, June 30*, July 5*, 17*, 1861, B-LP. For an explanation of the Lee–Montgomery Blair difficulties, see E. B. Smith, *Francis Preston Blair*, 286–87, and *Wartime Washington and Letters of Elizabeth Blair Lee*, 271 n).

2. Isaac Sherman to FPB, May 27, 1861, FPB to FB, June 18, 1861, MB to Edward Bates, June 19, 1861, BLC; EBL to SPL, June 19, 23, 26*, 30*, 1861, B-LP.

Congress convened in special session on July 4. Among those now serving in the House with Frank was his friend James Rollins, elected from Missouri's central district. The two would become increasingly closer as the war continued and Frank moved progressively into the conservative wing of the Republican Party. Clement L. Vallandigham of Ohio immediately rose to challenge the right of Blair and three others to take their seats because of their presumed entry into military service. Frank promptly countered that, while he had seen military action in Missouri, he had never been sworn into service, whereupon Vallandigham withdrew his objection. The Speaker's race was decided quickly. Originally anticipated as a three-person race, it evolved to two following the withdrawal of Schuyler Colfax of Indiana. In the ensuing balloting, Frank garnered forty votes to seventy-one for Galusha Grow of Pennsylvania with forty-eight scattered. With the trend obvious, and Grow only nine votes short of a majority, Frank rose and asked his supporters to switch their votes to the Pennsylvanian. Twenty-eight did, and Frank helped escort the new Speaker to the well of the House to be sworn in.[3]

Grow moved promptly to name the committee chairmen for the critical session ahead. He initially offered Frank the chairmanship of the Ways and Means Committee, considered, next to the Speakership, the most important position in the House. Frank, however, demanded and received the chairmanship of the House Military Affairs Committee as more attuned to his interests. After Colfax also turned down Ways and Means, it went to Thaddeus Stevens of Pennsylvania, with whom Frank would clash often in the days and years ahead.[4]

In the ensuing weeks, Frank worked vigorously to secure support for President Lincoln's agenda to defend the Union against the secession menace. Within three days of securing the Military Affairs chairmanship, he reported two bills: one to promote the efficiency of the regular army and the other authorizing the employment of volunteers in the defense of the Union. The former called for increasing the army staff and facilitating the retirement of disabled or incapacitated officers of the various service branches. Many thought this was directed toward Winfield Scott and other aging generals, whose removal the Blairs and others had been urging to make way for younger leaders. The latter bill countered a proposal by Secy. of War Simon Cameron and General Scott simply to expand the standing army by eleven

3. *CG,* 37:1:3–4; EBL to SPL, July 5, 1861*, B-LP; Robert D. Ilisevich, *Galusha A. Grow: The People's Candidate,* 202–3.

4. W. E. Smith, *Blair Family in Politics,* 2:119; Leonard P. Curry, *Blueprint for Modern America: Nonmilitary Legislation of the First Civil War Congress,* 26.

regiments. Frank's committee contended that such was not necessary; but, in conference with the Senate, the standing-army concept prevailed. Frank, however, managed to provide that it be reduced to twenty-five thousand at the end of the war.[5]

When the special session adjourned, sixty-one acts had been passed in thirty-three days, essentially underwriting the war powers that President Lincoln had exercised already during the interim. The Washington correspondent for the *Missouri Republican* observed: "[Blair] is one of the hardest working men in the house; and his are not political or Utopian schemes. . . . Any one who reflects for a moment on the enormous pressure upon his time and attention, will know how to appreciate his immense additional labors on the Military Committee, of which he is chairman, and in this connection he has certainly developed a very strong practical and discriminative talent in military affairs."[6]

While the debate over the proper form of military organization raged in the halls of Congress, Maj. Gen. Irvin McDowell was pressed to move his ninety-day recruits southwest from Washington toward Manassas Junction, Virginia. Many in the capital expected that a short, quick victory would convince the Confederates of the futility of secession. When the two armies clashed along Bull Run on Sunday, July 21, however, the Confederates routed the Union forces, who fled headlong back into Washington. In their flight they became entangled with many congressmen, government officials, and their ladies, who had come out with their carriages and picnic baskets to watch the action. The Union suddenly realized that it faced a much longer and more difficult challenge than it had thought. Frank had missed the debacle, as he and Apo had gone with friends to Fort Monroe for the weekend.[7]

In the heated aftermath, the president and the Blairs, among others, came in for their share of blame. On August 1, Frank rose to defend his family and Lincoln against an attack by Thurlow Weed, the New York political boss, in his *Albany Evening Journal*. He reminded his colleagues that accusations that his Military Affairs Committee had emasculated Senate and administration attempts to enlarge the standing army were clearly false. While his family had urged a vigorous prosecution of the war so had Weed upon his recent visit

5. CG, 37:1:3–4, 56, 72–73, 94–102, 117–18, 128, 147–49, 228–30, 244–46, 273–74, 304–5, 332. The final military acts are in ibid., Appendix:30–34.

6. Howard Glyndon, *Notable Men in "the House": A Series of Sketches of Prominent Men in the House of Representatives: Members of the Thirty-seventh Congress*, 49.

7. EBL to SPL, July 19*, 20*, 1861, B-LP.

in Washington. As to charges that he and others had unduly pushed General Scott into the advance against Manassas, Frank reported that the president, among others, had urged delay for a day or two to allow for reinforcements. Blair emphasized that his main concern was that "the President retain the confidence of the people of this country—of all who are in favor of preserving the Union." That would remain his major goal throughout the war.[8]

At the end of the session in early August, Frank rejoined his family in Connecticut, where they had been staying with friends in the aftermath of the anxiety over the Bull Run disaster. It proved to be a brief visit. Apo wrote Montgomery that Frank had left Washington so hurriedly that he had forgotten some books he wanted forwarded. Frank planned to return to St. Louis, while Apo stopped with friends near Canandaigua, New York, where she hoped to put their oldest son, Andrew, in school. Wistfully, she wrote, "I hope we will all be well thro' this dreadful war business by winter & have some rest." Little did she or Frank realize the tumultuous months that lay ahead of them, which would embroil them in endless controversy and alter friendships and alliances of long standing.[9]

While in Washington, Frank had become increasingly concerned by reports from Missouri. In early July, the Blair protégé Fremont had received appointment as major general and commander of the Department of the West with headquarters in St. Louis. For various reasons, most of them legitimate, he had continued in Washington and New York for several weeks. Arriving in St. Louis on July 25, Fremont found military affairs in a state of chaos. With Lyon in southwest Missouri pursuing the pro-Confederate state forces, little coordination existed in St. Louis. In the light of the Bull Run battle, the War Department placed its emphasis on the eastern theater. Indeed, as seen previously, much of what Frank and Lyon had been able to accomplish in Missouri in arming and supplying their regiments had been done with private assistance from friends in New York and elsewhere.

Jessie Fremont wrote her longtime friend Lizzie Blair Lee shortly after their arrival, "Its making bricks without straw out here & mere human power can't draw order out of the chaos by force of will only." Fremont himself complained to the president that he found "this command in disorder, nearly every county in an insurrectionary condition, and the enemy advancing in force on different points of the southern frontier. . . . I am sorely pressed for

8. *CG*, 37:1:386–88; EBL to SPL, July 27*, August 3, 1861, B-LP.
9. EBL to SPL, July 22*, 23*, August 13, 1861, B-LP; Apo to MB, August 9, 1861, BLPLC.

want of arms. . . . Our troops have not been paid, and some regiments are in a state of mutiny, and the men whose term of service have expired generally refuse to enlist."[10]

Fremont plunged into this disorderly scene with a determination to bring organization and assistance to the badly neglected and threatened region. He wrote Montgomery, "I am working right up to my full capacity and although it is rough the ship rides tolerably easy." Although he made numerous mistakes in the one hundred days that followed, many of which would contribute to his downfall, Fremont could not be cited for lack of effort. He had tarried in the East in an effort to secure munitions and supplies and to put together a staff. Only partially successful in the first effort, the second quickly aroused antagonism in St. Louis when he drew many of his appointees from among foreign émigrés and California friends. He rented the mansion of Col. J. B. Brant, a relative of Jessie's, on Chouteau Avenue for his headquarters, which many considered ostentatious. This gave him not only space for living quarters, however, but also a work area for the entire administrative network that he established. The latter was extensive and proved one of his handicaps, as the staff kept him well protected from the many military officers, contractors, well-wishers, and others who immediately sought his attention. These soon complained of long delays in getting to see the commander and of Fremont's inaccessibility generally.[11]

Fremont faced two conflicting demands. Lyon, at Springfield, Missouri, reported that he faced a large army of pro-Confederate Missouri State Guards under Sterling Price, with Confederate reinforcements moving up from Arkansas under Ben McCulloch. With only 7,000 ill-equipped men, many of whose ninety-day enlistments were about to expire, Lyon bombarded headquarters daily with messengers seeking help. Meanwhile, Brig. Gen. Benjamin M. Prentiss warned of a Confederate concentration at the junction of the Mississippi and Ohio Rivers, which threatened his strategic command at Cairo, Illinois. Although many, including the Blairs, assumed that Fremont had a large supply of reserves at hand, his adjutant later reported that he had only 15,943 men to meet an enemy pressing his department on the several fronts. Fremont hoped to secure more troops from Illinois and Indiana, and many volunteers began arriving in St. Louis by early August. Most of

10. Jessie Fremont to EBL, July 27, 1861, BLC; *OR*, 1:3:416–17.
11. John C. Fremont to MB, August 12, 1861, BLC; Allan Nevins, *Fremont: Pathmarker of the West*, 476–77, 493–95; Pamela Herr, *Jessie Benton Fremont: American Woman of the 19th Century*, 326–28.

them came unarmed and untrained, however, and Fremont did not possess sufficient transportation beyond water and rail to move them to where they might be needed.[12]

Fremont ordered Lyon to fall back on the terminus of the Southwest Pacific Railroad at Rolla, 120 miles to his rear, and await reinforcements if he did not consider himself strong enough to maintain his position at Springfield. Considering the threat to the lower Mississippi to be the greater danger, the new commander then personally took 4,000 reinforcements to Cairo in support of Prentiss. His action had a positive effect, for the Confederates apparently became frightened and no attack occurred.[13]

Lyon received Fremont's message on the morning of August 9. Frustrated by the lack of support from St. Louis, he declined retreat even though some of his officers recommended it. The next morning, he attacked the numerically superior combined forces of Price and McCulloch at Wilson's Creek, southwest of Springfield. Although his troops fought valiantly, Lyon's plan of attack weakened his already small force. The Confederates carried the day, and Lyon fell dead on the field of battle. That night the shattered Union forces retreated to Rolla.[14]

Lyon became the first great Union hero-martyr. His earlier exploits against the Missouri Confederates had captured the imagination of the nation, in large part because of a favorable press corps. Now the nation, including the Blairs, received the news of his death with considerable shock. The Blairs' concerns were compounded by the death of Frank's cousin Cary Gratz on the Union side and the knowledge that Cary's stepbrother, Jo Shelby, had been on the Confederate side in the battle.[15]

Frank returned to St. Louis in the wake of the Wilson's Creek disaster. His First Missouri Regiment had been with Lyon's troops, and he had many friends among the casualties. He had come to regard Lyon almost as a brother and long had taken a special interest in Cary Gratz, the youngest son of his beloved uncle Ben. Deeply grieved, Frank took charge of Cary's body and made arrangements to have it returned to Kentucky. He also joined the military escort that accompanied Lyon's body to his home in Connecticut with

12. William E. Parrish, "Fremont in Missouri," 6; Nevins, *Fremont*, 486; John C. Fremont to MB, August 5, 1861, Lincoln Papers.

13. Parrish, *Turbulent Partnership*, 51–52; Phillips, *Damned Yankee*, 248; John M. Schofield, *Forty-six Years in the Army*, 39–40.

14. Phillips, *Damned Yankee*, 248–56; Schofield, *Forty-six Years*, 39–43.

15. Phillips, *Damned Yankee*, 257–61; EBL to SPL, August 14*, 15*, 1861, B-LP; EBL to FPB, August 15, 1861, BLC.

stops en route at Cincinnati, Philadelphia, New York, and Hartford, where large numbers of mourners paraded by the closed casket.[16]

Greatly alarmed by this turn of events, Frank wrote Montgomery prior to his departure with Lyon's body, "Affairs here are rather threatening but if the Government will send Fremont a strong reinforcement & at once he will turn the tables on the enemy & make him sorry that he left home. Let us have all the men [and] money that can be spared." Fremont had earlier dispatched a member of his staff to President Lincoln with the same message, but the beleaguered chief executive replied that he had sent "all available force" already.[17]

The Missouri political scene was also changing as Fremont arrived to take his command. On July 22, the state convention, which had decided earlier against secession, reconvened at Jefferson City. Over the next nine days it deposed the Jackson regime and the state legislature and established a provisional government headed by Hamilton R. Gamble of St. Louis and Willard P. Hall of St. Joseph. A conservative former Whig, Gamble determined to keep as much of the state's destiny in local hands as possible, including the protection of slavery. He had direct access to the Lincoln administration through Atty. Gen. Edward Bates, his brother-in-law; and he sought to use this entrée to advantage wherever he could. Lincoln promptly recognized the new government and promised cooperation where possible.[18]

Concerned to establish his authority over the new political regime, Fremont immediately wired Gamble to make no appointments in the state volunteer regiments until he could write him. The following day Fremont forwarded a list of certain officers he wanted to head these battle groups. Gamble responded that his constitutional powers were limited inasmuch as each regiment could elect its own officers. He agreed, however, to appoint the Fremont nominees for adjutant general and quartermaster general.[19]

Shortly after this, Jessie brought her husband a letter she had received from Preston Blair. In it, he proposed "a copartnership in the West." He would be

16. F. A. Dick to FPB, August 16, 1861, BLC; Rebecca Gratz to Ann Boswell Gratz, n.d., in David Philipson, ed., *Letters of Rebecca Gratz*, 423–25; FB to John M. Schofield, n.d., John M. Schofield Papers; John Thomas Scharf, *History of St. Louis City and County*, 1:506. Lyon's body had badly decomposed from having lain unattended on the battlefield for hours after the battle and was considered unsuitable for viewing (Phillips, *Damned Yankee*, 259–61).

17. John C. Fremont to Abraham Lincoln, August 11, 1861, FB to MB, August 15, 1861, Lincoln Papers; Lincoln to Fremont, August 15, 1861, in *Collected Works of Lincoln*, 4:484–85.

18. Parrish, *Turbulent Partnership*, 35–47.

19. J. C. Kelton to Hamilton R. Gamble, August 2, 1861, John C. Fremont to Gamble, August 3, 1861, Hamilton R. Gamble Papers.

her agent in the East if she would be his in St. Louis. He rebuked her gently, "You treated me with great scorn in passing me by without a recognition as 'westward your star of empire took its way,' nevertheless, you are followed by [my] affections." Most specifically, the senior Blair requested that Fremont ask Governor Gamble to make Frank a major general in the state militia, for which the state convention had recently made provision. He reported that Frank had declined a military commission at the hands of the president because this would compromise his congressional seat under the Constitution. A state appointment would enable him to have an active military career between sessions, however, without jeopardizing his other role.[20]

To what extent this letter galled the Fremonts at the time is uncertain. They later made an issue of it after the blowup between them and the Blairs had occurred. Significantly, at the time, Fremont forwarded a request to Governor Gamble almost immediately. Declaring, "In organizing my force for the field I am embarrassed by the want of superior officers to whom trust may be confided," he asked that Frank, "now Colonel of the 1st Missouri Volunteers," be appointed brigadier general.[21]

The governor responded directly to Frank that he could not make the appointment with his constitutional limitations. He suggested that Blair write the president to get him to make the various commissions that Fremont had previously requested. Frank wired Montgomery on August 21 and followed this with a letter elaborating the need for the commissions and arguing that Fremont should be "clothed with power to do just as he pleases & have all the money he wants and be held responsible for the results." Becoming obviously concerned about Fremont's inaction, Frank declared that the commander needed to move within two weeks to counter Price's forces in western Missouri.[22]

Eight days later, on August 29, Governor Gamble left for Washington to consult with Lincoln and the War Department on militia matters. By that time, Frank was becoming thoroughly disillusioned with Fremont and "reluctantly" expressed some of his concerns in a letter to Montgomery, which Gamble carried with him. Frank reported that he was losing confidence in "Fremont's capacity to manage affairs here successfully" and complained

20. FPB to Jessie Fremont, August 13, 1861, Lincoln Papers.
21. Fremont to Gamble, August 18, 1861, Gamble Papers.
22. FB to MB, August 21, 1861 (telegram), Lincoln Papers; FB to MB, August 21, 1861, Edward Bates Papers. The president agreed to the appointments the same day (Lincoln to FB, August 21, 1861, in *Collected Works of Lincoln*, 4:495).

that the general occupied himself with trifles "and does not grasp the great points of the business." Fremont had isolated himself from the public through "a sort of court," so that "officers and men of influence who do not wish to impart their business to the clerks are denied admission altogether and many spend days & hours and weeks trying to get an interview upon important business without success." These included Governor Gamble prior to his departure for Washington. Frank had suggested that Fremont set aside one hour a day to receive any and all who wanted to see him, but the commander had resisted this. If Fremont had an action plan, Frank reported the general had not disclosed it to him, and what little he had discovered on his own did not merit his confidence.[23]

Within another three days, on September 1, Frank agonizingly wrote again, reiterating his concerns. "Oh for one hour of our dead Lyon," he cried. While he felt responsible for Fremont's appointment, he now announced that he believed the commander ought to be replaced. Montgomery showed this letter to the president, together with others from James O. Broadhead, John How, and Lincoln's good friend Samuel T. Glover. Attorney General Bates also passed on reports he had been receiving, and Governor Gamble added his complaints during his interview with the president.[24]

Fremont later claimed that his break with Frank stemmed from difficulties over his refusal to grant contracts to Blair's friends. There can be no doubt that Frank pressed hard to see that St. Louisans got their fair share of army business and resented that many awards seemed to be going to Fremont's California friends. While this may have been a contributing factor, the change in Frank's attitude between August 21 and 29 seems to have been triggered by an interview that he and Maj. John M. Schofield had with Fremont toward the end of August. Schofield had served with Frank's regiment at Boonville and became Lyon's aide in the subsequent campaign in southwest Missouri. He had come to St. Louis to report on the events at Wilson's Creek. After being kept waiting for an extended time, the two men were ushered into Fremont's office. Much to their surprise, the commander asked not one question about the recent battle they had come to discuss. Instead, he engaged in an enthusiastic one-sided conversation about his coming campaign against

23. FB to MB, August 29, 1861, BLC.
24. FB to MB, September 1, 1861, FB to Apo, n.d. [1861], A.S. to MB, September 3, 1861, BLC; John How to MB, August 21, 1861, John Poyner to Lincoln, August 27, 1861, MB to Lincoln, n.d., enclosing Glover to MB, September 2, 1861, and Broadhead to MB, September 3, 1861, Lincoln Papers.

the Confederates in southern Missouri. The two men came away dazed at his egotistical insensitivity.[25]

Fremont compounded his problems, at least in the eyes of Lincoln, with a proclamation on August 30 establishing martial law throughout the state. The commander declared that anyone discovered armed within Union lines would be shot upon being found guilty by court-martial. This was controversial enough, but even more disturbing was the general's decision to confiscate the property of those who had taken up arms against the Union, including slaves, who would subsequently be freed. With no preliminary warning, the proclamation took the country by storm. Radicals applauded it as an important first step toward moving the war from one to save the Union to one to secure emancipation. Both the *Missouri Democrat* and the *Missouri Republican* responded favorably to the emancipation policy, the latter conservative paper not aware of its full implications. For all his misgivings about other matters, Frank told Montgomery, in his September 1 letter, that he considered it "the best thing of the kind that has been issued but should have been issued when he first came when he had the power to enforce it & the enemy no power to retaliate."[26]

President Lincoln had strong reservations about two aspects of the Fremont proclamation and quickly made them known to the commander. He dispatched a special messenger to St. Louis on September 2, expressing his concern about the order to shoot those taken with arms, which he feared would lead to Confederate retaliation. He, therefore, ordered that no such action be taken without his consent. He then requested Fremont to modify his emancipation policy to conform with an August 6 act of Congress that limited emancipation to those slaves forced to take up arms or otherwise actively participate in the war on the Confederate side. The president worried particularly lest Fremont's emancipation program drive neutral and conservative Kentucky into the arms of the Confederacy. The patient Lincoln closed significantly, "This letter is written in a spirit of caution and not of censure."[27]

25. *Report of the Joint Committee on the Conduct of the War*, 75–76, 176–79, 210–12 (hereafter cited as *JCCW*); Schofield, *Forty-six Years*, 49. For a discussion of the contract issue, see W. E. Smith, *Blair Family in Politics*, 2:67, and Nevins, *Fremont*, 497–98, 623–27.

26. *OR*, 1:3:466–67; FB to MB, September 1, 1861, BLC; *Missouri Democrat*, September 13, 1861; *Missouri Republican*, September 3, 13, 1861; Nevins, *Fremont*, 504–5.

27. *OR*, 1:3:469–70. For Kentuckians' concerns, see James Speed and Greene Adams to Lincoln, September 2, 1861, Joseph Holt to Lincoln, September 12, 1861, Lincoln to Holt, September 12, 1861, Robert Anderson to Lincoln, September 13, 1861, Lincoln Papers.

Fremont stubbornly refused to back down on the emancipation issue. He wrote the president, "If upon reflection your better judgment still decides that I am wrong in the article respecting the liberation of slaves, I have to ask that you will openly direct me to make the correction. . . . If I were to retract it of my own accord, it would imply that I myself thought it wrong, and that I had acted without the reflection which the gravity of the point demanded. But I did not." Lincoln, thereupon, directed Fremont to modify his proclamation to conform to the congressional action.[28]

Concerned by the rising tide of complaints about Fremont, the president decided to send Montgomery Blair and Q.M. Gen. Montgomery C. Meigs to St. Louis to investigate matters and counsel Fremont. En route, they stopped in Chicago to deliver a presidential letter to Maj. Gen. David Hunter. "General Fremont needs assistance which it is difficult to give him," Lincoln wrote Hunter. "He is losing the confidence of men near him, whose support any man in his position must have to be successful. . . . He needs to have by his side a man of large experience. Will you not, for me, take that place?"[29]

The three men arrived in St. Louis at midnight, September 12. Although the official reason given for their mission was an examination of the overland mail, this deceived no one. The press reported that the government was concerned about contract irregularities as well as Fremont's independent nature. The general himself later wrote that he "began to feel the withdrawal of the confidence and support of the Administration." He had already received a visit from Governor Gamble upon the latter's return from Washington a day earlier, during which the Missouri chief executive had given him a letter from Lincoln indicating his desire that the two cooperate in establishing and equipping the new state militia.[30]

After talking with Frank and others, Montgomery wrote the president on September 14 that most of the Union men in Missouri had lost faith in Fremont and his ability to take sufficient action to keep Sterling Price and the pro-Confederate State Guard at bay. Price currently threatened Lexington in western Missouri, and Fremont seemed to have little in the way of a plan to thwart him. Montgomery recommended his removal. Meigs, meanwhile, had been examining the accounts of the department and found them sorely in disarray. He became particularly displeased with the work of

28. *OR*, 1:3:477, 485–86.
29. Lincoln to Hunter, September 9, 1861, in *Collected Works of Lincoln*, 4:513.
30. Parrish, *Turbulent Partnership*, 63–64; W. E. Smith, *Blair Family in Politics*, 2:75; Nevins, *Fremont*, 513–14.

Maj. Justus McKinstry, Fremont's quartermaster general and provost marshal. Other impartial observers also reported McKinstry's supply operation totally ineffective. Originally a protégé of the Blairs, like Fremont, the major had later turned against them over contract disputes. Realizing that McKinstry had become a handicap, Fremont requested a replacement as quartermaster general. Meigs gladly obliged. Still, McKinstry remained as provost marshal.[31]

Even as Montgomery Blair, Meigs, and Hunter made their way to St. Louis, Jessie Fremont headed east to see the president with a confidential letter from her husband detailing his views on the Western Department. She arrived in Washington on the evening of September 10 after an exhausting two days of travel by train. Taking rooms at the Willard Hotel, she immediately dispatched a note to Lincoln seeking an interview that evening or the next morning.

Although it was nearly nine o'clock, the president saw her that evening. Jessie went, accompanied by Judge Edward Cowles of New York, a staunch abolitionist friend of the Fremonts. Lincoln read the letter she had brought from Fremont, containing the general's refusal to back down on the emancipation issue. The president reminded her that he had already indicated his wishes to her husband. Jessie presented counterarguments to which Lincoln responded, half in humor, "you are quite a female politician." He then added that he had sent Frank to St. Louis "to advise [Fremont] and to keep [himself] advised about the work," and admonished her that her husband "never would have done it [emancipation] if he had consulted Frank Blair."

Jessie could reply only that she and her husband had been unaware "that Frank Blair represented you—he did not do so openly." When she asked how soon she might expect a reply to Fremont's letter, Lincoln responded that it would take a day or two. After she left, he told John Hay, one of his secretaries, that Jessie had "taxed me so violently with so many things that I had to exercise all the awkward tact I have to avoid quarreling with her."[32]

The next morning Jessie received a visit from Preston Blair, who accused her of making an enemy of the president. He informed her of Frank's letter of September 1 and indicated that it had caused Lincoln to send Montgomery and Meigs to St. Louis to investigate the department. The two argued for several hours. Jessie had known the senior Blair since childhood, his daughter

31. MB to Lincoln (telegram and letter), September 14, 1861, J. W. Shaffer to Winfield Scott, September 14, 1861, Lincoln Papers; Russell F. Weigley, *Quartermaster General of the Union Army: A Biography of M. C. Meigs,* 191–95.
32. "The Lincoln Interview: Excerpt from 'Great Events,'" in *Letters of Jessie Benton Fremont,* 264–66; *Lincoln and the Civil War in the Diaries and Letters of John Hay,* 133.

Lizzie being her best friend and confidante. Preston Blair reminded Jessie of the many favors his family had done for the Fremonts, which only irritated her more. The former friends parted bitterly, and this interview effectively ended any friendship Jessie had for the Blairs.[33]

After waiting another day, Jessie wrote the president requesting his reply, as well as a copy of Frank's letter. Lincoln responded that, not having heard from her, he had sent his answer (the dispatch directing Fremont to rescind the emancipation order) to her husband the previous day. As for Frank's letter, he did not feel he could furnish her "with copies of letters in my possession without the consent of the writers." Not having a report yet from the trio he had sent to St. Louis, the president sought to assure Jessie that Montgomery Blair had gone to St. Louis to "converse with Gen. Fremont as a friend" and closed, "No impression has been made on my mind against the honor or integrity of Gen. Fremont; and I now enter my protest against being understood as acting in any hostility towards him." Lincoln, meanwhile, wrote Orville Browning that he was astonished that Frank had supported Fremont's proclamation after helping pass the law that nullified it at the special session.[34]

Jessie returned to St. Louis to find Montgomery still closeted with Fremont. Utterly suspicious of his intentions after her visit to Washington, she spewed out her newfound hatred of the Blairs to her husband and later reported that she refused to speak to Montgomery then "or ever again." Lizzie Blair Lee, upon learning of all this from the papers, expressed her dismay to her father at the prospect of losing Jessie's friendship, "A personal quarrel fills me with a terror I can't articulate."[35]

Lizzie's terror quickly turned to anger, however, when she learned of Jessie's next move. Immediately upon Montgomery's departure, Jessie persuaded her husband to take one of the most foolish steps in this whole controversy. On September 16, Fremont telegraphed Asst. Adj. Gen. E. D. Townsend in Washington that he had ordered the arrest of Frank Blair because of his "insidious & dishonorable efforts to bring my authority into contempt with the Government." The commander promised to "submit charges to you

33. "The Lincoln Interview," in *Letters of Jessie Benton Fremont*, 267; EBL to SPL, September 17*, 1861, B-LP; MB to W. O. Bartlett, September 16, 1861 (marked not sent), BLC.
34. "The Lincoln Interview," Jessie Fremont to John Charles Fremont, September 11, 1861, Jessie Fremont to Lincoln, September 12, 1861 (two letters), in *Letters of Jessie Benton Fremont*, 267–71; Lincoln to Jessie Fremont, September 12, 1861, Lincoln to Browning, September 22, 1861, in *Collected Works of Lincoln*, 4:519–20, 531–33.
35. Herr, *Jessie Benton Fremont*, 341; EBL to FPB, September 15, 1861, BLC.

for his trial." Lizzie, who was staying in Bethlehem, Pennsylvania, because of the post–Bull Run scare in Washington, wrote to Phil, "Were there ever people who were so false to themselves & to others. . . . I have felt bitterly all day—but have held my tongue." She promised to go to Philadelphia, where Apo was staying, and offer her "all the attention & kindness I can proffer."[36]

Frank's arrest caused tremendous excitement, with both the local and the national press having a field day. To the dismay of Frank and his friends, the *Missouri Democrat,* which long had been his staunch supporter, now turned against him, defending Fremont's action in a series of stinging editorials. The paper had clearly favored the general's emancipation policy and had gained favor with the Germans, who enthusiastically approved that course. Frank and his supporters claimed that McKinstry, as Fremont's agent, had conspired with the paper's editor, William McKee, to attack Blair, holding out patronage plums as an incentive. McKee and George W. Fishback, the principal owners of the paper, had been having financial problems. Frank still held a financial interest in the paper and deeply resented its actions but could do little about it. He sent the *Democrat* a scathing letter, accusing it of lies and unfair representation. Asserting that he had no personal quarrel with Fremont, Frank, nevertheless, admonished that he considered him responsible for "the pompous threats which appeared in your columns."[37]

The German press followed the lead of the *Missouri Democrat.* A constant stream of anti-Blair and antiadministration invective poured from these organs and aroused many of the Germans to violent action, as they believed they saw a conspiracy to remove their newfound hero. Frank's only press defender during this period was the small *St. Louis Evening News,* which had a circulation of only twenty-two hundred. After it criticized Fremont, following the fall of Lexington on September 20, Provost Marshal McKinstry had its editors arrested and the paper temporarily suspended.[38]

36. Fremont to Townsend, September 16, 1861, Lincoln Papers; EBL to SPL, September 17–18*, 1861, B-LP.

37. *Missouri Democrat,* passim, September 1861 (Frank's letter is in September 18, 1861); *Missouri Republican,* passim, September 1861; Peter L. Foy to MB, September 17, 1861, Arden R. Smith to MB, September 17, October 20, 1861, John M. Wimer to MB, September 18, 1861, Smith to FPB, September 19, 1861, FB to William Dennison, September 19, 1861, Gratz Brown to FB, December 21, 1861, John How to FB, October 7, 1862, BLC; T. Blank to MB, September 24, 1861, G. F. Filley to Henry T. Blow, October 7, 1861, Lincoln Papers.

38. Rowan, *Germans for a Free Missouri,* 283–88; W. E. Smith, *Blair Family in Politics,* 2:77–81, 211–16; Hart, "*St. Louis Globe-Democrat,*" 64–65. Jessie Fremont later reported that a group of Germans stoned John How when he attempted to address them and "made a committee of fifty to take Frank Blair & hang him as the source of the trouble," a move

Montgomery quickly sought to ease the situation. He wired Fremont on September 19, "I will send Frank's letter. It is not unfriendly. Release him. This is no time for strife except with the enemies of the country." Much to Frank's anger, Montgomery followed by sending the general a copy of the September 1 letter. "I admit that I have been excessively annoyed by the telegram and letter you sent to Fremont," Blair wrote his brother on the twenty-sixth, "but I know that you were moved by considerations of my advantage." Frank made it clear to his father, however, that he did not intend to be silenced. Encouraged by the many visitors to the arsenal, where he was being detained, he told Preston that Fremont and Jessie had been spreading lies about him; and he intended to retaliate. "All the talk about this quarrel being detrimental to the public service is *bosh*," he boldly asserted. "If Fremont is not removed the public service will go to the devil."[39]

Greatly concerned by the continuing controversy, Lincoln instructed General Scott on September 27 to order Frank's release, unaware that Fremont had already done so three days earlier. Lincoln asked Montgomery to write his brother, advising patience, something of which Frank and others were growing increasingly short. Not wishing to prolong the controversy, Fremont and Jessie had accepted Montgomery's efforts as a face-saving way out. In doing so, however, Fremont informed his adversary that he had been arrested because he had used his family's influence to disrupt the rapport between the commander and the president, thereby "seriously impairing the efficiency of this Department." Fremont expected that Frank would avoid any such "breach of military propriety" in the future.[40]

Fremont's and Lincoln's hopes for an end to the controversy were in vain. Outraged by the general's charge that he had used his influence with the president unwisely, the hot-tempered Frank wrote Adj. Gen. Lorenzo Thomas, threatening to prefer formal charges against the commander. Although counseled by both his father and his brother against such action, the angry Blair would not restrain himself. Two days later, Fremont had him rearrested and sent to Jefferson Barracks. Greatly concerned about her husband, Apo made arrangements to rejoin him. She asked Lizzie, who still

---

that she helped to thwart (Jessie Fremont to Isaac Sherman, October 15, 1861, in *Letters of Jessie Benton Fremont*, 277–78).

39. MB to Fremont, September 19, 20, 1861, Arden R. Smith to FPB, September 19, 1861, FB to MB, September 26, 1861, FB to FPB, n.d. [September 1861], BLC. Frank made similar complaints to his father in three undated letters from this same period, B-LP.

40. Fremont to FB, September 24, 1861, B-LP; MB to FB, September 27, 1861, BLC.

remained in the Philadelphia area, to take the three youngest children to Silver Spring for the time being, while she and nine-year-old Christine returned to St. Louis with Schofield, who had been consulting with authorities in Washington.[41]

President Lincoln hesitated to move against Fremont, who had finally taken the field after the fall of Lexington to Price on September 20. Many in Missouri blamed the commander for that disaster. Price and his Missouri State Guard had moved against the river city in the aftermath of Wilson's Creek, finding it defended by only a small force under Col. James Mulligan. Although Fremont had directed reinforcements to the place upon learning of Price's advance, a series of misunderstandings and incompetence on the part of their respective commanders had prevented them from arriving. As complaints rolled into Washington from all sides, Fremont moved quickly to meet Price, who, having gathered gold from the Lexington banks and recruits, retreated back toward southwest Missouri.[42]

General Scott once again ordered Frank's release while he studied the charges brought against Fremont. In an effort to get a better grasp on the situation, Lincoln, in early October, dispatched Secretary of War Cameron and Adjutant General Thomas to Missouri. Cameron had been getting regular reports from J. W. Schaffer, an agent he had sent there the previous month. He had passed these messages, which indicated a deteriorating situation both in St. Louis and in the field, along to the president. Lincoln gave the secretary an order removing Fremont, with authority to deliver it at his discretion. Cameron and Thomas reached St. Louis on October 11, where they conferred with Brig. Gen. Samuel R. Curtis, in command of Benton Barracks, Blair, Broadhead, and other leaders. Curtis, who had resigned his Iowa seat in Congress to accept a commission, had come reluctantly to believe that Fremont needed to be replaced, and wrote the president that Fremont "lacks the intelligence, the experience & the sagacity necessary to his command." He

41. FB to Thomas, September 26, 1861, FB to Asst. Adj. Gen. Chauncey McKeever, September 30, 1861, FB to MB, October 1, 1861, Lincoln Papers; MB to FPB, September 30, 1861, EBL to SPL, October 1*, 6, 1861, B-LP; EBL to FPB, September 27, October 1, 1861, BLC. In the end, Apo left all of the children with her sister, Midge Dick, who was staying with her in-laws in Philadelphia (EBL to SPL, October 6, 1861, B-LP).

42. Fremont to E. D. Townsend, September 23, 1861, Charles Gibson to Lincoln, September 27, 1861, enclosing Gamble to Lincoln, September 20, 1861, J. W. Schaffer to Simon Cameron, September 29, 1861, James O. Broadhead to MB, September 30, 1861, Lyman Trumbull to Lincoln, October 1, 1861, John How to MB, October 3, 1861, Samuel T. Glover to MB, October 4, 1861, Lincoln Papers; Edward Bates to Broadhead, September 28, 1861, Broadhead Papers.

sagely reminded the president, "Public opinion is an element of war which must not be neglected."[43]

Leaving St. Louis on the twelfth, Cameron and Thomas proceeded to Tipton, where they found Fremont encamped with his forces. The secretary immediately conferred with the commander and presented him with the order for his removal. Shocked, Fremont asked for a chance to prove himself in the field, which Cameron reluctantly granted. The secretary agreed to withhold the order until after he returned to Washington on condition that Fremont would resign if he failed to engage the enemy in the interim.

Thomas, meanwhile, had been doing some consultation on his own, primarily with Frank and his circle. He also talked with General Hunter, who informed him that, although he was presumably second in command, Fremont kept him at arm's length and never discussed his plans with him. Upon their return to Washington, the adjutant general submitted a caustic report to the secretary reflecting the Blair group's concerns about extravagance and contract irregularities. Frank wrote his father that he had seen Cameron upon his return to St. Louis and was dismayed at the outcome of the Tipton conference. He again asked Preston to intervene with the president.[44]

Thomas's report precipitated a cabinet showdown over Fremont's removal. Attorney General Bates confided to his diary on October 22 that Lincoln seemed to think that the adjutant general's findings, backed by the testimony of Hunter and Curtis, indicated a need for change. Secy. of State William H. Seward "came again, as twice before, to the rescue—and urged delay," much to Bates's disgust. Chase and Cameron "gave in and timidly yielded to delay," so "the President still hangs in painful and mortifying [sic] doubt." Frank told Montgomery in disgust that "Cameron has *flummuxed* on the Fremont business. . . . I never since I was born imagined that such a lot of poltroons & apes could be gathered together from the four quarters of the Globe as Old Abe has succeeded in bringing together in his cabinet."[45]

43. J. W. Schaffer to Cameron, September 14, 22, 29, 1861, Cameron to Lincoln, October 12, 1861, Curtis to Lincoln, October 12, 1861, Lincoln Papers; Edward Bates to Broadhead, October 9, 1861, Broadhead Papers; *Collected Works of Lincoln*, 4:549. For Jessie Fremont's reaction to the Cameron-Thomas visit, see Jessie Fremont to Frederick Billings, October 12, 1861, Jessie Fremont to Isaac Sherman, October 15, 1861, in *Letters of Jessie Benton Fremont*, 273–79.

44. Cameron to Lincoln, October 14, 1861, Lincoln Papers; FB to FPB, October 12, 1861, B-LP; *OR*, 1:3:540–49.

45. Bates, *Diary of Bates*, 198; FB to MB, October 25, 1861, FPB to Bigelow, October 26, 1861, BLC. Seward forwarded to Lincoln a letter from William K. Strong of New York,

While the cabinet debated, a congressional subcommittee arrived in St. Louis to begin investigating the numerous complaints of contract irregularities and fraud. Elihu B. Washburne of Illinois, the subcommittee's chairman, sent Lincoln increasingly adverse reports of their findings. "The disclosures of corruption extravagance and peculation are utterly astounding," he wrote. Washburne indicated that such prominent Unionists as Governor Gamble, James Broadhead, Samuel Glover, and others "are really under the ban," while "a gang of California robbers and scoundrels rule, control and direct everything." McKinstry seemed to be at the center of the difficulties; and, although he had been relieved as quartermaster general, the committee had found his replacement a disgusting drunk.[46]

Other reports proved equally disturbing. Charles G. Hulpine wrote Thurlow Weed from Tipton that Fremont's advance to Warsaw had been "one of continuous devastation without the least respect to political opinions or antecedents." The general suspected all regular officers, Hulpine reported, while putting his trust in lower subordinates, many of whom were irresponsible and some of whom smuggled supplies to Price. He noted that McKinstry, who had accompanied Fremont into the field, was the special favorite. A similar report came directly to Lincoln from J. M. Lucas, captain of the post commissary at Tipton. Both men complained of J. C. Woods, Fremont's "so-called 'Master of Transportation,'" who lacked experience and discipline. They received reinforcement from Lincoln's close friend Ward H. Lamon, who also visited Tipton and wrote: "Things are in a terribly unorganized state here, and I find great complaints about the Commanding General (and some jealousies)." Lamon indicated that "there is about as much likelihood of his catching Price as there is of his being struck by lightning."[47]

In light of these complaints, Lincoln decided that he could no longer delay. On October 24, he sent the order for Fremont's removal to General Curtis at St. Louis with the request that he forward it to the commander by courier. The order should be withheld only if the messenger found Fremont at the conclusion of a successful battle, upon the battlefield, or facing the enemy with

dated October 24, 1861, together with a clipping from a St. Louis paper, indicating that Strong had been dispatched by Fremont to take care of unsettled accounts and contracts in the hope of speeding supplies to the army in the field (Lincoln Papers).

46. Washburne to Lincoln, October 17, 19, 21, 1861, Lincoln Papers. The Simon Cameron Papers contain numerous letters during October 1861 from St. Louis banks and merchants detailing large sums of money owed them for government purchases.

47. Hulpine to Weed, October 17, 1861, Lamon to Lincoln, October 21, 1861, Lucas to Lincoln, October 23, 1861, Lincoln Papers.

immediate prospects for battle. Curtis took special precautions to accomplish the task. He made duplicates and sent two men to deliver them in case one did not get through. Fremont had advanced to Springfield at the end of October, occupying that town after a gallant charge by his personal bodyguard under the command of Maj. Charles Zagonyi, which scattered the Confederate rear guard there. Price had retreated to the far southwestern corner of the state, hoping to give battle with the aid of Confederate general Ben McCulloch, who had previously joined him at Wilson's Creek. Still, such plans were nebulous.[48]

While Fremont might have been hopeful of fighting soon, Curtis's messengers had no way of knowing this. The first, "dressed like a country farmer," arrived at the commander's camp outside Springfield at five in the morning of November 3. After waiting five hours for an audience, he finally gained admittance to the general's tent and presented the removal order. Fremont asked how he had gotten through his lines and if General Hunter, who had been ordered to replace him, knew of the order. When told that another messenger had gone to Hunter, who remained some distance away, Fremont dismissed him. As word of what had happened made the rounds of the encampment, a feeling of gloom pervaded the troops; and many of the officers, particularly the Germans, talked of resigning. Some of Fremont's officers wanted the commander to lead an attack the next morning, and he promised to do so if Hunter did not come quickly. Such hopes proved short-lived as Hunter arrived that evening at ten o'clock. The following morning, Fremont issued a farewell address to his troops and relinquished his command. Hunter immediately sent cavalry patrols in all directions but found no enemy in the immediate vicinity.[49]

Returning to St. Louis with his bodyguard, Fremont received a strong welcome from the German community, whom he had won over with his emancipation policy and who blamed Frank for his removal. The *Missouri Democrat* reported that twenty thousand demonstrated on his behalf, but Lincoln's agent, Leonard Swett, who had brought the removal order to Curtis, wrote the president that "Last night there was a perfect failure of a demonstration here. It was very small confined to the Germans & Fremont actually made no speech at all." The truth undoubtedly lay somewhere in between.

48. Curtis to Lincoln, November 1, 16, 1861, Leonard Swett to Lincoln, November 9, 1861, Lincoln Papers; *OR*, 1:3:731–32; Jessie Benton Fremont, *The Story of the Guard: A Chronicle of the War*, 137–51.
49. Swett to Lincoln, November 9, 1861, Curtis to Lincoln, November 16, 1861, Lincoln Papers.

A few nights later some of Frank's friends gathered outside the home of Ben Farrar, where he and Apo were staying, to serenade him. Although some pro-Fremont Germans tried to make a brief counterdemonstration, police quickly brought them under control. Blair addressed the crowd briefly and stated simply, "What I did, I did from a sincere desire to serve God and my country."[50]

Much has been written about the Blair-Fremont controversy, with most historians seeing the affair as a clash of strong personalities whose egos simply could not be reconciled. There is some truth in this, although, in Fremont's case, Jessie's may have been the stronger ego. Fremont came to St. Louis with a limited military background. He found himself thrust into a chaotic situation that demanded quick and decisive action. He later claimed that he had been given no specific directions while in Washington, although there had been general conversations about the desirability of a thrust down the Mississippi. He undoubtedly worked hard to bring some order to the scene. He built a strong defense network around St. Louis, although at considerable expense and somewhat with Frank's disapproval.

Fremont acted decisively with his expedition to reinforce Cairo. Whether he had sufficient force to do that and support Lyon as well will long be debated. His order to Lyon to withdraw to Rolla and await reinforcements was undoubtedly wise; but that impetuous commander, who had battled long and hard, politically as well as militarily, to arrive at his position, believed he could not abandon southwest Missouri without a fight. It cost Lyon his life, and it cost Fremont much-needed support, including that of the Blairs, particularly as Sterling Price proceeded to move freely through the western part of the state and the commander seemed oblivious to what was happening. The crucial interview of Frank and Schofield with Fremont in late August appeared to mark a major turning point in their relationship.

Frank had fought hard with Lyon to save Missouri for the Union. Together with his brother and father, he had then recommended Fremont for the western command. Whether the Blairs thought that Fremont would be a puppet, as some, including the Fremonts at a later date, have implied from the senior

---

50. *Missouri Democrat*, November 9, 11, 12, 1861; Swett to Lincoln, November 9, 1861, Lincoln Papers. Franklin Dick wrote Preston Blair, "A large portion of the Germans seem to be infatuated with Fremont & hostile to Frank. Frank has made many friends amongst the Americans, but as they are all that class of men, old Whigs, who when the pinch comes have always gone away, I do not place any reliance upon them. But undoubtedly Frank stands in a very high position in the community" (Dick to FPB, November 25, 1861, B-LP).

Blair's letter of August 13, is doubtful. Rather, they hoped for a genuine "co-partnership" to complete the work that Frank and Lyon had begun earlier. Many, including Frank, testified that, until their break in early September, he was one of the few who had almost unlimited access to the commander. Both men seemed to get along well, although Blair complained that Fremont seldom confided his plans, if any, to him. In his letter of September 1, Frank expressed more disappointment than anger over what was happening. He even supported Fremont's proclamation of martial law, somewhat to Lincoln's dismay where the emancipation clause was concerned.

All of the Blairs, whether in St. Louis or in Washington, continually worked throughout August to secure adequate supplies for the Western Department, even as Frank had done earlier in supplying the Home Guards through the assistance of eastern friends. Frank continued to urge greater action by the administration as late as August 21. Certainly he hoped that friends and supporters, who had staunchly stood by the Union cause in the preceding difficult days, could benefit from government contracts for needed materials. Whether he adequately screened those he recommended can be argued. In the concern for quick action, mistakes are often made. Frank later testified that no contract he recommended had been denied, although some exceptions obviously existed. It galled him and others in the St. Louis community to see many of the contracts going to the "California gang," as they called them: friends and associates of the Fremonts from their stay in the West. The times were chaotic, and the government found the supply problem unprecedented on all fronts. Corruption and venality frequently rear their ugly heads in such circumstances. Both Blair and Fremont undoubtedly made mistakes in this regard, but probably none deliberately. There is little reason to doubt that Frank had a genuine concern with the chaotic management of the whole supply problem as it would affect the armies in the field. Quartermaster General Meigs, Congressman Washburne, and others who visited St. Louis reiterated the same concern.

Fremont's style of operation also bothered Frank. Although he had un-limited access to the commander, others, including key military and civilian officials, found it difficult to get through Fremont's overly protective staff. That many of these staffers were Hungarians and Italians alienated western-ers, who were used to informality, even more. Constantly at the commander's side stood his strong-willed wife, Jessie, who took it upon herself to serve as her husband's confidante and protector. Those who encountered her quickly styled her "General Jessie" and resented her influence in what they considered to be a male-dominated atmosphere. There is no evidence that Frank, who had been well acquainted with her for years, held such a view until after her fateful trip to Washington in early September.

Jessie's visit to the capital marked the decisive turning point in the relationship between the two families. Always defensive in support of her husband, she overreacted, out of ignorance and suspicion, to what she considered unjust attacks on his motives. Throwing longtime friendships to the winds, she encouraged Fremont to launch a deadly counterattack against Frank by arresting him and by a constant barrage of charges in the local press. The hot-tempered Frank retaliated in kind, even as Montgomery, his father, and an overly patient president sought to soothe the troubled waters. Once these two strong personalities crossed swords in this fashion, only decisive military action by Fremont could have prevented his removal. The reports reaching Lincoln and other officials of continued chaos during his march to the interior of Missouri merely reinforced the image of the commander's general incompetence.[51]

The blowup between the Fremonts and the Blairs would have long-range consequences for both families as well as for Lincoln. Fremont became the hero of the radicals in Congress and elsewhere and of many of the Germans in St. Louis, who increasingly supported a policy of immediate emancipation. Indeed, some have accused Fremont of deliberately seeking to use this issue as a stepping-stone for another presidential run in 1864. Frank, meanwhile, moved increasingly into the ranks of the conservatives, alienating many like Gratz Brown and Henry Blow, as well as his German constituency, who had stood by him during the struggles of the 1850s and early 1861. While not opposed to emancipation, the Blairs favored a gradual, compensated manumission with continued emphasis on colonization. War made this increasingly untenable.

The Fremonts departed St. Louis in late November for New York City, embittered over what had befallen them. They had not fought the last round in their battle with the Blairs and the administration. When the Thirty-seventh Congress convened for its second session on December 3, 1861, many of its members began a crusade to regain some control over the conduct of

---

51. The two standard treatments of the Blair-Fremont controversy, each from its own particular perspective, are Nevins, *Fremont*, and W. E. Smith, *Blair Family in Politics*. E. B. Smith, *Francis Preston Blair*, presents a strong defense of Frank. For a spirited recent defense of Fremont, see Robert L. Turkoly-Jozik, "Fremont and the Western Department." Jessie's role is sympathetically treated in Herr, *Jessie Benton Fremont*.

the war, which they had lost to the administration during the preceding months when they had not been in session. The string of recent Union military defeats, including Balls Bluff, Wilson's Creek, and Lexington, gave them the ammunition they needed to establish the Joint Committee on the Conduct of the War. Dominated by the radical faction of the Republican Party, this committee began a series of hearings aimed at placing the blame for the military defeats on the president and his advisers.[52]

High on the joint committee's agenda stood the exoneration of Fremont, whom many considered a martyr to the emancipation cause. Jessie and his friends had been rallying outside support for his defense from the time the Fremonts arrived in New York. Foremost among their allies stood Horace Greeley, editor of the *New York Tribune*. Fremont made his first brief appearance before the joint committee on January 10, 1862, at which time its chairman, Sen. Benjamin F. Wade of Ohio, asked him to prepare a written statement for a subsequent meeting. A week later the former commander presented a lengthy defense in which he refuted all charges made against him by Frank and others. Most of the committee members followed this with sympathetic questioning. Indeed, one of them, Cong. George W. Julian of Indiana, had already made a long defense of Fremont on the floor of the House; and Senator Wade had assured Jessie by mid-January "that it was all proved up & every charge against Mr. Fremont exploded."[53]

Montgomery and Frank appeared before the joint committee on February 5 and 7, respectively. The former read only a brief prepared statement and received only one short question. Frank, however, delivered a long and detailed rebuttal to Fremont's testimony and was questioned extensively. He told his family that evening that he believed his appearance had gone well. Yet, in the weeks that followed, the committee's determination to vindicate Fremont became obvious as it called only those witnesses who would collaborate his case. Samuel Glover, whom Montgomery had suggested as an aide to the joint committee when it went to St. Louis, wrote in frustration that the members blocked his every move to gather testimony. On February 7, the same day that Frank testified, committee members approached Secy. of War Edwin Stanton seeking a new command for Fremont. Although the joint committee had

52. Herr, *Jessie Benton Fremont*, 351; *CG*, 37:2:17, 32, 40, 110, 153; Bruce Tap, "Reconstructing Emancipation's Martyr: John C. Fremont and the Joint Committee on the Conduct of the War," 40–41.

53. Tap, "Reconstructing Emancipation's Martyr," 41–43; T. Harry Williams, *Lincoln and the Radicals*, 104–9; *JCCW*, 33–77; *CG*, 37:2:327–32; *Letters of Jessie Benton Fremont*, 309.

vowed to keep its proceedings confidential, the *New York Tribune* published the general's full testimony with supporting documents in early March, claiming that it had the approval of the committee to do so.[54]

Increasingly concerned over the direction that the joint committee seemed to be going, Frank decided to counterattack. He asked Schofield in late February to send him his report on Wilson's Creek to help buttress the case. Although Montgomery and his father urged him to let matters rest, Frank rose on the floor of the House of Representatives on March 7 and made a blistering attack on Fremont's testimony, which had just appeared in the *Tribune*. In response to the radical press's claims that Lincoln had treated Fremont unfairly and dismissed him simply because of the emancipation fiasco, Frank defended the president and called the general's testimony "an apology for disaster and defeat; ingenious upon its face by the omission of important facts, and by the suggestion of others which never existed." Citing an *Atlantic Monthly* article titled "Fremont's One Hundred Days," written by one of the general's staff officers, Frank laughed at its attempt to compare Fremont to Napoleon: "Can imagination conceive of Bonaparte returning to Paris, and announcing that he had lost two armies, liberated two negroes, and published a bombastic proclamation?" For two hours Frank held sway and later told his sister that he was well pleased that he had held his temper in check.[55]

Frank's elation proved short-lived. Four days after his House appearance, President Lincoln handed Fremont a new command in the Mountain Department of Virginia. While Lincoln had not consulted him, Montgomery saw this assignment as a way to assuage the radicals without placing the general in an important command. Since the radicals had been attacking General McClellan for his lack of action on the eastern front, there had been some concern that they might pressure Lincoln into putting Fremont in his place.[56]

Although the joint committee's majority vindicated Fremont's conduct in the Western Department and commended him for his stand on emancipation, three minority members declined to sign the final report and chose instead

54. *JCCW*, 154–83; Glover to MB, January 8, 13, February 8, 13, 1862, BLC; EBL to SPL, February 8, 1862, B-LP; Tap, "Reconstructing Emancipation's Martyr," 46–48.

55. *CG*, 37:2:1118–24; FB to Schofield, February 28, 1862, Schofield Papers; EBL to SPL, March 6*, 7*, 8, 1862, B-LP. Frank's attack did not go unanswered as Schuyler Colfax, with whom he had worked closely in previous sessions, rose to defend Fremont, providing another example of the increasing split between Frank and many of his previous supporters (*CG*, 37:2:1124–29).

56. EBL to SPL, March 13*, 1862, B-LP.

to print the testimony without comment. In the meantime, two other groups, which had been sent to investigate the allegations of contract fraud, brought in unfavorable reports. The House subcommittee, of which Washburne was a member, criticized Fremont's handling of that aspect of his administration and recommended censure, which the House passed 103 to 28. In the debates on their report, Frank remained silent. Then a presidential commission, headed by Joseph Holt of Kentucky, made a similar widely circulated report. As for Fremont, his Mountain Department command proved short-lived and undistinguished; and in June 1862 he resigned when Lincoln sought to add his command to the new Army of Virginia under John Pope, a Fremont subordinate in Missouri.[57]

Frank had much to occupy him besides the continuing Fremont controversy. He and Apo had returned to Washington in late November 1861 to rejoin their children, splitting their residency between No. 4 and Silver Spring. In the ensuing session, Frank continued to play a major role as chairman of the Military Affairs Committee. He strongly supported the construction of gunboats by James B. Eads, begun under Fremont, which would play an important role in subsequent river campaigns. He quickly pushed through the House a bill to compensate those who had fought in the Western Department, whether actually mustered into service or not. He secured passage of another measure giving the secretary of war the authority to take possession of the telegraph lines and railroads when necessary for military purposes. This law included a provision that civilians employed by those utilities might be drafted into military service if they refused to work. Frank also led the fight to authorize the president's moving men from disbanded regiments to other units and transferring individuals between cavalry and infantry units as needed. Yet another measure sought to enhance the army medical department.[58]

One of Frank's most ambitious proposals, which ultimately proved unsuccessful, called for the construction of a ship canal from Chicago to the Illinois River to enhance navigation between the Great Lakes and the Mississippi River. Such a canal would greatly benefit St. Louis. In an effort to gain eastern support, he later amended his bill to provide funding for the enlargement of the Erie and Oswego canals in New York State. Presenting it

57. *CG*, 37:2:116, 1745–53, 1835–39, 1849–53, 1862–71, 1887; EBL to SPL, April 30*, 1862, B-LP; Tap, "Reconstructing Emancipation's Martyr," 50–51; Nevins, *Fremont*, 550–62.

58. EBL to SPL, February 14*, 1862, B-LP; FB to Eads, January 6, 1862, FB to G. V. Fox, n.d. [1862], James B. Eads Papers; *CG*, 37:2:117–18, 548, 948, 1268–72, 1587.

as a "twin measure" to the Pacific Railroad Act, which had recently passed, Frank actively promoted its passage throughout the session. Other vested transportation interests worked equally hard against the measure, which the House finally tabled by a vote of sixty-five to sixty-three. Meanwhile, Frank labored successfully, as a member of the select committee on the Pacific railroad, to secure the initial authorization for a transcontinental railroad, something he had been actively promoting for nearly a decade.[59]

On yet another front, Frank displayed his steady drift toward the conservative wing of the Republican Party with his stance on the burning question of emancipation. The issue arose early in the session over Order No. 3, issued by Maj. Gen. Henry W. Halleck, the new commander of the Western Department at St. Louis. Halleck sought to prevent fugitive slaves from entering his lines on the grounds that they frequently proved a source of intelligence for the enemy. Frank upheld Halleck's position in open debate with Thaddeus Stevens and Owen Lovejoy. He warned the general, however, that it might make him appear antagonistic to Fremont's policy, which had forbade the return of runaways to their masters, and thereby jeopardize his nomination for permanent rank. At the same time Frank began sitting on the Democratic side of the aisle, prompting Stevens to accuse him bitterly of deserting the Republican Party. To this Frank replied, "Well, if so—I go with a majority of its members—who vowed with me to support the Constitution Union [sic] about which we care more than we do the niggers."[60]

The radical faction in Congress pushed increasingly for a stronger stand on emancipation as Lincoln tried to steer a moderate course. On March 6, 1862, the president recommended the adoption of a joint resolution placing the federal government on record as willing to "cooperate with any State which may adopt gradual abolishment of slavery," supporting it with some type of compensation. Meeting with border-state representatives four days later, he received little encouragement for his proposal. When the joint resolution finally passed the House on March 11, only Frank, within the Missouri

59. Curry, *Blueprint for Modern America*, 117, 121, 135, 137–41.
60. FB to Halleck, December 4, 1861, BLC; *CG*, 37:2:33–34, 57–60; EBL to SPL, December 15*, 1861, B-LP. By act of March 13, 1862, Congress prohibited the military's return of runaway slaves. On July 17, 1862, it went one step further in declaring the slaves of disloyal owners free if they entered Union lines (James G. Randall, *Lincoln the President*, 2:131). Halleck subsequently insisted that he wished to leave the question of master-slave relationships to civil authorities. He specifically forbade the practice of St. Louis police holding runaways for sale if their owners could not be found (Parrish, *History of Missouri*, 88).

delegation, supported it. The others, except Elijah H. Norton, who opposed, abstained. Missouri's two senators split on the issue when it passed that chamber on April 2, with John B. Henderson in favor and Robert Wilson opposed.[61]

In early April, Congress, with Frank's support, voted for compensated emancipation for the District of Columbia. In the midst of this debate, Frank rose to make a spirited defense of the president on April 11. To those who said that Lincoln had no policy, Frank argued that the president's main concern lay in preserving the Union. Refusing to believe that the South had seceded strictly over the issue of slavery, Frank recalled those Southern leaders who had tried to pursue moderation, and then made it clear that he considered the real cause of the war to be the *"negro question* and not the *slavery question."* "The rebellion originated chiefly with the non-slaveholders resident in the strongholds of the institution," he argued, "not springing, however, from any love of slavery, but from an antagonism of race and hostility to the idea of equality with the blacks involved in a simple emancipation."

With regard to emancipation, Frank warned,

> No wise man desires to increase the number of enemies to the State within the hostile regions, or divide its friends outside. Mr. Lincoln knew that a decree of emancipation simply would have this effect. Such an act he knew was calculated to make rebels of the whole of the non slaveholders of the South, and at the same time to weaken the sympathy of a large number of working men of the North, who are not ready to see their brethren in the South put on equality with manumitted negroes.

Blair urged support for Lincoln's plan of compensated emancipation where the individual states were willing to undertake it. He then returned to his well-worn theme of the 1850s that the freed slaves should be encouraged to colonize in Central America or the Caribbean.[62]

Lincoln had been examining the last of these possibilities that winter. The area of the Chiriqui Lagoon in present-day Panama seemed particularly attractive for a colonization project. Ambrose W. Thompson, a wealthy Philadelphian, had recently acquired several hundred thousand acres in that

    61. *CG,* 37:2:1102–3, 1179; Parrish, *Turbulent Partnership,* 124.

    62. *CG,* 37:2:1631–34. For reactions to Frank's speech, see EBL to SPL, April 19*, 1862, B-LP; *New York Times,* April 17, 1862; *Missouri Democrat,* April 29, May 13, 1862; Rudolf Doehn to FB, May 21, 1862, BLC. W. E. Smith says that Lincoln must have been aware of Frank's intended remarks given the close friendship that existed between him and the Blairs at the time (*Blair Family in Politics,* 2:136–37).

region. The lagoon presumably was deep enough to serve as a naval base; and the region reportedly held rich stores of coal, which Thompson indicated he could make available to the navy at a bargain price. In addition, it appeared suitable for cotton production. To the Blairs and Lincoln, the Chiriqui Lagoon seemed an ideal spot to colonize American freedmen. The president asked Ninian W. Edwards, his wife's brother-in-law, to look into the matter, but the project met with a mixed response in the cabinet. Although Congress included one hundred thousand dollars in the District of Columbia bill for those freedmen wishing to emigrate, nothing further came of the Chiriqui Lagoon proposal.[63]

The congressional session finally closed in early July. Frank had been at the forefront of many battles, becoming increasingly Lincoln's conservative spokesman in the emerging struggles with the radicals. Shortly before adjournment, he turned down a place on General McClellan's staff, which his father had wanted him to take, after visiting that officer's camp with the president. Secretary of War Stanton had approached him, undoubtedly at Lincoln's instigation, about raising troops in the West in connection with the president's call for three hundred thousand additional volunteers; and Frank eagerly agreed.[64]

Apo decided to keep the children in the East and took a house for the remainder of the summer at Newport, Rhode Island. She had had a difficult spring with considerable illnesses among the children, the most serious being young George's bout with typhoid fever. After a quick trip to Newport to ensure that his family was safe, Frank headed west to St. Louis to shore up his political base and to undertake a new mission: the recruitment of a brigade for possible service down the Mississippi. The next three years would find him performing an intricate balancing act between politics and military service.[65]

63. David Herbert Donald, *Lincoln*, 344–48.

64. Ward Hill Lamon, *Recollections of Abraham Lincoln, 1847–1865*, 204; EBL to SPL, July 2, 5, 10, 11, 12*, 1862, B-LP; Miers, *Lincoln Day by Day*, 3:126–27; FB to Apo, n.d., BLPLC; *Missouri Republican*, July 16, 18, 1862.

65. EBL to SPL, February 26*, March 1*, 4*, 6*, 7*, April 4*, 6*, May 17*, 25*, 26*, June 9*, 10, 16*, 23, 1862, B-LP; FB to Apo, July 2, 1862, BLPLC.

Frank Blair (courtesy State Historical Society of Missouri, Columbia)

Montgomery Blair (courtesy State Historical Society of Missouri, Columbia)

Francis Preston Blair (courtesy National Archives)

Maj. Gen. Frank Blair and his staff. Andrew Hickenlooper is on Blair's right. (courtesy Massachusetts Commandery Military Order of the Loyal Legion and the U.S. Army Military History Institute)

Apolline Alexander Blair (courtesy Washington University School of Medicine Library)

Elizabeth "Lizzie" Blair Lee (courtesy P. Blair Lee family)

7

The Vicksburg Campaign

Frank faced a double challenge in the spring and summer of 1862: his reelection campaign and the recruitment of two brigades for the proposed Mississippi expedition. Fortunately for him, Missouri's state and congressional elections had been moved from their earlier August time until November, thus giving him more time to mend his political fences. His principal concern was to recapture as much of his still angry German constituency as possible. A local German doctor, Rudolf Doehn, a member of the Missouri General Emancipation Society recently organized by Gratz Brown, wrote Frank in early April seeking a clarification of his views. Blair replied at length, calling for a program of gradual compensated emancipation coupled with the separation of the races, citing Carl Schurz as a supporter of colonization. Doehn turned the letter over to the *Missouri Democrat*, which published it on May 10. The *Democrat* denounced the Blair plan as perpetuating slavery indefinitely, while the *Westliche Post* called it a blatant attempt to win back German votes. It certainly did little to influence many of the more radical Germans, who then were further alienated by Blair's May 23 speech in Congress defending the gradual approach that Lincoln sought to pursue at the time.[1]

Even before Frank's return to Missouri, several moderate Republicans had expressed their concern about the seeming disintegration of their party. In late May, Henry Blow wrote Henry Boernstein, deploring the emerging factionalism. One of Frank's closest allies in organizing the Republican Party in the late

1. *Missouri Democrat*, May 10, 1862; W. E. Smith, *Blair Family in Politics*, 2:208.

1850s and through the crisis of 1861, Boernstein had been rewarded by Lincoln with the American consulship at Bremen, Germany. Blow urged Boernstein, whom he considered one of the most influential Missouri German Americans, to use his influence to try to reconcile the Lincoln-Blair policy with Missouri's Germans. He followed this letter with a trip to Washington, at which time he urged the president and Montgomery Blair to secure Boernstein's return to the editorship of the *Anzeiger des Westens* to counteract the anti-Blair sentiments of the *Missouri Democrat* and the *Westliche Post*. Boernstein proved amenable and received four months' leave, together with the vague promise of a higher echelon job. In the months that followed, he and Charles Bernays, an earlier associate who had been given a consular position in Zurich, Switzerland, but was now recalled, provided a strong counterpoint to the increasingly radical *Democrat* and *Post*.[2]

Emancipation matters had begun to come to a head in Missouri in June when Governor Gamble called the state convention back into session to reschedule legislative and congressional elections from August to November while postponing until 1864 those for statewide officials. Although Gamble made no mention of emancipation in his call, several St. Louis conservatives attempted to provide for gradual compensated emancipation, taking advantage of the April congressional offer. Although the convention refused to consider this, Gamble, in the waning days of the meeting, asked the members to make some kind of response to the congressional offer. So, while thanking Congress for its "liberality," the convention proclaimed that it did not feel authorized to take action on such "grave and delicate questions of private right and public policy."[3]

Two days later, the state Republican Party met in convention at Jefferson City. In his call, State Chairman B. Gratz Brown had urged consideration of a plan to take speedy advantage of the congressional proposal for gradual compensated emancipation, as well as the selection of a statewide ticket. The 195 delegates from twenty-five counties included numerous German Americans from the anti-Blair opposition. The actions of the recently adjourned state convention in postponing the election of statewide officials negated the need for an electoral slate. In view of the convention's lack of action on emancipation, however, the Republicans adopted resolutions, prepared by

2. Blow to FB, July 30, 1862, MB to FB, August 3, 1862, Boernstein to FB, October 2, 1862, FB to FPB, on back of Boernstein letter, BLC; Boernstein, *Memoirs*, 444–49; Stevens, *St. Louis, the Fourth City*, 1:217–19; W. E. Smith, *Blair Family in Politics*, 2:208–11.
3. Parrish, *Turbulent Partnership*, 126–32.

Brown, calling for gradual emancipation while rejecting colonization. Brown, who had been distancing himself from Frank politically ever since leaving the editorship of the *Missouri Democrat* in 1859, now moved increasingly to the forefront of what would become the Radical Union Party of Missouri. He declined, however, to stand as a congressional candidate in opposition to Frank, as many of his followers were urging.[4]

Frank, meanwhile, continued to shore up his political base. In mid-August, he sold his one-sixth interest in the *Missouri Democrat* to Daniel Houser for four thousand dollars after a heated argument with William McKee in the *Democrat* office had failed to dislodge that editor from his anti-Blair stance. Frank had already joined with a number of loyal friends, including John How, Bart Able, and O. D. Filley, to establish the *St. Louis Union* in the hope that it could serve as a stronger vehicle for his campaign than the favorable but circulation-weak *Evening News*. Peter Foy, who had succeeded Gratz Brown as editor of the *Democrat* and later received a presidential appointment as St. Louis postmaster, was installed as editor in chief, while continuing his patronage job. He joined Boernstein and the *Anzeiger des Westens* in counterattacking the *Missouri Democrat* and the *Westliche Post*.[5]

The new paper carried on its masthead Andrew Jackson's famous quotation, "The Federal Union, it must be preserved." News of Frank and the exploits of his military command appeared regularly in its columns. A typical editorial trumpeted,

> The true patriot [Blair] who took his life in his hand and repaired to the field last December [1862], there to perish gloriously or triumph over his foe, has already placed petty malice and detraction under his feet. His vindication, his valor, his virtue, and his patriotism are proofs such as seal the lips even of personal enemies. As his fame rises purely and brightly from ensanguined fields, his malingers [*sic*] slink away and hide their guilty heads from sight.

For all the *Union*'s efforts, however, Frank's foes did not disappear. Maintaining the paper proved an uphill battle. Subscriptions to the *Union* did not meet expectations, and only government advertising and that from friends kept it operating. Eventually, Frank assumed sole ownership except for a small amount of stock held by Foy. The *Union* continued to operate throughout

4. Peterson, *Freedom and Franchise*, 113–14, 121; Parrish, *Turbulent Partnership*, 133.
5. R. J. Howard to MB, April 15, 1862, Apo to MB, February 19 (no year), Apo to FPB, March 18, 1863, FB to Apo, April 26, 27, 1863, BLC; Scharf, *History of St. Louis*, 2:925–26; Stevens, *St. Louis, the Fourth City*, 1:214.

the war, with Apo later playing a major role in keeping it going while Frank remained absent in Congress and the military.[6]

Meanwhile, the congressional campaign became increasingly ugly as it moved into late summer and fall. In early August, Foy, in his capacity as postmaster, denied the list of German general-delivery letters to the *Westliche Post*. The paper protested this move to the postmaster general's office, claiming it had the largest circulation among German Americans in St. Louis. After referring the matter to Foy, an assistant postmaster general replied in late August that *"your journal has made itself notorious as a malinger [sic] of the President and his administration and a bitter and pertinacious opponent of enlistments under the new call for Volunteers."* Such activity was considered sufficient justification for the action taken. When the president received numerous protests, including one from Henry Blow, in September, he apparently directed a reversal of the policy, lest it further alienate substantial numbers of Germans. The list reappeared in the *Post* by the end of the month.[7]

Meanwhile, ward meetings were being held throughout Frank's district to choose delegates to a Union convention that would select candidates for Congress and the legislature. To the chagrin of his opponents, that meeting quickly nominated Frank for reelection. He accepted in a lengthy address, which appeared in all of the newspapers friendly to him, as well as being printed in pamphlet form for wide circulation. He noted that he had nearly finished raising his brigade and would soon leave for the front. This responsibility made it difficult for him to conduct an extensive canvass, as he had in the past.

Turning on his enemies, Frank attacked "the petty despotism under Fremont," which had instigated slanderous lies against him. He then outlined the treachery of McKee and Fishback, as he saw it, in selling out to the Fremont forces. Contrary to their claims that he had taken both congressional and military pay, Blair reported that he had refunded the latter when he took his seat in Congress. He noted that he had always been opposed to slavery but believed that it should be ended constitutionally and not "according to the demand of these howling Dervishes and fanatical revolutionists." He had voted to abolish slavery in the District of Columbia with compensation for

6. *St. Louis Daily Union*, June 9, 12, 1863; W. E. Smith, *Blair Family in Politics*, 2:211–12.

7. Theodore Olshausen and Ernest W. Heemann to 3rd Asst. Postmaster General, August 5, 1862, St. John B. Skinner, acting 1st Asst. Postmaster General to Olshausen and Heemann, August 25, 1862, Blow to Lincoln, September 3, 1862, Olshausen and Heemann to Lincoln, September 8, 1862, Lincoln Papers.

loyal owners and money for colonization. He had also supported the Confiscation Act, which freed the slaves of rebels, although he strongly opposed the use of blacks in the armed forces. Frank reminded his constituents that he had worked hard for local interests during the last session of Congress, pushing the Pacific Railroad Act and the Michigan Ship Canal Bill, both of which would greatly benefit St. Louis. In a later rousing speech on October 25, he urged his constituents to compare his wartime record with that of his naysayers, outlining an impressive list of accomplishments in both the military and Congress.[8]

The emerging radical wing of the Republican Party countered with a meeting of the Missouri General Emancipation Society at St. Louis with Gratz Brown and Charles D. Drake as the principal speakers. They attacked the Lincoln administration for failing to make emancipation a major war aim and accused the president of being a dictator. Brown argued that the war necessitated emancipation and urged the enlistment of freed blacks to join in the struggle for freedom. He saw no need for colonization, while hinting that he might eventually support equal rights for the freedmen.[9]

Drake, a St. Louis attorney and rising star in the radical ranks, echoed these sentiments with vehemence. A recent convert to the emancipation cause, he had been successively a Whig, a Know-Nothing, and a Democrat in the 1850s. He had taken a strong stand against German interests while in the legislature in the late 1850s. Drake had clashed with Frank on the eve of the war over the sale of Missouri's railroads to eastern capitalists, whom Blair represented; and a strong enmity had since existed between the two. As late as July 1861, Drake had denounced antislavery agitation. He now emerged, however, as the foremost radical leader behind Brown, and he would become the dominant force within the postwar Radical Union Party.[10]

President Lincoln threw a bombshell into the midst of the continuing controversy in Missouri with the announcement of his preliminary Emancipation Proclamation on September 23, following the battle of Antietam. The president had been considering such a move since July; but the cabinet, including Montgomery Blair, had persuaded him to wait until after the early congressional elections and until the military picture looked brighter

---

8. *Address of F. P. Blair, Jr., to His Constituents, October 8, 1862* (pamphlet, MHS); *Missouri Republican*, October 13, 1862; *Missouri Democrat*, October 28, 1862.

9. Peterson, *Freedom and Franchise*, 118–19.

10. William E. Parrish, *Missouri under Radical Rule, 1865–1870*, 4–5, 20; David D. March, "The Life and Times of Charles Daniel Drake," 56–58.

for the Union. Both Frank's supporters and the radicals accepted Lincoln's proclamation at face value. Apparently some of the latter, including Brown, expected that the final version, due January 1, would include Missouri, however, and expressed bitter disappointment when they learned that it would not.[11]

Failing to persuade Brown to become a candidate for Frank's congressional seat, the radical Republicans turned to Samuel Knox, a local attorney, while proslavery Democrats nominated Lewis V. Bogy. Frank continued a rigorous round of campaign appearances throughout September and October while working strenuously to raise his brigade. He also received invitations from Union men to address rallies elsewhere but generally avoided these unless he could use them as recruiting tools. In late October, John C. Fremont returned to St. Louis, ostensibly to testify at the court-martial trial of his former aide, Justus McKinstry. The radicals exploited this opportunity to stir up the German vote for Knox. The Blairs, Apo particularly, expressed deep resentment over this ploy, especially since Gratz Brown had played a major role in arranging the primary Fremont rally. Frank had made a hasty trip to Newport in late September to bring Apo back to St. Louis, and she entered into the campaign with great vigor.[12]

Missourians finally went to the polls on November 4. The state's population growth had resulted in the gain of a congressional seat, which split St. Louis County into two new districts. In the southern district, Frank's old friend and ally Henry Blow ran unopposed. Blair carried the northern district over his two opponents, defeating Knox by a bare 153 votes, while Bogy trailed by another 2,000. Both Frank and Knox claimed fraud on the part of each other's supporters, and Knox later formally challenged the election.[13]

Congratulations for Frank came from around the state, together with reports of efforts by his supporters to secure a strong showing for President Lincoln's policies generally. In response to an inquiry from Lincoln, Frank

11. W. E. Smith, *Blair Family in Politics*, 2:203–7; Peterson, *Freedom and Franchise*, 120–21.

12. *Missouri Republican*, passim, September–October 1862; Thomas J. C. Fagg to FB, August 24, 1862, EBL to FPB, September 11, Apo to FPB, October 22, 1862, BLC; EBL to SPL, October 22, 28, November 13*, 1862, Apo to FPB, November 7, 1862, B-LP. Apo also had another campaign during this time, namely to secure an appointment to the Naval Academy at Annapolis for their oldest son, Andrew, aged fourteen. It also proved successful (Apo to FPB, September 28, 1862, B-LP; FPB to FB, October 3, 1862, Apo to Andrew, October 24, 1862, Andrew to Apo, November 11, 22, 1862, BLC).

13. Abstract of Election Returns, St. Louis County, November 4, 1862; FB to MB, November (n.d.), 1862, BLC.

exultantly wired the president: "We have elected 5 Republicans, one Eman-
cipationist Democrat, 2 Unconditional Union & 2 proslavery Democrats to
Congress. The Legislature is emancipation in both Branches on your plan
& secures two senators to support the Administration." This proved overly
optimistic, as did Preston Blair's reaction that "Frank's election has got us
out of the Fremont slough for all time." While a swing had obviously begun
toward some form of emancipation, it remained unclear at this point what
form it would take. The ensuing session of the legislature could not agree
on a course of action and so did nothing. Three of the new congressional
Republicans—Henry Blow, Benjamin F. Loan, and Joseph W. McClurg—
quickly moved into the ranks of the radicals. The issue of emancipation
continued to plague Missouri politics throughout the next two years as the
radicals forced Frank to move increasingly toward the right and eventually,
in the postwar era, work for the revival of the state's Democratic Party.[14]

In the midst of all this political activity, Frank also labored to recruit his
brigade. He had begun to grow restless about his long-term political future as
early as February 1862. Concerned with his continuing debts, which a political
career did little to help erase, he began to think about a military career as an
alternative, at least for the duration of the war. On February 11, Missouri's
two U.S. senators and four of her congressmen, including Frank's friend
James Rollins, petitioned President Lincoln to consider Frank for appointment
as major general and the command of an expedition "to operate against
Columbus and other points below on the Mississippi river." Three days
later, during a cabinet meeting, Secretary of War Stanton suggested a similar
arrangement. Attorney General Bates reported in his diary that the president
responded by saying the Mississippi expedition "was the greatest business
of all, and needed the highest general in that region. He added that it was
generally thought that a man was better qualified to do a thing because he
had learned how; and that in this case it was Mr. Blair's misfortune not to
have learned," which apparently ended the matter. To what extent Frank or
the other Blairs may have been involved in this particular move cannot be
ascertained.[15]

14. F. Rodman to FB, November 6, 1862, William S. Moseley to FB, November 11, 1862,
BLC; Lincoln to FB, November 14, 1862, in *Collected Works of Lincoln*, 5:496–97; FB to Lincoln,
November 14, 1862, Lincoln Papers; EBL to SPL, November 8, 1862, B-LP; Parrish, *Turbulent
Partnership*, 123–48.
15. EBL to SPL, February 3, 24, 28, 1862, B-LP; John B. Henderson and others to Lincoln,
February 11, 1862, BLC; Bates, *Diary of Bates*, 232.

Apparently the matter lay dormant for the remainder of the congressional session. As previously noted, Frank's father and others in early summer began urging his appointment as an aide to General McClellan, then on the Virginia peninsula. After visiting that front with the president, however, Frank declined, presumably preferring service in the West, which Stanton offered him. The *Missouri Republican* reported on July 18 that recruiting offices had opened in St. Louis in response to Lincoln's call for three hundred thousand volunteers but noted that the "business of recruiting is deadly dull." It expressed the hope that Blair's return would spur enlistments.[16]

By July 21, Frank was back in St. Louis, staying at Rose Bank with the Dicks, who occupied it as a wartime residence. He wrote Apo that he kept busy with recruitment efforts, which were going well. At a meeting in the Ninth Ward, Frank sought Irish recruits by alluding to "the threatening position of England—our hereditary enemy, and the hereditary enemy of the Irish race," apparently in reference to that nation's actions in the Trent affair. A few days later a mass meeting was held at the courthouse to encourage enlistments. Detained elsewhere, Blair did not appear until midway through the rally. In the interim, James Peckham, on his behalf, presented resolutions calling for the appointment of a fund-raising committee composed of two persons from each ward to assist in the organization. These resolutions also included demands for one hundred thousand dollars from the city council and county court to support the families of the volunteers during their absence. The crowd received these resolutions with "great demonstrations of applause," following which Charles D. Drake spoke on behalf of the effort—the last time he and Blair would appear on the same platform. When he finally arrived, Frank made a strenuous appeal that partisanship be laid aside in the effort to save the Union.[17]

By early August, Frank had filled five regiments and hoped to raise two or three more to make two brigades. Inquiries came from some who had served with him in the 1861 campaign, but were now assigned to other units, as well as from overseas wanting to know whether Prussian officers resigning their commissions there might expect American appointments if they came to the United States. With regard to Missouri Germans, however, Frank noted that "not a hundred Germans have enlisted under the last two calls of the President in this state and three or four Regiments have

16. *Missouri Republican,* July 16, 18, 1862.
17. FB to Apo, July 21, 1862, BLPLC; *Missouri Republican,* July 24, 28, 1862.

been disbanded for mutinous conduct. They have been utterly poisoned by Fremont's revolutionary programme." Blair alternately received both support and condemnation from the St. Louis press. The *Missouri Democrat* and the *Westliche Post* pursued an ambivalent posture, with the former professing support while also publishing damaging denunciations from the latter. The *Anzeiger des Westens,* now managed by Boernstein, gave its strong support as did the faithful *Evening News* and Frank's own *Union.* The more conservative *Missouri Republican* also came to his assistance.[18]

By mid-August, Blair had received his commission as brigadier general, which he promptly accepted. The question now remained as to where and when his troops would be called into service. Frank had written his father at the end of July asking him to ascertain the president's reaction to his leading an expedition against the Texas coast, a command that eventually went to Nathaniel Banks. He reminded Preston of the earlier appeal of the Missouri congressional delegation that he have an active command as a major general. One of Blair's concerns dealt with General Halleck, who recently had been called east as general-in-chief. Frank believed him friendly but also feared that Halleck might hold his lack of a military background against him. In a separate letter to Montgomery, he put it succinctly, "The robes of West Point must cease to be sacred and the President must let the nation go 'on its muscle.'" Still, he urged that Montgomery "cultivate [Halleck] to advantage."[19]

Before this issue could be resolved, additional complications arose. In late July, a group of prominent Unionists, including Frank, met in St. Louis to discuss their concern over the chaotic environment throughout the state. When General Halleck left St. Louis in early April to take personal charge of operations in Tennessee and Mississippi, prior to his promotion to Washington, Brig. Gen. John Schofield received temporary command with the brief instruction to "take care of Missouri" in Halleck's absence. Eventually Halleck agreed on June 1 to the establishment of the Military District of Missouri under Schofield's command. The latter forwarded many of the regular troops from Missouri to the campaign east of the Mississippi, leaving the state largely dependent on local militia. Although Schofield, working with Governor Gamble, sought to beef up this force by conscription and take

18. EBL to SPL, July 31*, August 5, 1862, B-LP; Fred Roever to FB, August 27, 1862, FB to FPB, October 8, 1862, BLC; Augustin J. Quinn to FB, July 21, 1862, Missouri State Archives; W. E. Smith, *Blair Family in Politics,* 2:146–47.
19. FB to FPB, July 31, 1862, FB to MB, September 13, 1862, B-LP; FB to MB, August 21, 1862, BLC.

other drastic measures to curtail guerrilla warfare, some of the more ardent
Unionists, especially in St. Louis, questioned this policy, doubting the loyalty
of many of the conscripted residents in the interior of the state.[20]

The St. Louis group decided to send a delegation, headed by Henry Blow,
to Washington to seek the appointment of a permanent military commander
who would act independently of Gamble in suppressing the guerrillas. They
wanted to make the state militia part of the regular Union military establishment while requiring a loyalty oath of all who enlisted. Frank became
embroiled in controversy when the Blow committee, in conference with
the president and Halleck, claimed that he had authorized them to ask for
Schofield's removal "for inefficiency." Halleck informed Schofield of this
move and wired Blair to confirm it. Frank denied seeking his good friend's
removal. Rather, "I think the State military organization should be disbanded
as soon as practicable, and a military commander in the State authorized
without respect to Gov. Gamble."

When Schofield sought personal assurances, Frank gave him a copy of
the letter to Halleck, while reiterating his concerns. To complicate matters
further, however, several of Blair's close friends, including his brother-in-
law Franklin Dick, sought Frank's appointment as Schofield's replacement.
The matter was finally resolved on August 12 by the appointment of Maj.
Gen. Samuel R. Curtis as commander of a newly created Department of the
Missouri with Schofield assuming command of a field army under him.[21]

In the wake of the St. Louis meeting, Frank wrote Montgomery that he
believed the state militia should be mustered into federal service, even as
his Home Guards had been a year earlier. The latter group had become
irritated because they originally understood that they would not see service outside the state. When they were ordered elsewhere, it increased the
disaffection of the German element generally in relation to Blair and his
campaign. After the matter escalated with the Blow committee's trip to
Washington, Frank explained to his brother that he had been called into
the St. Louis meeting at the last minute and without a prior agenda. He

20. Parrish, *Turbulent Partnership*, 90–95.

21. Resolutions of St. Louis group, August 4, 1862, Halleck to FB, August 12, 1862, FB
to Halleck, August 12, 1862, Schofield Papers; S. T. Glover to MB, August 6, 1862, FB to
MB, August 8, 1862, Blow to Lincoln, August 12, 1862, Glover to Lincoln, August 20, 1862,
Lincoln Papers; Arden R. Smith to FPB, August 19, 1862, F. A. Dick to FPB, August 25,
1862, B-LP; Schofield, *Forty-six Years in the Army*, 60–62; *OR*, 1:13:552, 562–4. Even Apo
supported the move "to get rid of Schofield & Gamble" in the hope that "they would make
you military governor" (Apo to FB, August 23, 1862, BLC).

outlined his general dissatisfaction over certain militia actions in relation to the guerrillas and cited specific examples. He disclaimed any knowledge that the resolutions would be carried to Washington and denied any desire to have Schofield's place. Frank reported that he had tried to smooth things over with Blow following his return but could not be certain of success. As it turned out, Blow moved into the radical ranks following the November election, and the two men became as bitter enemies as they had once been close friends.[22]

Yet another crisis arose in September when Frank received a letter from William D. Wood, the acting adjutant general of Missouri, accusing several Blair officers with illegal impressment. Apparently a Captain Welsh had roused several citizens from their beds and compelled them to enlist. In the other cases, according to Frank, "under the direction of an officer of Police [his agents] made arrests of some bad characters who afterwards enlisted in the Regiment preferring it to the punishment usually inflicted upon vagrants." Frank deplored such action as "reprehensible" but did not believe that it warranted the withholding of the officers' commissions. When Wood proceeded to revoke the commissions anyway, Frank protested that such authority rested solely with the president. Wood responded that under War Department General Orders 75 the officers remained "under the exclusive control of the Governors" until the regiments had been fully organized and the muster rolls completed. Unwilling to accept this interpretation, Blair argued that the special order authorizing him to recruit substituted his authority for that of the governor. While Wood protested, Frank apparently won out in the end.[23]

With the November election behind him, Frank became increasingly anxious for his military orders. He told his father and Montgomery that he would willingly serve either with the Nathaniel Banks expedition in Texas or under Maj. Gen. John A. McClernand, like Blair a civilian soldier but one who had

22. FB to MB, August 8, 1862, Lincoln Papers; FB to MB, August 19, 1862, B-LP. Montgomery wrote Frank that he needed to talk to Blow about keeping the faith. "He is I believe personally attracted to you but is swinging off from you politically under the fancy that his political interests demand it" (MB to FB, August 29, 1862, BLC). Secy. of the Treasury Salmon P. Chase noted in his journal for September 9, 1862, that he proposed at a cabinet meeting that day the creation of a Trans-Mississippi Department with Cassius Clay as commander and Frank as his associate, but there is no other record of this (*The Salmon P. Chase Papers*, 1:376).

23. Wood to FB, September 18, October 16, 17, 1862, FB to Governor Gamble, September 18, October 16 (two letters), 1862, BLC; F. A. Dick to FPB, September 12, 1862, Dick to MB, September 12, 1862, B-LP.

seen fighting at Shiloh. McClernand had recently sold Lincoln and Secretary of War Stanton on a campaign to open the Mississippi River. Frank's orders finally came from the president on November 17, directing him to Helena, Arkansas, to join the McClernand expedition.[24]

Preston Blair wrote Apo that Lincoln was "very anxious to promote all Frank's aspirations, but I think his War Secretary and his General-in-Chief do not accord a cheerful acquiescence." Frank, meanwhile, protested that Curtis had detached some of his units to other places and asked Montgomery to have them restored. This produced the desired effect; and, in early December, Frank boarded boats at St. Louis with six regiments (five infantry and one cavalry) and "the battery of my old regiment." Just prior to his departure a committee of Union ladies of St. Louis called on him at his home to present him with a ceremonial sword, which he received with the hope that it "may prove an incentive to deeds which will entitle me to wear it."[25]

Arriving in Helena on December 18, Frank found that most of the essentials had made it down the river, but the unit also had a great deal of equipage that they did not need. He informed Apo that there was considerable sickness (measles, smallpox, varioloid) in the camp, while the troops were raw and would need discipline. He was homesick for her and the children already, particularly in the morning, but this wore off as the day went on and he got busy.[26]

Action came quickly. On December 22, Blair and four of his regiments found themselves part of an expedition under Maj. Gen. William T. Sherman, to whom Frank had offered the Missouri command a year and a half earlier. Sherman headed downriver as part of a three-pronged operation to take Vicksburg. The new campaign called for Sherman to attack the Confederates on the north approach to the city while Grant operated in the vicinity of the Yalobusha River in northern Mississippi to prevent its reinforcement. Banks, commanding in northeastern Louisiana, would move up against Port Hudson below Vicksburg. Meanwhile, McClernand, who thought he was to head the expedition but who was anathema to Grant and Sherman, dallied in Illinois,

24. FB to FPB, n.d., FB to MB, November 11, 1862, BLPLC; FB to MB, n.d., November (n.d.), November 17, December 6, 1862, FPB to Apo, November 24, 1862, BLC; FB to FPB, n.d., Apo to FPB, December 12, 1862, B-LP; Lincoln to FB, November 17, 1862, in *Collected Works of Lincoln*, 5:498–99; *OR*, 1:13:794; 1:17:2:348–50.

25. FB to MB, December 6, 1862, Committee of Union Ladies to FB, November 10, 1862, FB to Ladies, November 12, 1862, FPB to Apo, November 24, 1862, BLC; Lincoln to Curtis, November 20, 1862, in *Collected Works of Lincoln*, 5:517; Apo to FPB, December 12, 1862, B-LP.

26. FB to Apo, December 18, 1862, BLPLC; FB to Apo, December 19, 1862, BLC.

unaware of the change of plans, which his two detractors hastened to put into effect before his arrival.[27]

The Sherman expedition left Helena on the afternoon of the twenty-second aboard seventy transports with six or eight gunboats. Sgt. Maj. E. Paul Reichhelm of the Third Missouri Infantry later remembered, "It was a grand sight and inspired us all with the greatest confidence of success." On the way down, they were harassed by Confederate guerrillas along the riverbank. Sherman landed troops, who chased the guerrillas and burned the neighboring plantations in retaliation. Reichhelm recalled "the horrible grandeur of hundreds of burning buildings."

The expedition arrived at the mouth of the Yazoo River on Christmas Day. Frank, commanding the First Brigade of Maj. Gen. Frederick Steele's Fourth Division, was confident of success, assuring Apo that the enemy "must suffer that they may realize the suffering they have inflicted." The troops disembarked the next morning and, hampered by driving rain, slowly made their way across a tangled avenue of swamps and bayous encrusted with Confederate abatis, pushing the enemy's pickets before them. Reaching Chickasaw Bayou, they found themselves confronting a considerable body of water beyond which stood steep bluffs atop an open plateau, again laced with abatis. From there the entrenched Confederates could lay down a direct and enfilading cross fire. Having silenced the battery protecting the approach to the bluffs on the twenty-seventh, the troops bivouacked for the night.

The following day, Frank pushed his men across the bayou under heavy fire, in support of a badly wounded Maj. Gen. Morgan L. Smith, and managed to silence the enemy batteries and rifle pits on the other side. Instructed by Sherman to reconnoiter the enemy positions on the far side of the bayou, Blair found the day too far spent to accomplish that mission.

On the twenty-ninth, Sherman ordered a general assault. Frank's brigade on the left of the advancing columns carried out its assignment with great bravery. Making their way with much difficulty through the abatis and across a small slough, the men scaled the high banks with impetuous abandon, with an enthusiastic Blair in the forefront of the fighting. His horse "floundered to his belly in the quick sand slough," but Frank gained the other side and, waving his sword, urged his men on. Having cleaned out one set of rifle pits halfway up the slope, some of the men sought cover there, but Frank

27. FB to Apo, December 22, 1862, BLC; Bruce Catton, *Grant Moves South,* 332–40; John F. Marszalek, *Sherman: A Soldier's Passion for Order,* 202–5.

routed them out with his sword. The other officers followed his example, and the assault continued. The brigade had nearly reached the summit when forced to fall back under heavy enemy fire. Sergeant Major Reichhelm, coming on the scene with Brig. Gen. C. E. Hovey's Second Brigade, remembered seeing what was left of Blair's force falling back. "The sight was horrible and discouraging," he wrote, "and the frightful description of the deadly struggle, and the strength and position of the enemy, which the Blair men gave us, was enough to discourage veterans." General Steele simply reported that Frank "led his brigade with intrepidity in the face of all these obstacles."[28]

A few days later Frank wrote Apo proudly, "My brigade did its duty & did the work allotted to it but it was not well supported & we failed. I did not receive a scratch altho I went up to the enemy's last entrenchments." Yet, the Confederates had successfully defended the bluff. Unbeknownst to Sherman, although he heard a rumor to that effect, Grant's campaign in northern Mississippi had bogged down as a result of raids against his supply line by Earl Van Dorn and Nathan Bedford Forrest. Banks, meanwhile, had gone up the Red River instead of moving against the Confederates at Port Hudson.

As the weary federal troops held their positions below the bluff the night of the twenty-ninth, a pelting rain made them even more miserable. Heavy fog set in the next morning and forced the abandonment of plans for a second attack at Haynes' Bluff farther up the Yazoo, which would have included Frank's brigade. Sherman now retreated back to the Mississippi. His forces had received some 1,800 casualties out of 32,000 engaged. Frank's brigade had suffered heavily with 636 killed and wounded, including 41 officers. Blair noted in his official report, "The list of casualties in the regiments under my command, embracing nearly one-third of the entire number who went into the field, attests the courage and obstinacy with which they struggled for victory, and which natural obstacles alone placed beyond our grasp."[29]

Arriving back on the Mississippi, Sherman found McClernand, who promptly took command of the troops. McClernand announced his plan to move back up the river to capture Arkansas Post, some fifty miles up

28. *OR*, 1:17:1:606–10, 637–39, 650–58; "Memorandum E. Paul Reichhelm, Sergeant Major, Third Infantry, Missouri Volunteers, U.S.A. 1862," unpublished manuscript, Edward Paul Reichhelm Papers; Arden R. Smith to MB, December 31, 1862, BLC; Sherman, *Memoirs*, 1:291–92; Franc B. Willkie, *Pen and Powder*, 242–43; Faunt L. Senour, *Major General William T. Sherman and His Campaigns*, 110.

29. *OR*, 1:17:1:606–10, 653–56, 17:2:888; FB to Apo, December 31, 1862, BLC; "Memorandum E. Paul Reichhelm," Reichhelm Papers.

the Arkansas River, which had been a source of irritation for some time against Union shipping on the Mississippi. In the subsequent battle there on January 12, 1863, Frank's brigade was held in reserve because of its earlier heavy losses.[30]

Frank and his brigade had fought valiantly at Chickasaw Bayou. He later contended that he could have taken the bluffs but for lack of support from Brig. Gen. George W. Morgan, commanding the Third Division on his right. The latter responded that the terrain facing him made this impossible, however, a claim others substantiated. A frustrated Blair found it difficult to accept failure, having come, as he believed, so close to success. Thomas C. Fletcher, who commanded the Thirty-first Missouri and was captured in the assault and later exchanged, encountered Frank during the siege of Vicksburg. As the two talked, Frank "laughingly remarked to me that I had literally obeyed his order and gone 'straight to Vicksburg.' " When Blair reiterated his charges against Morgan, Fletcher replied that even with that general's support, he did not believe they could have taken the bluffs.[31]

Frank never really accepted that. Tired and frustrated, he wrote his father a long letter while en route to Arkansas Post. He complained bitterly that the expedition had failed because of Sherman's inability to concentrate what forces he had against a central point along the Vicksburg defenses. Even so, Frank wrote, they could have carried the Chickasaw Bluffs if Morgan had not held back six or seven regiments while he was "skulking" behind the lines. Blair also criticized Col. John F. DeCourcy, commanding the Third Brigade of Morgan's Third Division, for not moving beyond the first rifle pits on the assault up the bluffs. Still seeking to wield political influence, even while in the field, he urged his father to speak against DeCourcy's proposed promotion to brigadier when it came before the Senate.[32]

In spite of the disagreeable aspects of the campaign so far, Frank told Apo that he had no regrets about coming south as opposed to returning to Congress. John Witzig, who served as Blair's courier, told Apo that many of the German officers and enlisted men alike believed that Sherman deliberately intended to sacrifice Frank, an observation she passed on to the family in Washington. In an effort to keep busy and learn more about her husband's activities, Apo daily visited the soldiers' hospitals in St. Louis to talk to

30. *OR*, 1:17:1:757, 768–70; FB to Apo, January 14, 1863, BLPLC; Senour, *Sherman and His Campaigns*, 115.

31. Sherman, *Memoirs*, 1:435–44.

32. FB to FPB, January 6, 1863, B-LP. DeCourcy subsequently resigned. *OR*, 1:17:2:888.

the wounded of Frank's brigade, all of whom, she reported, "speak kindly of him."[33]

Frank and other officers of Steele's division voiced additional negative sentiments to reporters accompanying the expedition back to Arkansas Post. Many of these correspondents were good friends from St. Louis. Sherman had a long-running feud with reporters over what he considered leaks of military information. He had banned them on the expedition to Vicksburg, but several had managed to get aboard the transports anyway and consequently had witnessed the disaster at Chickasaw Bayou. Blair's observations simply reinforced their already negative feelings concerning Sherman's competency. Arden R. Smith, Frank's adjutant, wrote Montgomery on January 3, "I might say things to you but I leave you to judge from the papers which will be very heavy on Sherman. The Herald, Times and World are represented here. I think they will do justice to Gen. Blair. I hope so. They are very bitter against Sherman as he sought to interfere with their press privileges."[34]

Whether Frank and his fellow officers considered their conversations off the record or not is unclear. Whatever the case, they poured out their frustrations. Two of Frank's reporter friends, Franc Willkie of the *New York Times* and Thomas W. Knox of the *New York Herald,* in particular, took it all in and proceeded to write blistering accounts from their somewhat limited perspective. They sought to avoid Sherman's censorship unsuccessfully, although in looking at Knox's initial letter, brought to him by his staff, the general did not seem unduly disturbed. Failing to get their original dispatches approved, the two reporters returned to Cairo and put together a second set from memory and with what notes they could smuggle out with them. Now even more embittered by their experiences, they excoriated Sherman and dredged up stories of his past difficulties at Shiloh and elsewhere, including rumors of insanity.[35]

Both Knox's and Willkie's stories appeared on January 18. Six days later copies reached Sherman's new headquarters at Milliken's Bend, Louisiana, above Vicksburg. Soon other papers, including the *Missouri Republican* and the *Missouri Democrat,* arrived with similar accounts. The former particularly praised Frank for his gallant assault. Enraged by the critical nature of the press

33. Apo to FPB, n.d., Apo to MB, January 15, 1863, BLC; EBL to SPL, January 23, 1863, Apo to FPB, January 24, 1863, B-LP.

34. Smith to MB, January 3, 1863, BLC; Crozier, *Yankee Reporters,* 291–93. On January 8, Smith forwarded a copy of General Steele's report, which had a strong commendation for Frank, for whatever use might be made of it (Smith to MB, January 8, 1863, BLC).

35. Crozier, *Yankee Reporters,* 293–97; John F. Marszalek, *Sherman's Other War: The General and the Civil War Press,* 118–24.

reports, Sherman determined to make an example of one of the reporters and settled on Knox, whom he arrested and questioned extensively. In the interview Knox indicated Frank as his primary source of information.[36]

Having already suspected that, Sherman had queried Frank earlier in the presence of Generals Steele and David Stuart, at which time Blair had denied any wrongdoing. Now Sherman addressed a blunt letter to Frank with twenty-two pointed questions relative to the latter's views of the action at Chickasaw Bayou. Incensed, Blair replied with equally pointed answers. "It is a matter of mortification to me to receive such a letter from you after the conversation which occurred between yourself, Generals Steele and Stuart, and myself," he remonstrated. He reiterated that none of his staff was responsible for an earlier critical letter in the *Missouri Republican*, but assured Sherman that he had since ascertained its author and reported the matter to General Steele.[37]

Sherman accepted Frank's denial at face value while telling him that he did not expect any repetition of the need for such correspondence. He also politely explained the larger picture at Chickasaw Bayou with the implication that those in the forefront of action might not always understand the total scene. A month later, Sherman wrote his foster father, Thomas Ewing, still reflecting his 1861 sentiments, that "Frank Blair is a 'disturbing element.' I wish he was in Congress or a Bar Room, anywhere but our Army."[38]

Both men eventually put this situation behind them. Indeed, Frank shortly thereafter wrote to Montgomery, "Sherman is the only man of brains in this army and he ought to have the command. Grant is disposed to take his advice and therein shows good sense but he is surrounded by a pack of fools who manage to make what Sherman recommends miscarry in the execution."[39] As subsequent events would show, Frank and Sherman worked harmoniously together throughout the rest of the war; and Sherman came to have great respect for Blair's military ability. Frank's opinion of Grant would also change by the end of the Vicksburg campaign.

To the consternation of McClernand and the delight of Sherman, General Grant arrived at Milliken's Bend at the end of January to take overall

36. Marszalek, *Sherman's Other War*, 119–29; *OR*, 1:17:2:896; EBL to SPL, January 23, 1863, B-LP.

37. *OR*, 1:17:2:581–86.

38. Ibid., 587–90; Joseph H. Ewing, *Sherman at War*, 109.

39. FB to MB, March 10, 1863, BLC. At Knox's subsequent court-martial trial, Frank served as a character witness for his friend, together with General Steele and William E. Webb, a reporter for the *Missouri Republican* (Marszalek, *Sherman's Other War*, 133).

command of the combined forces. He found his troops scattered along the west bank of the Mississippi just above Vicksburg in camps placed on narrow levees or still on their transports because of heavy rains, which left the swampy ground saturated. With Vicksburg well protected on its high bluffs along the opposite bank, Grant puzzled over the best approach to that city as the high water levels made it difficult for him to move in any direction. Frank wrote regularly to Apo during this time and even managed an occasional letter to his daughter Christine. He reported that he was sharing a house with General Steele. He had been quite sick from swamp fever and bad water but was cheered by the arrival of Apo's brother George, who had visited him en route to Paducah, where he was beginning a new enterprise.[40]

Grant had begun work on a canal along the west bank in the hope of using it to bypass the Vicksburg batteries on the Mississippi, and some of Frank's troops were busily engaged in this enterprise. Although he understood Grant's reasoning for digging the canal, Frank complained, "[T]his business of working our men to death when there are hundreds of thousands of negroes who could be had to do the work in the mud & water is disgusting beyond all measure." About this time, a horse kicked him on the right leg during an inspection tour of the levee along the river. Arden Smith reported that his heavy riding boot saved Frank's leg from being broken. He returned to work after a few days' recuperation, but the leg continued to bother him for weeks thereafter. Frank's sentimental side revealed itself when he sent Apo some hair from the mane of "my old sorrel horse," who had died of lockjaw caused by a slight wound in the rump. "It is like losing a dear friend," he wrote. "He was a noble animal, spirited but gentle and fearless in battle."[41]

Promotion to major general finally came in mid-March. Lincoln had first proposed it at the end of January; but, with a number of others, it got caught

40. FB to Apo, January 23, February 10, 1863, BLC; FB to Christine, February 16, 1863, Blair Family Papers, MHS. George Alexander, Apo's oldest brother, had lived with the Blairs in St. Louis throughout much of the 1850s, engaging in various businesses. Most recently he had failed in the cartridge business and had talked of enlisting in the army, but he apparently changed his mind. He continued off and on with Frank at Youngs Point prior to Grant's final assault on Vicksburg. About that time he leased two Louisiana cotton plantations. Sometime later, he approached the *Times* reporter Franc Willkie for assistance with General Grant in getting a permit to ship his cotton out, which Willkie provided. After the war, Frank would join George in a similar enterprise (EBL to SPL, April 8, June 27*, July 7*, 1862, February 28, March 29, 1863, Apo to FPB, May 2, 1863, B-LP; George Alexander to Mira Alexander, April 21, 1864, BLC; Willkie, *Pen and Powder*, 225–27).

41. Apo to MB, February 9, 1863, FB to Apo, February 23, 1863, BLPLC; Smith to Apo, February 24, 1863, B-LP; FB to Apo, February 27, April 2, 1863, BLC.

up in the political game between the president and the radicals in the Senate. Disgusted, Lizzie wrote Phil, "Even his ultra friends for whom he has done so much are no longer friends." Preston Blair lobbied behind the scenes to push the promotion through and finally carried the day with the help of a number of Democratic senators on March 13 by a vote of twenty-eight to seven.[42]

When the news reached the Mississippi, Grant gave Frank command of the Second Division of Sherman's Fifteenth Corps, replacing David Stuart, whose permanent appointment as brigadier had failed to win Senate approval. Some of Stuart's men expressed resentment at the change, considering Blair's appointment as "being notoriously a political one." Brig. Gen. Morgan L. Smith, who had been wounded at Chickasaw Bayou, spoke to the division and praised Blair for his actions there, which allayed many of their concerns. Frank wrote Apo that, although pleased with the new responsibility, it meant leaving his old brigade, which would remain in Steele's division. He had been swamped with applications for staff positions but intended to have "a plain and unpretending sort of staff who will do the work I appoint and no more." Concerned about reports that she had not been well, Frank urged Apo and the children to spend the summer in Newport, where son Andrew was in naval training, and promised to join her there if he could get a short furlough at the end of the campaign.[43]

Arden Smith wrote Apo about this same time that General Steele had presented Frank with a new horse, a "really very handsome present," to replace the one he had lost. Frank was still having trouble with boils on his injured leg, which had to be bandaged each morning, but "in all other respects he is in capital health and spirits." He had issued "something like a special order for the staff to have their hair cut." After one of the lieutenants submitted first to the operation and emerged "with a full penitentiary chop, the effect was unique and contagious," whereupon Frank and the other officers followed suit. "It will be healthy if not handsome in style," Smith assured her. "It is not too much to say that the General is by far the most popular general officer here," the adjutant boasted. "You can almost at any time see half a dozen horses of generals, colonels and such small fry tied to the fence."[44]

42. EBL to SPL, January 31, February 1, 21, 26, March 2*, 4*, 10*, 13*, 1863, B-LP.

43. *OR*, 1:24:3:171–72; *The Story of the Fifty-fifth Regiment, Illinois Volunteer Infantry in the Civil War, 1861–1865*, 229; FB to Apo, March 15, 26, April 2, 6, 14, 1863, BLC; Apo to Apolline Hankey, April 10, 1863, BLPLC.

44. Smith to Apo, March 9, 1863, BLC. James E. Yeatman, the head of the Western Sanitary Commission at St. Louis, reported similarly to Apo upon his return from a visit with Frank

Franc Willkie, the *New York Times* reporter, who saw a great deal of Frank during this period, later provided an excellent description:

> He was a most interesting man in every respect. Tall, well-formed, with a "sandy" complexion, light-gray eyes, heavy mustache, clean-shaved face, and a fine forehead covered with a mass of reddish hair, *distinguished* in style and bearing, he was handsome and commanding. He was slow and deliberate in speech, like one accustomed to addressing large audiences; he was versatile, doing everything well, from leading a charge to uncorking a bottle, and in all instances characterized by a calm, dispassionate manner and a movement full of dignity. He never seemed to have the slight knowledge of the composition of fear,—if he did, he concealed the fact so completely that on no occasion was its existence discovered. In conversation he was a polite, attentive listener, and an engaging, unassuming talker. Beneath all his outward calmness he had a tremendous force,—a fact which was demonstrated by the momentum with which he threw his columns against the bristling, deadly heights of Chickasaw Bayou.[45]

During this lax time, Adj. Gen. Lorenzo Thomas came to the Mississippi valley to enlist former slaves into military service. Frank, who had previously opposed such a policy, now came around to its support, perhaps, in part, because Thomas was empowered "to dismiss and to commission officers according as they were for or against the new policy without referring their cases to Washington." On April 21, Frank assembled his division at his headquarters, forming it into a hollow square. There they heard Thomas explain the new policy and listened to speeches from Sherman, Blair, and one of the German colonels in his native language, favoring arming the blacks and placing them under white officers. The men responded with mixed emotions. One recalled that the Fifty-fifth Illinois voted overwhelmingly for the plan. The troops quickly turned their attention to other matters, however, as the campaign heated up.[46]

In mid-April, Grant made his move. A Union fleet of seven ironclads, three transports, and ten barges ran the Vicksburg batteries on the night of April 16,

---

that spring. She wrote her father-in-law, "I hear he is *the* man among the soldiers" (Apo to FPB, March 18, 1863, BLC). Frank finally went to Milliken's Bend and had his leg lanced by one of the army surgeons there (FB to Apo, April 6, 1863, BLC).

45. Willkie, *Pen and Powder*, 244.

46. John Eaton, *Grant, Lincoln and the Freedmen: Reminiscences of the Civil War*, 53–55; Walter George Smith, *Life and Letters of Thomas Kilby Smith, Brevet Major General United States Volunteers, 1820–1887*, 289–90; Edward E. Schweitzer Diaries and correspondence; Owen Francis Diary; C. E. Affeld Diary; *Story of the Fifty-fifth Illinois*, 226–27.

with the loss of only one boat, putting them below the city from whence they could be utilized to move troops across to the east bank. Six days later, another six steamers pulling twelve barges duplicated the feat. A later attempt to move a towboat and barges did not prove quite as successful and resulted in the capture of four newspaper correspondents, who had sneaked aboard the towboat. First reports said the reporters had been killed, which brought a sarcastic note from Sherman to Frank that none of them had "floated" because they "were so deeply laden with weighty matter that they must have sunk. . . . In our affliction we can console ourselves with the pious reflection that there are plenty more of the same sort."[47]

On April 30, the transports began ferrying the first of Grant's troops, who had marched down the west bank, across the river from whence they would drive north to threaten Vicksburg. Much to their disappointment, Frank's division did not take part in this initial movement. Rather, they had been directed on the twenty-eighth, as part of Sherman's corps, to make a feint on Haynes' Bluff to the north as a diversion from the main attack. They steamed up the Yazoo River the following day and made a landing in force, putting up a show of making a strong assault. Once Grant's main body had gotten across, however, they were called back to Milliken's Bend to await further orders. Sherman placed Frank in charge of the entire Louisiana area as far west as Richmond with responsibility for providing escorts for the provision trains, which were moving supplies down the west bank to Hard Times in support of the Mississippi invasion.[48]

Finally ordered forward on May 7, the First and Second Brigades of Frank's division arrived at Hard Times on the tenth and crossed the following day. Along the way, they observed considerable destruction, including many mansions and outbuildings "having been burned to the ground." At one point along the line of march from Milliken's Bend, several wagons tipped over while crossing a stream. Among them was Frank's, from which the troops salvaged numerous bottles of whiskey and several barrels of beer. Even in the midst of an arduous campaign, Blair managed to care for the thirst of himself and his staff.[49]

47. Catton, *Grant Moves South*, 414–18, 430; *OR*, 1:24:3:278.

48. *OR*, 1:24:3:244–46, 260–64; W. G. Smith, *Life of Thomas Kilby Smith*, 39; FB to Apo, May 3, 1863, BLC; Terrence J. Winschel, "The First Honor at Vicksburg: The 1st Battalion, 13th U.S. Infantry," 4.

49. *OR*, 1:24:2:254–55, 3:284–86; W. G. Smith, *Life of Thomas Kilby Smith*, 39, 46; FB to Apo, May 7, 1863, BLPLC; Affeld Diary; Francis Diary.

Once across, Frank's column moved slowly. Contrary to Grant's later contention that he cut himself loose from his supply line at this point, Blair, in addition to all the wagons of his own division, escorted some two hundred other wagons with supplies needed for the rest of the army. Frank's troops encountered numerous blacks from surrounding plantations who announced they were en route to Grand Gulf to join the army. The weather was typical Mississippi May: warm and sultry. A brief shower made the roads difficult for a time. They finally reached Raymond on the fifteenth, having been joined en route by A. J. Smith's division. Here, the two divisions were ordered to cooperate with McClernand's Seventeenth Corps as the army moved cautiously west toward Vicksburg.[50]

The following day, May 16, brought the last major battle prior to the siege of Vicksburg, at Champion Hill. Blair's division, arriving late, moved quickly to join the attack on the left of the Union line in support of A. J. Smith. The forces opposite them had effectively covered the withdrawal of the remainder of the Confederate troops toward Vicksburg but were not impregnable. Some later believed that a more vigorous drive by Smith and Blair might have carried the day and resulted in the capture of the rebel force. The responsibility for failure lay with Smith, however, who halted their forces in spite of an order from McClernand to "attack the enemy vigorously."[51]

In the aftermath of Champion Hill, Frank was ordered to take his division quickly to the Big Black River and lay a pontoon bridge across to accommodate the rest of Sherman's corps. He moved out promptly on the morning of the seventeenth, pushing past Smith's division. By the time Sherman arrived at noon, he found Blair with the pontoon train in position, having dispersed a Confederate outpost on the opposite bank. The pontoon bridge was quickly put down, and two of Sherman's three divisions crossed before nightfall with the third following the next morning. Some of Frank's men captured a group of Confederates, whom they found "universally despondent" and despairing of any hope of holding Vicksburg against the advancing Union forces.[52]

50. *OR*, 1:24:2:254 55, 3:300, 306–7; W. G. Smith, *Life of Thomas Kilby Smith*, 46; "The Vicksburg Campaign, 1862–1863," W. T. Gardner Memoir, 28, 33; Francis Diary; Affeld Diary.

51. *OR*, 1:24:2:31–32, 254–56, 3:300, 306–7, 311–19; W. G. Smith, *Life of Thomas Kilby Smith*, 46–47; Edwin C. Bearss, *The Campaign for Vicksburg*, 2:523–24, 548, 570–71, 591, 617, 625; M. L. Haney, *Pentecostal Possibilities*, 179.

52. *OR*, 1:52:1:358, 24:2:143, 256, 3:322; W. G. Smith, *Life of Thomas Kilby Smith*, 40; Ulysses S. Grant, *Personal Memoirs*, 1:523–27; Senour, *Sherman and His Campaigns*, 126–27; Bearss, *Campaign for Vicksburg*, 2:660–61; Sherman, *Memoirs*, 1:349.

Frank's division led the advance toward Vicksburg early the next morning, May 18, hardly having time to eat breakfast before taking up the march. Once there, they formed on the left of Sherman's corps, which occupied the extreme right of the line against the Confederate entrenchments. These ran for miles from the hairpin bend of the Mississippi above the town to the muddy bottomlands below it. Grant, believing the Confederates demoralized, lost little time in moving against fortress Vicksburg. Sherman ordered Frank's men to storm Stockade Redan in their front. The Confederate defenses were strong, standing high above deep ravines, littered with felled timber, concealing treacherous sinkholes.[53]

Advancing to the felled timbers that afternoon, Frank's skirmishers laid down a withering fire against the rebels in the redan above them while his artillery blasted the Confederate positions. In the ensuing encounter, Missourians fought Missourians as the redan was defended by rebels under the command of Col. Francis M. Cockrell, who would later join Frank in rebuilding Missouri's Democratic Party after the war. Although Blair's men fought valiantly, it proved a hopeless task. Falsely believing that the enemy would quickly surrender once attacked, there had been no thought of providing scaling ladders for a final assault up the steep front of the rebel entrenchments. Frank and Sherman now found themselves confronted with the problem of withdrawing their forces with minimum further losses. They wisely decided to wait for the cover of night to accomplish the difficult maneuver. While James B. McPherson's and McClernand's corps had also been engaged that day, their line of action had been more remote from the main defenses than Sherman's. Blair's losses totaled more than six hundred killed, wounded, and missing, far exceeding any other unit of the army.[54]

Although the effort of the nineteenth by Frank's division and the others had met with a stinging repulse, Grant and his corps commanders decided to make yet another all-out assault on the Vicksburg defenses on the twenty-second. In the meantime, they were concerned with getting supplies from the Mississippi by way of the Yazoo. They found an acceptable road down through the Chickasaw Bluffs and quickly sent word to clear it of fallen trees and build a few bridges. The final leg comprised a levee along the eastern shore of Thompson's Lake, which proved convertible into a road. Frank

53. *OR*, 1:24:2:256–57; W. G. Smith, *Life of Thomas Kilby Smith*, 47–48; Catton, *Grant Moves South*, 450–52.

54. *OR*, 1:24:2:257; W. G. Smith, *Life of Thomas Kilby Smith*, 40–41, 48–52; Bearss, *Campaign for Vicksburg*, 3:745–46, 756–85.

assigned Capt. Herman Klosterman and the Eighty-third Indiana, which had been in the thick of the fighting the previous day, to get the job done; and the valiant Hoosiers managed it in less than twenty-four hours. Soon supplies rolled up to Grant's army along the route that Sherman, Frank, and the others had tried vainly to capture the previous December. One hardened veteran of the Fifty-fifth Illinois rejoiced, "The Hard tack and coffee were especially acceptable as we had been living for the three weeks on little else than the fresh meat that we got by foraging in the country through which we passed supplemented occasionally with a small quantity of corn meal."[55]

In preparation for the planned assault on the twenty-second, Sherman determined on the need for stronger artillery support, which also called for the construction of better roads along the periphery to move the weapons. With his men closest to the enemy lines, Frank sent sharpshooters along the abatis fronting Stockade Redan to protect the working parties. By the morning of the assault, he had a heavy artillery emplacement ranging in distance from three hundred to five hundred yards from the salient angle of the redan. Blair also assembled, at Sherman's orders, a storming party of 150 volunteers, who came to be known as the "forlorn hope." Made up of equal numbers from each of Frank's three brigades, it had the responsibility to charge up Stockade Redan at precisely ten o'clock, followed by Brig. Gen. Hugh Ewing's Third Brigade, while the artillery sought to soften up the enemy in their front. As Sherman and Blair listened, Col. Giles A. Smith promised the men sixty days' furlough if they captured the fort.

This time planks and ladders had been provided with which to traverse the ditch and scale the heights. The men were ordered to take sixty rounds of ammunition each and a canteen of water. When someone asked if they should take their haversacks, Frank curtly replied, "No, you can go without your dinners; you'll be inside the walls of Vicksburg or in hell for supper." Then, he jocularly added that they ought "not to eat and drink all the good things they found." This did little to endear Frank to his men, but "it served to indicate then the peril of our undertaking." Shortly before the charge, a commissary sergeant asked Pvt. John O'Dea of the Eighth Missouri if he would like some whiskey. He reminisced later that he declined the drink because "I then thought I had nine chances of going into eternity to one for escape, and did not care to knock at St. Peter's gate with thick tongue or

55. *OR*, 1:24:2:187–88; Bearss, *Campaign for Vicksburg*, 3:791–92; Gardner, "The Vicksburg Campaign," Gardner Memoir, 44–45.

tangled feet." O'Dea survived and won the Medal of Honor for valor while also claiming the whiskey later, "with scruples removed."

The rebels, many of them from the Confederate First and Fifth Missouri brigades, quickly realized what was happening and laid down a withering fire. In spite of the pleading of their officers, Frank's men took cover where they could find it, blocking the advance of those behind them. A few climbed the parapets, but it was impossible to hold them. Two men of the Eighth Missouri managed to plant the Union colors in front of the fort before one was cut down and the other captured. The Thirtieth Ohio, seeing it, had one of their sharpshooters guard the flag and "kill every man that attempted to haul it down." Blair ordered reinforcements from the Forty-seventh Ohio and Fourth West Virginia across the abyss along parallel approaches, but little was gained except to cover the "forlorn hope" as its survivors struggled to get back and reform behind newly established lines. Of the 150 who composed the "forlorn hope," nineteen were killed and thirty-four wounded, including two senior officers.[56]

At least Sherman's corps did not act alone in the assault of the twenty-second. All units of Grant's army advanced simultaneously although not altogether in harmony. Shortly before noon, Grant received a communiqué from General McClernand indicating that he was close to scoring a breakthrough but needed support. "A vigorous push ought to be made all along the line," McClernand urged. A second dispatch an hour later promised even better results, so Grant ordered part of McPherson's corps to his support. When Sherman learned of McClernand's concerns, he ordered a renewal of the attack by Frank's forces at two that afternoon. Although supported by part of Brig. Gen. James M. Tuttle's Third Division, the results were the same. In the end, Blair's division took three hundred casualties, including twenty-two officers, and Tuttle's two hundred with little to show for their heroic efforts. Flanking movements by other units of Sherman's corps also accomplished little.[57]

Grant now decided against further assaults and undertook siege operations. In late May, he received word that Confederate general Joseph E.

56. *OR*, 1:24:1:756–57, 2:162–63, 257–64, 268–73, 282, 52:1:62–63; "George Theodore Hyatt," newspaper clipping from *Chicago Sunday Times-Herald*, March 21, 1897, in 127th Illinois file, VNMP; John O'Dea, "A Forlorn Hope," in *Transactions of the McLean County [Illinois] Historical Society*, 1:477, in 8th Missouri file, VNMP; W. G. Smith, *Life of Thomas Kilby Smith*, 41–45, 53–56, 295–96; *Story of the Fifty-fifth Illinois*, 242–46; Gardner, "The Vicksburg Campaign," Gardner Memoir, 45–47; Affeld Diary; Francis Diary; J. W. McElravy to J. B. Allen, April 16, 1904 in 30th Ohio file, VNMP.

57. *OR*, 1:24:2:162–63, 259; Bearss, *Campaign for Vicksburg*, 3:819–58, 865–66.

Johnston might be gathering a force to the east in an effort to relieve Gen. John C. Pemberton. Reacting quickly, Grant organized an "Expeditionary Force" to investigate and entrusted its command to Frank, whose leadership and vigor thus far in the campaign had impressed him. Blair left the Vicksburg area on May 26 with twelve thousand men. During the next five days his force reconnoitered the region as far as the small village of Mechanicsburg, meeting no resistance. Still, he received reports from his cavalry that rumors had forty-five thousand Confederates concentrating near Jackson. While considering the numbers greatly exaggerated, Frank passed this information on to Grant with the added report that should he encounter Confederates in force he would fall back on the Yazoo in the hope that the gunboats there might offer support. Blair did find in the Mechanicsburg corridor an abundance of forage and supplies, which Johnston's army could use should it come that way. The fertile valleys yielded more than one thousand head of cattle and some two hundred horses and mules, which Blair's force seized. In addition, they destroyed some five hundred thousand bushels of corn, large quantities of bacon, and considerable cotton. Frank wrote his family that he was heartsick at the devastation he had wrought, but that wartime necessity demanded it.[58]

By the thirty-first, Frank had returned to Snyder's Bluff on the Yazoo, having experienced no opposition. From there his force could thwart any advance by Johnston should he come down the Mechanicsburg corridor. With the arrival of the Fifth Illinois Cavalry on June 1, Blair sought Grant's approval for another cavalry thrust up the corridor. Supported by infantry taken to Satartia by boat, this force could destroy a vital railroad bridge at Way's Bluff. While Grant approved this move, he did not allow Frank to accompany it. Rather, Blair, with most of his "Expeditionary Force," returned to their section of the investing lines before Vicksburg.[59]

Although the Confederate threat would ultimately prove greatly exaggerated, Grant took it seriously and appealed in several directions for reinforcements, which were soon forthcoming. Frank supported his entreaties with letters to Montgomery to be passed on to the president. He expressed his pleasure at hearing that the new military draft had been extended to Missouri. He hoped that it would catch a few radicals, "who busy themselves with assessments and with banishing helpless women and a few secesh from

58. *OR*, 1:24:1:89–92, 2:435–36, 3:352–56, 361–62; Grant, *Personal Memoirs*, 1:543–44; Affeld Diary; EBL to SPL, June 13, 1863, B-LP.
59. *OR*, 1:24:1:92–93, 3:373–74, 380.

the state and who make it a test of loyalty that a man shall be in favor of emancipation today rather than tomorrow or the next week."[60]

The reference to the banishment of women quite possibly reflected a letter he had received during the siege from his cousin Jo Shelby. Writing from his Confederate outpost at Jacksonport, Arkansas, Shelby "demanded" that his cousin take care of his wife who had recently been banished from Missouri to Kentucky and from there to Illinois. "I am surprised that any set of men should resort to such means as to vent their feelings on some innocent women," Shelby raged. Full of the same braggadocio and daring that characterized Frank, Jo sent his love to "cousin Apo," promising to call upon her as soon as Confederate forces entered St. Louis. Frank subsequently assisted Mrs. Shelby by arranging for her satisfactory return to Lexington and the home of Uncle Ben Gratz.[61]

Frank's division remained on the siege lines until Vicksburg's surrender on July 4. He told Montgomery that his troops had gotten so close to the enemy entrenchments that "I pitched a clod of dirt into one of their bastions from a point which we can work without exposure." One of his men later noted that, unlike Grant, who frequently visited the troops with only one or two orderlies accompanying him, Blair, when he went along the lines, was "usually attended by his whole staff and an escort of hundreds of cavalry, and the dust they kicked up shrouded half of Vicksburg."[62]

In mid-June, Frank picked up a copy of the *Memphis Evening Bulletin* and discovered an item titled "Congratulatory Order of General McClernand." In it, the general praised his troops for their exemplary behavior in the assaults of the twenty-second, leaving the impression that they, as opposed to McPherson's and Sherman's men, had borne the brunt of the fighting. Blair, whose men had been in the thick of the action on both the nineteenth and the twenty-second, naturally resented McClernand's insinuations, as did Sherman, to whom he showed the paper. Sherman passed the paper up to Grant, accompanied by protests from both himself and McPherson. The commander, who had been suspicious of McClernand's excessive claims during the battle of the twenty-second, now had the excuse he needed to get rid of his military rival. He did so. War Department regulations required the submission of all orders to headquarters prior to publication, something McClernand

60. FB to MB, June 8, 16, 1863, BLC; *OR*, 1:24:3:390.
61. Shelby to FB, May 11, 1863, B-LP; O'Flaherty, *General Jo Shelby*, 188.
62. FB to MB, June 16, 1863, BLC; J. J. Kellogg, *The Vicksburg Campaign and Reminiscences*, 60; cf. Catton, *Grant Moves South*, 459–60.

had failed to do. Given this circumstance, Grant relieved McClernand of his command and sent him back to Illinois, where he would remain for the rest of the war.[63]

Frank's division did not join the triumphal march into Vicksburg following the city's surrender. Grant had ordered Frank's men to join Sherman in a sweep to the east to keep an eye on the Confederate Joe Johnston, who was at Jackson. The federal forces began a siege of that city on the eleventh. Frank wrote Apo three days later that most Mississippians he had encountered seemed tired of the war. Johnston decided not to wait and see whether Sherman would launch an all-out attack. He evacuated Jackson on the seventeenth and retreated further east, leaving behind a ruined city, whose officials quickly surrendered to the Sherman forces.

Sherman designated Frank's division as the occupying force with orders to burn all cotton and other public property that might be used "for hostile purposes." Blair later told his family that he followed so closely on Johnston's heels that, upon arriving in Jackson, he was able to eat a dinner prepared for his rival, which the latter had left too hastily to enjoy. The next morning, while having breakfast, he found some papers dropped by John C. Breckinridge, containing "the curl of a childs hair." Both Johnston and Breckinridge had been close friends of the Blairs before the war, and such incidents revealed the sad reminders of prewar days. Meanwhile, Frank's cavalry joined other units of Sherman's command in destroying the railroads within a sixty-mile radius to prevent their use by the enemy in the future. Having accomplished this, Sherman's corps went into camp on the Big Black River to enjoy a well-earned rest.[64]

Frank quickly applied for and received a furlough. It had been a long campaign, and he and his men had experienced hard fighting at Chickasaw Bayou and throughout the Vicksburg siege. As such, they had participated in one of the critical turning points of the war; and, given Robert E. Lee's retreat from Gettysburg at the same time, many of them realized it. With General Banks's capture of Port Hudson and the successful defense of Helena against the combined Confederate forces of Theophilus Holmes and Sterling Price, Frank could truly admit to Apo that things looked hopeful for the final

---

63. *OR*, 1:24:1:162–65; Grant, *Personal Memoirs*, 1:546–47; FB to MB, June 23, 1863, BLC; EBL to SPL, July 3, 1863, B-LP.

64. *OR*, 1:24:3:524–43; FB to MB, July 4, 1863, BLC; FB to Apo, July 14, 1863, EBL to SPL, August 14*, 1863, B-LP; Virginia Jeans Laas, "Elizabeth Blair Lee: Union Counterpart of Mary Boykin Chesnut," 397; Marszalek, *Sherman*, 229–30; Catton, *Grant Moves South*, 482–83.

triumph of Union arms. Many of his comrades had been lost or captured, and Blair found himself emotionally drained. He could be proud of what his men had accomplished while saddened at the cost. For Frank, however, the war was far from finished, either militarily or politically. As he headed for St. Louis, he could not be certain of what lay ahead.[65]

Grant would observe of Frank in his *Memoirs:*

> General F. P. Blair joined me at Milliken's Bend a full-fledged general, without, having served in a lower grade. . . . I knew him as a frank, positive and generous man, true to his friends even to a fault, but always a leader. I dreaded his coming; I knew from experience that it was more difficult to command two generals desiring to be leaders than it was to command one army officered intelligently and with subordination. It affords me the greatest pleasure to record now my agreeable disappointment in respect to his character. There was no man braver than he, nor was there any who obeyed all orders of his superior in rank with more unquestioning alacrity.[66]

65. FB to Apo, July 14, 1863, EBL to SPL, August 4, 1863, B-LP; *OR,* 1:24:3:568.
66. Grant, *Personal Memoirs,* 1:573–74.

8

Fighting on Two Fronts

Frank returned to St. Louis on August 2, 1863, to a hero's welcome. Accompanied by his staff, aboard the steamboat *John Warner,* he was met some forty miles below the city by enthusiastic friends, who had hired the *City of Alton.* The two steamboats were tied together for the return upstream. Arriving at the St. Louis docks at ten o'clock that evening, they found hundreds of St. Louisans waiting to welcome them with torches and flags. A band played "We'll Rally round the Flag, Boys," as Blair and the celebrants from the two boats moved ashore. From there Frank was taken by carriage to his home on Washington Avenue. He declined speaking, undoubtedly tired after the long trip upriver. Two nights later, when his friends returned to serenade him, amid fireworks and band music, he spoke briefly, praising Generals Grant and Sherman for their leadership during the Vicksburg campaign. Invited friends then remained for a ball, which lasted the rest of the evening.[1]

Within a few days, Frank headed east to see Apo and the children, who were spending the summer in Newport. Apo met him in New York with Christine and Jim, and the group stopped in Philadelphia before continuing to Washington. Apo's brother, Andrew Alexander, who had joined the army in 1861 and risen to the rank of colonel, was now stationed in the capital. All the Blairs were eager to see him, especially in view of his rumored engagement to Eveline "Evy" Martin, the daughter of old family friends. When Frank

---

1. *Daily Union,* August 3, 5, 1863; *Missouri Democrat,* August 3, 5, 1863; *Missouri Republican,* August 4, 7, 1863; EBL to SPL, August 12*, 1863, B-LP.

returned to the army later that year he took Andrew with him as his assistant adjutant general.[2]

Frank, Apo, and the children reached Silver Spring on August 13, and the family sat up late that night listening to him report on his campaign exploits. The following day Frank visited Secy. of the Navy Gideon Welles, whom he regaled with his account of the Vicksburg campaign. Welles summed up his guest well in his diary: "Frank is as bold in words as in deeds, fearless in his utterances as in his fights [he] is uncalculating—impolitic it would be said—rash, without doubt, but sincere and patriotic to the core."[3]

On the fifteenth, Frank and Montgomery met with the president. The three discussed the recent Vicksburg campaign and recent requests from Texas refugees that Frank be sent there with troops. Lincoln, as well as the Blair family, was more concerned with having Frank in Washington for the upcoming congressional session. They agreed that he should remain in the House, where he could better serve as a spokesman for Lincoln's program, rather than stand for the Senate, as some of his Missouri friends were urging. In the meantime, the president extended Frank's military leave, giving him the opportunity to rest and spend more time with his family. Lizzie told Phil, "I rejoice that Frank has got his leave for I think tho he is sunburnt & red looking but not fat I doubt if he is as heavy as when he went south. Still he looks corpulent. He is covered with prickly heat like a child only far more thickly than any child I ever saw."[4]

On the sixteenth, Frank accompanied Lizzie into the city to go to church and then hurried off to No. 6 for an interview with Charles Dana of the *New York Tribune* before leaving for Newport for a month's respite. He was anxious to see the two younger children, whom Apo had left there with the Dicks. Apo remained exhausted after the long winter in St. Louis and concerned by the recent death of one of the Dick children from diphtheria. They found all well when they got to Newport, however. From there Blair wrote Grant, telling him about his leave being extended until October 1, while assuring him that "if you desired me to report for duty sooner than that date I should do so immediately." Grant replied promptly that since his division was "laying

2. FB to Apo, April 26, 1863, BLC; EBL to SPL, August 6*, 8, 12*, 1863, Eveline Martin to FPB, June 28, 1864, B-LP; Wilson, *Life of Alexander*, 49.
3. EBL to SPL, August 14*, 16*, 1863, B-LP; *Diary of Gideon Welles*, 1:405.
4. EBL to SPL, July 24*, 28*, 30*, August 16*, 1863, B-LP; Lincoln to FPB, July 30, 1863, Lincoln to FB, August 15, 1863, in *Collected Works of Lincoln*, 6:356, 388; MB, "Life of Senator F. P. Blair, Jr." (draft manuscript), BLC.

idle," there was no need for his immediate presence. He also thanked Frank for "the very flattering way in which you spoke of me in your St. Louis speech."[5]

Three weeks later, Frank and family were back in Silver Spring for a brief visit. Lizzie wrote Phil that her brother and the children seemed well but that Apo was thin and looked sick. Frank made the rounds of various offices, including the White House, and took a quick side trip to Virginia to visit the Army of the Potomac. Several individuals gave him encouragement to stand as the conservative candidate for Speaker in the new House in the hope of bringing the conservative Republicans, War Democrats, and old line Whigs together in a coalition in support of the president's policies. Not yet having given up on a return to the military, Blair remained noncommittal.[6]

Frank returned to St. Louis at the end of the month and quickly threw himself into the emerging political contest between the conservative and radical factions of Missouri's Republican Party. His conservative friends such as Sam Glover and James Broadhead, among others, had been warning of the radicals' growing political power since their late spring sweep of the St. Louis city elections.

Glover had written the president on April 13 of a further possible danger. Two recent arrivals from Ohio, one of whom came as a revenue agent, the other as a new editor of the *Missouri Democrat*, were devoted admirers of Secy. of the Treasury Salmon P. Chase. The *Democrat*, which had become increasingly critical of the Lincoln administration since the Fremont affair, was now building up Chase "as the very hope of the country." Glover claimed that the paper received money from cotton speculators, who benefited from their connections with the secretary. Chase had long been anathema to many conservative merchants because of his licensing restrictions on Mississippi River traffic. They had sent a committee to Washington in early September to seek the restoration of free trade but secured no major concessions. The conservatives strongly suspected Chase and his agents of using the licensing system to play to his political advantage. In addition, Glover indicted Secy. of War Edwin M. Stanton as a partner in the attempt to build up the *Democrat* with an order to military officials in St. Louis to print their notices only in that paper.[7]

5. EBL to SPL, August 17, 1863, B-LP; *OR*, 1:30:3:73; Grant to FB, August 23, 1863, in *The Papers of Ulysses S. Grant*, 9:199.

6. EBL to SPL, September 4, 5*, 7, 8, 9, 10*, 1863, B-LP; *Missouri Republican*, August 7, 1863; *Missouri Democrat*, August 14, 1863; *Diaries and Letters of John Hay*, 87.

7. Glover to Lincoln, April 13, 1863, Lincoln Papers; *Missouri Republican*, September 17, 1863. The impact of the trade restrictions on St. Louis is well analyzed in Wyatt Winton Belcher, *The Economic Rivalry between St. Louis and Chicago, 1850–1880*, 139–57.

To the conservative Glover and others, the emancipation issue further complicated the situation. The president's Emancipation Proclamation affected only those slaves in states still in rebellion, which left Missouri and the other border states to deal with slavery on their own. Glover claimed that provost marshals had begun freeing slaves in Missouri "on the mere statements of the slaves," even though their owners were loyal Unionists. Maj. Gen. Samuel R. Curtis, who had come to the command of the Missouri Department in the fall of 1862, had exacerbated the situation by instituting a policy of assessments and banishments against those suspected of disloyalty and establishing a rather broad definition of that term. In addition, the conservatives suspected Curtis of being secretly involved with the cotton speculators. Governor Gamble and others had pressed for his recall and finally secured his replacement by John Schofield in the late spring of 1863.[8]

The newly elected state legislature, while clearly favoring some form of emancipation, could not agree on how to accomplish it that spring. This led Governor Gamble in June to recall the old state convention, which had been governing in the legislature's place for the last two years. After much debate, the convention approved emancipation but postponed it until 1870, much too long for the growing radical coalition to accept.[9]

The radicals countered with their own convention in early September at Jefferson City, where they launched the Radical Union Party. Spearheaded by Charles D. Drake, they applauded Fremont's 1861 emancipation proclamation. They condemned the recent action of the state convention and demanded the immediate abolition of slavery in Missouri and the enlistment of free blacks into the armed forces. The Radicals also called for the termination of Missouri's Provisional Government and the removal of General Schofield. The latter had earlier arrested the *Missouri Democrat*'s editor, William McKee, for, among other "anti-Radical acts," publishing a confidential letter to Schofield from the president. The Radicals appointed a committee of seventy, headed by Drake, to go to Washington and lay their demands personally before Lincoln. Joined by a similar group from Kansas, the Radical delegation arrived in the capital on September 27, where they waited three days before securing an audience with the president. Meanwhile, the conservatives fired off their own

8. Glover to Lincoln, April 13, 1863, Lincoln Papers; Thomas T. Gantt to MB, April 25, May 1, 12, 1863, BLC. The controversy over Curtis is detailed in Parrish, *Turbulent Partnership*, 101–22, 149.
    9. Parrish, *Turbulent Partnership*, 136–48.

letters of support for Schofield to Montgomery Blair and Atty. Gen. Edward Bates for transmission to Lincoln.[10]

It was into this highly volatile atmosphere that Frank returned from Washington in late September, having passed the Radical delegation heading east en route. Before leaving Washington, he had written the president assailing Chase for misusing the licensing system to play favorites for political purposes and had the letter published in the *Missouri Republican*. The *Missouri Democrat* promptly accused him of supporting St. Louis's copperhead merchants, who, it said, wanted unrestricted trade with the rebel South. Revealingly, the *Democrat* claimed that Blair sought to thwart any attempt by Chase to secure his party's presidential nomination.[11]

Frank followed his letter with a biting speech to an overflow crowd at Mercantile Library on September 26. He attacked those who, he said, sought to prescribe their own conditions to the Union cause, namely, agreement with their stand on immediate emancipation. The whole question of emancipation and reconstruction should wait until the end of the war, he argued. Blair then advocated the organization of a broad-based Union Party, similar to those already coming into existence elsewhere, looking to the 1864 elections. To the dismay of the Radicals, he opposed proscription of the rebels after the war. Rather, he urged that they should be restored to a full franchise once they had taken a new oath of allegiance to the federal government. He once again assailed Chase's restrictive policies on the Mississippi in bitter terms and openly accused the secretary of being a political Judas, sitting in the cabinet while seeking to replace Lincoln. Frank reasserted his strong support for the president against all comers.[12]

Lizzie told Phil that Frank "has taken the course which I have urged for many weeks on Father. When F.[rank] was here he was silent & it was agreed

10. *St. Louis Daily Union,* July 11, 21, 1863; Parrish, *Turbulent Partnership,* 149–51, 161–64; Hart, "*Saint Louis Globe-Democrat,*" 75–78.

11. *St. Louis Daily Union,* September 21, 22, 1863; *Missouri Republican,* September 21, 1863; *Missouri Democrat,* September 23, 1863; *New York Times,* September 27, 1863.

12. *St. Louis Daily Union,* September 26, 28, 1863; *Missouri Republican,* September 27, 1863. Upon hearing of Frank's speech, Adm. David Porter, who commanded in the lower Mississippi, wrote General Sherman, only somewhat facetiously, "I have also been waiting to see General F. P. Blair, jr., come out with a book on trade generally in these waters, telling how the matter is to be arranged. He says the trade should be free and unrestricted, but he does not say how much of it will go to the rebels and how much to the plantations. I think the whole matter is contained in a nut-shell. The military status must determine the direction of trade" (*OR,* 1:31:1:781).

by others that the best thing to do was to do & say nothing in Missouri just now—I considered silence in active politicians as consent to schemes which seemed to me akin to Secession & so it seems I was not alone." The spirit was obviously catching. On October 5, Montgomery made an equally strong defense of the president's reconstruction policy, in opposition to that of the Radicals, at an Unconditional Union meeting in Rockville, Maryland. The two speeches essentially marked the beginning of an open war between the Blairs and the Radicals, which would have strong consequences for both.[13]

On September 30, Lincoln received the two Radical delegations from Missouri and Kansas in the East Room of the White House. Drake read a lengthy address of grievances and responded to detailed questions from the president, who refused to consider their request to remove Schofield while taking their other concerns under advisement. Schofield, meanwhile, unaware of all this activity, had forwarded through General Halleck a series of incendiary articles from the Radical press, mincing few words in his denunciation of their effects on the tense Missouri situation.

Lincoln certainly realized that his true support came from the state's conservatives, even as he sympathized somewhat with the Radicals' efforts for swifter emancipation. He confided to his secretary, John Hay, that he could not condone the Radicals' methods: "They are utterly lawless—the unhandiest devils in the world to deal with—but after all their faces are set Zionwards." On October 5, he sent a formal reply to Drake, which conceded little. Eventually, however, as the political cauldron heated further, Lincoln, in December, gave Schofield a field command and replaced him in St. Louis with Maj. Gen. William S. Rosecrans, who had recently suffered a strong defeat at the battle of Chickamauga, south of Chattanooga.[14]

Having shored up his conservative friends, Frank left St. Louis to resume his military career two days after his Mercantile Library speech. He rejoined Sherman at Memphis on October 4 and promptly received orders to proceed to Corinth, Mississippi, to prepare for the army's advance to Chattanooga. Enemy patrols operated throughout the region, and Blair dispatched troops across northeastern Mississippi into northern Alabama to secure the area for the advance.

13. EBL to SPL, October 2, 1863, B-LP; W. E. Smith, *Blair Family in Politics*, 2:227–45.
14. Parrish, *Turbulent Partnership*, 163–66, 175. For a lengthy Lincoln analysis of the Radical versus Conservative situation in Missouri, see *Diaries and Letters of John Hay*, 135–36.

Sherman himself reached Corinth on the thirteenth after a near disastrous trip from Memphis during which Confederate cavalry attacked his train. On the sixteenth, the War Department combined the Departments of Ohio, Cumberland, and Tennessee under Grant's overall command, placing him in charge of the entire western theater. He quickly replaced Rosecrans with Maj. Gen. George Thomas as commander of the Army of the Cumberland at Chattanooga and hastened there to take personal charge of operations. Sherman became commander of the Army of the Tennessee. He promoted Frank to the command of the Fifteenth Army Corps on October 25, praising him for the "good service" he had rendered thus far, as Union forces edged their way toward Chattanooga.[15]

By November 13, the advance columns of the Fifteenth Corps had reached Bridgeport, Alabama, some thirty miles south of Chattanooga. Frank arrived there on the seventeenth with the remaining troops. Although there had been some brief skirmishes en route from Corinth, no major opposition had been encountered as the troops averaged twenty miles a day. The last thirty miles would be a different story, however, as the army sought to advance over steep terrain with Confederate forces keeping a tight circle around the beleaguered city.

Sherman began moving his entire force forward on the eighteenth, with Grant eager for an attack to relieve the Confederate pressure. He finally had them in place opposite the mouth of Chickamauga Creek by the twenty-third. The battle plan called for Sherman to occupy the left of the Union advance with orders to take Missionary Ridge. When the attack came the following day, not all of Frank's Fifteenth Corps took part. Brig. Gen. P. J. Osterhaus's First Division had been diverted to Maj. Gen. Joe Hooker's Corps, which swept Lookout Mountain on the right of the Union attack while Maj. Gen. George H. Thomas's Corps carried the center. Sherman's attack on the left, which had been designed as the primary one, stalled initially but ultimately carried out its objective. Grant had total losses of 5,616, of which Frank's Fifteenth Corps sustained 1,172. In the aftermath of the battle, Sherman complimented the corps: "I cannot speak of the Fifteenth Army Corps without a seeming vanity, but, as I am no longer its commander, I assert here there

15. *St. Louis Daily Union*, September 29, 1863; EBL to SPL, September 30*, 1863, B-LP; Sherman to FB, October 16, 1863, BLC; *OR*, 1:30:4:73, 122, 146, 172–73, 278, 410, 730–32, 31:2:568–72; Marszalek, *Sherman*, 240.

is no better body of soldiers in America than it, or who have done more or better service."[16]

Frank's appointment to command the Fifteenth Army Corps during this campaign proved to be a temporary one. En route to Chattanooga, Blair learned that the permanent command had been given to John A. Logan of Illinois, like himself a political general, by the War Department at the recommendation of General Grant. He wrote Apo, "I confess that I am a good deal mortified at losing the command of the 15th Army Corps to which I am greatly attached, having served with it through so many defeats and victories and a part of which I am sure is equally attached to me; still I am not disposed to make any difficulty and if I can get a proper command I will remain with the army." While Frank accepted his fate, Apo complained to the family at Silver Spring in bitter terms about her husband's replacement. Preston Blair replied that Logan's appointment had been made before the president knew of the vacancy, and Lincoln had promised that Frank should have another military appointment if he wanted it.[17]

Logan, who commanded a division in McPherson's corps, had been left behind at Vicksburg as Sherman's forces moved north to Memphis en route to Chattanooga. Now he had to follow their circuitous route to reach that place himself, arriving too late to participate in the battle. Once there, Logan discovered the corps ready to move out to Knoxville as a part of Sherman's force designed to relieve Maj. Gen. Ambrose Burnside's troops. The Knoxville garrison was reported to be near starvation because of Confederate operations under Gen. James B. Longstreet in that area. Logan believed that Frank should have the honor of leading the corps on this follow-up campaign because of his experience and rapport with the men. Sherman agreed. It proved to be a quick operation as Burnside was not as beleaguered as he had reported, much to the disgust of Sherman and Blair. Sherman's troops destroyed a great deal of enemy property in the area and, by December 10, had returned to winter quarters near Chattanooga. There Frank turned command of the Fifteenth Corps over to Logan on the eleventh and took his leave. He wrote Montgomery, "[Logan] behaved very handsomely & I was not sorry . . . to turn [the corps] over to one who has shown me so much good feeling." Sherman, in his official orders of

16. Marszalek, *Sherman*, 241–45; S. H. M. Byers, *With Fire and Sword*, 102–10; *OR*, 1:31:2:64–67, 86–87, 572–76, 583–653, 3:159, 168, 185; FB to Apo, November 17, 1863; J. S. Fullerton to Apo, November 19, 1863, BLC; W. E. Smith, *Blair Family in Politics*, 2:170.

17. FPB to Apo, November 7, 1863, FB to Apo, November 17, 1863, BLC; EBL to SPL, November 26*, 1863, B-LP.

transfer, thanked Blair "for the zeal, intelligence, courage, and skill with which he had handled the corps during the eventful period he has commanded it."[18]

Blair now hastened to resume his other career. In late October, Montgomery had asked Lincoln, on Frank's behalf, whether his brother should take his seat during the upcoming session of Congress or remain with the army. The president responded on November 2 that he preferred that Frank come to Washington, "put his military commission in my hands, take his seat, go into caucus with our friends, abide the nominations, help elect the nominees, and thus aid to organize a House of Representatives which will really support the government in the war. If the result shall be the election of himself as Speaker, let him serve in that position; if not, let him re-take his commission, and return to the Army." While Frank would have much preferred to remain with the military, the appointment of Logan temporarily curtailed that opportunity. Unfortunately, the intensity of the Chattanooga campaign and its aftermath prevented his returning to Washington in time to participate in the opening of Congress. The House easily elected Schuyler Colfax, now in league with the Radicals, as Speaker. Lincoln told the Blairs that Frank might have prevented that outcome had he been there, but the president understood the necessity for his staying with his men.[19]

By the time Frank left Chattanooga, Congress had already adjourned for the Christmas holidays. Consequently, he headed for St. Louis to spend time with his family before going to Washington. Apo and the children had not been well, and he had become increasingly concerned about them. He also needed to straighten out his finances, which continued to be complicated by past indebtedness, the drain from the *Union,* and wartime inflation. Apo had reluctantly agreed to sell Rose Bank, the country home that meant so much to her, and now Frank arranged for Samuel Simmons to dispose of various business properties and rentals as well.[20]

Frank also needed to strengthen his political base. Within a few days of his departure for the field in early October, following his Mercantile Library

18. FB to MB, December 20, 1863, BLC; *OR,* 1:31:3:354; *St. Louis Daily Union,* December 29, 1863; James P. Jones, *"Black Jack": John A. Logan and Southern Illinois in the Civil War Era,* 184–86; Marszalek, *Sherman,* 246–47.

19. FB to Apo, October 17, 1863, BLPLC; Lincoln to MB, November 2, 1863, in *Collected Works of Lincoln,* 6:554–55; Apo to MB, October 31, 1863, FPB to Apo, November 7, 1863, FB to MB, December 20, 1863, BLC; EBL to SPL, December 8*, 1863, B-LP; W. E. Smith, *Blair Family in Politics,* 2:251.

20. EBL to SPL, October 3*, November 30*, 1863, Apo to FPB, November 8, 1863, B-LP; *St. Louis Daily Union,* December 15, 18, 1863; Simmons to FB, January 7, 1864, BLC.

speech, Henry T. Blow, Frank's former ally but now bitter foe, had delivered a stinging reply in the same forum. In it, he excoriated his former associate for failing to espouse the Radical stand on emancipation and came out with a strong defense of Secretary Chase. Blair, upon reading the account of it in the *Missouri Democrat*, promptly sent a lengthy reply to Apo to be printed in the *Union*. In response to Blow's contention that Frank should not only "save the Union" but also "make Missouri free," Blair responded, "Now I have done quite as much 'to make Missouri free' as Mr. H. T. Blow and I shall probably continue to use as great efforts to that end." Frank asked,

> Did it ever occur to Mr. Blow that there are tens of thousands of conservative men "in the field of conflict," shedding their heart's blood for the cause, while he remains safely at home to malign them with doubts as to their loyalty to the Union. The "soul of him" is not big enough to do Justice to the brave and loyal soldiers who are fighting for the Republic but whose opinions do not square with his ideas adopted to suit his "most Radical district."

Frank then accused Blow and other Radicals of trying to secure Grant's removal from command and claimed that the general had in his possession a letter to that effect.[21]

Before printing Frank's letter, a reluctant Apo wrote Preston Blair for advice. She wanted Frank to give Blow "silent contempt" rather than add fuel to the fire. She also hated to publish anything that reflected on the president's cabinet; but, at Frank's insistence, she did so on October 19. Attorney General Bates confided in his diary, upon seeing Frank's letter: "At all events the war is openly begun between Mr. C.[hase] and the Blairs." In reality, Frank had fired the opening salvos upon his return from Vicksburg, and it had been accelerated by Montgomery's Rockville speech.[22]

In late October, the Radicals struck back with detailed charges against Frank, filed by a "Merchant." These accused him of corruption while on duty with Grant's army at Vicksburg. Blair had allegedly arranged for the

21. *St. Louis Daily Union*, October 5, 1863; FPB to FB, December 23, 1863, FB to *St. Louis Daily Union*, October 10, 1863, BLC. The accusation against Blow concerning Grant brought an appeal from the Radical leader to the general asking for the evidence. Grant denied ever having seen such a letter nor did others admit to knowing anything about it (Grant to Blow, October 25, 1863, in *Papers of Grant*, 9:318–19; *St. Louis Daily Union*, November 16, 1863).

22. *St. Louis Daily Union*, October 19, 1863; Salmon P. Chase to Blow, September 23, 1863, Blow Family Papers; Apo to FPB, October 16, November 8, 1863, EBL to SPL, October 24*, November 30*, December 19, 1863, B-LP; FB to Apo, October 17, 1863, BLPLC; FB to MB, December 20, 1863, BLC; Bates, *Diary of Bates*, 311.

shipment of some eighty-six hundred dollars in liquor, cigars, and other supplies, which the *Missouri Democrat* claimed would bring twenty to twenty-five thousand dollars in resale. General Grant had stopped the shipment, the *Democrat* stated, so that it never reached Blair, but the intent was there. Frank reacted furiously, charging forgery by one of Chase's Treasury officials. While not denying that he had ordered such supplies for himself and some of his officers in the amount of a few hundred dollars, he claimed, and later proved during congressional hearings, that one Michael Powers, a Chase agent, had deliberately expanded the amount for his own purposes. In the meantime, however, Radical papers across the country printed and reprinted the charges with great delight.[23]

By the time Frank reached Washington in early January 1864, the battle lines between radicals and conservatives within the Republican Party, both in Missouri and elsewhere, were being clearly drawn, with the Blairs serving as the primary defenders of the president. Shortly before Frank left St. Louis, several of his friends met "for the purpose of considering the propriety of placing Old Abe's name at the head of the columns of the 'Union.' " R. J. Howard, who worked at the customs house, attended and informed Montgomery that while Broadhead, Glover, and others agreed with the course, "considerable opposition was manifested by some of our truest and best men," particularly former mayor John How, who owned the *Anzeiger*. Everyone agreed on the necessity for How's cooperation: "If we can have the two papers come out flatfooted for the President I think two months will not roll round before there will be an open war between two Govt functionaries."[24]

The pro-Lincoln group prevailed, the *Union* announcing for the president's reelection the last week of December. By mid-January, William McKee, the editor of the *Missouri Democrat*, wrote Blow, describing "the bitter enmity of Blair toward Secy Chase," as evidenced by the columns of the *Union*. McKee complained that the paper derived its main support from customs-house printing and advertising because of the influence of Howard, who, in effect, served as an employee of Chase since the customs house was a Treasury Department operation. "I am satisfied Mr. Chase is not aware of these things," McKee wrote, "and yet while he might not wish to directly interfere, he could

23. *Missouri Democrat*, October 23, 26, 27, 30, November 3, 1863; *St. Louis Daily Union*, October 26, 1863; General Orders No. 36, June 15, 1863, in *Papers of Grant*, 8:363–68; MB to Lincoln, November 12, 1863, BLC; EBL to SPL, November 16*, 1863, B-LP; Noah Brooks, *Washington in Lincoln's Time*, 132–33.
24. Howard to MB, December 28, 1863, BLC.

compel Mr. Howard to offer proposals for printing as in all the other govt offices here."

Herein lay one of the increasing concerns of the Missouri Radicals: control of patronage. With many of Frank's friends, like Howard at the customs house and, more particularly, Peter Foy as St. Louis postmaster, in key patronage positions, the Radicals argued with their Washington supporters that the administration was playing an unfair game. At the same time, the conservatives complained of Chase's discrimination against them in political favors. A similar struggle was occurring in Maryland, where Montgomery Blair's conservative friends contended with the radical faction led by Cong. Henry Winter Davis. Montgomery, of course, controlled vast patronage in the postal service, and these jobs would be put to good use in the coming campaign.[25]

Frank arrived in Washington on January 9, having been delayed en route by storms in the West. With Apo and the children staying in St. Louis, Lizzie had been busy arranging rooms at No. 4 for his stay. She told Phil that Frank looked well and was in good spirits. Friends and colleagues, including James Rollins, quickly inundated him. Even Gratz Brown, who recently had been elected to the Senate, made his appearance to welcome his cousin back to the capital, although this sometimes strained the atmosphere because of their political differences over emancipation. Gratz also opposed John Schofield's promotion to major general, which Frank supported in the wake of his friend's removal from his Missouri post and return to field duty. Nevertheless, Brown remained a favorite with Lizzie, who kept house for Frank at No. 4 and served as her brother's unofficial secretary. So, he was usually a welcome visitor.[26]

Frank had deferred the question of returning to the House until his arrival, but the president quickly put that matter to rest by agreeing to hold Blair's resignation from the army in abeyance until spring, while assuring him that he needed him in Congress in the meantime. The radicals, meanwhile, operating through Speaker Schuyler Colfax, refused to give Frank a seat on any of the major House committees. Preston Blair, together with former governor William Dennison of Ohio, a longtime Blair ally, met with Lincoln the day after Frank's arrival to discuss their plans for derailing the Chase locomotive.

25. *St. Louis Daily Union*, December 29, 1863; McKee to Blow, January 19, 1864, Blow Family Papers; Truman Woodruff to Lincoln, April 9, 1863, S. T. Glover to Lincoln, April 13, 1863, John L. Bittinger to J. B. T. Todd, February 27, 1864, Lincoln Papers; Thomas T. Gantt to MB, May 1, 1863, BLC; Carman and Luthin, *Lincoln and the Patronage*, 199–200, 204–12; E. B. Smith, *Francis Preston Blair*, 335–36; William Frank Zornow, *Lincoln and the Party Divided*, 45.

26. FB to Andrew Johnson, January 19, 1864, in *The Papers of Andrew Johnson*, 6:567; EBL to SPL, November 18, 1863, January 11*, 12*, 14*, 15, 22*, 26, February 12*, March 1*, 1864, B-LP.

Frank and Lizzie spent the evening with the Lincolns on the sixteenth, as Blair reviewed the Chattanooga campaign for the president. Undoubtedly, they also discussed politics, for Lizzie wrote Phil, "The Presidential question is rife—& Abe has the inside track & he has the other candidates—they think so fixed that they will have to make a break from him & against him to get on the track even[.] [T]is for that emergency F[rank] is here."[27]

That the Chase machine was gearing up to make its move quickly became evident. The president's "Proclamation of Amnesty and Reconstruction," issued December 8, 1863, which outlined rather easy terms for the reconstruction of the postwar South, provided a catalyst for a small group of Lincoln critics. They came together the following day as the "Organization to make S. P. Chase President." This soon became the "Republican National Executive Committee," chaired by Sen. Samuel C. Pomeroy of Kansas, who felt discriminated against by the Lincoln administration in patronage matters. Chase encouraged his friends to participate. The Pomeroy committee went public in February with two important campaign documents. It first published a pamphlet titled "The Next Presidential Election," which it circulated widely under the frank of several congressmen, including Henry Blow. Many Northern newspapers also printed it. The argument was that the president had forfeited the public confidence by his mishandling of the war. Without endorsing a specific candidate, it called for "a statesman profoundly versed in political and economic science, who fully comprehends the spirit of the age in which we live." The committee followed this pamphlet with a document called the "Pomeroy Circular," naming Chase as the logical person to replace Lincoln.[28]

Whatever their hopes for these trial political balloons, Chase's supporters must have been greatly disappointed. A determined public reaction in favor of Lincoln set in, particularly in Chase's home state of Ohio. Most Americans favored the president's moderate course, as opposed to the more extreme views of the Radicals. An embarrassed Treasury secretary, while admitting his knowledge of the committee's existence, insisted that he had no prior knowledge of its publications. He apologized to Lincoln and offered to resign. The president waited a week before responding. He told Chase that he

27. EBL to SPL, January 12*, 14*, 17, 1864, B-LP; *Diary of Welles*, 1:509; *St. Louis Daily Union*, January 22, 1864.

28. Frederick J. Blue, *Salmon P. Chase: A Life in Politics*, 221–23; John Niven, *Salmon P. Chase: A Biography*, 357–61; Zornow, *Lincoln and the Party Divided*, 47–49; Burton J. Hendrick, *Lincoln's War Cabinet*, 412–16; Carman and Luthin, *Lincoln and the Patronage*, 231–33.

had not read the documents, knowing only so much as his friends told him, and requested the beleaguered secretary to continue in office. Chase formally withdrew from the race in early March. Although some of his friends continued to work on his behalf, the Chase candidacy was dead.[29]

Meanwhile the Blairs and other Lincoln supporters counterattacked. Montgomery made a careful address before the Maryland legislature on January 22, in which he endorsed the concept of a broad Union Party, which would embrace War Democrats as well as Republicans, to secure Lincoln's reelection. In state after state, support was forthcoming from legislatures, party caucuses, and other groups. In Missouri, many of the War Democrats in the legislature and elsewhere endorsed the president's candidacy.[30]

On February 1, Frank made his move against Chase, introducing a resolution that called for the appointment of a special five-man committee to investigate the work of Treasury officials in the Mississippi valley. Speaker Colfax and others opposing Lincoln managed to block the resolution, much to Blair's disgust. During the next few days, a lengthy debate ensued on a proposal to expand the confiscation of rebel property. This gave Frank his chance to defend the president. In a long speech on February 5, he extolled Lincoln's more liberal reconstruction policy while excoriating those, like his old enemy Thaddeus Stevens, who would make reunion more difficult by their confiscation bill. He also took the opportunity to lash out against the Missouri Radicals and their press for opposing Schofield's promotion after agreeing to it as part of the arrangement for his transfer from St. Louis. Together with Rollins and other conservatives, Frank then left the House floor in the hope of preventing a quorum for a vote. This failed to accomplish its purpose, however, as the confiscation bill passed eighty-three to seventy-four. Frank did not participate in the final vote on the measure, having left the Capitol to catch a train to Newport to visit his son Andrew, who was attending the Naval Academy, which had been moved there for the duration of the war.[31]

29. Blue, *Chase: A Life*, 223–25; Niven, *Chase: A Biography*, 361–62; Zornow, *Lincoln and the Party Divided*, 49–57; Hendrick, *Lincoln's War Cabinet*, 416–17; Carman and Luthin, *Lincoln and the Patronage*, 233–35.

30. W. E. Smith, *Blair Family in Politics*, 2:253–54; Zornow, *Lincoln and the Party Divided*, 51–52, 58; Carman and Luthin, *Lincoln and the Patronage*, 234–42; EBL to SPL, February 2*, 1864, B-LP; *Missouri Republican*, March 9, 1864.

31. *CG*, 38:1:509–14, 519; *New York Times*, February 6, 1864; Hendrick, *Lincoln's War Cabinet*, 424; Wood, "James Sidney Rollins," 329; FB to Schofield, March 31, 1864, Schofield Papers; EBL to SPL, February 2*, 12*, 1864, B-LP.

Frank's speech of February 5 has been overlooked by earlier historians in relation to the ones he made later in the session. Yet, it is crucial to an understanding of them, for it touched off the whole series of speeches, which would embroil him and his family, together with the president, in lengthy controversy. His Radical opponents seethed at his attacks on them and planned their response during his absence in Newport. They struck back on several fronts. The *Missouri Democrat* condemned him for his opposition to the confiscation resolution, claiming that he acted with the "Copperhead Democrats." Henry Blow took the House floor on February 23 to deliver a lengthy reply to Frank's remarks of the fifth. He accused Blair of self-aggrandizement in slandering his former friends. Blow denied that the *Missouri Democrat* and the *Westliche Post* had sold out to the Fremont interests. They had "never to this hour flinched in their devotion to this Government." He extolled the virtues of Chase while condemning Frank for his attacks on the Mississippi trade policy. If Blair did not like the trade arrangements, he should hold the president equally responsible, as Lincoln had "carefully examined and approved every one of them." Turning to the quarrel over Schofield, Blow defended the Drake committee while reiterating the old charge that Frank had been among those seeking that general's removal a year earlier. In conclusion, Blow contrasted the Missouri Radicals' view of emancipation with that of the Blairs. Who, he asked, were the true friends of the government?[32]

Although in great pain from a severe case of piles, Frank responded four days later with "The Jacobins of Missouri and Maryland," which he had reprinted for wide circulation. He reviewed the chaotic situation that had existed in those two states throughout the war and accused his opponents of seeking "to keep up the strife in States in which the rebellion has been put down, instead of fighting to put down the rebellion where it exists." He saw no need to review his own course with regard to the war. The "Jacobins," as he now referred to them, "seek to make a direct issue with the President, to defeat his reelection, in order that they may enjoy the license of another French Revolution under some chief as malignant as themselves." He accused his four Radical colleagues from Missouri of having been proslavery before the war while he had been the leading advocate of Free-Soilism. In addition, they had belonged to what Blair called "the dark-lantern fraternity," namely,

32. EBL to SPL, February 2*, 12*, 1864, B-LP; *Missouri Democrat*, February 19, 1864; *CG*, 38:1:779–85.

Know-Nothingism. Now, "they denounce us as unfaithful to the cause of human freedom."

Frank insisted that he had always been ready to accept any form of emancipation, "whenever the people of Missouri or any other State desire it" and Congress provided the money to compensate the owners. He reminded his listeners of the course he had taken in this regard in 1862. He then contrasted his support of colonization with the Radicals' position, as he saw it, of elevating the freed blacks to equality with whites, something he contended most whites would never accept.

Frank next turned to the issue that had motivated Blow's remarks in the first place: Secretary Chase and his licensing policy. He briefly dissected that policy's questionable application and results in both the lower Mississippi valley and Virginia and asked why the Radicals had opposed his call for an investigation if Chase had nothing to hide. In conclusion, he asserted that the Radicals had only one purpose, namely, the defeat of President Lincoln. Blair vowed he would continue to try to thwart their designs.[33]

The speech brought strong reaction in the partisan press, with the friends of Chase demanding that the president repudiate Frank and dismiss Montgomery from the cabinet, while conservatives chortled at the Treasury secretary's embarrassment. Frank's conservative colleagues from Missouri, James Rollins and Austin King, came to his support with speeches on the House floor.[34]

Frank's many battles continued to bring on physical problems. In addition to his piles, he experienced severe headaches, something that bothered him throughout his life. These became so painful that Lizzie had to bind his head with chloroform to give him temporary relief. Preston Blair wrote Apo that he wished the family could all be together at Silver Spring; but, despondently, she replied that she felt it necessary to stay at home so as not to interrupt the children's education.

Apo was obviously tired of her husband's constant absences and complained about them regularly in her letters. Frank responded in exasperation, "I explained to you when I was in St. Louis that it was necessary for me to

33. FB to Apo, February 29, 1864, BLC; *CG*, 38:1:Appendix:46–51; FB to Schofield, March 31, 1864, Schofield Papers.

34. W. E. Smith, *Blair Family in Politics*, 2:258; *CG*, 38:1:878, 980, 1831–32. Attorney General Bates would later confide to his diary: "How the President will take it I know not; but if he'll just let me 'take the responsibility,' I'll make short work of Mr. Chase's knot of ignorant and rapacious swindlers, from the Balise to C[a]iro" (*Diary of Bates*, 382).

make bread for you & the children & that nothing now was left open to me by which I could do this but by a public career." To try to resolve the conflict between them, he reported that he was considering running for governor, which, if successful, would allow them to be together. "I hope therefore you will feel satisfied or if not satisfied that as I cannot help it and as the children must be fed that I may escape further censure & complaint which is both useless and annoying."[35]

The thoughts about the governorship proved short-lived. Five days later Frank again wrote Apo with the news that General Grant had offered him, and he had accepted, the command of the Seventeenth Corps in Sherman's army. He hoped she might join him for a few weeks before he returned to active duty. Blair had met Grant ten days earlier during a dinner at Secy. of State William H. Seward's and found him "very cordial." Shortly after that Lincoln had written the general asking him to make room for Frank in his command. After conferring with Sherman, Grant responded positively. A few days later Frank had accompanied Lizzie to a tea for Mrs. Grant and encountered the general, who filled in Blair on his concerns for the upcoming campaign.[36]

Frank's congressional activity continued unabated during March. The elections committee was considering Samuel Knox's contest for Frank's seat, stemming from the disputed 1862 returns. Blair met with them on March 3, and Lizzie informed Phil that he "seems to feel very little concern as to the result." Frank told Rollins a few days later that Knox had made less of a case than he expected. On the eighteenth, Lizzie reported that her brother had finished his response to Knox "& I now hope he will get well of his headache which still follows him."

The headaches continued to recur, however, undoubtedly aggravated by the tensions of the committee investigations and by Apo's refusal to come east, which, Lizzie told Phil, "he takes bitterly." Their mother had urged Lizzie to write Apo asking her to come. At one point, she did so, then when her niece Betty Blair "begged me not to send it as it would be [hardly] appreciated, I put it in the fire." In the end, by whatever persuasion, Apo did come and

35. FB to Apo, March 13, 1864, BLC; EBL to SPL, March 16*, 26, 1864, B-LP.

36. EBL to SPL, March 9, 17, 23*, 26, April 4, 1864, B-LP; FB to Apo, March 10, 18, BLPLC; *OR*, 1:32:3:72, 81, 191, 221, 322, 465, 34:3:27, 35:2:48. Lincoln had originally asked that Frank be given his old Fifteenth Corps with Logan being transferred to the Seventeenth, whose command had become vacant because of the promotion of McPherson to command of the Army of the Tennessee. When Logan balked at that arrangement, Blair received the Seventeenth (Lincoln to Grant, March 15, 1864, in *Collected Works of Lincoln*, 7:248).

spend ten days. She then went to Newport to see Andrew before returning to New York, where Frank later met her as he headed west to rejoin Sherman's army.[37]

Before Frank could return to the military, he had unfinished business in Congress. In addition to the elections issue, Frank faced yet another challenge from one of his Jacobin colleagues. Not content to leave matters alone in the wake of Frank's reply to Blow, Joseph W. McClurg of Missouri, on March 9, dredged up the controversy about Frank's purported illicit traffic in liquor and tobacco during the Vicksburg campaign. Blair demanded and secured the appointment of a select three-person committee to investigate the charges. He asked various members of his staff to come from St. Louis to testify on his behalf. In the course of its hearings, the committee called as a star witness Michael Powers, whom Frank had accused of forging the manifest in question. To the dismay of the Radicals, Powers quickly acknowledged his guilt, saying that he did it to enrich himself, with "no intention of injuring Genl Blair." The committee had no recourse but to completely exonerate Frank of any wrongdoing. John G. Nicolay and John Hay, Lincoln's private secretaries, reported, "It was a striking instance of the bewildering power of factious hatred that such charges should ever have been brought. Anyone who knew Blair, however slightly, should have known that personal dishonesty could never have offered him the least temptation." An elated Frank now planned a final dramatic flourish before he returned to the army.[38]

On April 20, Frank formally requested the command of the Seventeenth Corps of Sherman's army with his brother-in-law Andrew Alexander as his adjutant. Lincoln endorsed the request the next day and sent it to Secretary of War Stanton, who, in turn, handed it to Adj. Gen. E. D. Townsend without comment. When Townsend informed Stanton that Frank had resigned his commission and, therefore, could not be given such an assignment, the secretary simply told him, "But the President orders it!" When Townsend still protested, Stanton told him to take his concerns to Lincoln. The adjutant general did so. The president responded, "Well, I am anxious to have it fixed up some way, so the order can be issued, if you can do it." Townsend replied

37. EBL to SPL, March 3*, 8, 18, 26, 28*, 30, 31*, April 1, 4, 13*, 22, 1864, B-LP; *Missouri Contested Election.*

38. CG, 38:1:1017, 1251–53, 1827–28; *Report of the Special Committee in the Blair Investigation Case, April 23, 1864; St. Louis Daily Union*, February 9, April 28, 1864; *New York Times*, April 24, 1864; FB to Apo, March 10, n.d., 1864, BLPLC; EBL to SPL, March 31*, April 1, 4, 5*, 21, 22, 1864, B-LP; John G. Nicolay and John Hay, *Abraham Lincoln: A History*, 9:80. Cf. John Maguire to MB, August 18, 1864, BLC.

that Frank would have to withdraw his resignation, for which precedent existed. Lincoln then asked him to take care of it. Upon being summoned to the War Department, Blair quickly complied; and Townsend drafted the orders on Saturday, April 23.[39]

Frank had no sooner received his new orders than he proceeded to the capitol to make his farewell. Aware that the committee assigned to the McClurg investigation would make its formal report exonerating him that afternoon, he wanted to have a final parting shot at his erstwhile opponents. Preston Blair and Lizzie sat in the packed gallery as Frank asked permission to address the House. Word had circulated that this might be his valedictory, and even many senators crowded into the chamber to hear Blair's anticipated assault on Secretary Chase and his supporters.[40]

Frank began with a summation of his military accomplishments and then lashed out at McClurg for attacking him unfairly. Realizing what was coming, Speaker Colfax quickly ruled him out of order, only to be overruled by the House itself. Frank apologized for his strong language but then plunged ahead to lay the blame for his difficulties directly at the feet of Chase, accusing the secretary of being directly behind "the forgeries committed and disseminated by his understrappers." Colfax again ruled Frank out of order unless he would confine his remarks to the committee's report, which made no mention of Chase. When Blair refused to be limited in that way, the Speaker lost control. As partisans on both sides clamored either for order or for Frank to continue, Blair attacked the move by the Radicals to bury his request for an investigation into Chase's activities in the Joint Committee on the Conduct of the War. He then assailed the secretary's alleged abuse of his office to promote his own presidential ambitions at the expense of Lincoln, citing numerous letters he had received to back his claims of favoritism in the Mississippi valley. After an hour, in which he had enlivened the House with some of the most colorful language it had ever heard, Frank turned on his heel and left the chamber to return to the army.[41]

That evening, "a troop" of congressmen, "mostly Democrats & western men," visited No. 4 and presented Blair with a superb sword, mounted in a

39. Lincoln to Stanton, April 21, 23, 1864, in *Collected Works of Lincoln*, 7:307, 312; E. D. Townsend, *Anecdotes of the Civil War in the United States*, 105–7.
40. *CG*, 38:1:1827–28; EBL to SPL, April 22, 23*, 1864, B-LP; Hendrick, *Lincoln's War Cabinet*, 426–27.
41. *CG*, 38:1:1828–32; EBL to SPL, April 23*, 1864, B-LP; Hendrick, *Lincoln's War Cabinet*, 426–29. Numerous letters can be found in BLC accusing Chase's agents of illegal operations.

solid silver scabbard with sash and spurs. Engraved on the scabbard were the words: "from his friends as a token for his gallant support of *'the Union.' "* Another supporter gave him "a beautiful seal ring."

Later, Frank crossed Pennsylvania Avenue to the White House, at Lincoln's request, for one last conversation. He suggested that it might be best if he did not return to the army, lest it cause fallout for the president. Lincoln replied that Frank's military commission had been his idea in the first place, and he did not mind the political heat that might come of it since it would be generated by his "personal & political Rivals." "We must not back down," the president told him. In relating this to Lizzie the next morning, Frank told her that Lincoln had recounted a conversation with Sen. Charles Sumner, who had been complaining about the Blairs. The president had reminded Sumner that the Radicals had really begun the conflict when they had supported Fremont in his arrest of Frank back in 1861. It was well known that "Frank was the most honest & best man of the two." Lincoln then continued, "Now Mr. S.[umner,] the B's are brave people & never whine—but are always ready to fight their enemies and very generally whip them."

Frank spent most of the rest of the long night writing out his remarks so that Lizzie could have them published. The following evening he left for New York to meet Apo before heading west to join his corps at Cairo, Illinois. Sherman had been urging Frank to hurry back for more than a week lest he miss the forthcoming campaign, something Blair had no intention of doing.[42]

The ferocity of Frank's attack on the House floor left the Radicals stunned, climaxing as it did three months in which he had kept Congress in continuous turmoil. They assumed that he had Lincoln's blessing, particularly when they discovered over the weekend that the president had restored him to a military command. James A. Garfield wrote a friend, "Lincoln's creature was sent here for a special purpose, which, when accomplished, he put him back in his place, thus ratifying all he said and did when here." Garfield eventually chaired a special committee, packed with Chase supporters, which Speaker Colfax appointed to investigate Frank's charges. Although Garfield later claimed that Chase was exonerated, in reality, the committee reached no conclusion either way with regard to the charges. How directly, if at all, Chase may have been involved in the activities of his agents will probably never be known.

42. *St. Louis Daily Union,* April 28, 30, May 3, 1864; EBL to SPL, April 23*, 24*, 26*, June 18*, 1864, B-LP; *Missouri Statesman,* May 6, 1864; FB to Apo, May 9, 1864, BLPLC.

There can be little doubt, however, that he played the patronage game for personal advantage, much like the Blairs and every other politician on the Washington scene did.[43]

Meanwhile, an enraged Chase talked openly with his friends of resigning unless the president repudiated Frank's remarks. The following Monday, April 25, former congressman Albert G. Riddle and Cong. Rufus P. Spalding, both from Ohio and friends of the Treasury secretary, sought an audience with Lincoln at the White House. The president received them "politely but with no pretence of cordiality." After a long, detailed discussion of his arrangements with Frank, going back to December, Lincoln reported that Grant had assigned Blair a corps in Sherman's command, and the latter had wanted him to report quickly. The president had obliged by rescinding Frank's resignation and restoring him to the army. He had not learned of the farewell speech until later, "when I knew *that another beehive was kicked over.*" While he had considered revoking the military commission, he thought better of it and intended for it to stick. Lincoln did not tell the two men of his conversation with Frank the evening after the speech. They left generally satisfied, and Chase remained in office for the time being. When he submitted his resignation two months later over a patronage disagreement, the president calmly accepted it.[44]

Frank wrote Montgomery during a temporary stopover in St. Louis, "I see that Chase's people have let loose upon me. Well let them rip. . . . As things now stand the President must take active measures to put down the Chase raid on him." Lizzie kept busy mailing copies of Frank's speech to various constituencies as "the papers all refuse to publish it." It "has made a *big fuss,*" she wrote Phil, "& it has a parthian arrow to those it was meant to hit." His foes, meanwhile, condemned him in scathing terms. In early May, the House Elections Committee, by a split five-to-four vote, recommended seating Knox in his place. Frank had understood that they were leaning the other way prior

43. Blue, *Chase: A Life*, 229–34. The Garfield quote is in Hendrick, *Lincoln's War Cabinet*, 429. Chase's most recent biographer states, "There was considerable truth to [Blair's] allegations, but he had little firm evidence" (Niven, *Chase: A Biography*, 348).

44. Riddle, *Recollections of War Times*, 266–77; Blue, *Chase: A Life*, 229–30, 234–36; Niven, *Chase: A Biography*, 349–51. That same day, April 25, Cong. Henry L. Dawes of Massachusetts introduced a resolution calling upon the president to explain Frank's military status. Lincoln replied three days later with a detailed report of his correspondence with Grant and Sherman concerning the matter and offering to submit copies of these if the House wished to see them, which he ultimately did (*CG*, 38:1:1859; Lincoln to the House of Representatives, April 28, May 2, 1864, in *Collected Works of Lincoln*, 7:319–20, 326–27).

to his departure. The House concurred by the narrow vote of seventy to fifty-three. It would mark the end of Frank's career in the House. His enemies had had the final word.[45]

Frank reached Cairo on May 4 and assumed command of the Seventeenth Corps, most of whom, like himself, were returning from veterans' furloughs after the Chattanooga campaign. En route, he gathered additional evidence against Chase, which he forwarded to Montgomery for whatever use his brother and father could make of it. Having brought together his various units, Frank left Cairo on May 11 with eight thousand men, thirty pieces of artillery, four hundred wagons, and twenty-three hundred beef cattle. He made his way south along the Tennessee River and across northern Alabama to join Sherman, who had begun his movement from Chattanooga to Atlanta a week earlier.[46]

Frank wrote Apo on May 23 from Huntsville that he had ridden forty-five miles that day and planned to push on to Rome, Georgia, in the next two days after the rest of his corps caught up with him. He badly needed her to forward additional clothes, "especially the light suit as it is very hot here." He told his father that much of the country through which they were marching had recovered from the devastation of the previous year's campaigns.[47]

Frank had orders to clear out any enemy forces he encountered and, particularly, to keep them away from the river. He was also to make feints south from Huntsville to keep the enemy off guard as to his plans, but he encountered only minimal opposition. His major difficulty came when he ordered "the non-veterans whose term of service was about to expire to escort the cattle to Chattanooga," where they would be mustered out. After he left Huntsville with the rest of the command, these men mutinied, but the Huntsville commander agreed to send one of his regiments forward with the cattle, which relieved Frank of the necessity of returning to discipline these men anxious to return home.[48]

Frank joined Sherman at Acworth, Georgia, on June 8 with nine thousand fresh troops and an immense drove of cattle. He had left two thousand men behind at Rome to garrison that post and another fifteen hundred at Altoona for the same purpose. That same day the reconstituted National Union Party,

45. FB to MB, April 30, 1864, BLC; EBL to SPL, April 28*, May 7*, 11, 26*, 29, 1864, B-LP; *CG*, 38:1:2861.

46. *OR*, 1:38:4:40–41; FB to MB, May 5, 7, 1864, BLC.

47. FB to Apo, May 9, 14, 23, 1864, BLPLC; EBL to SPL, May 29, 1864, B-LP.

48. *OR*, 1:38:3:539–40, 4:52, 146, 305; EBL to SPL, June 9, 1864, B-LP.

meeting at Baltimore, nominated Abraham Lincoln for a second term as president. Two Missouri delegations had appeared at the convention, one Radical (anti-Blair), whose members went uncommitted, and one conservative (pro-Blair), committed to Lincoln. The other delegates seated the Radicals by an overwhelming vote, to the embarrassment of the convention managers. The Missourians then cast the only votes against Lincoln, going for Ulysses S. Grant. They did, however, make the nomination unanimous at the end of the ballot. The majority of Missouri Radicals had come to realize that they could be seriously damaged in the fall elections unless they outmaneuvered the conservatives in embracing the National Union ticket. A small group, led by Gratz Brown and a number of Germans, refused to go this route, however, and instead had helped coordinate a convention in Cleveland a week earlier that nominated Fremont for the presidency on the Radical Democracy ticket.[49]

Frank had little time to concern himself with these matters. He did report to Apo, however, that Lincoln's renomination had been received "with acclamation by the army." In a letter to Bart Able, which found its way into the public press, he expressed his distress that Lincoln's "real friends from Missouri" had been excluded from the convention in favor of those "who stand in the record as his most bitter enemies." Fortunately, that did not prevent the president's renomination, and he urged his friends to stand by Lincoln in spite of the convention's rude treatment.[50]

Blair brought badly needed reinforcements to Sherman, who had been fighting his way down the Georgia corridor for the past month in a series of encounters against Confederate forces commanded by Gen. Joseph E. Johnston. Blair's troops became part of James B. McPherson's Army of the Tennessee occupying the left of Sherman's advance. McPherson rode out to meet Frank upon his arrival, taking with him his aide, Capt. Andrew Hickenlooper. During the ride over, the latter expressed his concern about a politician, rather than a military man, commanding the Seventeenth Corps, which had previously been McPherson's. Hickenlooper told his commander that he had been "very unfavorably impressed" by newspaper stories he had read about Blair. McPherson asked him to withhold his judgment until he met Frank; and Hickenlooper later wrote, "Contrary to my expectations, I

49. *OR*, 1:38:4:433; Andrew Hickenlooper Reminiscences, 53; Parrish, *Turbulent Partnership*, 182–86; Zornow, *Lincoln and the Party Divided*, 72–104.
50. EBL to SPL, June 26, 1864, B-LP; *New York Times*, July 17, 1864.

was very favorably impressed to General Blair's frank manners and cordial greeting."[51]

Frank told Hickenlooper how much he had heard about him from the other officers in the corps and invited him, with McPherson, to come back that evening "to meet my old friends." Somehow Frank had managed to bring through "great hogsheads of ice and numerous baskets of champagne," and the company thoroughly enjoyed it. John Schofield, who had joined Sherman's forces as commander of the Army of the Ohio, rode up as the party got under way and reported, "[W]e did not disdain such an unusual treat in the enemy's country." Hickenlooper later wrote, "The occasion was a most enjoyable one and the reunion of old friends, in many cases, quite touching."[52]

The occasion did not go unnoticed by men in the ranks. A soldier in the Thirty-second Illinois Regiment wrote his hometown paper complaining of such luxuries for officers when those in the ranks had to be content with hard tack and bacon. The *Missouri Democrat* picked up the story and added it to its anti-Blair campaign.[53]

There was no time for such celebrations in the days ahead. On June 10, Sherman moved his forces out of Acworth to continue his relentless march to Atlanta. In a series of fight-and-flank encounters, during which the Seventeenth Corps saw its share of action, Sherman brought his army to the banks of the Chattahoochee River, northwest of Atlanta, by July 9, as Johnston retreated into the outer defenses of the city. Here Sherman rested his men for five days in preparation for the hard fighting ahead. Frank's corps crossed the Chattahoochee on July 17, as Sherman ordered his army forward, and took up a position along Peach Tree Creek at the extreme left of the line. Here Frank received word of a daring raid against Washington by the Confederate general Jubal Early, which resulted in the burning of Montgomery's home at Silver Spring. He wrote Apo that the news had hit him hard, and he offered

---

51. Marszalek, *Sherman*, 269–71; Hickenlooper Reminiscences, 53.

52. Hickenlooper Reminiscences, 53; Schofield, *Forty-six Years in the Army*, 138. A native of Ohio, Hickenlooper had served under Fremont in his Missouri campaign. Later transferring to Grant's command, Hickenlooper distinguished himself at Shiloh. He became chief engineer of the Seventeenth Corps and had charge of the engineering operations during the siege of Vicksburg. During the march to the sea, he joined Frank's staff as inspector general and served with him throughout the remainder of the war, during which time the two became warm friends (Allen Johnson and Dumas Malone, eds., *The Dictionary of American Biography*, 9:3–4).

53. *Missouri Democrat*, June 27, 1864.

six thousand dollars, recently acquired from the sale of a lot in Washington, to his father to help them rebuild.[54]

That same day, July 17, Jefferson Davis, frustrated by Johnston's retreat, replaced him with Gen. John Bell Hood, one of his corps commanders. Hood, in a vain attempt to avert the impending siege of the city by Sherman's forces, unsuccessfully attacked the troops of Schofield and Thomas along Peach Tree Creek to the right of McPherson's position on the twentieth. On the next day, Frank ordered Brig. Gen. Mortimer Leggett's Third Division to take what would become known as Bald Hill to his front. This high ground became extremely important in the ensuing battle of Atlanta the following day.

Undaunted by his failure of the twentieth, Hood moved next against McPherson's forces on the afternoon of July 22. McPherson, Blair, and Logan heard the opening shots while lunching with their staffs in a nearby oak grove, and the last two immediately rode off to join their respective corps. The Confederates had struck the flank and rear of Frank's corps. Fortunately, for them, Brig. Gen. Grenville Dodge's Sixteenth Corps was moving into position there and thus took the brunt of the initial attack. The Confederates tried to move between the two corps, but Blair's men held firm.

In the fierce fighting that followed, McPherson was killed as he rode to confer with Blair. Frank, not more than three hundred yards away, later reported, "I saw him enter the woods and heard the volley which probably killed him." He immediately notified Logan as the senior to command; and Sherman, upon hearing the news, confirmed that temporary designation. The Seventeenth Corps fought well and managed to hold Bald Hill. By early evening the enemy had been repulsed and pushed back into their fortifications. Blair's casualties for the two-day fighting stood at 2,582, including 245 men of the Sixteenth Iowa, cut off from the rest of the corps and captured during one of the Confederate thrusts.[55]

McPherson's death affected Frank deeply. The two had served together all through the Vicksburg and Chattanooga campaigns, although Blair had not been under McPherson's direct command. The Ohioan was only thirty-five at the time of his death, and Frank mourned him as "the youthful illustrious leader of the Army of the Tennessee, who in this battle, laid down

54. Albert Castel, *Decision in the West: The Atlanta Campaign of 1864*, 269–347; Marszalek, *Sherman*, 271–76; FB to Apo, July 18, 1864, BLPLC.

55. *OR*, 1:38:3:21–29, 542–51; FB to Walter Q. Gresham, August 20, 1864, in Matilda Gresham, *Life of Walter Quintin Gresham, 1832–1895*, 1:306–10; Oliver Otis Howard, *Autobiography*, 2:3–15; EBL to SPL, August 6*, 1864, B-LP; Castel, *Decision in the West*, 365–410.

his unsullied life for the cause to which he had consecrated it." There were those who blamed Blair for McPherson's death, including his newspaper foes the *Missouri Democrat* and the *New York Tribune*. Again, they dredged up the question of his fitness for command as a political general. Unperturbed, Frank wrote Apo that they would be no more successful in this attack than they had been in the whiskey affair. He had already given her his account of the battle, which she forwarded to the Washington Blairs in the hope that it could be used to counteract these stories. Sherman, in a casual discussion with some of his staff, simply remarked that *"'twas false"* to blame Frank for McPherson's death or the heavy casualties of the twenty-second, noting that Blair had been "brave, cool and of ability."[56]

When it came time to appoint a successor to McPherson a few days later, however, Sherman passed over Logan and Frank "as politicians by nature and experience," and gave the command of the Army of the Tennessee to the West Pointer O. O. Howard at the urging of George Thomas. Frank had encouraged his old friend Schofield to hope for the assignment, but the latter carefully hid his disappointment. Blair had not expected his own promotion and accepted Howard without question. The two served well together during the rest of the war.[57]

Considerably diminished by the fighting of July 22 to little more than four thousand men, the Seventeenth Corps, nevertheless, performed well in the remainder of Sherman's Atlanta campaign, although one historian has noted that it seemed "that the XVII Corps, as a consequence of its ordeal on July 22, has such an intense fear of being attacked in the open that it is incapable of offensive action." Frank had been trying to restore the corps' strength "by rounding up detailed soldiers and convalescents from as far north as St. Louis." He had also urged on Montgomery the necessity of having the president vigorously enforce the draft so as to provide more recruits. By the end of August, he had increased the Seventeenth's strength from sixty-four hundred to eleven thousand.[58]

At some point in the campaign, Frank hurt his hand so badly that Andrew Alexander had to handle his correspondence. With the fall of Atlanta in early

56. W. E. Smith, *Blair Family in Politics*, 2:178; EBL to SPL, August 5, 6*, 16*, September 8, 1864, B-LP; FB to Apo, August 23, 1864, BLPLC; Henry M. Hitchcock, *Marching with Sherman*, 54–55.

57. Castel, *Decision in the West*, 418–22; Sherman, *Memoirs*, 2:558–59; Jones, *"Black Jack,"* 219–22; Howard, *Autobiography*, 2:17.

58. Howard, *Autobiography*, 2:16–46; *OR*, 1:38:5:244, 305, 314–15, 470, 554–55, 744, 39:2:301–2, 377; Castel, *Decision in the West*, 425, 435, 513–21, 620 n.

September, both Frank and Logan obtained leaves to return home in the hope of shoring up their respective political fronts. The successful conclusion of the Atlanta campaign would prove to be a critical turning point in the president's reelection bid, but the concern to get out the vote remained a real one.[59]

Frank had once again proved himself an able commander who continued to gain the confidence of Sherman and his fellow officers. Hard-driving himself, he expected the same motivation from his men and pushed them accordingly. That the Seventeenth earned an enviable reputation indicates that they responded well. Even as Frank had performed creditably on the battlefield, Lincoln now needed him to help ensure success at the ballot box, and Blair once again gladly answered the call to duty on the political battlefront.

59. Alexander to MB, September 10, 15, 1864, BLC; Apo to FPB, October 1, 1864, B-LP.

9

Marching through Georgia and the Carolinas

Taking a thirty-day leave from the army, Frank headed for St. Louis by way of Lexington, Kentucky, where he spent several days visiting Uncle Ben and other relatives. En route, he learned that Montgomery had resigned as postmaster general at the request of the president. Much had occurred on the political front since Blair's departure from Congress. Even as he joined in the advance on Atlanta, he kept abreast of political developments. Both Frank and Montgomery had come under increasing attack from the Radicals since the Baltimore convention. The Blairs had received setbacks there in the seating of the Radical Missouri delegation. The platform included a plank, presented by the Missouri delegation, announcing that "harmony should prevail in the national councils, and we regard as worthy of public confidence and official trust those only who cordially endorse the principles proclaimed in these resolutions and which should characterize the administration of the government." Most observers assumed that this was directed at Montgomery and other conservatives, including Attorney General Bates and Secretary of the Navy Welles.[1]

In the weeks after his return to the army in May, Frank had been denied his seat in Congress; and the Radicals had put continuing pressure on the president to explain the reinstatement of his military commission. Fremont had continued to be a thorn in Lincoln's side through the summer of 1864, refusing

1. Hickenlooper Reminiscences, 73–74; W. E. Smith, *Blair Family in Politics*, 2:266–68; E. B. Smith, *Francis Preston Blair*, 342–43.

to withdraw from the contest even after losing the Democratic nomination to George B. McClellan. The Radicals, meanwhile, had launched a spirited campaign in Congress and elsewhere against Lincoln's conciliatory plan of reconstruction. Sen. Benjamin Wade of Ohio and Cong. Henry Winter Davis of Maryland had pushed a bill through Congress calling for a much harsher reconstruction, only to have the president apply a pocket veto. This move led them, in turn, to deliver a blistering manifesto against Lincoln's action. The Radicals later hinted, through Sen. Zachariah Chandler of Michigan, that they might be more conciliatory if the president removed Montgomery from the cabinet. Reluctantly, Lincoln agreed in an effort to promote party harmony. Montgomery had offered to resign earlier and now stepped aside gracefully, pleased with the knowledge that he would be succeeded by the Blairs' longtime friend, former governor William Dennison of Ohio. Frank wrote his father that Montgomery did right in resigning, as no sacrifice was too great to ensure the president's reelection, although he greatly resented the triumph it gave to their enemies.[2]

Frank arrived home very thin and worn and with his injured hand still bothering him. His limited leave would not allow him to come to Washington, so Apo urged his parents to make the trip west; but this proved impossible. Blair faced a major challenge upon his return. Following their rejection by the Baltimore convention, a number of conservatives had reorganized the Missouri Democratic Party and supported the nomination of McClellan at the Democratic National Convention at Chicago. They later nominated a slate of candidates for state office headed by Thomas L. Price, a staunch Benton Democrat in the 1850s, for governor.[3]

The Radicals, meanwhile, had chosen Thomas C. Fletcher as their gubernatorial candidate on a Radical Union ticket. One of Blair's officers in the Vicksburg campaign, Fletcher had been wounded and captured during the fighting at Chickasaw Bayou. Later paroled, he rejoined Frank as a brigade

2. *Missouri Contested Election;* W. E. Smith, *Blair Family in Politics,* 2:276–88; E. B. Smith, *Francis Preston Blair,* 343–47; EBL to SPL, September 30*, 1864, B-LP; FB to FPB, September 30, 1864, BLC. On September 22, the day before Montgomery's resignation, Fremont withdrew from the presidential race. Some early historians have tried to tie the two events together, but more recent analyses would indicate that the Pathfinder realized the hopelessness of his quest after failing to secure the Democratic nomination and that his withdrawal was not predicated upon Montgomery's subsequent action (Zornow, *Lincoln and the Party Divided,* 144–46; David E. Long, *The Jewel of Liberty: Abraham Lincoln's Re-election and the End of Slavery,* 239–42).

3. Apo to FPB, October 1, 1864, EBL to SPL, October 5*, 1864, B-LP; Parrish, *Turbulent Partnership,* 187–88.

commander in the Chattanooga and Atlanta campaigns. The Radicals also stepped up their campaign to remove Peter Foy from the St. Louis post-mastership in the wake of Montgomery's resignation. Frank dispatched Foy to Washington and wrote his father to have Postmaster General Dennison stand firm against this, which he did. The *Missouri Republican* endorsed the Democratic ticket, while most of the Radical press, including the *Missouri Democrat*, announced their support for Lincoln and Fletcher. Fletcher made no open statement of his feelings concerning the presidency until the end of October, a month after Fremont had withdrawn from the race, for fear of alienating the German vote.[4]

With the Radicals endorsing Lincoln and claiming the Union banner, Blair had no choice but to support them, while trying to hold as many of his conservative friends in line for the president as possible. Some of these men had been ready to denounce Lincoln for his action against Montgomery, but Frank arrived in time to stop them. At a meeting of the various factions, Peter Foy, as Blair's representative, sought to make common cause with the Radicals by proposing that all candidates run on an unadorned Union ticket, united only by their support of Lincoln. The Radicals refused to drop the Radical label, however, so the conservatives withdrew from the meeting, although several found places on the county slate. Thereafter, the pro-Lincoln conservatives generally expressed their support quietly, while Frank concentrated his efforts on getting out the soldier vote in Missouri and Indiana. In the end, fifty-two thousand fewer Missourians went to the polls in 1864 than four years earlier. The Radicals made a clean sweep. Lincoln won the state by not quite forty thousand votes, and Fletcher ran slightly ahead of that. The voters also approved the Radicals' call for a new state convention to reconsider the emancipation issue. They simultaneously elected its delegates, three-fourths of whom were Radicals.[5]

Frank's return home coincided with a new invasion of the state by Confederate forces led by his old enemy, Sterling Price. Moving up through the southeastern corner of the state, Price hoped to strike at St. Louis and then move west to reinstall the pro-Confederate state government at Jefferson City. Stymied by a gallant federal defense at Pilot Knob, he abandoned the St. Louis

4. FB to FPB, September 30, 1864, BLC; Parrish, *Turbulent Partnership*, 184–88.

5. EBL to SPL, October 4*, 1864, B-LP; Lincoln to Rosecrans, September 26, 1864, Rosecrans to Lincoln, October 3, 1864, C. D. Drake to Lincoln, October 5, 1864, John G. Nicolay to Lincoln, October 10, 18, 1864, Lincoln Papers; FB to FPB, November 10, 1864, BLC; Benjamin Thomas, *Abraham Lincoln: A Biography*, 450; Parrish, *Turbulent Partnership*, 195.

maneuver. He then headed west along the south bank of the Missouri River, pursued by federal troops, who ultimately defeated him at Westport near Kansas City and drove him back into Arkansas.

During the crisis, Maj. Gen. William S. Rosecrans, who now commanded the Department of Missouri, accepted Frank's offer to help with the defense of the city and put him in charge of constructing temporary fortifications. In typical fashion, Blair immediately took charge, touching off a tremendous protest from the Radicals. Apo and Peter Foy reported that Gratz Brown and Henry Blow stirred up the Germans by telling them that Frank planned to march them off to Arkansas to repay them for their defection. A mob stormed city hall in protest until the mayor agreed that Brown "will have immediate command of the exempts" to organize the city's defense. Rosecrans used the arrival of Brig. Gen. Alfred Pleasanton the following day to announce that Frank's services, although greatly appreciated, were no longer needed. The Blairs were amused, although Apo expressed great bitterness against cousin Gratz and announced that she hoped the family would keep their distance from him when he came to Washington for the congressional session.[6]

Frank returned to active duty in late October. During his stay in St. Louis, he and Apo had had several long talks about the future. His financial fortunes had continued to suffer during his absence, and Apo had been forced to sell off several additional properties. She had written him in early September, "You will see that our fortunes are growing smaller & bountifully less but it will not take one iota from my happiness to be poor if you are satisfied to live a quiet poor life. I am used to it but you are not." With the advent of the Radical triumph in Missouri, Frank anticipated his personal retirement from politics, something that Apo had sought for a long time. Concerned about the future of Missouri, they discussed the possibility of moving to California to make a new beginning. Ever desirous of his family's input, Frank informed his father, "When this war is over it will be time enough to talk over my plans for the future. . . . I hope to receive your sanction but I have had enough of politics. I do not think that anything will again induce me to enter upon that career." His father acquiesced, whether reluctantly or not is not clear.[7]

6. *OR*, 1:41:3:441–42, 480, 508; *Missouri Democrat,* September 30, 1864; *Missouri Republican,* October 1, 1864; Apo to FPB, October 1, November 24, 1864, EBL to SPL, October 4, 1864, B-LP. In spite of Apo's admonition, Gratz Brown continued to be welcome at No. 4 and Silver Spring (EBL to SPL, December 13*, 1864, B-LP).

7. *OR*, 1:39:3:533; Apo to FB, September 8, 1864, FB to FPB, November 10, 1864, FB to Apo, November 10, 1864, BLC; Christine Blair to FB, November 12, 1864, EBL to SPL, November 20, 1864, B-LP.

Ecstatic over this decision, Apo assured her in-laws, "[Frank] has a political & military record of which his children can well be proud. I believe no man of his age has rendered greater or more disinterested services to his country & now that he is determined to devote the rest of his life to his family I can be thankful that he has been useful in his day & generation."[8]

Such thoughts had to be put aside for the time being, however. Upon his return to Atlanta, Blair discovered that Sherman had made plans to cut his lines of supply and communication and begin his famous "March to the Sea." Frank wrote Apo on November 10 from near Marietta not to worry if she did not hear from him for some time. Undaunted as ever, he promised to take good care of himself. One of his concerns was the loss of his brother-in-law Andrew Alexander as his assistant adjutant general. Andrew had stayed behind during Frank's leave to wind up the affairs of the Seventeenth Corps, then had hastened on his own leave to marry Eveline Martin in Willowbrook, New York. Frank and Apo, to their great regret, had been unable to attend the wedding. Andrew's leave had prolonged his absence beyond Sherman's departure from Atlanta, and Frank rearranged his staff accordingly.[9]

On November 9, Sherman issued Special Field Orders No. 120, outlining in very general terms the campaign ahead. Frank's Seventeenth Corps would form the right wing of the march, together with the Fifteenth, whose commander, Logan, would not rejoin them until they reached Savannah, under the overall command of Maj. Gen. O. O. Howard. The Fourteenth and Twentieth Corps composed the left wing under Maj. Gen. H. W. Slocum. The total force numbered about sixty thousand men. They were to march on four parallel roads with no general train of supplies. Rather, the orders called for the army to "forage liberally on the country during the march," with the corps commanders alone being given "the power to destroy mills, houses, cotton gins, &c." Such destruction would occur only in areas where they met guerrilla or other resistance. Where the army was allowed to pass unmolested, no such destruction should occur. Horses, mules, and wagons could be taken liberally as needed for replacements. Slaves attempting to follow the army could do so only if able-bodied and capable of service because supplies would be limited.

---

8. Apo to FPB, November 24, 1864, B-LP.

9. *OR*, 1:39:3:716; FB to Apo, November 10, 1864, BLC; Apo to FPB, October 1, 1864, EBL to SPL, November 2, 1864, Eveline Martin Alexander to FB, November 8, 1864, A. J. Alexander to FPB, November 26, 1864, B-LP; Wilson, *Life of Alexander*, 73–75. Eveline's parents were close friends of the senior Blairs, and she had been their guest many times at Silver Spring, where she met Andrew. This relationship would become even more important during Frank's final illness (Cornelia Williams Martin, *The Old Home, 1817–1850*, 1:41–45).

The army received no indication of its destination, and surprisingly no one seriously questioned their commander.[10]

The last trains chugged off to the north on November 12, and Frank's corps then had the assignment of destroying the rails between Big Shanty and Atlanta in preparation for the march. Quickly completing this work, they marched to White Hall just south of the city. On the morning of November 15, Blair's staff arose for breakfast at two in the morning in the stately mansion that had been their headquarters. Concluding just before dawn, they piled up the furniture in the center of the dining room, applied a match, and watched the building go up in flames, "having paid the penalty of its owners disloyalty." They then headed east with their corps, the entire movement covering a front thirty miles wide with the cavalry serving as an advance force to sweep aside any enemy they might encounter.[11]

As one member of the Eighteenth Missouri later recalled, what ensued was "a pleasant campaign with little fighting and plenty to eat." The army moved into the Confederate heartland—"a perfect garden," as one of Sherman's officers described it. They found plenty of fodder for their horses and mules, and another one of the Missourians remembered enthusiastically, "those hams, cured with but little salt were the nicest we had ever eaten." Blair's staff had to constantly keep the line of march moving as plenty of motive existed for straggling through the abundant countryside. At night his staff headquarters and Sherman's would frequently be in the same vicinity. The two generals had come to have a strong respect for each other over the past year and a half; and Frank became a regular evening visitor at Sherman's camp, where the two men sat around the campfire and reviewed the day's activities.[12]

Sherman's army met little opposition. The Confederates had only about fifteen thousand available men in the vicinities of Augusta and Macon. The Confederate cavalry commander, Maj. Gen. Joseph Wheeler, could do little beyond hovering on the flanks of the advancing Union troops, trying to guess at their destination and reporting periodically to his superiors on their destructive course.[13]

10. *OR*, 1:39:3:713–14; Marszalek, *Sherman*, 298.
11. *OR*, 1:39:3:716–17, 751; Hickenlooper Reminiscences, 78–79; Joseph Sladen Diary.
12. Leslie Anders, *The Eighteenth Missouri*, 273–76; Hickenlooper Reminiscences, 79; Marszalek, *Sherman*, 298; Hitchcock, *Marching with Sherman*, 109–10, 120, 136, 141, 153–57, 166.
13. Lewis, *Sherman*, 441; *OR*, 1:44:859, 870.

The Seventeenth Corps reached Gordon on the Georgia Central Railroad on November 21 and accomplished its destruction as far as the Oconee River. Here, they met their first opposition; but they quickly routed the rebel force and placed pontoon bridges, which allowed the Army of the Tennessee to cross with no difficulty on Saturday, November 26. Although the following day was Sunday, the men received no rest. Sherman joined Frank that morning to watch the men of the Seventeenth continue their destruction of railroad property east of the river as the army marched steadily on toward Savannah.

By December 2, the corps had reached Millen at the intersection of the Georgia Central and Augusta Railroads. Blair ordered the depot and warehouses burned. Four miles further north, his men discovered a three-hundred-yard square with a log stockade used to house federal prisoners. The Millen prison pen had no shelter from the weather and no source of water. Adjacent, Frank's men found seven hundred unmarked graves. The survivors had been hastily evacuated and moved south. Lt. Col. Andrew Hickenlooper, Blair's chief of staff, later recalled, "I sadly contemplated the abundant evidence of the exposure, suffering, starvation and death of our brave boys, through acts of savage brutality." The troops learned of a nearby plantation whose owner kept a pack of bloodhounds with a contract to hunt down any escaping prisoners "at so much per head." Frank ordered the place destroyed and the dogs killed, which Hickenlooper promptly accomplished.[14]

The army now stood fifty miles north of Savannah, and Sherman gathered his staff around a blazing seven-foot stump to contemplate their next move. The Confederates had entrenched themselves at Savannah behind a series of earthworks, protected by a crescent-shaped cypress swamp. Sherman told Frank that he anticipated flanking the first of these to get at Savannah from the south, where he could link up with the Union blockading squadron. Blair's forces found this last stretch of territory more desolate than the country they had just traversed. As they plunged into the swamp, the men of the Eighteenth Missouri frequently waded in water waist deep, concerned as much with alligators as with the enemy.[15]

On the seventh, while riding with the cavalry advance, Hickenlooper came across an enemy troop. The Federals charged them, only to find the road

14. Hickenlooper Reminiscences, 79–80; Sladen Diary; Anders, *Eighteenth Missouri*, 276–79; Thomas W. Osborn, *The Fiery Trail: A Union Officer's Account of Sherman's Last Campaigns*, 65. For background on Hickenlooper, see note 52, chapter 8.

15. Hitchcock, *Marching with Sherman*, 141; Anders, *Eighteenth Missouri*, 279–81; Sladen Diary; Osborn, *Fiery Trail*, 67.

pockmarked with buried torpedoes, which killed the horses and seriously wounded several of the troopers. When Hickenlooper and Lieutenant Tupper dismounted to investigate, they unavoidably discharged yet another torpedo, blowing off Tupper's leg. Upon hearing of this incident, Frank ordered his prisoners forward and forced them, under penalty of being shot, to dig up the rest of the torpedoes, ahead of his advancing men. When Sherman rode up, the prisoners begged off, but the general supported Frank, denouncing the Confederates who had placed the mines there as cold-blooded assassins. Shortly after this, Blair, himself, had a close call when a twelve-pound shot came down the road and passed directly over his head with little room to spare, killing a captain and his horse directly behind him.[16]

By December 10, Sherman had reached Savannah only to discover Confederate general William J. Hardee well entrenched behind high parapets. Realizing the futility of a frontal assault, Sherman moved along the Ogeechee River to the south of the city, where, on December 13, he sent Brig. Gen. William B. Hazen's division of the Fifteenth Corps against Fort McAlister. Hardee abandoned the city, escaping across the Savannah River into South Carolina. Almost simultaneously, the armies of George Thomas and John Schofield, whom Sherman had sent north to Tennessee following the fall of Atlanta, defeated the Confederate forces of John Bell Hood near Nashville. Frank wrote Apo from Savannah, "The Southern Confederacy is like an egg & you encounter nothing more after once breaking the shell." He sent a captured pistol to his son Jimmy, "as he begged me to get him one from the rebels." Meanwhile, Sherman presented Lincoln with a more appropriate Christmas present: the city of Savannah.[17]

Frank selected as his headquarters in Savannah the home of a Mrs. Shaaff, who entertained him and his officers cordially. She had relatives near Washington who were good friends of his father, and Blair appreciated her hospitality. Her husband, a former major in federal service, had accepted a Confederate commission and was with their forces elsewhere.

Mrs. Shaaff had a younger sister, aged nineteen, staying with her, who attracted the attention of several of Frank's officers. One evening, "in a playful spirit of bandage," one of them remarked that he "would very much like to marry and transplant to Northern soil so beautiful and charming a

16. Hickenlooper Reminiscences, 80–81; Hitchcock, *Marching with Sherman*, 161–65.
17. Marszalek, *Sherman*, 306–9; FB to FPB, December 14, 16, 1864, BLC; FB to Apo, December 16, 1864, B-LP.

Southern bud." The next day Mrs. Shaaff asked the officer to call on her. She proceeded to question him about his personal antecedents with the assurance that she had already talked with General Blair, who had given him the highest recommendation. She then told him that, as the young lady's closest relative, she assented to their engagement. Embarrassed, the young officer tactfully explained that he had not meant his proposal to be taken seriously, thus putting a strain on their relations during the remainder of the stay.[18]

Once again mail could be sent and received. Frank had written Apo on December 16 that he was not certain what Sherman intended doing next but that he planned to remain with his corps until the end of the fighting. A distraught Apo replied that she was happy for his safety but wished to have him out of the army and home. "There are so many people who could command the 17th army corps but no one to take your place at home," she wrote tearfully. "Our lives are passing away in these separations & I cannot see that the sacrifices you are making are appreciated or that they have brought the satisfaction that a different life would have done." She and Samuel Simmons had been selling off property to make ends meet, and she had received an offer on the home where they were living. She longed to leave St. Louis where the Radicals were "sweeping everything before them." The children were well but missed their father. In addition, she had not heard from Frank's father and feared that Lizzie had turned the family against them because of their announced desire to leave St. Louis at war's end. "I shall be perfectly willing to go anywhere if you should ever settle down & I have no doubt you will do what is best. All places are alike to me & any would be pleasant with you and my children," she wearily concluded.[19]

By the time Frank received these despondent notes from home, he was already well into South Carolina on the final phase of Sherman's campaign. General Howard had dropped by his headquarters on January 1, 1865, to discover "a New Year's festival." "It was a jolly table that I found with Blair that day, he doing the honors of the occasion," the Army of the Tennessee's commander later reported. Howard came to deliver orders that the Seventeenth Corps would lead the advance into the Palmetto State beginning January 3,

18. FB to MB, January 17, 1865, BLC; Hickenlooper Reminiscences, 88–89. After Frank left Savannah, he asked Montgomery to intercede with the War Department to exempt Mrs. Shaaff from the order banishing all wives of rebel officers from Savannah (William E. Ware to MB, February 15, 1865, BLC).

19. FB to Apo, December 16, 1864, Apo to FB, December 28, 1864, January 9, 18, 1865, B-LP; Apo to FB, January 27, 1865, BLC.

moving by ship to Beaufort, where the Federals had earlier established a base on Port Royal Island. The corps completed its transfer by the eleventh; and Frank was then ordered forward to Pocotaligo, an important supply base on the Charleston-Savannah Railroad. He stayed there until the end of the month, waiting for good weather and the arrival of Logan's Fifteenth Corps.[20]

It rained every day, creating a cold, clammy atmosphere in the camps and impassible roads. Frank complained to Howard about having to leave his black "pioneers" (laborers) in Beaufort. He had plenty of fatigue duty for them to perform at Pocotaligo, for which he was currently compelled to detail his own troops. Further, he wanted to get the pioneers "out of the hands of the recruiting agents of the different States, who are tampering with the men and officers, offering them bribes to enlist for particular States." Such interference, if it proved successful, he disparaged, revealing his innate prejudice, would "deprive me and my corps of a good body of pioneers and encumber the Government with another regiment of negroes to lay around in barracks." There is no indication of the outcome of his request.[21]

Frank established his headquarters at Pocotaligo in "an old dilapidated frame with but two habitable rooms." Sherman caught up with him there on the twenty-sixth and stayed two nights. The two generals spent the time in lengthy conversations concerning "the political situation, government policy, and army movements." Hickenlooper, who shared the quarters, described them as "more confidential and companionable than any other two officers of our army."[22]

Following Sherman's departure, Frank made a quick overnight trip back to Savannah on personal business, accompanied only by Hickenlooper. Staying again at Mrs. Shaaff's, they were sleeping soundly when Hickenlooper was awakened "by volleys of musketry and exploding shells." Assuming that the rebels were trying to retake the city, he hastened to wake the general and warn him. Frank calmly replied, "Well suppose they have, it's none of our fight. Go to bed and we'll see about it in the morning." The next day they discovered that someone had set fire to the arsenal, whose burning and exploding shells had created all the noise. They returned to Pocotaligo that night "without anyone being aware of our temporary absence."[23]

20. Howard, *Autobiography,* 2:96; Hickenlooper Reminiscences, 90; Anders, *Eighteenth Missouri,* 287–90.
21. *OR,* 1:47:2:92, 99.
22. Hickenlooper Reminiscences, 90–91.
23. Ibid., 91–92.

By the end of January, the weather improved, and the roads rapidly dried out. The Army of the Tennessee moved slowly toward Columbia with one of Frank's divisions being sent to make a demonstration so as to create the impression that Charleston might be the army's destination. The outmatched Confederates threw numerous obstacles in the Federals' way as they retreated. At Whippy Swamp, barricaded roads and burned bridges necessitated Blair's men wading, sometimes up to their armpits, into the icy waters to make repairs and scour out the enemy. This scenario would be repeated several times as they advanced.

Sherman made every effort to keep foraging under control, but it became difficult as the men expressed their hatred of South Carolinians, whom they considered the perpetrators of the war. Some of Frank's men had been guilty of depredations in the Beaufort area when they first arrived, and Howard had asked Blair to "ascertain, if possible, approximately, the amount of damage wantonly committed on the island, and have it assessed on the brigade or regiment guilty." Howard issued similar orders to both Blair and Logan later as the march continued across South Carolina. Frank, concerned particularly by reports of wanton pillaging by his First Alabama (Union) Cavalry, warned its commander that he would hold his men to strict accountability. It became increasingly difficult, however, to control individuals who saw nothing wrong with acquiring a variety of souvenirs from the hated South Carolinians.[24]

By February 7, the army had reached Midway on the South Carolina Railroad. From there it moved up the railroad to Orangeburg. As in Georgia, Sherman ordered the road torn up, which Frank's men, by now experts at the work, quickly accomplished. From Orangeburg the army turned west toward Columbia, continuing its destructive pattern.[25]

Some eight miles from the South Carolina capital, the corps camped overnight. Hickenlooper rode up to a nearby plantation to see about its use as Blair's headquarters for the night. Surprisingly, the mistress of the mansion received him kindly. She assured him of her hospitality, expressing only regret at the illness of her daughter, who had been unable to procure any medical attention. Hickenlooper informed her that one of their doctors

24. *OR*, 1:47:1:375–77, 385–89, 405–6, 2:33, 291–92, 505–6; Jacob D. Cox, *The March to the Sea, Franklin and Nashville*, 168–69; Howard, *Autobiography*, 2:103–8; Hickenlooper Reminiscences, 92–95; Anders, *Eighteenth Missouri*, 294–302; Joseph T. Glatthaar, *The March to the Sea and Beyond: Sherman's Troops in the Savannah and Carolinas Campaigns*, 150–51; Lewis, *Sherman*, 493–94.

25. *OR*, 1:47:1:377–79, 2:333–34, 405–8; Osborn, *Fiery Trail*, 106–25; Sherman, *Memoirs*, 2:755–56; Hickenlooper Reminiscences, 94–96; Howard, *Autobiography*, 2:109–12.

would be happy to examine and prescribe for the girl. The lady thanked him and then inquired, "Is all our army coming this way?" At this point Hickenlooper realized that she had mistaken him for a Confederate. When he told her it was Sherman's army at her doorstep, she became quite flustered. Admitting her lack of knowledge concerning the difference in uniforms, she told Hickenlooper, "you deported yourself so like a gentleman that I supposed of course you were a Southern soldier. Had you robbed my house and insulted me and my family I would of course [have] recognized you as a Yankee, but by assuming the character of a gentleman you totally misled and deceived me." Thereupon, she turned and fled to the upper floor of the house.

When Frank and his staff arrived, Hickenlooper took them to the mansion, telling them nothing of his earlier encounter except that the home's mistress had indicated that she had a sick daughter who had been unable to get medical attention. Blair promptly dispatched one of his doctors to check on the girl. Shortly thereafter, as Frank and Hickenlooper were reviewing the events of the day, their hostess burst into the room demanding to see the general. Upon being introduced to Blair, she cried out, "General is it absolutely necessary that I and my family be subjected to the humiliation and brutal indignity of having your officers force their way into my private apartments and demand the privilege of examining my daughter, for the purpose of deciding for themselves whether my representations as to her illness are true? Spare, oh! spare me this pain and humiliation." Frank sent Hickenlooper to check on the situation. He encountered the doctor, holding his hand to a blood-soaked face and cursing. When the aide stopped him for an explanation, he reported that he had knocked on the upstairs door to explain his mission only to have the lady slam it so hard in his face that it broke his nose. Hickenlooper informed Blair of what had happened, but no further attempts to explain the misunderstanding could persuade the woman to unlock her door until after the army had moved on the next day.[26]

Sherman gave the Fifteenth Corps, which had been moving against Columbia from the southwest, the honor of taking the city after the Confederates evacuated it on February 17. Frank's feint against Charleston had been so successful that the Southerners had left the capital virtually undefended. On the day before the city fell, Sherman casually mentioned to Brig. Gen. W. W. Belknap, one of Blair's brigade commanders, that he "would appreciate the men who first made lodgement in Columbia." Belknap quickly authorized

26. Hickenlooper Reminiscences, 96–97.

some of the men of the Thirteenth Iowa to sneak across the Congaree River at dawn and enter the city. Commandeering a buggy, and with a color bearer in tow, they hurried to the center of the town and quickly raised their colors over the city hall and the capitol. Their division commander, Brig. Gen. Giles Smith, then proudly informed Frank that the colors of the Thirteenth Iowa had been floating over the city since eleven that morning, forty-five minutes before the chagrined Fifteenth Corps arrived.[27]

The remainder of the Seventeenth Corps did not enter Columbia, camping two miles north of town. That evening Frank and Hickenlooper went into the city to visit the headquarters of Generals Sherman and Howard. They could already see signs of "growing demoralization." Although Sherman, following his custom, had established a provost guard from men of the Fifteenth Corps to keep order, pillaging became inevitable. Columbia served as a storehouse of liquor, which had been brought into the capital from Charleston and the surrounding countryside. Sherman's men found these stores and quickly confiscated them for their own use. The city quickly turned into a riotous scene of celebration by the occupying troops, released federal prisoners, freed slaves, and anyone else who wanted to join in. The soldiers, realizing that they were in the heart of secession, had little concern for private property. In addition, immense quantities of cotton had been stored throughout the city, tinder for an inferno in the making and already smoldering when Sherman arrived.

As Frank and Hickenlooper returned to their headquarters north of the city, they observed "columns of dense black smoke circling over the doomed city, and with the deepening darkness flashed here and there the fiery tongues of a growing conflagration." En route, they encountered stragglers, many of them women and children "with bundles of clothing hastily snatched from burning or endangered homes." "Occasionally," Hickenlooper later reported, "we met a squad of drunken and demoralized soldiers making light of the pitiful scene, or bands of pilfering citizens, both white and black, loaded down with plunder taken from abandoned stores and dwellings." Since the occupying troops were not from their command, they could do little to bring discipline; but Blair quickly summoned his own headquarters guard, once back at his own location, and stationed them to protect the buildings in his area.[28]

27. *OR*, 1:47:2:462; Hickenlooper Reminiscences, 98; John G. Barrett, *Sherman's March through the Carolinas*, 72.
28. *OR*, 1:47:1:379; Hickenlooper Reminiscences, 99; Barrett, *Sherman's March*, 72–86; Marszalek, *Sherman*, 322–24.

Meanwhile, Sherman became aware of the growing disorder as various citizens came to his headquarters seeking aid. Realizing that his provost guard was not up to the task of keeping order, he brought additional troops into the city for that purpose. As men of the Seventeenth Corps were not required, Frank and Hickenlooper sat on the porch of their occupied residence for a time, discussing what they had observed, before retiring. A distraught Harriett Ravenel, who lived nearby, sent her nurse and a servant to Blair's headquarters at some point seeking protection for her home, which was being constantly threatened. The nurse returned empty-handed, reporting that "General Blair was very sorry, but was too sleepy to do anything." The truth of this cannot be ascertained. One wonders if the guard outside Frank's headquarters simply declined to wake him. Mrs. Ravenel eventually did find help from a young Irish soldier, who took pity on her because she shared his brogue. During the night various groups of miscreants approached Blair's headquarters only to turn away when they saw the guards. About four in the morning, however, "one drunken and smoke-begrimed soldier and two depraved and desperate negroes, while attempting to force an entrance, were summarily dealt with."[29]

The burning of Columbia created one of the most intense controversies of the American Civil War. By the morning of February 18, one-third of the city lay in ruin. Federal generals in their reports stated that they had made serious attempts to halt the flames, lest they destroy the entire town. High winds had quickly fanned the fires, however, and had made their task virtually impossible. Most Columbians later agreed. Sherman blamed the winds and the Confederates who had left huge piles of cotton scattered about the city. The Southern generals refuted this and sought to throw the responsibility back on Sherman and his men. Whether Sherman could have kept better control of the situation remains a more serious question; but, given the circumstances of tired troops suddenly released in a city loaded with whiskey, which had been the cradle of secession, this is doubtful. Historians have generally agreed that the destruction of Columbia left an unfortunate but unavoidable legacy that would long overshadow South Carolina's relations with the rest of the nation.[30]

29. Hickenlooper Reminiscences, 99–100; Katharine M. Jones, *When Sherman Came: Southern Women and the "Great March,"* 162; Marion Brunson Lucas, *Sherman and the Burning of Columbia,* 93–95.

30. Lucas, *Burning of Columbia,* 163–67; Marszalek, *Sherman,* 324–25; Barrett, *Sherman's March,* 88–92.

Except for the small contingent from the Thirteenth Iowa and a few uncontrollable stragglers, the Seventeenth Corps did not enter Columbia on the seventeenth. The following morning, General Howard ordered Frank to assign an officer to maintain order in the northeastern part of the city, with authorization to call upon him for such forces as might be necessary. Blair assigned two brigades to this duty. The bulk of the Seventeenth Corps proceeded north to Winnsboro, destroying the Charlotte and South Carolina Railroad en route. Having accomplished this by the twenty-second, they passed through Winnsboro and continued on to the small village of Liberty Hill.[31]

Here, Hickenlooper approached one of the homes to establish a temporary headquarters. He found "a beautiful and spirited girl," whom he asked for permission to utilize her kitchen and its equipment for the preparation of the staff's meals. The officers themselves would stay in tents, which they would erect upon the lawn. The fiery Southern belle retorted, "No sir! Never would any self-respecting Southern lady consent that Yankee lips should pollute a vessel from which they would afterwards be compelled to drink, or use for the preparation of food." Hickenlooper replied that he regretted her bitterness but would respect her privacy and then began looking around for an adjacent building for his purpose. He discovered near the kitchen a large one-story framed building piled high with bags of peanuts and decided that it would do. He quickly ordered his men to toss the peanuts into the yard to clear out the place.

Immediately, a more contrite young lady appeared to say that she was sorry for the inconvenience she had caused earlier and that the kitchen could now be utilized to save the men the trouble of clearing the outbuilding. Hickenlooper replied that the work had already begun, and they would not bother her or her family again. She suddenly became adamant that the peanuts not be disturbed and mounted the pile already on the lawn to try to stop the work. The men continued, however, causing the growing pile to slide and "making it exceedingly difficult for the young lady to maintain her place on so unstable a foundation without exposing her shapely limbs to the vulgar stare of the rude soldiers."

Finally, the cause of the young woman's concern became evident as the detail discovered that the peanuts had been hiding "one of the richest stores of provision we had yet found." They uncovered all kinds of hams and cured meats, pickles, jellies, liquors, and wines, "sufficient to supply all the various headquarters of the corps during the remaining days of the campaign." With

31. *OR*, 1:47:1:379–80, 475–76, 485.

that, their hostess quickly disappeared, and the corps continued its march the next morning with its newfound loot safely in tow.[32]

The army encountered little opposition until it advanced on Cheraw, the last major town on its line of march within the Palmetto State, although Col. Oscar L. Jackson of the Sixty-third Ohio noted in his diary that at least three soldiers had been killed "a short distance from the road," presumably while straggling or foraging. The Federals pushed the Confederates back through Cheraw and across the Pee Dee River on March 3 in heavy fighting. The occupying force found a considerable array of artillery pieces, armaments, and ammunition, as well as a large complex of ordnance and machine shops. Hickenlooper selected a large imposing mansion for the corps' headquarters. It turned out to be the home of a blockade runner. While clearing out its large basement for use as a mess room, he discovered, among other valuables, "one of the largest and finest stocks of choice wines and liquors that I had ever seen." They had been sent up from Charleston for safety. Frank quickly sent out ambulances "loaded up with choice assortments" to the hospitals and headquarters of every command, while reserving enough supply, which, coupled with what they had taken at Liberty Hill, sufficed them until the end of the campaign.[33]

That evening General Sherman and his staff joined Blair's officers for dinner. As the time wore on, others, including General Logan, stopped by to thank Frank for his earlier thoughtfulness. It was a rainy night, and everyone enjoyed the warmth of the evening as the wine flowed freely. Someone produced a violin, and Logan favored the company with a song. They called upon Adj. S. H. M. Byers to recite his recently completed poem, "Sherman's March to the Sea." Sherman left fairly early. As he was leaving, Frank asked if he would like some saddle blankets or a rug for his tent. Leading the general upstairs, he pointed out a pile of carpets that had also been sent up from Charleston. Sherman later sent his orderly over, and he "came back staggering under a load of carpets, out of which the officers and escort made excellent tent-rugs, saddle-cloths, and blankets." The others continued their merrymaking into the early hours of the morning, and some were pretty drunk by daylight.[34]

32. Hickenlooper Reminiscences, 100–101.

33. *OR*, 1:47:1:381, 2:661, 666–67; Oscar L. Jackson, *The Colonel's Diary*, 187–90; Hickenlooper Reminiscences, 103–4; Sherman, *Memoirs*, 2:773–74; Byers, *With Fire and Sword*, 182.

34. Hickenlooper Reminiscences, 104; Byers, *With Fire and Sword*, 182; W. B. Hazen, *A Narrative of Military Service*, 357; Sherman, *Memoirs*, 2:773–74.

There were somber moments at Cheraw as well. The carelessness of one of the soldiers caused an immense pile of captured powder to explode, shaking the town badly, and killing and maiming several of his fellows. On March 2, Frank ordered a rebel prisoner shot in retaliation for the Confederates having captured one of his foragers and murdering him on the spot. The man, chosen by lot, claimed to have a large family of small children. Nevertheless, the lot had been drawn. After allowing the prisoner time for prayer, he was stood up against a large tree while twelve men of the Thirtieth Illinois did the shooting. "Such," wrote a diarist, "are the necessities of war."[35]

At nearby Bennettsville, Frank had to deal with a problem of another kind. An Ohio sergeant was accused of raping a teenager by three witnesses from the Tenth Illinois, who reported that they saw part of the act and observed the victim and her parents frightened and crying. The sergeant claimed that he had paid for the sexual favors, but a court-martial found him guilty, ordered a dishonorable discharge, and sentenced him to two years in the state prison. Blair remitted the sentence; and the soldier later received a full pardon from President Andrew Johnson, based on additional testimony, with full restitution to his previous rank and unit. In two earlier cases involving his men, Frank had remitted the life imprisonment of an Illinois soldier accused of murdering a friend while intoxicated, after the man served five months, and ordered him restored to rank because of previous good behavior. In another instance, involving an Illinois private, Blair let stand a five-year prison sentence for a month's desertion, even though the soldier produced a letter from an army surgeon that he had been in the hospital the entire time.[36]

The army marched out of Cheraw on March 6, replacing the destroyed bridge over the Pee Dee and heading for North Carolina. Again, they encountered the inevitable late winter rains that plagued the region and made the roads difficult if not impossible to maneuver. They found retreating Confederate cavalry in their front, who destroyed the bridge over the Cape Fear River before Fayetteville as they went. While there, the troops were startled but agreeably surprised to hear the shrill whistle of a steamer flying the Stars and Stripes ascending the Cape Fear. Cheers immediately went up as the gunboat *Eolus* and the tug *Davidson* appeared with mail and intelligence— the first the corps had had in six weeks of campaigning. The boats brought the welcome news that Maj. Gen. Alfred Terry had captured Wilmington,

35. Sherman, *Memoirs*, 2:774; *OR*, 1:47:2:649–50; Cyrus Marion Roberts Diary, 86.
36. Glatthaar, *March to the Sea*, 73–74, 86–87.

which could provide a base of supply for the North Carolina campaign. That afternoon the *Davidson* returned to Wilmington, carrying the first mail the corps had been able to send to loved ones since they had left Pocotaligo. It included a letter from Frank to his father reporting that they had had a trying campaign, although primarily because of the nature of the country through which they had been going rather than the opposition of large enemy forces. He assured Preston that he remained in good spirits and told his father that he believed the Southern people were ready for peace.[37]

Hickenlooper and Jackson reported a remarkable change in the troops' attitude after they crossed the border into North Carolina. They had regarded South Carolinians "as a body and, practically without individual exception, as life long enemies of the Union, and as primarily responsible for the war," which made it extremely hard for the officers to control their pillaging. Indeed, Frank had called the excesses of foraging to Howard's attention on March 7 and asked that it be discontinued as necessity no longer required it. Three days later Blair issued specific orders that "Nothing should be taken except what is absolutely necessary for the use of the army." Once beyond the confines of the Palmetto State, "the whole demeanor of the army changed, and the men yielded with alacrity to the restraints of discipline." It quickly became evident, however, that the fairly easy progress they had made through South Carolina would not be duplicated further north.[38]

General Sherman had managed to keep the rebel army divided by the interposition of his larger force through secrecy and skill. But the troops soon realized that the Confederates, whom they had driven from Cheraw, were being reinforced. Sherman also learned through a chance newspaper at Cheraw that his old antagonist, Joseph E. Johnston, had replaced P. G. T. Beauregard as commander of the Confederate forces in the Carolinas.[39]

Sherman made several important decisions at Fayetteville. He sent word to the recently arrived General Schofield and General Terry to meet him at Goldsboro with all their available forces. He had hoped that the *Davidson* would bring him badly needed clothing and shoe replacements, but Terry reported that they could not be had at Wilmington. Instead he sent forage for the army's animals, which Sherman hardly needed, given the effectiveness of his bummers. Sherman also decided to rid himself of the immense crowd of refugees,

37. Hickenlooper Reminiscences, 104–5; FB to FPB, March 12, 1865, B-LP.

38. *OR*, 1:47:2:714–18, 760–61, 783; Hickenlooper Reminiscences, 105–6; Jackson, *Colonel's Diary*, 198.

39. Barrett, *Sherman's March*, 111–12; Marszalek, *Sherman*, 327.

both white and black, who had followed him north from Columbia, thereby further impeding his progress. He wrote Terry that "They are dead weight to me and consume our supplies." He ordered Blair's men to accompany the refugees as far as Clinton, from where they would turn south to Wilmington.[40]

The army moved out of Fayetteville on March 15, again divided into two wings: Slocum on the left and Howard on the right. The latter met little resistance, but Slocum was first confronted by Hardee at Averasboro, where he quickly outflanked the Confederates and forced them back, and then by Johnston at Bentonville, in what became the major battle of the campaign on March 19. Johnston had decided to concentrate his forces against the left wing in the hope of surprising and defeating it before the right wing, including Frank's Seventeenth Corps, could come to its rescue.[41]

Forewarned at the last moment, Slocum quickly sent word to Sherman to bring up the remaining troops while he entrenched to await Johnston's attack. Howard sent Logan's Fifteenth Corps forward quickly, followed by the Seventeenth. Fighting was light on the twentieth as the two sides felt each other out. Frank and his staff met with Sherman at Falling Creek Church at three o'clock the following morning and received their marching orders. The Seventeenth Corps was to occupy the far right of the Union line. Not fully aware of the size of Johnston's force, Sherman wanted to avoid major fighting, if possible, hoping to keep casualties to a minimum at this late stage while awaiting "cooperating forces."

Blair's corps was in line by daybreak. Brig. Gen. Joseph A. Mower's division on the extreme right encountered annoying fire from the enemy and moved aggressively forward. Howard quickly ordered Frank to reinforce Mower with his entire corps. Sherman countermanded the order, however, ordering Mower back as well, in line with his earlier announced plan, much to Blair's disgust. That night Johnston withdrew to the north, leaving the field to Sherman. The Federals lost 1,604 men during the three days of fighting, with 193 of them from the Seventeenth Corps. Sherman later admitted his mistake in not supporting Mower's breakthrough, which, if followed, might have resulted in the destruction of Johnston's army. Yet, he had been motivated by a desire to avoid unnecessary bloodshed at this late stage of the war.[42]

40. Barrett, *Sherman's March*, 135–49; Jackson, *Colonel's Diary*, 192–93; Hickenlooper Reminiscences, 106; Howard, *Autobiography*, 2:139–40; *OR*, 1:47:2:823, 848; Osborn, *Fiery Trail*, 192.
41. Barrett, *Sherman's March*, 148–63; Marszalek, *Sherman*, 328–30.
42. Barrett, *Sherman's March*, 163–85; Marszalek, *Sherman*, 330–31; Howard, *Autobiography*, 2:143–51; Hickenlooper Reminiscences, 106–8; *OR*, 1:47:1:67–73, 382–83.

The Seventeenth Corps continued its advance, arriving in Goldsboro on March 24 and finding Schofield already there. For all intents and purposes, the war in the Carolinas had ended, and most of the soldiers realized it. They had marched nearly five hundred miles since leaving Savannah, through swamps and over dusty roads, which frequently turned to quagmires in the rain. They had fought numerous skirmishes and one major battle and had taken the war to the heart of the enemy's country. As they marched into Goldsboro, the troops were a bedraggled, if not a comic, lot. Many had acquired pets along the way, which they carried on their shoulders or in knapsacks or dragged along on a rope. Few of them had much left in the way of a standard uniform. Indeed, Hickenlooper, in taking inventory of the Seventeenth Corps, reported that "there were 5,023 men without uniform pants, 3,888 destitute of boots and shoes, 2,726 without regulation hats or caps, and 2,298 without uniform coats."[43]

Frank invited Sherman to an impromptu review of his men as they filed into Goldsboro, en route to their camps. Schofield and the other officers joined them. Schofield's clean-shaven and well-dressed soldiers lined the thoroughfare, laughing at the passing ragamuffins and receiving catcalls from the weary men of the Seventeenth in return. Many of the passing troops had lost their pants legs to the knees, and Frank was heard to remark to Sherman, "See those poor fellows with bare legs." The general quickly replied, "Splendid legs! Splendid legs! I would give both of mine for any one of them." He soon realized the difficulty the men were encountering in trying to keep some kind of formation after their long march and called off the rest of the impromptu review after two regiments had passed.[44]

Shortly after stacking their guns and lighting their campfires, the men of Sherman's army heard the welcome shriek of a locomotive indicating that railroad communication had been opened from their new base of operations at Wilmington one hundred miles away. Over the next few days, regular runs brought all kinds of supplies, including clothing, shoes, and repair equipment for wagons and harnesses. Workmen began preparing the army for renewed marching. In less than fifteen days, all was in readiness.[45]

43. Barrett, *Sherman's March,* 186; Hickenlooper Reminiscences, 108; Hazen, *Narrative of Military Service,* 360.

44. Hickenlooper Reminiscences, 108; Barrett, *Sherman's March,* 186–87; Burke Davis, *Sherman's March,* 241–42.

45. Hickenlooper Reminiscences, 108.

Sherman's effective strength now stood at 88,948 men, of whom 80,968 were infantry, 2,443 artillery, and 5,537 cavalry. Of these, 12,600 belonged to the Seventeenth Corps. The corps had 385 wagons and 77 ambulances, 3,107 mules, and 2,156 horses. While at Greensboro, Frank requested and received permission to raise an additional regiment of black troops from among the hundreds of refugees flocking into the army's lines. This stood in remarkable contrast to his opposition to such enlistments two years earlier. Proud of his corps' accomplishments, he ordered a new badge to distinguish the Seventeenth. It consisted of an arrow, because "In its swiftness, in its surety of striking where wanted, and in its destructive powers when so intended, it is probably as emblematical of this corps as any design that could be adopted." Some of his men fashioned their own arrows from silver spoons and wore them proudly on their hats. No one asked where the spoons had come from.[46]

Hickenlooper resumed his duties as inspector general and "aided in divesting the command of much of impedimenta by gathering in and confiscating the personal plunder which the boys had accumulated during their march through South Carolina." He accomplished this by having the men muster for parade and inspection while his assistants went through their belongings back in quarters. In the process they collected "the largest and most heterogeneous mass of booty ever gathered together by pilfering soldiers. There were probably 25,000 different articles, embracing everything that mind can conceive, from a paper of pins to a woman's nightdress. Some, such as watches, rings and jewelry, were of considerable value, but the great mass of the find, stuff for which the possessor could have no earthly use either present or prospective, but which had been accumulated simply from an unreasoning spirit of acquisition." Hickenlooper realized, of course, that such pilfering was not limited to the rank and file. Officers, too, had accumulated their own souvenirs. While some had been taken from occupied residences, Hickenlooper surmised that much of it had been acquired from secret caches, often miles away from their homes, to which freed slaves led the bummers in gratitude for their freedom.[47]

46. *OR*, 1:47:1:43, 3:21, 117, 122, 3:5:394; Albion Gross to wife, March 30, 1865, Albion Gross Letters and journal. Frank also took time while at Goldsboro to submit a detailed report of the corps' activities over the past two months (*OR*, 1:47:1:375–85).

47. Hickenlooper himself acquired a thoroughbred horse belonging to Roger Pryor during a raid against Confederate cavalry on that individual's plantation. He turned it over to the quartermaster and then ten days later paid the government-established price of

The opening of communication to the coast brought the first mail the men had received in two months. In two days alone, 514 bags of mail arrived for Sherman's army. Frank received a letter from Apo that contained lots of family news. She reported all the children well except young Jimmy, who had the measles. Apo noted, somewhat nostalgically, "I missed the attentions of your friends very much at first but find now I get on just as well without them & more independently. I can buy coal & go to the gas office & the meat contractors very well myself & ask no favors of anyone. But it is [a] rather strange thing to note the change from a year ago when there were so many who seemed such good friends." Apo looked forward to the end of the war and eagerly awaited word from Frank as to when she should join him in Washington.[48]

On April 10, the army moved out of Goldsboro and headed for Raleigh. Retreating Confederate skirmishers slowed their advance. Brig. Gen. Mortimer Leggett's Third Division encountered entrenched Confederate infantry at Smithfield on the eleventh but finally forced them to retreat across the Neuse River, burning the bridge as they went. At Smithfield, the corps learned of Lee's surrender to Grant two days earlier. Hickenlooper later recalled, "Our banners were unfurled, the bands sent forth their sweetest strains, cheer upon cheer echoed far away over hill and dale, and evidence of intense joy and satisfaction were everywhere apparent."[49]

In the wake of this news, Sherman received word that Gov. Zebulon Vance was sending two commissioners to negotiate a suspension of hostilities in that area and to arrange for the peaceful occupation of the state capital. One of the commissioners was former governor David L. Swain, the president of the University of North Carolina during Blair's student days in Chapel Hill. Upon their arrival at Sherman's camp, Swain asked about Frank, whom Sherman immediately summoned. The two men talked far into the night, reminiscing about earlier days. Sherman treated the commissioners courteously, but he made no commitments other than to ask them to tell Vance to remain in

---

$125 for such an animal. Pryor sought to reclaim the animal after the war, but was turned down by the War Department after Sherman demonstrated the legality of Hickenlooper's claim. Frank's aide then sold the horse to Lawrence Jerome, one of Frank's sporting friends in New York City, for $3,000, giving him "a nice little nest-egg to carry home upon my return from the war" (Hickenlooper Reminiscences, 108–10).

48. Barrett, *Sherman's March*, 192; Apo to FB, March 15, 1865, B-LP.

49. Barrett, *Sherman's March*, 204–7; Hickenlooper Reminiscences, 113; Roberts Diary, 91.

Raleigh and keep the state government functioning. The governor, having had no word from his commissioners, however, had already fled the city, leaving its surrender to the mayor.[50]

Sherman's army reached Raleigh on April 14. The general issued strict orders against burning and looting. Anyone caught setting fire to any building would be shot. He established sentinels at each occupied house along the road into the city. The Seventeenth Corps marched through Raleigh and went into camp three miles northwest, along Hillsborough and Chapel Hill Roads. Frank made his headquarters at the home of an old friend from Chapel Hill days, Dr. Richard Haywood, in a lovely Georgian brick mansion near the capitol. When Haywood confided that he had buried the family's silver service in the garden and that the well hid a pair of massive brass andirons, Frank told him to reclaim them as those were among the first places that bummers looked. A few days later, Sherman stopped by the Haywood home and joined the two men in a toast to the end of the war.[51]

In the late afternoon of his arrival in Raleigh, Sherman received a message from Johnston asking for a cessation of hostilities, in light of Robert E. Lee's surrender, "to permit the civil authorities to enter into the needful arrangements to terminate the existing war." Sherman quickly replied, indicating his willingness to meet his opponent to accomplish that end. They made arrangements to confer near Durham's Station. Just as he was about to board the train to take him there on the morning of April 17, Sherman received a coded telegram telling him of Lincoln's assassination. He determined to withhold the information until his return and continued to the meeting. Once there, Sherman showed Johnston the telegram in confidence. Both generals agreed that this forebode tragic circumstances for both sides. After a lengthy discussion, Johnston offered to surrender all Confederate forces still under arms, thereby brushing aside civilian authority, which Sherman had indicated he could not recognize anyway. Without reaching a definite conclusion, the two agreed to continue their discussions the next day.[52]

Upon his return to Raleigh, Sherman sent a confidential memorandum to Frank telling him of Lincoln's assassination. He summoned Blair to a meeting at his headquarters, where the "feeling of depression and apprehension was

50. Barrett, *Sherman's March*, 210–17; Lewis, *Sherman*, 529–32.
51. *OR*, 1:47:2:187–88; Hickenlooper Reminiscences, 113–14; FB to MB, April 12, 1867, BLC; Davis, *Sherman's March*, 256.
52. Marszalek, *Sherman*, 341–43; Lewis, *Sherman*, 532–36; Barrett, *Sherman's March*, 226–35.

indescribable." Sherman did not want to release the news generally until he had strengthened the provost guard throughout the city, lest his soldiers get out of hand at the news and try to take some kind of revenge upon the Raleigh community. Once they heard the announcement, most of the men reacted with anger. "We'll hang Jeff Davis to a sour apple tree" could be heard in many camps, and a large group of Logan's men actually began a march on the city, only to be turned back by their commander's threat of artillery. Undoubtedly, Frank shared the tremendous feeling of sorrow at the loss of a close friend. Lizzie wrote Phil immediately upon hearing the news, "I am full of terror for you—for Father[,] Frank & all my dear ones."[53]

Sherman met with Frank and his other generals the following morning to solicit their advice for his second meeting with Johnston that afternoon. Without exception they urged him to work out peace terms with his Confederate counterpart. Indeed, the night before, Frank had excitedly told Dr. Edward Warren, who had accompanied Governor Vance's peace commissioners, to write out a memorandum to the effect that North Carolina would be "immediately restored to the Union without the loss of a single element of her sovereignty, and with all the machinery of her existing government," which he proposed giving to Sherman as a suggestion the following day.[54]

When Sherman rejoined Johnston on the afternoon of the eighteenth, the two men haggled for several hours before the former finally took pen in hand and wrote out his terms, which were generally quite lenient. As Sherman saw them, they reflected his understanding of Lincoln's plans for the postwar South as transmitted to him during a recent meeting in Virginia. Confederate armies would surrender their arms at their respective state capitals and agree to obey federal authority. Even as Frank had proposed with regard to North Carolina, existing state governments would be recognized and the federal court system reestablished. There would be a general amnesty so long as Southerners resumed peaceful pursuits. There was no mention of slavery. In the interim, until Washington approved the terms, a truce would exist between the two armies.[55]

When Sherman showed the proposed terms to his commanders, both Frank and Logan expressed their strong agreement. Indeed, the only apparent dissenter was Carl Schurz, serving as Slocum's chief of staff. Schurz felt

---

53. *OR*, 1:47:3:239; Hickenlooper Reminiscences, 115; Marszalek, *Sherman*, 343–44; EBL to SPL, April 14*, 1865, B-LP.
54. Edward Warren, *A Doctor's Experiences in Three Continents*, 345–46.
55. Lewis, *Sherman*, 533–36; Marszalek, *Sherman*, 344–45.

that the general had been too generous and predicted the terms' rejection by Washington. In this, he proved correct, for a cabinet, still in shock from the assassination, quickly pronounced the terms too lenient. Secretary of War Stanton, in particular, attacked Sherman in the press, accusing him of overstepping his authority. As a result, an even more decided reaction set in. General Grant was dispatched to Raleigh to inform Sherman that he must resume hostilities unless Johnston accepted unconditionally the same terms that had been approved by General Lee. Frank's old adversary, Salmon P. Chase, also appeared in Raleigh and reiterated the Washington sentiment that this was no time for leniency.[56]

Although shocked by the negative reactions, Sherman quickly arranged a new meeting with Johnston. Accompanied by Blair, Howard, and Schofield, he presented his counterpart with the same general conditions previously offered Lee by Grant. Johnston accepted. The troops received the news enthusiastically. The men of the Seventeenth Corps called on Frank for a speech, and he obliged, telling them that they would march into Raleigh the next day and then head for Richmond and Washington. The war had ended. The troops could begin the long journey home.[57]

On April 29, Sherman's army moved out of Raleigh and headed for Petersburg, with the Seventeenth Corps serving as the "regulating column" for each day's march. Sherman issued strict orders against foraging. The army reached Petersburg on May 7. That evening Frank and Hickenlooper called on Sherman, who had just returned from Washington, where apparently he had discovered the full extent of the venomous attacks upon him by Stanton and General Halleck, who had long been a friend.

Halleck had just been placed in charge of military affairs in Richmond and had ordered that the troops pass in review before him the following day. Hickenlooper reported, "I never before saw [Sherman] in such a towering passion, or even angry, and never believed that he was capable of using such scathing and denunciatory language as he did in reference to General Halleck." Frank, who had become quite close to Sherman during the past two years, sympathized with the general's position. He had written Montgomery earlier that the whole army was annoyed by the secretary of war's attack

56. Hickenlooper Reminiscences, 115; Roberts Diary, 93; FB to MB, April 30, 1865, BLC; Marszalek, *Sherman,* 346–51; Barrett, *Sherman's March,* 243–44, 267–69; Lewis, *Sherman,* 536–55.
57. Hitchcock, *Marching with Sherman,* 315; Roberts Diary, 93–94; *OR,* 1:47:3:308; Barrett, *Sherman's March,* 270–71.

on Sherman and warned that if President Johnson retained Stanton it would make him "odious" to every man in the army. Sherman repudiated Halleck's order, and the Seventeenth Corps marched through Richmond before daylight to their camps on the Chickahominy. Frank now took temporary leave of his men, turning the command over to General Leggett to bring them to Washington, where he planned to rejoin them.[58]

Frank had been anxious to leave for some time. He had applied for a leave in Raleigh, but Sherman and Howard had been unwilling to release him that soon so he did not insist on it. General Grant later ordered him to march up from Richmond with his men, but Blair had left before receiving this letter. Lizzie wrote excitedly to Phil that the entire family eagerly awaited his coming. They also expected Apo momentarily. Apo had written Frank that she would leave St. Louis in late April to go to Silver Spring. She was anxious to see him and begin planning their future. She reported gratefully that Phil Lee, who was in St. Louis at the time, had been to see her several times and on one occasion had left an envelope containing three hundred dollars with which to buy shoes for the boys.[59]

Frank surprised the family at Silver Spring at noon on May 10, as they had not expected him until his corps arrived from Richmond. He brought several horses with him: a pony for Montgomery's daughter Betty and two others for his mother's carriage, while retaining Van Dorn, who had been given to him by General Steele at Vicksburg, and two others. He regaled the family with his adventures at a lengthy dinner. Apo and the boys arrived the following day, having left Christine in Philadelphia with her grandmother and the Dicks. Lizzie made arrangements for them to stay at No. 4. Her son Blair was particularly happy to see his cousins. As for Apo, she "has a new plan for the future every day," Lizzie wrote disparagingly. The latest apparently called for Frank to retire to Alabama and oversee a plantation there, "where he will end in loafing & its usual accompanyments [sic]." Lizzie gave Phil a private assessment that Apo's family "has always been in hot haste to make money & are the most unprofitable visionary people I know." So far, however, Lizzie had kept her own counsel and was getting along with her sister-in-law "as smooth as 'a rich woman' generally does."[60]

58. *OR*, 1:47:3:325, 423; Roberts Diary, 94–95; Hickenlooper Reminiscences, 118; FB to MB, April 30, 1865, BLC; EBL to SPL, May 8, 1865, B-LP.

59. FB to MB, April 30, 1865, BLC; Apo to FB, April 4, 6, 15, 1865, EBL to SPL, May 5, 8, 9, 10, 1865, B-LP.

60. EBL to SPL, May 10, 12, 17, 1865, B-LP.

The Seventeenth Corps arrived at Alexandria on May 19, and Frank quickly joined them. President Johnson had ordered a two-day review of all the armies through the streets of Washington for May 23 and 24, and Blair wanted to make sure his men were ready. The Army of the Potomac had its turn the first day, followed by the Army of the Tennessee on the twenty-fourth. Frank proudly led the Seventeenth Corps down Pennsylvania Avenue, riding Van Dorn, as the band played the "Bonnie Blue Flag" for the last time. Noah Brooks, the Washington correspondent of the *Sacramento Union,* noted that Blair "looked stouter and browner than when he was in Congress. He was frantically cheered by the populace as soon as he was recognized, riding there with a certain military grace and alert manner that were characteristic of his admirable soldierly reputation." Hickenlooper reported the enthusiasm of the crowd as "something indescribable. We had not reached 'Willard's' until we were so ladened down with gorgeous flowers that we could carry no more." After they passed the presidential reviewing stand, Frank and Hickenlooper dismounted and ascended the platform, where they sat next to Generals Grant and Sherman until the completion of the parade. Having finished their march, the men of the Seventeenth returned to their camps across the Potomac to await the long process of mustering out.[61]

That night Frank and his father entertained Sherman and some nineteen other generals and numerous politicians with a lavish dinner party at No. 4. Grant declined at the last moment. Lizzie, in charge of arrangements, told Phil that the table was so crowded with dignitaries that the ladies had to give up their spaces. This led to protests from Frank's mother and Apo, among others, but to no avail. Lizzie, however, was only too happy to be excused, being exhausted from the preparations. In addition to the dinner, many of Frank's corps had "drank & lunched here today" after the parade.[62]

Immediately after the review, the Seventeenth Corps was ordered to Louisville for mustering out. Frank did not go with them. For all intents and purposes, his military career had ended. He rejoined the corps briefly and issued his farewell orders on July 11, promising, "In whatever position I may hereafter be placed I shall regard it as a duty to devote myself to your interests." Having been involved in all of the major campaigns of the West for the past three years, he had earned the commendation of his superiors as one

61. EBL to SPL, May 18, 19, 24, 1865, B-LP; Brooks, *Washington in Lincoln's Time,* 320; Hickenlooper Reminiscences, 120–21; Roberts Diary, 98.
62. EBL to SPL, May 24, 25, 1865, B-LP.

of the best of the political generals. As fearless on the battlefield as he was on the political stump, he had gained the approbation of his men as well as his peers. In the afterglow of the Grand Review and the splendid dinner at No. 4, his future remained uncertain. For a little while, he could bask in the glory of his military accomplishments, but in the long run that would not pay the bills. Apo still hoped that Frank would eschew a political role in the postwar era, but that remained to be determined.[63]

63. *OR*, 1:49:2:1076–77; Roberts Diary, 98.

10

Reconstruction Politics

In late March 1865, Montgomery Blair received a letter from A. R. Corbin, offering to serve as Frank's "press agent" once the war was over.

There are 50 prominent Generals under Grant & Sherman—all have friends breathlessly watching & praying for the developement [sic] of an incident which will enable them to place their friend *favorably* before the country [he exuded], all merits, but those of their friend will be totally *ignored*. I have among them *one* friend who is equal to the best of them in Genius—F. P. Blair by name. Please let me know, by first mail, from time to time, *whatever affects him*, & thus enable me to serve him with the press here [New York].

There is no indication that Montgomery or Frank took advantage of Corbin's services. With war's end, Frank continued to make his own headlines—not always favorable—without the assistance of a press agent. With the Radicals in the driver's seat in Missouri and moving to get there in Washington, the Blairs and other conservatives had their work cut out for them if they would play any significant role in the reconstruction of Missouri, Maryland, and the South. In the ensuing struggle over Reconstruction, Frank would pursue his goal of quick reconciliation with the same vigor that he had previously taken in the fight for free soil.[1]

Frank became a man on the move in the months following the Grand Review. Worn out from his months of active campaigning with Sherman, he eagerly sought to make time for rest and family but found that politics could

---

1. Corbin to MB, March 26, 1865, BLC.

not be totally avoided. Politically, Frank, together with Montgomery and his father, was concerned to support the new president, Andrew Johnson, who seemed to be pursuing the course of moderate reconstruction outlined by Lincoln.

The Blairs had cultivated Johnson even before he became vice president. Frank had stopped with Johnson at the governor's mansion in Nashville early in 1864, en route to take his seat in Congress. Pleased with Johnson's nomination as vice president on the Union ticket, Preston Blair wrote him immediately following his election to solicit his support for the Blairs' political agenda. Still pursuing the vain hope of some type of colonization in the wake of the coming emancipation, the senior Blair suggested "[s]etting apart a portion of Texas on the Rio Grande for a Refuge for such of the freedmen of the South to go to as might choose." Such a policy, he argued, could avoid racial tensions in the South in view of Radical proposals for black suffrage in that region. Above all, Preston sought Johnson's support for Lincoln's moderate reconstruction.

Following Lincoln's second inauguration, at which Johnson had made a rambling, incoherent, drunken speech, the Blairs secluded him at No. 6. He spent several weeks there recuperating from what was really the aftereffects of a bout with typhoid fever. When Johnson took the oath as president on April 15, Montgomery and Preston were among the guests, much to the disgust of Secretary of War Stanton. By midsummer, the Radicals were beginning to fear, as Senator Sumner wrote, that "[t]he ascendancy is with the Blairs."[2]

The postwar scenario of the Blairs anticipated not merely a speedy reunion as envisioned by Lincoln and, they hoped, Johnson, but also the ascendancy of the Southern yeoman class, something with which the new president undoubtedly sympathized. Although highly paternalistic with their own black slaves, the Blairs feared wholesale emancipation, as witness their strident support for colonization. When colonization proved unfeasible they opposed civil rights for the freedmen because of their strong racial bias, based on their intense feeling of black inferiority and their fears that the ruling white classes could manipulate the black vote to the detriment of the poorer whites. In addition, their strong Jacksonian background caused them to fear not only the expansion of federal power that would be needed to ensure black civil

2. FB to Johnson, January 19, 1864, FPB to Johnson, November 17, 1864, in *Papers of Johnson*, 6:567, 7:293–94; W. E. Smith, *Blair Family in Politics*, 2:326–46; E. B. Smith, *Francis Preston Blair*, 386–93.

rights but also the possibility that a new financial and industrial complex could undermine a return to Jeffersonian-Jacksonian agrarianism with the former slaves as pawns in the process. Frank reflected these themes in speech after speech across Missouri and throughout the rest of the country during the next seven years. In this regard, he and his family were typical of most of the conservatives of the era.[3]

In early June, Frank joined Grant, Logan, and other generals and politicians in a massive rally at Cooper's Institute in New York in support of the Johnson administration. Ten thousand packed the hall, which was bedecked with portraits of the president and his generals with immense flags wreathed about them. The crowd went into ecstacy when Grant appeared, but the general merely waved and then departed, leaving the speaking to his two subordinates. Blair and then Logan addressed the crowd briefly, giving their endorsement to the moderate policies of the administration. Frank told his listeners that Johnson was pursuing the policies that Lincoln would have adopted had he lived and that the president deserved their support. At about the same time, Frank joined Logan and others in extending an invitation to a reunion of the members of the Army of the Tennessee at Saratoga Springs, New York, to celebrate the second anniversary of the fall of Vicksburg. Blair had played a major role in organizing the Society of the Army of the Tennessee while at Raleigh, and he continued to play an active role in its reunions.[4]

Following the New York appearance, Frank and Apo, together with Christine, headed to Newport for a brief visit with son Andrew before Blair returned to St. Louis. They left the other boys with Montgomery and Minna to enjoy the pleasures of Silver Spring for the summer. Eleven-year-old Jimmy took it upon himself to organize a school for freedmen, which he held every evening "in a little room over the dairy." Apo split her time between Washington and Philadelphia, anxiously awaiting Frank's return and clearly concerned about their plans for the future.[5]

Frank was anxious to shore up his political base in St. Louis. The Radicals had gained control of the Missouri government in the 1864 elections, holding a constitutional convention in early 1865. Dominated by Charles D. Drake, the

3. E. B. Smith, *Francis Preston Blair,* 382–84; Wurthman, "Frank Blair: Jacksonian Orator," 116–32.

4. *New York Times,* June 8, 1865; Reunion invitation, June 1, 1865, B-LP; Gresham, *Life of Gresham,* 1:462.

5. EBL to SPL, June 7, 9, 16, 30, 1865, B-LP; Minna Blair to Mrs. A. H. Lowery, July (n.d.), 1865, BLC.

convention produced a highly proscriptive new document, which included an ironclad oath for voting, officeholding, jurors, preachers, lawyers, teachers, and corporation officials and trustees. It also ousted all of the state's judiciary from the Supreme Court to the local level and replaced them with Radical appointees. The constitution's stringency had threatened to split the Radical camp, and conservatives universally opposed it when it was sent to the electorate for ratification. The vote, taken in early June, provided only a narrow approval, and the conservatives hoped to capitalize on this to rally continued opposition to its enforcement and Radical rule.[6]

Both Edward Bates and James Rollins, among others, had written Frank in mid-May denouncing the new constitution and urging his support for the conservative cause. As Blair arrived back in St. Louis on June 20, even the *Missouri Democrat* seemed willing to put past grievances aside temporarily to welcome him as a hero. "The citizens would generally delight to do him honor for his eminent services in the field," it intoned, "and many have expressed the wish that the General's political friends should not make this thing impossible." Frank was greeted by a serenade the following evening. On the twenty-second, some three hundred gathered at the Lindell Hotel for a banquet in his honor. Blair used both occasions to reiterate the views he had expressed at Cooper's Institute, preaching reconciliation and support for President Johnson's reconstruction policies. At the same time, he denounced the new Missouri state constitution with its ironclad oath and heavy proscriptions for flying in the face of that policy. The speech gained a positive response from the conservative press both in Missouri and elsewhere. The *New York World* called it the "best and soundest popular speech made since the close of the war." In the months ahead Frank would take an active lead in both the political and the legal attacks on the proscriptive features of the new state code, as well as seeking a political reorganization of conservatives to back the Johnson program.[7]

Frank spent the remainder of the summer in the East getting a much needed rest. En route east he stopped over in Kentucky briefly, where he urged its citizens to ratify the Thirteenth Amendment in order "to make the best of the circumstances which surround them." He participated in the Army of the

6. The ironclad oath required an individual to swear that he had never committed any one of eighty-six different acts of supposed disloyalty against the state and the Union (Parrish, *Missouri under Radical Rule*, 26–49).

7. Bates to FB, May 12, 1865, Rollins to FB, May 20, 1865, B-LP; *Missouri Democrat*, June 21, 26, 1865; *Missouri Statesman*, June 30, 1865. The *New York World* quote is in W. E. Smith, *Blair Family in Politics*, 2:339–40.

Tennessee reunion at Saratoga Springs on July 4. After spending a few days in New York, he stopped off in Cape May, New Jersey, where Lizzie had taken a cottage for the summer. He then moved on to Washington to rejoin Apo and the children. Apo had been having considerable difficulty with her eyes, and Frank wanted her to see an oculist in New York to find a remedy. That accomplished, they divided time between Cape May and Philadelphia with their Biddle and Gratz relatives. Lizzie told Phil that Frank acted "as if he was 25 instead of the old gentleman he is." At the beginning of August, Frank and Apo left on what one relative described as their "bridal tour," a chance for relaxation and renewal after their long separation. After spending a week at Saratoga, they joined a group of friends for a two-day boat ride up the coast to Portland, Maine. Frank wrote his sister-in-law Minna, "We had a jolly time. I did not know from the time we left until the day it ended whether I was on my head or heels."[8]

While in the East, Frank had ample time to consult with his father and Montgomery as to the clan's political future. All were convinced of the need to reinforce President Johnson's moderate reconstruction. With little concern for the newly freed slaves, whom they would have colonized elsewhere if they could, they concentrated their energies on ensuring as painless a reconciliation as possible with Southern whites, many of whom were relatives or prewar friends.

The Blairs remained convinced that the vast majority of white Southerners had been led into the war by a handful of leaders. They had responded where they could to numerous pleas for assistance from beleaguered friends and acquaintances, as already demonstrated in Frank's case by his intercession for Mrs. Shaaff, his Savannah hostess. The senior Blair had undertaken a private mission to Jefferson Davis, an old family friend, in Richmond during the closing days of the war, in which he proposed Confederate cooperation with Union forces, possibly under Frank's command, to expel the French from Mexico. Nothing came of this; but, at war's end, western Confederate forces under Frank's cousin Jo Shelby were openly encouraged by Lincoln through Blair to escape to Mexico, to join the *Juarista* movement against Maximilian. Following her husband's imprisonment, Varina Davis appealed through Preston Blair for better treatment for the former president of the Confederacy.[9]

8. *New York Times,* July 15, 1865; EBL to SPL, July 9, 16, 21, 22, 26, 30, August 4, 1865, B-LP; FB to Minna Blair, August 16, 1865, BLC.

9. W. E. Smith, *Blair Family in Politics,* 2:344; E. B. Smith, *Francis Preston Blair,* 363–89; Stevens, "Lincoln and Missouri," 115–18; O'Flaherty, *General Jo Shelby,* 352.

Fearful of the growing Radical influence, both in Washington and in their fiefdoms in Missouri and Maryland, the Blairs agreed on the need to counteract it at both levels. In Washington, they urged Johnson to replace Secretary of State Seward and Secretary of War Stanton, whom they suspected of sympathies with the Radicals. Although Preston Blair's first choice to replace Stanton was General Grant, he also mentioned the possibility of Frank's taking that post, something that a number of the latter's friends in Missouri and elsewhere had been urging on the president since early June. Johnson proved immune to these importunities while seeming to lend a more sympathetic ear to the Blairs' patronage concerns in Missouri and Maryland.[10]

Realizing that thousands of War Democrats and conservative Republicans who had supported Lincoln were, like themselves, feeling alienated by the Radicals' ascendancy in Republican counsels, the Blairs determined to create a new conservative coalition to back Johnson and, they hoped, ensure the success of a moderate reconstruction program. To that end, Frank returned to St. Louis in early October to try to unite the conservatives there behind the Blair plan, while Montgomery toured New York State for the same purpose. An announcement was soon forthcoming, signed by numerous Conservative Unionists, calling for a mass meeting at Verandah Hall in St. Louis on October 26 to endorse Johnson's reconstruction program and devise means for thwarting the new Radical constitution. It asked each county to elect delegates, and conservatives throughout the state quickly responded with local meetings to accomplish that task and to pass preliminary resolutions.[11]

To drum up enthusiasm, Frank and others toured outstate Missouri. At Rolla, Blair delivered a blistering speech in which he denounced the new state constitution as "begotten of malice and concocted by a clique who were destitute alike of heart, head, or conscience." He condemned the Missouri Radicals for their opposition to Lincoln in 1864 and argued that Drake and the others had done little to help secure the state for the Union in 1861. He then went on to praise President Johnson for his magnanimous policy toward the conquered South and linked him with his martyred predecessor as among the noblest of men. The crowd responded enthusiastically, adopting resolutions

10. W. E. Smith, *Blair Family in Politics*, 2:330–31; E. B. Smith, *Francis Preston Blair*, 398–99; Parrish, *Missouri under Radical Rule*, 56–57, 80–81; Jean H. Baker, *The Politics of Continuity: Maryland Political Parties from 1858 to 1870*, 144–45.
11. W. E. Smith, *Blair Family in Politics*, 2:329–30, 344–46; T. T. Gantt to MB, October 6, 1865, BLC; *Missouri Statesman*, October 13, 20, 27, 1865.

that endorsed Frank's positions down the line. From Rolla, Blair went on to several other towns, carrying the same message.[12]

Some one thousand delegates from all corners of the state gathered at Verandah Hall on October 26 and remained in session for three days. Sam Glover, who currently stood under indictment for refusing to take the ironclad oath as a lawyer, presided, while Peter Foy served as chairman of the resolutions committee. Frank, James Rollins, and other conservative leaders worked the crowd into an enthusiastic frenzy, denouncing Drake and the state constitution while praising Johnson and his reconstruction policy. On the final day of the meeting, the group adopted a wide range of resolutions and appointed two committees: one to visit Washington and present the convention's proceedings to President Johnson; the other, made up of one member from each congressional district and six members at large, "to organize the people of the State in opposition to the new Constitution."[13]

Frank wrote his father a few days later, "Our political prospects in this state are looking very bright." Although this proved somewhat optimistic, the Verandah Hall convention had created a foundation on which the conservatives could build. After their return home, many of the delegates called county meetings to ratify the St. Louis proceedings with the intention of keeping the fires alive for the 1866 electoral campaigns at the local and state levels. Indeed, the conservatives scored well in municipal elections that fall and the following spring before the Radical legislature had the opportunity to put a stringent new registry law into effect.[14]

In early November, Frank accompanied James O. Broadhead to Hannibal, where he spoke at a large enthusiastic rally. En route up the river, Frank wrote Montgomery that he planned to test the validity of the ironclad oath at an upcoming local election in St. Louis the following week. Glover had already contested the oath for lawyers. In addition, Frank reported that he had encountered Fr. John A. Cummings on the same boat. Cummings, a Roman Catholic priest at Louisiana, Missouri, stood under indictment for having refused to take the ironclad oath as a clergyman. He had just lost his case in the Missouri Supreme Court and was returning from St. Louis where he had been preparing an appeal to the federal level. Frank now asked Montgomery to take

12. *Missouri Democrat*, October 23, 1865. The Radicals did not let the conservative rhetoric go unanswered. Governor Fletcher responded at Sedalia, and Drake wrote a long letter to the *Democrat* answering Frank's charges (ibid., November 1, 1865).

13. *Missouri Statesman*, November 3, 1865.

14. FB to FPB, November 2, 1865, BLC; *Missouri Statesman*, November 17, 1865.

Cummings's appeal to the United States Supreme Court. It would give his brother the opportunity to stand well with Maryland Catholics, Frank argued, while also allowing him to try the constitutionality of a similar Maryland oath, which Montgomery had already publicly challenged. Montgomery agreed and, with the aid of two other eminent attorneys, David Dudley Field and Reverdy Johnson, won Cummings's case at the federal level in January 1867.[15]

Upon his return to St. Louis, Frank appeared at the polls with his own oath, which simply attested his allegiance to the state and nation. When the election officials demanded that he take the ironclad oath, he declared that he could not do so because he had taken up arms against the Claiborne Jackson government in 1861. Certainly with his staunch Union record he could not be accused of disloyalty. This did not satisfy the election judges, who rejected his ballot. Frank thereupon brought suit in the St. Louis Circuit Court, asking ten thousand dollars in damages from the two election officials while challenging the validity of the ironclad oath as an ex post facto measure in violation of the federal constitution. Sam Glover agreed to represent Blair in the circuit court, while Drake considered the case so crucial that he undertook the defense of the two election officials. The circuit court issued its decision in June 1866, deciding for the defendants on a split two-to-one vote. Frank immediately appealed to the Missouri Supreme Court.[16]

While politics held his first interest, it did not pay the bills. Apo, reluctantly accepting Frank's political passion and their return to St. Louis, wrote their son Andrew that his father had "several plans for making money & I dare say he will succeed as he generally does at anything he sets his mind to." Still, she continued realistically, "I do not set my heart upon it for after all riches do not make happiness." Frank's resignation as major general had been accepted at the end of October, and his law practice had yet to be reestablished. He asked his father to seek an appointment for him with the Johnson administration. The conservative delegation sent to Washington by the Verandah Hall convention had promoted him for secretary of war, but he correctly doubted that Johnson would replace Stanton. Consequently, he sought the post of collector of revenue for the St. Louis district, which would tide him over until other prospects brightened.[17]

---

15. FB to MB, November 4, 1865, BLC; Parrish, *Missouri under Radical Rule,* 65–75.

16. *Missouri Democrat,* November 10, 1865, January 5, June 27, 1866; *New York Times,* November 11, 1865. A copy of the circuit court proceedings is in BLC.

17. Apo to Andrew Blair, October 25, 1865, FB to FPB, November 10, 1865, B-LP; FB to FPB, November 2, 1865, BLC.

By mid-November 1865, Frank was on his way down the Mississippi River
to Memphis and New Orleans in a risky attempt to rebuild his financial
base. He had agreed to go into partnership with his brother-in-law George
Alexander to raise cotton. George had engaged in cotton growing in Louisiana
during the war, but had been forced out of the business by the harassing
activities of Bill Quantrill, the noted Confederate guerrilla who had operated in that vicinity after leaving Missouri, and by government cutbacks
in plantation leases. The new partnership was originally part of a much
larger projected scheme involving several Memphis cotton brokers headed
by Dan Able, a brother of one of Frank's St. Louis associates, Bart Able, and
various Northern adventurers interested in leasing plantations throughout
the Mississippi delta. Frank wrote Apo from Memphis on November 21 that
the group had already leased eleven thousand acres, and "no doubt we can
get all we want subscribed as stock" in a proposed company with venture
capital, which Frank hoped to raise in New York from some of his banking
friends. He had been elected president of the new operation at ten thousand
dollars a year. He hoped that labor could be secured through the Freedmen's
Bureau and his connection to General O. O. Howard, its head.[18]

Whether this larger scheme ever reached full fruition is doubtful. Nothing
further is indicated in the available correspondence. However, Frank and
George Alexander leased 259 acres, known as Cabin Teele Plantation, at
Milliken's Bend, Louisiana, where Frank had spent much time during the
Vicksburg campaign, for three years beginning January 1, 1866. The rental
was twenty thousand dollars per annum. They borrowed the initial down
payment from Dan Able. George was to manage the place, hiring available
black labor, while Blair generally remained a silent partner, helping only
when necessary. Although his father and other family members expressed
skepticism, in part because of George Alexander's previous poor business
record, Frank, like many other Union officers who had served in the South,
was convinced that this enterprise held great promise.[19]

From the outset, Cabin Teele presented nothing but problems. Heavy
spring rains in 1866 delayed planting. Levees neglected by the war allowed
water to pour in from the swollen Mississippi and other streams. Labor

18. George Alexander to Mira Alexander, April 21, 1864, FB to Apo, November 13, 21,
1865, BLC; Apo to FB, December 10, 1864, FB to FPB, November 10, 1865, B-LP.
19. Madison County, La., Notarial Record Book G, 111–12; FB to FPB, November 10,
1865, B-LP; FPB to FB, December 23, 1867, MB to FB, December 23, 1867, BLC; Ted Tunnell,
Crucible of Reconstruction: War, Radicalism and Race in Louisiana, 1862–1877, 140–41.

problems were constant as George found overseers unreliable, and labor contractors who promised field hands frequently failed to deliver. He toyed with the idea of hiring recently emigrated Dutch families during the spring of 1866, as some of his neighbors had done, anticipating that he could keep them separate from the blacks he had hired and get more work out of them; but nothing came of this apparently. By May, Alexander had thirty hands, to whom he was paying two dollars a day, as well as providing housing. Weeds were threatening to smother the cotton he had planted, although he "did heavy execution" on them. His suppliers frequently did not deliver promised goods, and George complained constantly about having to borrow from his neighbors. Still, by July, his and Frank's cotton crop was looking pretty good, and George celebrated with a big feast for the black hands on the Fourth.[20]

Shortly thereafter, George and Mary Alexander left for a much needed rest, and Frank went south to take charge of things. He wrote Apo that he was looking forward to the solitude of the place to give him an opportunity to do some serious thinking after the hectic political activity of the spring and summer in Missouri. He told his father that they expected a good cotton crop from the front part of the property, where the soil was sandy, but the success of the crops further away from the river would depend on rain. After the spring floods, drought had set in; and they had had no rain for more than a month. There was also concern about cotton worms, which had invaded the neighboring plantation. No record exists of the final 1866 accounting for Cabin Teele. Given the complications of flooding and cotton worms, which plagued the entire state in 1866, however, Joe Gray Taylor, the historian of Louisiana Reconstruction, reports that from the million acres of cotton planted in the state that year, only 131,000 bales were realized.[21]

Frank returned to St. Louis in time for the fall elections but was back at Cabin Teele by the end of the year. For 1867 he and George worked out a sharecrop arrangement with some of the freedmen, with the latter to keep one-third of the crop for their labor while Blair and Alexander furnished mules, land, seed, utensils, and so on. The new year brought difficulties similar to those of 1866, including an intense labor shortage. George rented out part of the land, taking a loss on it. Spring rains again brought heavy flooding; and, in June, a hailstorm slashed much of the new crop that he had planted

20. George Alexander to FB, February 27, May 28, July 5, 1866, Mary Alexander to Apo, July 13, 1866, BLC.

21. FB to Apo, August 1, 1866, Apo to FPB, August 1, 1866, FB to FPB, August 7, 1866, B-LP; Joe Gray Taylor, *Louisiana Reconstructed, 1863–1877,* 344.

in the wake of the earlier disaster. By the end of June, George's health began to fail under the strain of the operation. Then cholera and cotton worms hit the plantation. In mid-August, George died of dysentery at Paducah, where he had gone in an attempt to recover his health. Montgomery wrote Minna, "There was no one left there [at Cabin Teele] at all but the servants when George left. The cholera had scared away white men off the place."[22]

Frank made the sad journey to Cabin Teele to take charge of operations, although plagued himself by piles and diarrhea. He told Montgomery, "I grieve for dear George as I did for my brother." He stayed through the fall and reported that the cotton crop looked good in late September as they approached harvest. His overseers had fallen ill, however, and "the whole labor fell on me and I was myself made sick by it." It was a hopeless cause; and, by the end of the year, the operation had to be surrendered to creditors. Frank's assets could not cover his debts, and he found himself once again in deep financial difficulty. It was a common story throughout Louisiana and much of the South that year. His father noted this in commiserating about his losses and then blamed much of it on Radical reconstruction policies, which he believed discouraged blacks from working. Whatever the case, it proved a bitter pill for Frank to swallow. Still, he emerged from the experience with his usual optimism. "I have done all I could to make it profitable," he wrote Montgomery in January 1868, "& feel a lightness of heart in getting rid of it that I have not experienced in many days and I look at the debt which I have incurred only as a spur to new efforts to repay it and make myself independent again."[23]

Although concerned with his plantation enterprise, Frank did not let it distract him from political matters. Following up on the success of the Verandah Hall meeting and its local counterparts around the state, he moved quickly in 1866 to solidify the opposition to the dominant Radicals under the Conservative Union label. By doing so, Frank and the other party leaders sought to steer clear of any association with the discredited "Copperhead" Democracy as an organization, while extending an open welcome to any of its followers who wished to join them. The new party emphasized adherence

22. Apo to EB, December 6, 1866, Apo to FPB, April 12, June 3, 1867, Apo to SPL, June 30, 1867, FB to MB, August 22, 1867, B-LP; George Alexander to FB, February 17, 18, 1867, MB to Minna Blair, August 13, 19, 1867, BLC. The sharecrop agreement is to be found in BLC.

23. MB to Minna, August 13, September 18, 1867, FB to Apo, September 2, 18, 23, October 3, 1867, FPB to FB, December 23, 1867, MB to FB, December 23, 1867, BLC; FB to MB, August 22, 1867, January 10, 1868, FB to FPB, September 25, 1867, B-LP.

to the Union and loyalty to the wartime Provisional Government of Missouri. Former Whigs such as James Rollins, James O. Broadhead, and William F. Switzler, publisher of Columbia's *Missouri Statesman,* joined Frank and other Benton Democrats such as Sam Glover, Thomas Gantt, and John S. Phelps to form a phalanx of leadership that could attract supporters around the state. The small remnant of the state Democratic committee, realizing the drift in sentiment, endorsed coalition at its meeting in February 1866. When a small group of Boone County Democrats thought otherwise, Frank "pitched into" them in a speech at Rocheport and directed Rollins to follow up in squelching their independence, which his ally did.[24]

With President Johnson's veto branding the Freedmen's Bureau extension and the civil rights bills as unconstitutional that spring, national issues began to take on greater prominence. Missouri Conservatives, including twenty-four members of the General Assembly, forwarded numerous letters of support to the president. They held county rallies endorsing his stand and began organizing "Johnson Clubs." An estimated ten thousand attended a Johnson rally in St. Louis, called by the Conservative Union state central committee. In early March, Frank visited Jefferson City, where he spoke to a large, enthusiastic crowd in the Hall of Representatives. In Washington, Preston and Montgomery gave Johnson their full backing, and rumor had it that the former had written the veto message.[25]

Missouri's Radicals, meanwhile, quickly lined up behind their counterparts in Congress, denouncing Johnson as a traitor to their party. Henry Blow wrote the president, "I am both grieved and disappointed at the course you have seen fit to pursue." The municipal elections held that spring brought the Radicals a number of stunning setbacks in St. Louis, St. Joseph, Kansas City, and elsewhere, giving the Conservatives increased hope. The stringent registry act, passed by the new General Assembly, had not yet gone into effect, however, and most Radicals confidently expected that it would help improve their position by November.[26]

24. *Missouri Republican,* February 19, 23, 26, June 6, 1866; *Missouri Statesman,* March 2, 9, 16, 23, 30, June 1, 1866; Lewis V. Bogy to Rollins, May 21, 1866, FB to Rollins, May 23, 1866, John M. Richardson to Rollins, July 13, 1866, Rollins Papers.

25. Andrew Johnson Papers, passim, February–April 1866; *Missouri Statesman,* passim, March 1866; E. B. Smith, *Francis Preston Blair,* 393–94. John H. Cox and LaWanda Cox have shown conclusively that none of the veto drafts bear the Blair imprint ("Andrew Johnson and His Ghost Writers: An Analysis of the Freedmen's Bureau and Civil Rights Veto Messages").

26. Parrish, *Missouri under Radical Rule,* 79, 81.

With a great deal at stake, an all-out war over federal patronage in Missouri got under way. Thomas E. Noell, one of Missouri's two Conservative congressmen, had written Frank in January, seeking his help with the president. Concerned himself to secure the post of collector of revenue for the St. Louis district, Blair sought Montgomery's assistance in these matters. In particular, he wanted his brother's help in maintaining Peter Foy as St. Louis postmaster. Frank had complained earlier that their old friend Postmaster Gen. William Dennison seemed to have a penchant for appointing Radicals to vacant post offices at a time when they were trying to rally Conservative support for the president's course. Now Frank wrote Johnson protesting the appointment of Radical John McNeil as port surveyor for St. Louis, something that had been done at the strong recommendation of Missouri's congressional Radicals. Although the president asked for a postponement of McNeil's appointment by the Senate, he was confirmed.[27]

When Johnson then declined to commission McNeil, it went badly for the Conservatives. In early March, the president forwarded to the Senate Frank's and Foy's nominations as St. Louis collector of revenue and postmaster, respectively. Among those endorsing Blair for the post was his old commander General Sherman, who wrote his brother, Sen. John Sherman, "No person knows or appreciates better than I do General Blair's services to the whole country from the beginning to the end of the war from *first* to last." This and other endorsements failed to sway the Senate, however, which rejected both appointments when Missouri's two senators, John B. Henderson and B. Gratz Brown, withheld their endorsement. Foy continued in his post, in the meantime, as Johnson declined to make another appointment. With the adjournment of Congress that summer and the appointment of a new postmaster general in July, the patronage outlook began to look brighter for Missouri Conservatives, who hoped that congressional elections in November might further enhance their position.[28]

Hoping to capitalize on their spring successes, the Conservatives sent Frank on an extensive speaking tour into the interior of the state in early

27. FB to MB, November 30, 1865, B-LP; Noell to FB, January 8, 1866, FB to MB, January 10, 14, 23, 1866, Thomas T. Gantt to MB, April 11, 1866, FB to FPB, May 2, 1866, BLC; FB to Johnson, January 20, 1866, in *Papers of Johnson*, 9:610–12.

28. W. T. Sherman to John Sherman, March 2, 1866, William T. Sherman Papers; *Missouri Democrat*, May 14, 1866; *Missouri Statesman*, August 3, 1866. Interestingly, Gratz Brown continued to be a welcome guest with the Washington Blairs in spite of his Radical tendencies and his opposition to Frank's appointments (EBL to SPL, December 14, 1866, January 23, 1867, B-LP).

May. He assured his father at the outset that "affairs in Missouri [looked] promising" and confidently predicted victory. Blair was at his colorful best on this tour, during which he spoke in a different town nearly every day. He met with a mixed reception. Conservatives came out in large numbers to hear him satirize and ridicule the Radicals, but trouble frequently erupted. The Radical press showered him with a torrent of abuse, with the *Missouri Democrat* calling him a "desperate demagogue."[29]

Frank wrote Rollins from Boonville that they "had a very good time & a large audience" there. Although the Radicals had threatened to disrupt the meeting, they failed to materialize. "I was interrupted once or twice by them," he reported, "but I took Old Bullion's [Benton's] plane & insulted them in the grossest terms. The people shouted & cheered & they quieted down very quickly." Afterward, however, some Radicals assaulted Conservatives as they left the meeting, Frank wrote his brother. The local Radical mayor arrested the Conservatives, saying that he regretted only that he could not arrest more such "rebels." Finally, the military were called in to restore order.[30]

Frank had been warned to stay away from Warrensburg; but, undaunted, he went anyway. Speaking from an improvised stand near the courthouse, he harangued the crowd for five hours. Midway, an old farmer named Bill Stephens became sufficiently incensed that he moved toward Blair, calling him a liar and seeming to threaten him. Giving him a cool look, Frank bitingly remarked, "I'll take care of the ——"; but a supporter seized Stephens by the neck and forced him back into his seat. Blair later told his host that he carried a small derringer pistol in his vest pocket and would not have hesitated it to use it if Stephens had come any closer. During the disturbance, one of Stephens's sons came at Frank from a different direction only to be stabbed by another of Blair's supporters, who feared for Frank's life. Dragged away, the wounded man soon died, while his attacker escaped in the crowd and was never found. Although part of the speakers' stand had given way, Blair continued as if nothing had happened.[31]

29. *Missouri Statesman*, May 4, 1866; FB to FPB, May 2, 1866, Johnson Papers; FB to FPB, May 6, 1866, BLC; Arden R. Smith to FPB, May 17, 1866, B-LP; *Missouri Democrat*, May 21, June 6, 13, July 2, 4, 1866; *People's Tribune*, May 23, June 6, 13, 1866.

30. FB to Rollins, May 23, 1866, Rollins Papers; FB to MB, July 1, 1866, BLC.

31. Huston Crittenden, "The Warrensburg Speech of Frank P. Blair." In early September, Preston Blair received two pistols from C. M. Derringer with the notation that he forward them to "General Frank," whom the gun manufacturer had heard had lost one of his. "He is so much exposed," Derringer wrote, "that they shd. know he is well armed with them" (Derringer to FPB, August 29, September 1, 1866, BLC).

In his speeches Frank preached the Conservative line that President Johnson must be upheld and the test oath and the registry act resisted. He assured his hearers that the United States Supreme Court had already decided the unconstitutionality of the ironclad oath and implied that the Court's ruling would include the invalidation of the oath for voting.[32] He urged all those who had not actually borne rebel arms to register and take the oath without hesitation. Frank wrote his brother on July 7 that he had delivered some forty or fifty speeches over the last two months and had literally worn himself out for the cause. In spite of the occasional threats and hostile demonstrations, both Blair and the state central committee expressed satisfaction with the results of the tour. The impact of his personality and the wide publicity he received had given the Conservative cause quite a boost.[33]

The Radicals did not remain idle in the midst of this threat. They imported Govs. William M. Stone of Iowa and Richard J. Oglesby of Illinois to speak at rallies across the state. Drake, Governor Fletcher, and other state officials also spoke widely. In addition, the Radicals cultivated the veterans' vote by organizing soldiers' leagues and soldiers' associations. In the call for the organizational meeting of veterans in St. Louis, the *Missouri Democrat* warned: "The copperheads and rattlesnakes hidden under Union flowers . . . are endeavoring to swindle us out of our victories . . . and to destroy this Republic." It went on to describe Blair as "a false Moses" who sought to lead the "rebels" back to their old power. It further accused him of fanaticism, which would not stop short of perjury at the polls or rebellion, if necessary, to accomplish its evil purpose. The German press echoed these sentiments.[34]

In early July, the Conservative Union Party held a state convention at Mercantile Hall in St. Louis. Edward Bates enthusiastically wrote the president that "for numbers, individual work, popular estimation and general weight of character" he had never seen its equal in Missouri. While admitting that the delegates ranked high in "social status," the *St. Louis Evening News* by contrast described them as "a collection of political driftwood, a floating together of all the political debris of the State." After the usual speeches by Frank and

32. In reality, the Supreme Court had postponed a decision in the Cummings and other test-oath cases. Supposedly, however, Justice Robert C. Grier had informed Frank that the priest would be upheld (Parrish, *Missouri under Radical Rule*, 70–71).

33. *Missouri Statesman*, April 25, June 29, 1866; *People's Tribune*, May 23, June 6, 13, 1866; Lewis Bogy to Rollins, May 21, 1866, Rollins Papers; FB to FPB, June 17, 1866, BLC; FB to MB, July 7, 1866, BLPLC.

34. Parrish, *Missouri under Radical Rule*, 83–87; *Missouri Democrat*, passim, June–July 1866. The quotation is from July 13, 1866.

others, the delegates adopted resolutions similar to those already drafted by the various county conventions to which Blair had been speaking. They also chose delegates to the National Union Convention in Philadelphia on August 14, which the Blairs had helped organize as a nationwide demonstration of support for President Johnson. To coordinate the campaign at home, the Conservatives established a steering committee composed of Frank, Lewis Bogy, James O. Broadhead, Thomas T. Gantt, and Sam Glover.[35]

An added incentive for both sides came when Gratz Brown announced in late June that he would not seek another term in the Senate. In ill health for some time, he had never been very enthusiastic about Drake's constitution. He also supported both black and women's suffrage, as well as a modification of the test oath, which left him out of favor with many Radicals. This certainly brightened Frank's hopes. He had confided earlier to his father, "It is almost a conceded thing that I am to be the Senator in case of our success." On the Radical side, Drake quickly made it clear that he also coveted the seat.[36]

Frank left for Cabin Teele soon after the Conservative state convention and consequently did not attend the National Union meeting in Philadelphia. Montgomery represented the family well, however, as Preston remained in the background. Frank also missed the visit of President Johnson to St. Louis during his "swing around the circle" in early September. The city turned out in large numbers to hear the president, but hostile Radicals led him to make some intemperate remarks that did not help the Conservative cause there. Frank, meanwhile, stopped in Memphis to speak on his way back upriver. Shortly before leaving Cabin Teele, he had received a letter from his father urging him to make the fall canvass more issue oriented. The senior Blair, writing in the midst of the generally disastrous Johnson western tour, indicated that he believed that the time for sheer vituperation against the Radicals had passed. Rather, he urged Frank to emphasize such concerns as the tariff, huge government expenditures, and the movement to establish black rights in the South at the expense of whites in a series of short, succinct speeches, which could easily be fitted into the county presses and thereby gain even wider circulation.[37]

35. *St. Louis Evening News*, July 5, 1866; *Missouri Statesman*, July 6, 13, 1866; Bates to Johnson, July 12, 1866, Gantt to Johnson, July 27, 1866, Johnson Papers; E. B. Smith, *Francis Preston Blair*, 398–99; W. E. Smith, *Blair Family in Politics*, 2:366–67.

36. FB to FPB, May 2, 1866, Johnson Papers; Evans Casselberry to MB, May 19, 27, 1866, BLC; Charles D. Drake, "Autobiography," Charles D. Drake Papers, 1192–95.

37. FB to FPB, June 22, July 7, 1866, B-LP; FPB to FB, July 5, 1866, BLC; FPB to FB, September 10, 1866, Blair Family Papers, MHS; *Missouri Democrat*, September 5, 10, 1866;

Although Frank generally tried to follow his father's advice as he toured outstate Missouri that fall, the Conservatives were fighting a losing cause. In the wake of the war's devastation, the state was still being racked by discord and turmoil as disparate elements roamed freely across the landscape. It frequently became necessary for Governor Fletcher to call on the state militia and federal military to take action. Conservatives protested to President Johnson that the militia, which consisted largely of Radical volunteers, often misused its authority; and they urged a stronger role for federal troops. Generals Sherman and Winfield S. Hancock, who commanded the Division of the Mississippi and the Department of Missouri, respectively, sought to allay these fears, while accepting Fletcher's assurances that he could keep order fairly.[38]

The Radical governor also had the power to appoint the local registry boards, who would oversee the fall electoral process. These were generally partisans, many of whom seemed determined to prevent as many Conservatives from registering as possible. Frank and other Conservative speakers urged their constituents to register, regardless of difficulties, and, if rejected, to appeal. It was important to keep a list of rejected voters in case the courts should rule against the ironclad oath and the registry process. Such a ruling did not occur before the election, however; and, after Missourians went to the polls, it quickly became evident that the registry laws had helped the Radicals significantly. The new General Assembly would have overwhelming Radical majorities. "There is no use mincing matters," one Conservative editor declared, "The registry act has laid us out cold. We went in lemons and came out squeezed." The Conservatives fared badly elsewhere as well, with the Republicans gaining a two-thirds' majority in both houses of Congress, enough to override any future Johnson vetoes.[39]

Frank went east in the aftermath of the election to join Apo and the children, who had been there all fall after spending the summer in the countryside south of St. Louis to escape the threat of cholera hanging over the city. The trip gave him the opportunity to consult with his father and brother about the future. With Cabin Teele not bringing in the profit he had anticipated, his quest for a patronage job thwarted, and his hopes for a Senate seat dashed by the election, Frank once again faced a questionable financial future. Both Phil

---

Missouri Republican, September 9, 1866; E. B. Smith, *Francis Preston Blair*, 399–400; W. E. Smith, *Blair Family in Politics*, 2:367–70.

38. Parrish, *Missouri under Radical Rule*, 88–96.

39. Ibid., 96–98.

Lee and Montgomery had helped finance him during 1866, the latter allowing him to keep the money gained from the sale of certain St. Louis properties.[40]

Although he continued to pin his hopes on Cabin Teele, Frank needed some kind of steady income in the meantime. He had sued the *Missouri Democrat* the previous July for two hundred thousand dollars in damages, claiming libel over an article it had published accusing him of keeping confiscated property for himself during the Carolina campaign. The paper's owners were fighting back, however, and threatening to take depositions at the scene, which would cause him extra expense to monitor the process.

Two opportunities with the Union Pacific Railroad, then under construction, consumed his attention while in the East. The first involved a position as one of the railroad's attorneys. Blair, with several friends on the board, pinned high hopes on this; but when that body met in late December, the decision went against him. Instead, he settled for an appointment from Secy. of the Interior Orville H. Browning as one of three commissioners to examine and approve completed sections of the Union Pacific and other railroads then under construction. This, at least, provided a steady income, although it meant extensive travel over the next two years.[41]

The following year, 1867, proved to be a busy one for Frank. Although his defeat was a foregone conclusion, his Conservative friends in the Missouri legislature nominated him as their candidate for the Senate to show they "have not forsaken him." The seat went to Drake by a large margin, although a number of Radicals, disenchanted with his leadership, opposed his election. Blair's new position as railroad commissioner took him frequently to Kansas and Nebraska on inspection trips. On some of these, once school was out that summer, he brought along Apo and his sons Jim and Pres to give them an outing. They were happy trips, as he had the rare opportunity to spend quality time with his family. He had written his father earlier in the year, "It is a comfort to turn from the disappointments of public life to the unalloyed happiness of home."[42]

40. Apo to FPB, August 1, 1866, FB to Apo, October 5, 1866, EBL to SPL, December 13, 20, 1866, B-LP; SPL to FB, June 11, 1866, FB to MB, July 28, 1866, MB to FB, n.d., BLC.

41. Apo to FPB, August 1, 1866, FB to MB, December 6, 15, 1866, EBL to SPL, December 19, 20, 1866, January 7, 1867, B-LP; FB to MB, December 13, 20, 1866, FPB to FB, December 24, 1866, Browning to FB, December 27, 1866, BLC. The suit against the *Missouri Democrat* was subsequently dropped in July 1867 after the paper admitted it was mistaken and apologized.

42. FB to MB, January 17, 1867, BLC; *Missouri Statesman,* January 18, 1867; Rollins to FPB, January 19, 1867, FB to FPB, January 24, 1867, Apo to FPB, June 3, 1867, Apo to SPL, June 30, 1867, B-LP.

Early in March, Frank hurried to Washington. He had been invited to make several speeches in Connecticut later in the month in support of the state Democratic ticket there and wished to get his father's advice on the approach to take in the wake of the fall disaster. His own experience with labor problems at Cabin Teele, together with recent correspondence with former Confederate vice president Alexander Stephens, had brought Blair to the conclusion that the old concern with colonization needed to be de-emphasized. Father and son generally agreed to attack the dangers of Reconstruction run rampant, given the recent congressional legislation that imposed military rule there. Emphasis would be placed on the threat of black suffrage in the South, and the argument would be made that the Southern whites must organize for their own protection. Frank subsequently wrote Montgomery from Hartford that his speeches had been well received. The Democrats did well in Connecticut with the election of James E. English as governor and the unseating of two of the state's Republican congressmen by their Democratic rivals.[43]

While in Connecticut, Frank received word that President Johnson had nominated him to be minister to Austria. Blair had no advance notice of this and wrote Montgomery that he would have preferred that the appointment go to his father, who he believed could be confirmed while he could not. Frank hoped the senior Blair might even take Apo and the children abroad with him, which could be a wonderful experience for them. As he had anticipated, the Senate refused to confirm his appointment; and Frank shortly thereafter returned west to continue his railroad inspections. At this same time, he received another setback when the Missouri Supreme Court decided against him in his test-oath case. Although some Conservatives had hoped for a different decision in view of the recent rulings of the United States Supreme Court against the test oath in the Cummings case and a similar one from Arkansas affecting lawyers, the Missouri high tribunal remained a faithful embodiment of Radical doctrine. Frank immediately appealed to the United States Supreme Court in the hope that it might reach a different decision prior to the 1868 elections.[44]

With the Radicals now seemingly in control of the Republican Party, the Blairs turned their full attention to consolidating the opposition within the

43. FB to FPB, January 24, 1867, B-LP; FB to Apo, March 5, 1867, BLPLC; Stephens to MB, February 3, 1867, FB to MB, March 24, 26, 1867, BLC.

44. *Diary of Welles,* 3:70–72; FB to MB, March 26, 1867, BLC; *Missouri Statesman,* March 29, April 5, 1867; FB to Johnson, March 30, 1867, in *Papers of Johnson,* 12:194. A copy of the Missouri Supreme Court Transcript of Record is in BLC.

Democratic Party as they looked toward the 1868 presidential election. Their hopes of moving forward with President Johnson had disappeared after the disastrous election of 1866. When Johnson finally removed Edwin M. Stanton from the War Department in August 1867, something the Blairs had been urging for two years because of his suspected Radical connections, Secy. of the Navy Gideon Welles urged Frank as his replacement. After consulting with Montgomery, however, the president gave the interim appointment to Grant, whom the Washington Blairs hoped to woo for the Democratic nomination in 1868.[45]

Frank, by this time, was rapidly becoming disenchanted with his former commander. He had just returned from an extensive speaking tour across Tennessee in an attempt to shore up the Conservative cause there in the August state election. He found conditions in the Volunteer State "indescribable" and "infinitely worse & more hopeless than in Missouri." The blacks were "insolent & overbearing," while "nine tenths of the white men are utterly disgusted and disheartened." During his speech at Knoxville, "the white and black Radicals did their best to break up the meeting"; but Frank repeated the speech the next day at the courthouse to a large enthusiastic audience. For all his efforts, however, the Radicals carried the day, retaining most of the state offices.

Blair blamed the difficulties of Tennessee and the other Southern states on "Grant's course and that of the Generals under him." He believed that Grant had come under the influence of Stanton and was in danger "of allowing himself to be made the tool of the Radicals." Frank urged his father to talk with Grant but held out little hope that the general could be made compatible with Democratic concerns for changes in Southern reconstruction. He reiterated these views a week later from Chicago, where he had gone to make yet another speech, and in another letter later in the month after Grant had accepted the interim war portfolio.[46]

Frank began considering a run for the presidency himself by early August 1867. His good friend Bart Able had told him the previous month that he was writing Montgomery to suggest that a "Frank Blair for President" movement be started. Rollins enthusiastically supported this idea, and Frank asked his brother and father to consider it "with candor & if possible divesting your minds of all partiality and let us know what you think [my] chances are

45. *Diary of Welles*, 3:165–66, 231–32; W. E. Smith, *Blair Family in Politics*, 2:386–88; E. B. Smith, *Francis Preston Blair*, 409–10.

46. FB to FPB, August 2, 22, 1867, B-LP; FB to FPB, August 9, 1867, BLC. The itinerary for the Tennessee tour may be found in *Missouri Statesman*, August 2, 1867.

worth." Montgomery sought to dampen the enthusiasm of both Able and Rollins, although he indicated that the Washington Blairs might become interested in pushing Frank if Grant proved unavailable. Frank responded by assuring his brother, "From conversations with many leading men, I fancy that Bart Able's candidate will prove acceptable in quarters hardly counted upon. I of course have never alluded to it but the matter has been pressed upon me several times." To show his seriousness about exploring his possible candidacy, Frank then outlined an extensive strategy for Montgomery and his father to consider.[47]

George Alexander's death and the subsequent difficulties at Cabin Teele occupied most of Frank's time for the remainder of the year, but thoughts of the presidency were never far away. In October, Blair took time out from plantation cares to speak at Vicksburg, outlining much the same sentiments he had expressed earlier in Connecticut and elsewhere. By mid-November, he had returned to St. Louis. He made a quick railroad-inspection trip to Kansas, where he discovered the Democrats confident, with "no idea of Grant." While he found Sherman popular there, he did not believe that his former commander would make a good candidate, as "he is very uncertain & unreliable tho I shall not say so to anyone."

Frank was pleased to hear from Montgomery that the Washington Blairs now agreed with him concerning Grant. Frank assumed that the general would be the Republican nominee, which could discourage a lot of Democrats from seeking their party's nomination because they would consider him unbeatable. This should "make a nomination more easily to be attained by Bart Able's man," he predicted. For the Democratic candidate to win, he must have a noteworthy military record, but also "be distinguished as a civilian and have some points upon which superiority could be claimed for him over his antagonist," Frank continued, with "Bart Able's man" obviously uppermost in his mind. He followed this the next day with a long, detailed agenda for his brother to follow in quietly pushing a "Blair for President" movement.[48]

47. FB to MB, August 9, 1867, BLC; FB to MB, August 22, 1867, B-LP; MB to Rollins, September 7, 1867, Rollins Papers. Bart Able had come to St. Louis in the 1840s as a riverboat captain and then retired to run a commission house from 1858 to 1864, when he was elected president of the St. Louis Merchants Exchange. An early Free-Soiler and admirer of Benton, he and Frank had been friends and political allies for many years. Able's brother Dan, a commission merchant in Memphis, had helped finance Frank's ill-fated plantation adventure (Scharf, *History of St. Louis*, 1:604–5).

48. FB to MB, November 29, 1867, BLC; FB to MB, December 19, 1867, B-LP; FB to MB, December 20, 1867, Blair Family Papers, MHS.

Upon hearing from his father that he had had one last conversation with Grant, whom he found generally supportive of congressional reconstruction, Frank wrote Montgomery, "You are wasting your time on Grant & Sherman." Then, in language he would use again forcefully in his famous letter to James O. Broadhead the following summer, he stressed:

> *We must have a President who will not permit it* [Radical reconstruction] *to be executed,* who will take the ground that it is void and inoperative because unconstitutional. This is the only way we can get rid of it & release the 10 southern states from negro domination. For in my count the Radicals will retain their power in the Senate for years to come and the reconstruction acts cannot be repealed. They must be overthrown by executive authority.

Frank reported considerable sentiment in the West for Gen. Winfield S. Hancock, who had a strong military reputation and was a lifelong Democrat. "I prefer him to any except Bart Able's man," he told Montgomery, "and I don't know but he is better than him even and yet I cannot forget your saying to me on a certain occasion that the Blairs had worked long enough for other people."[49]

The campaign for Frank went quietly forward during the early months of 1868. Shortly after his return from Louisiana, where he had closed out the plantation disaster, he headed for Washington. He reported to Apo that his political affairs looked good. He had sounded out many influential men from all parts of the country. "It has been our policy not to allow anything to be said or done publicly," he told her, "as the business will in the end depend more upon the judgment of the sound and discreet men than upon any popular movement. I shall not be the choice of the body of the Democratic Party but if selected at all it will be for the reason that it is necessary to draw support from the other party in order to command success." He closed, "I feel it is a possible thing but will not be disappointed if it fails."[50]

Increasingly, Frank found that his main rivals, particularly in the West, were Hancock, who had strong support among Democratic veterans, and former congressman George H. Pendleton of Ohio, who had been the party's vice presidential candidate in 1864. The latter was the enthusiastic sponsor of what came to be known as the "Ohio Idea," a proposal to pay off the nation's debts with greenbacks, which appealed to many debt-ridden westerners, including

49. FPB to FB, December 8, 1867, FB to MB, December 10, 1867, BLC. Cf. also David M. Jordan, *Winfield Scott Hancock: A Soldier's Life,* 218–19.
50. FB to Apo, February 8, 1868, BLC.

Frank. Blair's old nemesis, Salmon P. Chase, now chief justice of the Supreme Court, also claimed support, as did Sen. Thomas A. Hendricks of Indiana. Rollins wrote Frank from Jefferson City that he was finding some Pendleton support, especially among the "old rebel element." He noted that one of Blair's weaknesses locally was his lack of patronage power. Still, he thought he could sway most of the Democratic legislators to come out in Frank's favor if the latter thought that helpful. Blair replied that he did not want to move that openly yet. He continued to prefer the more behind-the-scenes approach, looking to the Missouri Democratic convention at the end of May.[51]

While he worked to shore up his home base, Frank did not overlook the rest of the field. He urged Montgomery to circulate widely James Peckham's recently published volume *General Nathaniel Lyon and Missouri in 1861*, "which is really a history of my early efforts here." Peckham, who had been closely associated with Blair then, lavished praise on his two heroes for their roles in saving Missouri. Montgomery sent copies of the Peckham book to all of the eastern delegates on the eve of the convention, while he continued to work quietly to promote his brother's candidacy, receiving several assurances of Frank's general acceptability. William F. Switzler, the editor of the *Missouri Statesman*, who was in Washington pursuing a congressional electoral challenge, wrote Blair that he and other Missourians at the capital were actively engaged on his behalf. Frank now urged Rollins to join them there, once the Missouri legislative session was over.[52]

While pursuing his dream of the presidency, Frank continued his work as a railroad commissioner. This kept him away from home but also allowed him to take political soundings along the way. Apo was expecting their sixth child and having a difficult confinement, which kept him apprehensive. The baby boy, whom they named Cary Montgomery, after his Gratz cousin who had been killed at Wilson's Creek and his brother, arrived on March 1 while Frank was on a railroad-inspection trip. Apo made a sufficiently good recovery that he was able to go east at the end of the month for a speaking engagement in Connecticut and for further consultations with his family and associates in Washington. En route home, he stopped in New York to see his friend Leonard Jerome and others who promised to work on the New York

51. Rollins to FB, February 23, 1868, B-LP; Rollins to FB, March 6, 14, 1868, BLC; FB to Rollins, March 8, 15, 1868, Rollins Papers; FB to John Maguire, September 1869, cited in Robert P. Sharkey, *Money, Class, and Party*, 106–7.

52. FB to Rollins, March 15, 1868, Rollins Papers; Switzler to FB, March 16, 1868, FB to MB, March 17, 1868, BLC.

press through their social contacts there. He returned to St. Louis generally encouraged.[53]

One other opportunity to project his image beyond Missouri loomed on the horizon. Frank had been invited a year earlier to deliver the principal address at the dedication of a statue of Thomas Hart Benton in St. Louis. The unveiling had now been set for May 27; and Blair believed that this would give him a unique opportunity to appear statesmanlike, with the hope that his remarks would be widely published. He sent his father and Montgomery a skeleton draft of his speech, asking them to put some bones on it, which they did. When the day arrived, thousands gathered to honor Old Bullion; and Frank proved to be at his oratorical best. As numerous Missouri dignitaries and his old foes John and Jessie Fremont, among others, listened from the platform, he talked of Benton's love for the Union and his many contributions to its preservation, while also emphasizing his vision for the Pacific railroad, now on its way to completion. Whatever his hopes for the speech, however, it got little attention in the press outside St. Louis.[54]

Missouri's Democrats met at the state convention the next day, May 28, with a record attendance. The spring municipal elections had gone well for them in spite of the registry law, which led the Radical legislature to further tighten some of its loose ends. Still, Democratic enthusiasm ran high. The delegates voted to send a twenty-two-man delegation to the national convention uninstructed. Frank reported that eighteen of those chosen favored him, with four leaning toward Pendleton. He had agreed with Rollins and his other friends on the uncommitted strategy in the hope that the Pendleton men could be brought around at the right moment. Blair was already receiving considerable assurances from elsewhere for his candidacy, if not in the form of first ballot votes then as a compromise candidate should the convention deadlock. Meanwhile, the Republicans met in Chicago and, as expected, unanimously chose Grant as their presidential nominee.[55]

The Democratic National Convention assembled at a newly refurbished Tammany Hall in New York City on July 4. Simultaneously, Democratic veterans convened a soldiers' convention at Cooper's Institute. Its delegates

53. FB to FPB, March 1, 19, 1868, FB to MB, March 19, 1868, B-LP; FB to FPB, March 6, 14, 1868, FB to MB, April 7, 25, 1868, BLC; FB to Rollins, March 23, 1868, Rollins Papers.
54. Wayman Crow to FB, June 17, 1867, FB to FPB, March 19, 1868, B-LP; FB to MB, March 17, May 23, 1868, MB to FB, May 17, 1868, BLC; FB to FPB, April 28, 1868, FB to MB, April 30, May 26, 1868, Blair Family Papers, MHS; *Missouri Republican,* May 28, 1868.
55. *Missouri Statesman,* April 10, 17, 1868; FB to MB, April 7, May 29, 1868, BLC; W. E. Smith, *Blair Family in Politics,* 2:397.

expressed their first preference for Hancock, with Frank a strong second. Blair had been invited to address this gathering but thought that might not augur well for his candidacy elsewhere. He left the lobbying there to Bart Able and other friends. Montgomery, serving in the Maryland delegation, had gone to New York a week early to lay the groundwork for a Blair dark-horse candidacy with Frank reminding him of the importance of maintaining the two-thirds rule for the selection of candidates. Frank, meanwhile, remained in Washington, where he held private talks with various delegates en route to the convention.[56]

On July 1, Frank sent Montgomery, through their father, a letter to be given to James O. Broadhead, who had been asked to nominate him before the convention. Blair told his brother that he might "change its phraseology but not its sentiment if you think proper to do so." This letter, which would play a dominant role in the campaign to follow, reiterated the views Frank had been harboring for some time and had outlined earlier in his December 10 letter to his brother. "There is but one way to restore the Government and the Constitution, and that is for the President elect to declare these acts [congressional reconstruction] null and void, compel the army to undo its usurpations at the South, disperse the carpetbag Southern governments, allow the white people to reorganize their own governments and elect Senators and Representatives." Frank wished his candidacy to rise or fall on this issue. Whatever his feelings about the letter might have been, Montgomery made only minor changes in the wording and passed it on to the editor of the *New York World*, with Broadhead's approval, for publication.[57]

A deadlocked convention finally chose Horatio Seymour as its presidential nominee on the twenty-second ballot, although the former New York governor was a reluctant candidate. Exhausted, the delegates then nominated Frank for vice president on a unanimous first ballot. Undoubtedly, this reflected a desire to balance the ticket east and west as well as north and south. Frank's military record would also counterbalance Seymour's seemingly lukewarm support of the Union war effort. The platform, which the delegates unanimously adopted, generally favored Blair's position on Reconstruction, although its language was not nearly as extreme, and Pendleton's views on the currency. The two candidates appeared to thunderous applause before a

56. FB to MB, June 29, 30, 1868, Blair Family Papers, MHS; MB to Minna Blair, June 29, 1868, FB to MB, July 1, 1868, BLC; W. E. Smith, *Blair Family in Politics*, 2:404; Coleman, *Election of 1868*, 191–93.
57. FB to MB, July 1, 1868, BLC; W. E. Smith, *Blair Family in Politics*, 2:404–8.

spontaneous mass meeting at Tammany Hall on the evening of July 10; and it appeared, in the immediate aftermath, that the ticket had general support among Democrats nationwide. Dispatches from numerous places, north and south, indicated that the party faithful had responded enthusiastically with demonstrations and parades in support of the candidates. The *New York Times* sounded a warning note, however, in its editorial columns of July 10: "Considering Mr. Blair's letter [to Broadhead] in conjunction with Mr. Seymour's record, and both with the platform adopted by the convention, we must conclude that the position and policy of the Democracy are hostile to the peace which above all the country needs."[58]

Frank left New York immediately after the convention for another railroad-inspection trip. En route west he stopped over at Leavenworth and St. Joseph, where he addressed large crowds, denying that his program, as outlined in the Broadhead letter, was "revolutionary." The Missouri Democratic convention met in St. Louis in early August and gave its strong endorsement to both the ticket and the platform. Frank sent a formal letter of acceptance to the Democratic National Committee from Omaha on the thirteenth, reiterating his concern about the usurpation of Congress and the effects of Reconstruction on the Southern whites. The family joined him on this trip, which took them as far as Fort Sanders, Dakota Territory (present-day Wyoming), and Apo wrote Phil Lee that they were thoroughly enjoying this time together. She even held out the hope that Phil might bring the senior Blairs west before the campaign began in earnest.[59]

Frank wrote his father from Fort Sanders that he wanted to wage an aggressive campaign in the fall "and make the Radicals defend their rascality if they can." As he had so many times in the past, he asked for Preston's help in putting together his speeches. His father had urged him to get into an extensive canvass immediately; but Frank replied that he could not afford to give up his position as railroad commissioner, which would have been necessary. He needed the salary it brought too badly to pay off his debts. He further reported that Samuel J. Tilden, a member of the national committee, had asked him to confine his campaigning to Missouri and Illinois for fear he

58. W. E. Smith, *Blair Family in Politics*, 2:408–13; Coleman, *Election of 1868*, 193–251; James D. McCabe Jr., *The Life and Public Services of Horatio Seymour, Together with a Complete and Authentic Life of Francis P. Blair, Jr.*, 273–80; *New York Times*, July 10, 11, 12, 1868.

59. FB to FPB, July 15, 1868, enclosing letter of July 13 to George W. Morgan, chairman, Democratic National Committee, Apo to SPL, August 20, September 2, 1868, B-LP; *New York Times*, July 22, August 1, 7, 9, 1868.

"would hurt the ticket" because of his stand on Reconstruction. Blair assumed that Tilden spoke for Seymour. While he had no desire to back down from the Broadhead letter, he did not want to be a hindrance to the ticket.[60]

The campaign quickly turned into a nasty, negative brawl on both sides. The Republican press pictured Seymour as a Copperhead because of his actions during the New York City draft riots of 1863. They contended that insanity ran in his family and argued that if a successful Seymour fell prey to this curse, the nation would see a reckless and irresponsible Blair in the presidency. With many Republican papers contending that the real issue was whether Frank should be elected president, Blair's Broadhead letter became a centerpiece of the Republican attacks. "A Soldier" wrote the *New York Times* that the Germans would repudiate their former hero because of his postwar stand against Radical reconstruction. Perhaps most telling were the cartoons of Thomas Nast in *Harper's Weekly*, one of which depicted Frank in Ku Klux Klan regalia, planning the assassination of General Grant, based on a purported Blair remark that his former commander would not live to leave the White House if elected. One Radical sent this scurrilous poem to the *New York Tribune:*

> Blair, Blair, Black sheep,
> Have you any wool?
> Yes, my master, seven bags full—
> Nigger scalps from Georgia,
> Ku Klux got them all,
> So many less nigger votes
> Against us in the fall.

Democratic leaders worked hard to counteract these attacks. They authorized two campaign biographies: one by David G. Croly, a reporter for the *New York World;* the other by Edward Martin, a Virginian living in Brooklyn, under the pseudonym James D. McCabe Jr. There were the usual medals, songs, badges, and shields with the pictures of either or both candidates. The Democratic press kept up a constant barrage against the Republican opponents. Democrats and temperance groups attacked Grant for his presumed proclivity to alcohol, while the Republican press retaliated with Frank's own supposed drinking problem. Gideon Welles confided to his diary the differences between the two men's drinking habits, as he saw them, "Grant loves drink for the sake of drink. He is not like Blair, convivial, social and given to

60. FB to FPB, July 15, 1868, B-LP; FB to FPB, July 17, 1868, Blair Family Papers, MHS; *New York Times*, October 21, 1868.

a spree, but a soaker behind the door and in the dark." The Democrats also accused "Useless" Grant of being anti-Semitic because of an order expelling Jews from his military department during the war and of keeping confiscated property for himself. Yet another Democratic tale had Grant with a second wife, an Indian squaw, whom he possibly married while drunk and with whom he had three children. So it went.[61]

Frank returned from Dakota in mid-September. Over the next month and a half he undertook extensive campaigning throughout the Midwest and was greeted by enthusiastic crowds at each stop. He made every attempt to answer his critics, claiming that Radical reconstruction had never really had popular acceptance in the North and that the Supreme Court had raised serious questions about it. Blair denied the charges that he was a revolutionist. Rather, he warned that a real revolution by whites could be expected if the Radical policy of giving power to the freedmen of the South was not halted. In strident racist language, typical of the nineteenth century, he argued for the complete separation of the races so as to preserve "the purity, beauty and vigor of our own race." Only by restoring the white race to its rightful place and discontinuing the attempts at black rule could fellowship and prosperity be restored to the country.[62]

While campaigning in Indiana, Frank declined to speak in one congressional district where Walter Q. Gresham, one of his comrades who had been wounded in the battle of Atlanta, was the Republican candidate. The Republican National Committee, concerned about Blair's effectiveness in Indiana, tried to persuade General Sherman to go there and campaign, but he refused to say anything against Frank.[63]

The October 13 state elections in Pennsylvania, Ohio, and Indiana went to the Republicans by narrow margins. There quickly arose the demand in

61. *New York Times*, August 26, September 1, 1868; Mark W. Summers, *The Press Gang: Newspapers and Politics, 1865–1878*, 43–45; Coleman, *Election of 1868*, 96–98, 253–60, 264–70; W. E. Smith, *Blair Family in Politics*, 2:413–18, 427–29. The cartoon is in *Harper's Weekly*, November 7, 1868. Thomas T. Gantt wrote Preston Blair his concerns about the charges regarding Frank's drinking and reported that he had warned Frank to exercise great care in this regard during the campaign. Gantt asserted that he had defended Frank against his critics: "tho Frank was certainly not a 'total abstinence' man, he was a temperate man in this, that he never gave liquor the dominion over him, and that he was always perfectly master of himself" during the twenty-six years that Gantt had known him (Gantt to FPB, August 22, 1868, B-LP).

62. See typical speech, that at Indianapolis, September 23, 1868, in BLC. Other Blair speeches at Galion, Ohio, and Pittsburgh may be found in *New York Times*, September 28, 29, 1868.

63. Gresham, *Life of Gresham*, 344–45.

certain quarters for a change in the ticket in the hope of salvaging the rest of the canvass. Rumors of disaffection had circulated for some time, particularly from the supporters of Chase. Frank had gone east at the end of September, ostensibly to speak at Bedford, Pennsylvania, but also to confer with the family at nearby Silver Spring. En route back to St. Louis, he stopped in Cincinnati to visit with several of the western leaders the day after the October results. They "are hopeless," he informed Cong. James B. Beck of Kentucky, "and they have a plan in fact to get Seymour to decline & have Chase put in his place. It seems that an intrigue has been going on for a great while looking to this plan." Simultaneously, he wrote Tilden that while Chase would be distasteful to him, he was willing to accept the change if it meant the defeat of Grant.[64]

Even as Frank wrote these letters, the *New York World*, the city's leading Democratic organ, suggested, on October 15, that both Democratic candidates retire, putting particular emphasis on Blair, whose Broadhead letter it considered too large a detriment to the campaign. Others wrote similarly to various leaders, including Seymour. Still others warned that such a change would be political suicide. In a speech at St. Louis on October 17, Frank defended his course but offered to step down if it would help the party. He also wrote his father to that effect. Montgomery responded with an indignant letter to the *World*, repudiating its suggestion. Incensed by the clamor, Preston Blair argued that it was merely a ploy by Chase and Seward, the Blairs' old enemies, to embarrass the party. He offered to come to New York for a conference on the matter if Tilden thought that desirable.[65]

The Democratic leadership quickly squelched the idea of a replacement ticket. After a lengthy meeting with Seymour on October 17, Tilden, August Belmont, and Augustus Schell sent telegrams to W. F. Storey, publisher of the *Chicago Times* and the former national committeeman from Illinois, and others, declaring the proposition for change "absurd, and is received by our masses with astonishment, derision, and indignation." Simultaneously, Tilden asked Preston Blair to come to New York to discuss strategy. They now decided to change tactics. In public letters, Belmont and Tilden came out strongly for the ticket, without referring to the article in the *World*. Seymour, who had not taken an active role in the campaign to this point, went into the canvass,

64. FB to James R. Doolittle, October 8, 1868, Doolittle Papers; FB to Beck, October 15, 1868, BLC; FB to Tilden, October 15, 1868, B-LP.
65. *New York Times*, October 16, 18, 21, 1868; *Missouri Democrat*, October 18, 1868; FPB to Tilden, October 19, 1868, in *Letters and Literary Memorials of Samuel J. Tilden*, 1:198–99.

seeking to steer the campaign away from the harshness of Frank's attacks on Radical reconstruction. While change was needed in the South, Seymour emphasized that this should be done only by lawful and orderly means. Civil authority must take precedence over military action. The president and the Supreme Court should be respected rather than attacked, as the Republicans had done. In short, the Democrats would move along conservative lines to reorder national priorities.

Frank had previously responded to the issue of the Supreme Court when James Howes of Lafayette, Indiana, asked if he would submit the Reconstruction Acts to that body "before proceeding to treat them as null and void." Writing from Fort Sanders, Blair asserted that the Court had already spoken to the issue in the Milligan and Bowles habeas corpus cases, overturning martial law in areas where civil courts were open and operating. He argued that the Court would have taken similar action in the McCardle case from Mississippi if Congress had not removed its jurisdiction in the matter.[66]

Frank made one last appearance in the East at a Tammany Hall rally on October 27, which the *New York Times* headlined: "The Lost Cause." Generally following the new line, he claimed that the South was being made into a "New Ireland . . . proscribed and persecuted and trodden down as the old Ireland is." Then he went home to St. Louis to await the results. He had registered to vote without incident before leaving for New York, taking the oath while claiming rather boisterously that it was not really binding on him. Although someone else in the room protested, the registrars made no attempt to put him on the rejected list, which was their prerogative under the Registry Act; and Blair was thus allowed to vote on election day.[67]

The final vote came quickly. Seymour and Blair polled a strong 47.29 percent of the popular vote, although they lost heavily in the electoral college, 214 to 80. The Democrats in the South had worked hard, but Radical regimes controlled the election machinery and carried all of the states there except Georgia and Louisiana. Along the border, Kentucky, Maryland, and Delaware went Democratic. In the West, the Democrats carried only Oregon. Seymour won his own state of New York and neighboring New Jersey; but Frank, largely because of the Radicals' registry system, failed to carry Missouri. The *Missouri Democrat* exulted: "General Blair is beaten in his ward, his city, his

---

66. Tilden, Belmont, and Schell to Storey, October 17, 1868, Tilden to FPB, October 20, 1868, in *Letters of Tilden*, 1:250–51; Coleman, *Election of 1868*, 355–57; Katz, *August Belmont*, 180–83; *New York Times*, October 21, 1868.

67. *New York Times*, October 26, 28, 29, 31, 1868.

county and his State." The Missouri Radicals elected their complete slate of officers, headed by Joseph W. McClurg for governor, and retained control of the legislature. A proposed amendment to eliminate the word *white* from the suffrage provisions of the constitution failed, however, by a margin of nineteen thousand votes, as many Radicals indicated they were not yet ready to carry their revolution that far.[68]

Apo wrote her father-in-law, "[Frank] is of course disappointed but takes the disappointment as he always does in the best possible spirit."[69] The postwar years had been difficult ones as Blair struggled financially and politically. Although deeply disappointed by his decision to return to politics, Apo had supported him loyally. She and the children had shared some of their happiest times with him on their western trips. Frank's schemes to stabilize his finances had met with disaster at Cabin Teele and elsewhere. Political patronage had been denied him personally by his enemies until he found a post that did not require their approval. He had worked hard to acquire the Democratic presidential nomination in 1868 and gladly accepted second place on the ticket, only to find himself the storm center of controversy. The tumultuous campaign had taken its toll; but, as he had done so often in the past, Frank swallowed his disappointment and went on.

68. E. B. Smith, *Francis Preston Blair*, 413–14; W. E. Smith, *Blair Family in Politics*, 2:429; Coleman, *Election of 1868*, 362–67; Parrish, *Missouri under Radical Rule*, 257–58.
69. Apo to FPB, November 30, 1868, B-LP.

11

The Final Years

In the aftermath of the election, Frank took solace in his work as railroad commissioner. He made two trips to the "end of track," which took him as far west as Salt Lake City, where the Mormon legislature extended him the "freedom of the House." Apo was thankful that he had the railroad trips to get him out of St. Louis, as "seeing his personal & most vindictive political enemies elevated into the highest state offices is a hard thing." Preston suggested that his son return to his law practice, but Frank responded that he had been too long out of law to resume that discipline as a career. Apo was more blunt, "The judges are all radical & few people would be willing to risk a case with Frank before the courts." With a growing family, they had decided that the home on Washington Avenue, where they had lived for the last ten years, was too small. They relocated further west to 2737 Chestnut Street, which Frank described as "a very large & comfortable double 3 story house." Apo was pleased with it because "the boys will have plenty of open lots all around to play ball & we shall not have so much coal smoke & dust." The 1870 census found them living there with Apo's mother and four Irish women servants.[1]

Frank promised his father and brother a short trip to Washington over the holidays. With President Johnson scheduled to leave office in March, Blair sought a last-minute appointment as one of the commissioners to adjudicate

1. FB to MB, November 24, December 18, 1868, Orson Pratt to FB, January 25, 1869, BLC; Apo to FPB, November 30, 1868, FB to FPB, December 1, 1868, B-LP; 1870 Missouri Census, St. Louis City, in U.S. Bureau of the Census, Roll 816, page 337.

claims under a recent treaty between the United States and Mexico. Since he understood some Spanish and had his New Mexico experience to draw on, he thought this could tide him over "until better days come to us." Nothing came of this; and, following Grant's inauguration, the new president removed Frank from his position as railroad commissioner, replacing him with Cyrus B. Comstock, a former aide who had married Montgomery's oldest daughter, Betty. Certain friends wished Frank to intervene with the new administration in a situation where Grant had revoked certain orders benefiting them, which President Johnson had signed just before leaving office; but Blair declined, saying he had no desire to seek any favors from the Grant regime.[2]

Frank spent the early months of 1869 in Washington and New York. In addition to his political and financial concerns on this trip, Frank also needed to prepare for the argument of his test-oath case before the United States Supreme Court. Montgomery and William M. Evarts, who had served President Johnson as attorney general, argued the case for Frank in mid-March. They asserted that the Radicals had used the oath to disfranchise Democrats generally rather to proscribe "rebels" and that such action set a dangerous political precedent. While this approach strayed somewhat from the legal aspects of the case, it had been determined upon after Sam Glover, who had represented Frank earlier, talked with Justice David Davis. The latter seemed to indicate that he thought Chief Justice Chase would look favorably on such an argument, and the Blairs considered their old enemy the key man in the decision.[3]

Charles D. Drake represented the defendants, as he had done before the Missouri courts. He based his argument on the sovereign power of the people, in framing their constitution, to set suffrage conditions and included a vivid description of the wartime turmoil in Missouri that necessitated proscriptive measures. Following Drake, Evarts concluded with a tight summation of the plaintiff's legal and constitutional arguments based on the familiar bill of attainder and ex post facto contentions.[4]

The Blairs anticipated a quick and favorable decision. Frank wrote Rollins on April 13 that he had "some reasons of a private nature for believing that

---

2. FB to MB, November 24, 1868, BLC; EBL to SPL, March 10, 12, 1869, FB to FPB, March 15, 1869, B-LP. Although Lizzie and her mother continued a friendly relationship with the Grant family, Minna, Montgomery's wife, became so incensed at Frank's dismissal that she refused all White House invitations (EBL to SPL, March 31, April 6, 22, May 22, 1869, B-LP).

3. FB to MB, February 26, 1869, BLC.

4. *Missouri Democrat*, March 22, 1869; *Missouri Statesman*, April 9, June 25, 1869.

the Court will in this case give a just decision." He reported that even Glover, "who always looks to the gloomy side of every question," and Montgomery were optimistic. Frank's brother discussed the case favorably with Gideon Welles, who observed, "He [Montgomery] is, however, a sanguine man, and never doubts that his brother Frank is always right." The Blairs' optimism faded as the weeks passed with no decision. Apprehensions and misgivings now began to set in with the announcement that the Court would carry the case over to the October term. A worried Frank wrote Montgomery on November 12, "Is it possible to hurry the Supreme Court in my case? Our people are getting into a great fever about it." The *Missouri Republican* prophesied pessimistically that there could be "very little hope in regard to the result of future elections" if the case went against Blair. The Court refused to be hurried, however. It had a heavy workload; and, with only eight justices, it had fallen behind in its schedule.[5]

Even as the case was being argued, Frank was en route to New Orleans with Apo and son James to settle his accounts on the Cabin Teele adventure. He told Montgomery that, with what he had made from the railroad and the sale of some of his remaining St. Louis properties, he hoped to pay off all of his debts, amounting to some thirty thousand dollars. His friend Leonard Jerome, the New York financier-speculator, joined him in New Orleans. To their surprise, the lending house, which held most of the debt, had fallen into bankruptcy; and Frank's lawyer settled the claim against Blair with the bank's creditors for thirteen hundred dollars, getting a receipt in full for all indebtedness. Friends entertained a happy Frank and his party with a gala supper at the Hancock Club of New Orleans before their departure for Vicksburg, where they also received a warm reception. Apo and Frank left Jerome at Cincinnati to return to St. Louis, while the latter continued on to Washington, where he spent the evening at Silver Spring, filling in the family on the trip's success.[6]

5. FB to Rollins, April 13, 1869, Rollins Papers; *Diary of Welles*, 3:566; *Missouri Republican*, June 9, 1869; FB to MB, November 12, 1869, BLC.

6. FB to FPB, March 15, 1869, EBL to SPL, March 18, 19, April 3, 9, 10, 1869, B-LP; FB to MB, April 9, 1869, BLC; *People's Tribune*, April 7, 1869. Precisely when and how Blair became acquainted with Leonard Jerome is uncertain. The Jeromes had a summer home in Newport, where the Blairs frequently summered. Their home in New York stood on Madison Square at Twenty-sixth Street, and Frank sometimes stayed there. Jerome had brought horse racing to New York City in 1866 with the establishment of Jerome Park Racecourse, the home of the American Jockey Club, where Frank could often be found enjoying the races. Jerome's daughter Jennie would later marry Lord Randolph Churchill and become the mother of Sir Winston. One contemporary noted: "[Jerome] spent money as freely as he made it and never was happier than when contributing to the welfare and amusement of others" (Anita

Jerome now invited Frank to join him and the younger James Gordon Bennett, son of the owner of the *New York Herald,* on a yachting trip to Europe in June; and Blair accepted. The whole family, except Montgomery, thought it would be good for him to have the much deserved break. He made arrangements for Apo and the children to stay at Silver Spring in his absence. Apo looked forward to a relaxing summer with some time spent at the New Jersey seashore, one of her favorite spots. Frank, now relatively free from debt for the first time in years, assured the family that when he returned from Europe, he would "go to work with a will" to make himself independent in money matters.[7]

Before he could begin this new adventure, however, Frank had to deal with one other family problem. His oldest son, Andrew, had been forced to take a leave of absence from the navy because of "incipient bronchitis." The young man, a recent graduate of the Naval Academy, had left the navy in San Francisco the previous spring of 1868. Hoping to regain his health, he spent the summer with his Uncle Andrew and Aunt Evy Alexander, who were serving in the postwar military at Fort McDowell, New Mexico. A physical examination that fall at Santa Fe revealed an ulcer in Andrew's lungs that had left a cavity. Doctors in St. Louis confirmed the diagnosis when he returned home. His parents sent him to Silver Spring to recover there. The doctors, however, recommended an outdoor life on the plains for at least twelve months. Remembering his own experience of twenty years earlier, Frank took Andrew to Colorado in early May 1869 where he had friends with whom his son could stay. He also made arrangements for Andrew to visit several mines in the area to prepare him for a career as a mining engineer, as he had decided. Young Jim Blair joined his brother when school was out, going with Tom Gantt on a hunting expedition. When Frank and Christine went west in September to check on Andrew, they found his health much improved. He had determined to stay the winter in Georgetown at the smelting furnace of one of Blair's acquaintances to further his mining education.[8]

Leslie, *Lady Randolph Churchill: The Story of Jennie Jerome,* 16; Edward W. Martin, *Behind the Scenes in Washington,* 170).

7. Apo to FPB, April 8, 1869, EBL to SPL, April 9, 10, 13, May 17, 1869, FB to FPB, May 10, 1869, B-LP.

8. Eveline Alexander to FPB, May 6, 1868, Apo to SPL, September 2, 1868, EBL to SPL, September 6, 1868, May 19, 20, 1869, Apo to FPB, November 30, 1868, FB to FPB, May 10, 1869, B-LP; FB to MB, November 24, 1868, Andrew Blair to Apo, January 19, 1869, Samuel Simmons to MB, May 14, 1869, BLC; FB to Apo, September 23, 1869, BLPLC.

Following his return from Europe, Frank joined the family on the Jersey shore. While there he received an invitation to attend the first reunion of the Army and Navy of the Gulf at the Stetson Hotel in Long Branch, New Jersey. Once the drinking and feasting had reached a happy conclusion, the company began a round of toasts. Frank sat with his feet on a chair puffing furiously at his cigar. As the toasts resounded the glory of the Union, he rose to add his own prophecy, "I will speak of the people who were once our enemies, and I know that when I speak of them before soldiers I speak before those who will heartily respond. Those against whom we contended, whom we aspersed as Rebels, and whom we triumphed over as well, they were worthy of the steel of our best. We have heard here tonight only of Farragut and Sheridan; but I tell you in the future we will yet hear of General Lee and Stonewall Jackson." This sent the crowd into an uproar, and Frank was not allowed to continue. The affair quickly found its way into the press with a strong negative reaction. Blair responded, however, with a public letter in which he argued that he meant no insult but rather "a compliment to our army to speak well of those over whom our army had triumphed as 'foemen worthy of our steel.'" He then concluded that his "intention and meaning could only have been perverted by men who had been taught by such heroes as [Benjamin F.] Butler to relish a different kind of *steal*."[9]

While in Colorado that September, Frank bought stock in the Marshall Silver Mining Company of Georgetown at half price and received authorization to sell additional stock on commission. He also made arrangements sometime in 1869 to serve as the St. Louis manager for the Life Association of America, a New York–based insurance company. Still, his mind never strayed far from politics.[10]

Upon his return from Colorado, Frank found that he had missed an invitation to address the Women's Suffrage Association of Missouri. Its members had been encouraged that he might support them because of remarks made during the campaign at Indianapolis. Frank hastened to assure the suffragists that, although he was "very willing to concede all that they demand in regard to a wider sphere of employment, better compensation for their labor, and the full control of their own property & earnings," he did not favor giving them the vote. He reprimanded the women for combining their crusade with

9. *New York Times*, July 10, 13, 1869.

10. *Edwards Eleventh Annual Directory in the City of St. Louis for 1869*, 175; *Missouri Statesman*, April 15, 1870, January 21, 1871.

that for the blacks. He then went on to attack the recently passed Fifteenth Amendment, which would not only enfranchise blacks but Chinese and other "undesirable" Asians as well. Frank's racism ran deep and remained the most negative aspect of his career.[11]

An unfortunate family matter, which would have deep, long-range complications for the entire Silver Spring clan, clouded the horizon for Frank that winter. Betty Blair, Montgomery's oldest daughter by his first wife, had been adopted by her grandparents after her mother's death, becoming in effect a second daughter. She remained a part of their household until her marriage to Cyrus B. Comstock in 1865. Sometime during 1869 Betty, in a conversation with Midge Dick, Apo's sister, criticized Frank, claiming that he had made himself so financially dependent upon his father that it had left the latter in slightly straitened circumstances. Midge, of course, passed this along to Apo, perhaps exaggerating the complaint a bit to make it appear that Preston had spent his fortune on Frank. While some truth existed in Betty's concern for her grandfather, she apparently had meant her uncle no harm.

In mid-November, Frank wrote Betty a gently reproving note. He did not doubt her love for him, but he reprimanded her for having spoken critically to his sister-in-law when she should have talked directly to him about her concerns. He would expect criticism from his enemies, Frank told her, but not from a close relative; and he hoped she would avoid such remarks in the future. At the same time, he reminded Betty of his father's generosity to her and asked her to reflect on how she would have felt had he criticized her for it. The whole episode caused a permanent estrangement between the two, with Betty refusing to come to Washington when Frank was there. The tragic conclusion to the affair occurred in August 1872 when Betty asked to come home while confined in pregnancy, only to be turned away by her grandfather because Frank's children occupied her old room. A few weeks later her husband wrote that she had died in childbirth, which left the entire family distraught for the failure at reconciliation.[12]

At the end of January 1870, the Supreme Court handed down an indecisive judgment in the test-oath case. The Court split four to four, with Chief Justice Chase voting against Blair. The split decision, in effect, left the Missouri Supreme Court's ruling intact, so that the test oath remained valid for future

---

11. FB to Mrs. Frances Minor, October 13, 1869, BLC.
12. FB to FPB, November 14, 1869, enclosing FB to Betty, November 11, 1869, and Betty to Mira Dick, EBL to SPL, May 13, August 15, 25, 1871, August 8, 1872, B-LP; E. B. Smith, *Francis Preston Blair,* 351–52, 420–21, 431–32.

elections. The family was greatly disappointed, but Montgomery urged Frank to remain silent in the hope that another case might carry better results.[13]

Frank spent the early months of 1870 in New York with Leonard Jerome, whose family had gone to Paris. He had a variety of financial prospects, including his mining concerns in Colorado, where Andrew continued to look after his interests while pursuing his mining career. By March, Andrew was back in Philadelphia, staying with Biddle relatives and continuing his engineering education. Frank wrote Apo that they had had dinner together and that Andrew looked "remarkably well & seems to be in excellent spirits." He had hoped to bring Christine east, but her ill health prevented this. Before leaving New York for Washington, however, he requested that Jerome send her a spring silk to cheer her up. At some point, Frank asked Montgomery to see the Prussian minister in Washington about the possibility of a military appointment with Prussia's armed forces. Such might serve him well politically in the future with the German voters at home. Yet, when some hope for this appeared on the horizon, Frank backed off because he considered the financial arrangements insufficient.[14]

The family joined Frank in the East for the summer, with Apo expecting their seventh child, a daughter born in August and named Eveline Martin after Apo's sister-in-law. They enjoyed a relaxing summer, dividing their time between Washington, the Finger Lake region of New York, Philadelphia, and the Jersey shore. When they returned to St. Louis in early October, Frank found Missouri politics in a turmoil. He undoubtedly had maintained contact over the summer, although there is no extant correspondence for the period. Indeed, Frank had earlier filed for a seat in the Missouri House on the Democratic ticket.[15]

The Radical Union Party at its state convention in September had split into Liberal and Radical factions, with each nominating a slate of state candidates. The division had come over the question of endorsing a proposed state constitutional amendment modifying the ironclad oath provisions for voting and substituting a simple declaration of support for state and national constitutions. The Liberals had insisted on official party endorsement. When

13. *Missouri Democrat*, February 2, 3, 1870; *Missouri Statesman*, February 4, 1870; *New York Times*, February 1, 1870; MB to FB, February 2, 1870, FPB to FB, February 4, 1870, BLC.

14. FB to Christine, December 16, 1869, March 26, 1870, BLPLC; Andrew to FB, January 10, 1870, FB to Apo, March 24, April 26, 1870, FB to FPB, April 14, 1870, FB to MB, n.d. [1870], BLC; FB to MB, n.d. [1870], Blair Family Papers, MHS.

15. FB to FPB, September 21, 1870, EBL to SPL, December 2, 1870, B-LP.

the Radicals refused to agree to this or to support a moderate gubernatorial candidate in place of the incumbent Joseph W. McClurg, the Liberals bolted and nominated B. Gratz Brown for governor on a Liberal Republican ticket.[16]

Many Radicals had been dissatisfied for some time with the strident leadership of Charles D. Drake. As previously seen, there had not been unanimity over the new constitution at the time of its adoption. Following the Radicals' electoral triumph in 1866, Brown had called a meeting of party leaders to propose that they endorse universal suffrage for both blacks and disfranchised whites and remove the test-oath restrictions for the professions. Drake and his supporters balked; and, retiring from the Senate because of ill health, Brown did not push the matter further. Frank's cousin and former partner had stirred up sentiment that would not go away, however. He found new allies in William M. Grosvenor, who arrived during this period to take over the editorship of the *Missouri Democrat*, and Carl Schurz, who had moved to St. Louis to become associated with the *Westliche Post*. The Radical legislature sent Schurz to the Senate in the wake of the 1868 election, defeating Drake's handpicked candidate and making it evident that all was not well within the party.[17]

The Missouri Radicals had placed the question of black suffrage on the 1868 ballot, only to have it soundly defeated. Now the Liberals determined that the issue could succeed only if coupled with the removal of all proscriptions on voting, as suggested by Brown two years earlier. The departing Governor Fletcher took the lead in his final message in January 1869; but, with the new Governor McClurg, a staunch Drake supporter, opposing, the legislature took no action until the spring of 1870. Then, following the Supreme Court decision in Frank's test-oath case and the final ratification of the federal Fifteenth Amendment, the proposal gained acceptance, laying the ground for the party split that fall.[18]

The Democratic Party had seen little hope earlier in establishing a state ticket, given the conditions of the registry system. Undoubtedly with Frank's approval, it had adopted what came to be known as the "possum policy." Under this strategy, it would concentrate on local and legislative races, refraining from putting up a state ticket, while waiting to see what happened with the proposed amendment and the growing Radical divisions. Through

16. Parrish, *Missouri under Radical Rule,* 280–81, 289–99.
17. Ibid., 100–102, 228–67.
18. Ibid., 269–72, 280–81.

all of his antagonism with Frank over their postwar political differences, Gratz Brown and his wife had continued to be regular welcome guests at Silver Spring and No. 4 during his Senate tenure. A reconciliation between the two men had taken place at Christmas of 1869 when their two families shared dinner together. The two cousins must have conversed then about Brown's growing concern with the existing Radical leadership. Even before his return from the East in the fall of 1870, Frank and other Democratic leaders had endorsed Brown's gubernatorial candidacy in the hope that a coalition in the new legislature could bring further change.[19]

The Democrats were not disappointed. With their support, Brown defeated McClurg for governor by forty thousand votes. The electorate approved the proposed amendment ending the ironclad oath, together with two others, overwhelmingly. Frank secured election to the legislature by twelve hundred votes, even though the abstract of returns noted that he had failed to file the required oath of loyalty. All told, the Democrats carried 77 of the 138 seats in the Missouri House. In the Missouri Senate races, the Democrats elected 6 and the Liberals 6, with 3 seats going to fusionists and 2 to the Radicals. Democrats won four of the five congressional races in which they had candidates, with the Liberals and Radicals splitting the four that the Democrats did not contest. The election drew national attention as an omen of what Grant and the national Republican Party might expect in 1872. Missouri's Liberal Republicans had been disaffected by several of the administration's patronage appointments, which favored the Drake wing of the party, as well as by its stand on the tariff and other issues. Grant had thrown his weight behind McClurg during the election, which further alienated the Liberals. The question remained as to what direction Brown and the Liberals might take in forming a coalition in the upcoming legislature to move for additional reforms.[20]

Frank had a more immediate concern: a potential seat in the U.S. Senate. On November 11, three days after the election, he wrote Montgomery about rumors floating around that Drake would resign his Senate seat to accept the position as chief justice of the U.S. Court of Claims. If this proved true, Blair wanted his brother to secure the votes of all the Democratic senators for Drake's confirmation, as "I will without doubt be elected by the Legislature

19. Ibid., 283–86; EBL to SPL, January 31, February 6, March 7, 1865, January 2, 1870, FB to FPB, September 21, 1870, B-LP; Charles Gibson to MB, September 30, 1870, FB to MB, November 2, 1870, BLC; *Missouri Statesman*, September 30, October 14, 1870.
20. Parrish, *Missouri under Radical Rule*, 307–10; Abstract of Election Returns, St. Louis County, November 8, 1870.

already chosen to fill the vacancy in the Senate which his appointment will create." Realizing the full impact of the recent election on his party leadership, Drake had lost little time in seeking this sinecure from the Grant administration. Shortly after Congress convened in December, the president sent forward Drake's nomination, which received quick confirmation.[21]

With the definite announcement of Drake's retirement from the Senate, it quickly became evident that Frank had strong support across the state as his replacement. His election to the Missouri House gave him the added advantage of sitting in the body that would help make the selection. When speculation centered on Blair as a possible candidate for Speaker, he wrote Rollins quite candidly that he had his eye on higher things. Apo again showed her reluctance about her husband's return to politics, asking her father-in-law to encourage Frank to resume his law practice. Montgomery also apparently cautioned him about seeking higher office, but Frank responded, "If Drake resigns and I am not chosen for his place, who will suppose that I have any strength in Missouri?" With an eye to the future, he continued, "If I am placed again in position in Congress I shall be brought more into the eyes of our people. . . . It is not enough to have the strength (and I believe that I have it) but I must show the world that I have it."[22]

Frank early sought to make common cause with the Liberal Republicans in the hope that this could work to his advantage in the long run, as the Drake term had only two years remaining. He wrote Rollins that the Democrats should invite the Liberals to meet with them for purposes of organizing the legislature. Simultaneously, he urged Montgomery to cultivate Carl Schurz, the other Missouri senator and a key Liberal leader. Schurz had addressed the Senate on December 15 in an attempt to define the Liberal Republican movement. Among other things, he had called for the removal of all national restrictions on "persons lately in rebellion," which seemed to fit with Frank's earlier platform. "Schurz," Blair told Rollins, "is as much the leader of the Germans in America as Bismarck is in Europe. With his aid, backed by the Germans of Missouri, we can carry the entire German vote in the next Presidential election."[23]

21. FB to MB, November 11, 1870, BLC; *Missouri Republican*, November 19, 1870; *CG*, 41:3:Appendix:1–8.
22. Apo to FPB, November 16, 1870, B-LP; John W. Henry to James O. Broadhead, November 18, 1870, Broadhead Papers; FB to Rollins, December 14, 18, 1870, Rollins Papers; FB to MB, November 27, 1870, BLC.
23. FB to MB, December 9, 1870, Blair Family Papers, MHS; FB to Rollins, December 18, 1870, Rollins Papers.

Although Frank did not approach Gratz Brown directly, he fully expected his cousin's support. The two men had made considerable progress in reconciling their differences over the past year; and Gratz, who also had higher political ambitions, realized the importance of the Democrats in his gubernatorial victory. He acknowledged as much when the St. Louis Democrats serenaded him shortly after the election to the dismay of Schurz, who was more concerned with purging the existing Republican Party and creating a new one than with merging with the Democrats. "He [Brown] has made use of me whenever he could do so," Frank informed Montgomery, "& it is time he should be made to return some value for what he has had."[24]

When the General Assembly convened in January 1871 the Democrats had little difficulty in organizing both houses, although they shared some offices with the Liberals and the fusionists in the Senate. Rollins invited the Liberals to join the Democratic caucus for a senatorial candidate, but only four accepted. Frank was not the unanimous choice. His old friend Sam Glover, together with John S. Phelps and Silas Woodson, also sought the post. But, when the caucus voted, Blair emerged with a clear majority over the other three and went on to defeat former senator John B. Henderson, the Republican choice, 102 to 59, which gave him 12 more votes than the total strength of his party.[25]

William Grosvenor, the editor of the *Missouri Democrat*, wrote Schurz somewhat philosophically that he thought Frank would not be too harmful in Washington. "He went, I know, with an idea of cooperating as far as he possibly could with liberal Republicans like yourself; and I believe, if you encourage instead of fighting him you can do much to keep him straight or straighter." Frank did indeed desire cooperation but strictly with an eye to his own political ambitions. Schurz realized this, having written earlier to Emil Preetorius, "The election of Blair has dealt the liberal cause a decided blow, from which it will not recover for a long time. . . . Did Gratz Brown really favor the election of Blair? . . . If this should be really true, I believe him guilty of a total sellout." The relations of the two Missouri senators would be tenuous

24. *Missouri Democrat*, November 15, 1870; Brown to Schurz, November 26, 1870, Carl Schurz Papers; FB to MB, December 11, 1870, BLC.

25. FB to MB, January 1, 1871, Arden R. Smith to FPB, January 15, 1871, B-LP; Rollins to FPB, January 13, 1871, BLC; *Missouri Republican*, January 13, 1871; *People's Tribune*, January 18, 25, 1871. An interesting behind-the-scenes view of the Democratic caucus may be found in William B. Napton Diary, William B. Napton Papers, 639–41. In comparing Frank to his cousin Gratz Brown, Napton aptly observed, "Blair is a practical man and Brown a theorist," and then concluded, "Blair never did anything without reference to his individual advancement."

at best over the next two years in spite of Frank's efforts to further cultivate his colleague.[26]

Another skeptic, writing under the pseudonym "A Novice," asked the *New York Times* if the Blair now going to the Senate was the same one who had sought to "destroy" that body as the Democratic vice presidential candidate two years earlier. When the *New York World* proclaimed that Frank had "the qualities essential for Democratic statesmanship," the *Times* tartly asked how the *World* could find Frank so acceptable now when it had considered him too controversial in the 1868 election. The *Times* editors asserted that the Blair of 1868 was the Blair of 1871, and they were negative on both.[27]

An exuberant Frank quickly resigned his seat in the House and, with Apo, headed for Washington. An excited Lizzie prepared No. 4 for their occupancy. She told Phil that Apo was very pleased at Frank's success, particularly because it meant a steady income. The happy couple arrived in Washington on January 24. Three days later Frank took the oath as Missouri's newest senator. Apo and Montgomery went to the capitol, hoping to see the ceremony, but they arrived too late. Apo stayed in Washington only briefly before going to Philadelphia to see her Biddle relatives and check on Andrew, who remained in school there. Lizzie observed, "I never saw her looking so well & happy. Happiness is a great beautifier." When Apo returned to Washington for an extended stay, it became evident that her happiness reflected more than Frank's election. Their son Andrew had been courting Annie Biddle, daughter of Apo's cousin Tom, "the richest banker in Philadelphia"; and by March, the young couple announced their engagement. Frank approved the match, although he confided to Lizzie that he hoped Tom Biddle's wealth would not "sap some of his [Andrew's] energies & make him a trifler."[28]

Frank immediately plunged into his role as senator. Lizzie reported to Phil that he "seems very happy & all right, works very hard. Several nights [he was] up late as one or two o'clock & [he] has a large book of names already recorded out of his correspondence." Copies of his speeches were much in demand; and, by the end of February, Lizzie and an assistant had sent out sixteen thousand copies. A welcome guest at many dinner tables, Frank finally asked his sister to help repay his social obligations by having a ten-course dinner at No. 4 for all the Democratic senators on February 11,

26. Schurz to Preetorius, January 27, 1871, Grosvenor to Schurz, February 16, 1871, Schurz Papers.
27. *New York Times*, January 18, 25, 1871.
28. EBL to SPL, January 14, 23, 24, 27, March 5, 18, 20, 29, 1871, B-LP.

which he later pronounced a great success. Blair quickly sought rapport with his Missouri colleague, observing candidly to Rollins that "Schurz & I are on excellent terms, he is very friendly and very talkative. He is an immense egotist, and it is very hard to get at him on that account. He has fine powers and if he was not so opinionated he would be much more effective."[29]

Frank's committee appointments included that on the Pacific Railroad as well as Education and Labor. He saw his major assignment, however, as the special committee to investigate the Ku Klux Klan and its activities, in the hope that this could give him a national platform with which perhaps to project another bid for the presidency in 1872 with Southern support. During this first session the special committee occupied most of his energies as he worked to put forward a strong minority position to prevent additional anti-Klan legislation. Congress had passed its first such law the previous year, providing heavy fines and imprisonment for anyone found guilty of intimidating citizens from voting by any of several means, with enforcement the province of the federal courts. As the Senate considered even more drastic enforcement measures in February 1871, Frank rose to the attack on the fifteenth and again on the twenty-fourth. "If the central Government can make and unmake States at pleasure; can reconstruct them, displace the duly elected authorities chosen by the people, and put others in their places by edicts to be executed by the military arm," he thundered, "then we are under a consolidated Government without limitation of power. Such has been and is the action of Congress and of the administration of General Grant." His words did not sway the majority, which passed a new anti-Klan measure by the end of the month.[30]

The following month Frank attacked the Grant proposal for annexing the Dominican Republic, using a sixty-nine-page indictment prepared by his father. Having failed in their attempts at black colonization elsewhere, the Blairs had little desire to see a predominantly black Caribbean nation annexed to the United States. On April 3 and 4, Frank resumed center stage for two days against yet another anti-Klan measure introduced by Sen. John Sherman. Lizzie, who sat in the Senate gallery the first day, told Phil that the Senate gave him its full attention. In the spirited debate that followed, Frank kept his temper throughout, she observed. A final effort came ten days later, at a

29. EBL to SPL, January 27, February 2, 10, 12, 17, 27, 1871, B-LP; FB to Rollins, February 16, 1871, Rollins Papers.
30. *Missouri Statesman*, February 17, 1871; *CG*, 42:3:Appendix:114–17, 157–60.

time when he was very sick with a chill and fever. Undaunted, he addressed the Senate for more than an hour, reiterating his arguments defending states' rights and the unconstitutionality of the proposed legislation. In spite of this, it passed a week later, just before adjournment. Frank was pleased, however, that Schurz had joined him in opposition; and he encouraged his friends in St. Louis to serenade Missouri's senior senator when Schurz returned home.[31]

Meanwhile, his Missouri friends, led by Rollins, sought to honor Frank with a subscription for a full-length portrait to be painted by George Caleb Bingham. Completed by the famous artist at his Kansas City studio during the summer, it depicted Frank standing beside his desk in the Senate chamber. The *Missouri Statesman*, upon seeing it, commented: "The tall, well proportioned form, and stern, handsome face, are delineated with wonderful vigor and fidelity." Intended as a gift to the state legislature for display in the capitol, the portrait toured several places around the state that summer and fall.[32]

A Washington reporter during this period made the following observation: "In person, Senator Blair is tall, squarely built, and though by no means a beauty, is one of the most manly looking members of the Senate. His lack of beauty has often been the source of amusement to his friends. A gentleman, not long since, an ardent admirer of General Blair, met him for the first time at the Jerome Park Racecourse in New York. A friend of the Senator who had witnessed the meeting asked after he had withdrawn, 'Well—what do you think of Frank Blair, now?' 'I am agreeably disappointed,' was the reply. 'Indeed!' asked the friend; 'in what respect, pray?' 'Why,' said the other, 'Blair isn't so d—d ugly after all.' "[33]

Frank and the family spent the summer at Silver Spring, with Blair commuting to No. 4. Apo initially had been reluctant to come because of the difficulties with Betty Comstock, but when the latter put her visit off until fall, the entire family came and had a delightful time in the country. Andrew and his fiancée joined them in early May and, according to Lizzie, obviously

31. *CG*, 42:1:Appendix:117–34, 231–39; EBL to SPL, March 30, April 3, 13, 14, 1871, B-LP; FB to MB, April 29, 1871, Blair Family Papers, MHS.

32. Bingham to Rollins, March 6, June 4, July 1, 1871, Rollins Papers; *Missouri Statesman*, May 5, August 25, October 27, 1871. The portrait was never placed at the capitol but found its way to the Mercantile Library in St. Louis where it hung in the reference room for some forty years. It was transferred to the Missouri Historical Society, St. Louis, in 1926 and, having deteriorated, was cut down to bust size. It is currently on permanent loan from the Society to the Blair House in Washington, where it is displayed in one of the downstairs rooms (John Francis McDermott, *Bingham: River Portraitist*, 152–53; *Missouri Historical Review* [October 1965]: 80).

33. Martin, *Behind the Scenes*, 170.

enjoyed each other's company. In June, Frank took Jim to look at Princeton, where he planned to enroll that fall.

In the wake of the recently passed Ku Klux Klan legislation, Congress had established a joint committee to investigate the group's activities. Familiarly called the "Outrage Committee," it scheduled hearings well into July concerning conditions in the South. Frank worked hard to see that the views of Southern whites received an adequate hearing. As the hot and humid Washington summer dragged on, he complained continually of not feeling well, having trouble with headaches and cramps in his feet and hand. His doctor attributed the complaints to excessive smoking and limited him to two cigars a day. Concerned by the stressful schedule her brother kept, Lizzie also feared that he was having difficulty adjusting to a regimen of abstinence from liquor, to which he had agreed earlier in the spring. In reality, the illness of that 1871 summer portended far more serious complications that would fell him by the late fall of 1872.[34]

In early August, as the Outrage Committee wound down its hearings, Frank managed to get away to Cape May on the Jersey shore for a week. He came back feeling better. In mid-August, he left for Maine to pick up Jim and Pres, who had been visiting friends there for the past month. The headaches came and went, with Lizzie complaining that he lounged around much of the day and needed more exercise. "I am sure a horse and cold bath," she wrote Phil, "is his best remedy until his plethora [of cigars] is reduced to a total abstinence standard."[35]

Politics was never very far from Frank's mind. While at Cape May he had a series of press interviews in which he endorsed what came to be known as "the New Departure." This movement had been launched the previous May by Henry Watterson, editor of the *Louisville Courier Journal*. Accepting the Fifteenth Amendment as a given, it urged the Democrats to move toward a "broad conservatism" by accepting the war's results and turning their attention to current issues. Building on the success of the Liberal Republican–Democratic coalition in Missouri the preceding year, Frank sought to move the Democrats to a similar passive policy of coalition nationally. Having abandoned his own presidential ambitions for the time being, in his interviews and correspondence that summer and fall he openly endorsed his cousin Gratz Brown for the presidency. He portrayed Gratz as a Kentuckian thoroughly

34. EBL to SPL, May 13, 15, 16, 20, 31, June 30, July 3, 4, 6, 7, 14, 18, 20, 31, 1871, B-LP.
35. EBL to SPL, July 6, 7, August 1, 2, 4, 7, 8, 18, 1871, B-LP.

sympathetic with the South while also sound on questions of tariff and finance. He deliberately overlooked that Gratz long had been an advocate of black suffrage.[36]

Frank continued to test these waters throughout the fall. With Liberal Republican movements springing up across the North, his colleague Schurz, having concluded that the Republican Party could not be reformed from within, began speaking broadly about the need for a new party. Blair toured the South during part of the fall as the Outrage Committee took its hearings there. In speeches at Montgomery and elsewhere, Frank stressed the theme of reconciliation and urged consideration of the New Departure. He reached St. Louis in time to hear Cassius Clay, who had been invited by Rollins, speak at the Cotton Fair in October. Blair sat on the platform with Rollins, Brown, and Confederate general P. G. T. Beauregard as the noted Kentuckian pushed the concept of third-party politics. Later that fall Frank urged Rollins to return to St. Louis with Brown so that the three of them could make plans and particularly discuss how to bring Schurz into their camp. They hoped to also pursue the possibility of a gubernatorial nomination for Rollins. Blair further directed Rollins to draw up resolutions of support for coalition by the legislature at its forthcoming session.[37]

Not all Democrats agreed with this projected course for their party. Frank found considerable opposition among the party's members in Congress. When Montgomery forwarded a letter in support of the policy to the *New York World*, he received a reply from Manton Marble, the paper's editor and a major Democratic figure, who said that he could not endorse the program editorially nor did he find much support among his acquaintances. Marble also played down Frank's speeches in the following months. Still, the movement gained momentum.[38]

Things began coming to a head in January 1872. Before leaving for the new congressional session, Frank traveled to Jefferson City, where he endorsed

36. *People's Tribune*, July 26, 1871; *Missouri Statesman*, August 25, 1871; Charles Gibson to FB, July 25, 1871, Rollins to FB, July 28, 1871, Arden R. Smith to FB, August 23, 1871, Gideon Welles to FB, August 26, 1871, FB to Alexander H. Stephens, September 2, 1871, BLC; EBL to SPL, August 17, 1871, B-LP.

37. *New York Times*, October 21, November 22, 1871; *People's Tribune*, October 25, 1871; *Missouri Statesman*, November 3, 1871; FB to Rollins, November 21, December 14, 1871, Rollins Papers; Rollins to Schurz, November 22, 1871, Schurz Papers; Hans L. Trefousse, *Carl Schurz: A Biography*, 197–200; Peterson, *Freedom and Franchise*, 202–3.

38. FB to Rollins, December 14, 1871, Rollins Papers; Marble to MB, December 10, 1871, MB to Marble, December 23, 1871, BLC.

the passive policy in a speech to the legislature on January 9. A week later the Democratic State Central Committee issued an address reviewing the progress of the past two years and advancing the idea of a coalition to overthrow the national administration in the same manner as Missourians had accomplished in 1870. The climax of all this activity came when Schurz engineered a convention of Missouri's Liberal Republicans. Gratz Brown delivered the keynote address. Outlining the sins of the Grant administration, he called for a new reform party that could redress the nation's ills. With regard to the Liberals' Democratic allies, Brown spoke emphatically, "Some of our friends seem to indulge in great timidity about what is known as the Democratic Party. I participate in no such apprehension." The Liberals adopted resolutions calling for reconciliation, tariff and civil-service reform, and an emphasis on local self-determination. Although it endorsed the Reconstruction amendments, the convention's devotion to black civil rights was lukewarm at best. Most important, the convention issued a call for those who agreed with its platform to meet in Cincinnati in May to consider forming a new party.[39]

Frank wrote Rollins enthusiastically that these proceedings were the "sensation" of Washington. He had been invited to a meeting of "leading liberals here (in private)" to plan how to get other states organized behind the movement. George Pendleton of Ohio had issued an open letter calling upon the Liberal Republicans to organize in such a way that Democrats could cooperate with them. Blair urged Rollins to get the Democratic members of the Missouri legislature to add their endorsement, which "will have the effect of riveting the attention of the country upon the state of Missouri and its candidate [Brown]." "No time is to be lost," he stressed a week later. Five-eighths of the congressional Democrats now favored the Missouri policy and would probably endorse any "judicious nomination" by the Liberals. In late spring, Frank sent a telegram to the Louisiana Democratic convention: "Our friends here think it would be good policy to defer the Democratic nominations until after the convention in Cincinnati."[40]

39. FB to FPB, n.d. [early 1872], BLC; *People's Tribune,* January 10, 31, 1872; *Missouri Statesman,* January 19, 26, 1872; FB to Rollins (three letters), n.d. [early 1872], Rollins Papers. Brown's speech at the Liberal Republican state convention may be found in pamphlet form, including a letter from Schurz and the convention proceedings, in BLC. Gratz sent the materials to Frank to have fifty thousand copies made at Brown's expense for distribution, which Frank had done (EBL to SPL, February 1, 15, 1872, B-LP).

40. FB to Rollins (three letters), n.d. [January 1872], February 1, 1872, Rollins Papers; *New York Times,* April 20, 1872.

As the coalition movement moved forward, Frank was also deeply involved with his old friend Cong. James B. Beck of Kentucky, in preparing a
minority report for the Outrage Committee. The group had held countless
hearings in Washington and across the South and gathered testimony from
a wide cross section of Southerners, white and black, enough to fill thirteen
volumes. Even as the committee traveled, President Grant had been applying
the Ku Klux Klan acts passed by the previous session to quell disturbances in
South Carolina. The resulting trials played into the hands of the Democrats,
who contended that the deplorable conditions in the South resulted from
Republican corruption. Frank and Beck played this theme relentlessly in their
three-hundred-page minority report, which the majority Republicans initially
refused to publish, only to have the Senate order it printed. Gleeful over this
turn of events, Blair believed that the controversy would only increase reader
interest.[41]

With this concluded, Frank made a hurried trip to New York in early
March to see the Jeromes and hold political consultations there. Among those
contacted was Gov. Henry Clay Warmoth of Louisiana, who had served under
him during the war. Warmoth intended to go to Cincinnati and assured Frank
of his support for Brown and the Blair agenda. Alexander H. Stephens also
expressed interest in Gratz's candidacy, which Frank found as an encouraging
sign. Blair wrote Rollins that the New York Democracy would come out
in favor of the Cincinnati convention the following week, although he was
not certain if Horace Greeley would agree. Bad weather had prevented him
from seeing the editor of the *Tribune* or Samuel Tilden, but he knew many of
Greeley's friends would sign on.[42]

Greeley was proving one of the enigmas in the complex Liberal scenario beginning to emerge. A strident critic of the Grant administration
through the pages of the *Tribune* and elsewhere, he nevertheless differed
with many Liberals over the issues of free-trade and tariff reform, things that
particularly appealed to Schurz and the Germans. Greeley, who appeared
to be having presidential ambitions, agreed to come to Cincinnati only if
the revenue question remained as a local issue. Gratz Brown reported by
late March that he had worked things well west of the Mississippi, and
Rollins wrote Schurz on April 14 that he hoped the senator could back the

41. EBL to SPL, February 11, 15, 18, 19, March 3, 1872, B-LP; *Testimony Taken by the Joint
Select Committee to Inquire into the Condition of Affairs in the Late Insurrectionary States.*
42. FB to Apo, March 8, 1872, BLC; EBL to SPL, March 9, 1872, B-LP; FB to Rollins,
March 11, 1872, Rollins Papers.

Missouri governor's candidacy. Schurz, however, remained uncommitted, having never fully trusted Brown because of his flirtation with the Democrats in the immediate wake of the 1870 election. Other potential candidates on the horizon included Charles Francis Adams, son and grandson of presidents and best known for his diplomatic skills during the Civil War, Sen. Lyman Trumbull of Illinois, and Justice David Davis of the United States Supreme Court.[43]

Frank returned to St. Louis in April, having no intention of going to Cincinnati. He was exhausted physically, and the swelling in his hand continued to bother him. Although his doctor and family had urged him to quit smoking, he contented himself with cutting his daily supply in half and going to smaller and milder cigars. Phil Lee did him no favor when he sent him a box from Havana. "Tobacco has poisoned his [Frank's] blood & the nicotine is coming out of his finger," Lizzie admonished her husband and then remarked eerily, "I am glad [it] does not go to the head." Apo was expecting their eighth child and having a difficult confinement, which also gave him cause for concern. Midge Dick had told Lizzie that Apo appeared quite distressed at the prospect since twenty-month-old Evy could not even walk yet. At age forty-four, Apo considered herself too old to be having a second family. On the positive side, son Andrew had returned to St. Louis and gone into the metallurgy business with Regis Chauvenet, and the business seemed to be thriving. Annie Biddle had come out to see him, and the two went ahead with plans for their wedding.[44]

In the midst of his badly needed rest, Frank received an urgent telegram from Rollins. Gratz Brown's candidacy was unraveling at Cincinnati, thanks to the machinations of Schurz and his lieutenants, Rollins reported. Blair and Brown needed to hasten to the convention city to salvage it. William McKee, the editor of the *Missouri Democrat*, whose paper was solidly in Grant's camp, had been covering the Liberal Republican convention and sending dispatches home as "Mack." Not without malice, he warned that Schurz had decided to support Adams and now had his lieutenants libeling the governor for his intemperance and other presumed liabilities. His April 29 dispatch reported the Missouri delegation weakening in its support for Brown. Grosvenor, according to "Mack," appeared two-faced, supporting Brown on the surface

43. Trefousse, *Carl Schurz*, 202–4; Peterson, *Freedom and Franchise*, 208–11; W. E. Smith, *Blair Family in Politics*, 2:451.

44. FB to Apo, February 12, 23, March 1, 8, 1872, BLC; EBL to SPL, March 3, April 11, 17, 22, 24, 30, 1872, B-LP; *Gould and Aldrich's Annual Directory of the City of St. Louis for 1872*, 160.

while working against him behind the scenes. Schurz's acceptance speech, upon taking the gavel as presiding officer, did nothing to reassure Gratz. "Personal friendship and state pride are noble sentiments," he declared, "but what is personal friendship, what is state pride, compared with the great duty we owe to our common country."[45]

Whether Schurz actively supported an anti-Brown movement, as McKee implied, or the *Democrat* editor was merely stirring up mischief, cannot be certain. Frank took the Rollins warning seriously. With Gratz Brown in tow, he caught a train for Cincinnati, arriving there on the evening of May 2. Horace White of the *Chicago Tribune* recalled that Grosvenor, apparently in a panic, ran up and down the hotel corridors knocking on doors with shouts of "Get up! Blair and Brown are here from St. Louis." White and others could not understand why they should become excited over this. Frank and Gratz quickly held consultations with Rollins and others.

Grosvenor was soon asserting that Blair and Brown had made a deal with the Greeley men during the night by which the Missouri governor would withdraw in return for second place on the ticket, and this report appeared in the *Cincinnati Commercial* the next morning. Before the results of the first ballot, in which he ran fourth behind Adams, Greeley, and Trumbull, in that order, were announced, Brown asked Schurz for permission to speak. When granted, he announced his intention to withdraw, asking his supporters to switch their votes to Greeley, much to Schurz's dismay. Still, the convention continued through four more ballots before stampeding to Greeley on the sixth. It then quickly finished its business by giving Gratz the vice presidential nomination. Whether a deal had been struck, "Mack" reported that the Greeley men felt obligated to Gratz, and hence went for him for second place on the ticket.[46]

While Gratz Brown returned to Jefferson City, Frank hastened on to Washington. Lizzie reported that her brother was in *"a crisis."* He told the family at dinner on May 5 that the turn of events at Cincinnati had come about by his persuading Gratz to withdraw, even before the first ballot, as his

45. Cassius Marcellus Clay, *The Life of Cassius Marcellus Clay,* 1:505; *Missouri Democrat,* April 30, May 1, 2, 1872; *Proceedings of the Liberal Republican Convention in Cincinnati, May 1st, 2d, and 3d, 1872,* 11–12.

46. *Missouri Democrat,* May 4, 1872; EBL to SPL, May 5, 1872, B-LP; *Proceedings of the Liberal Republican Convention,* 3–4, 28–33; Horace White, *The Life of Lyman Trumbull,* 382–83; Peterson, *Freedom and Franchise,* 214–17; W. E. Smith, *Blair Family in Politics,* 2:452–53. For a thorough analysis of the Cincinnati convention, which downplays the Blair-Brown role in Greeley's nomination, see Matthew T. Downey, "Horace Greeley and the Politicians: The Liberal Republican Convention of 1872."

cause looked hopeless. Frank had hoped that the nomination might then go to Trumbull, whom the other Blairs had been favoring. It became evident, however, that with Trumbull and Davis both from Illinois, and that state's delegation unable to decide between them, the only way to stop Adams, who represented "the money power of the North aided by Schurz," was to endorse Greeley. Blair strongly believed that the *Tribune* editor's nomination was in the best interests of the South. Although unstated, the enmity of Frank and Gratz against Schurz, upon whom they had counted to push Brown's nomination, undoubtedly played a role in the scenario they followed. There is also the possibility that Frank saw Schurz as a potential threat to his political leadership in Missouri if the Liberal Republican ticket with Adams succeeded.[47]

The major concern of the Blairs beyond this point became the selling of the Greeley-Brown ticket to the Democrats. Frank thought his father should go to New York to visit with the party leadership there, but Montgomery persuaded Preston differently. After much maneuvering, the Democrats, meeting at Baltimore on July 9, accepted both the candidates and the platform of the Liberal Republicans. The latter pledged civil-service reform while promising to restore political morality and traditional constitutional principles. While the platform upheld the postwar constitutional amendments, the Liberals agreed that their enforcement should rest with the states. At the behest of the Greeley men, the platform left a stand on the tariff and revenue matters to local constituencies. All of this proved palatable to the Democrats in their desire to overthrow Grant.[48]

Frank informed Rollins, meanwhile, that Schurz "has not yet got over the unexpected turn of events at Cincinnati. His self esteem was terribly shocked and his ruffled plumage has not yet been smoothed." Indeed, Schurz had been in a constant depression, and his friends feared that he might abandon the movement he had done so much to organize. Grosvenor wrote him at the end of May, "You cannot now desert the party . . . and thereby leave all your friends in the lurch; its only result will be the election of Grant and betrayal of those who trusted you." Schurz realized that Greeley was anathema to the Germans, who also detested the tariff compromise; but he thwarted any attempt at a Liberal split, and the anti-Grant forces went into battle at least nominally united.[49]

47. EBL to SPL, May 5, 1872, B-LP.
48. EBL to SPL, May 7, 8, 9, 10, 21, 25, 1872, B-LP.
49. FB to Rollins, May 25, 1872, Rollins Papers; Grosvenor to Schurz, May 26, 1872, Schurz Papers; Trefousse, *Carl Schurz*, 206–8.

Frank had to deal with a number of personal problems before he could plunge into another campaign. Much to the dismay of the expectant and depressed Apo, who wanted him at home, he remained in Washington, exerting leadership to secure the passage of an amnesty bill, which restored the suffrage to all but some seven hundred former Confederates. Consequently, he was not at home when Apo delivered their eighth child, a son, whom they named William Alexander. When the congressional session finally ended in early June, Lizzie reported that Frank looked exhausted and still experienced difficulty with his hand. For all his effort to bring order to his financial house, money problems continued to plague him as his family grew and he sent the older children to expensive schools. He regularly gave his congressional paychecks to Apo to take care of expenses in St. Louis as his living arrangements at Silver Spring and No. 4 kept his needs there at a minimum. Still, he was forced to sell his horses and buggy shortly before leaving the capital to raise additional money.[50]

Upon his return home, Frank found Apo in a very weakened condition from her pregnancy. Lizzie kept up with family matters in St. Louis by corresponding with the baby's nurse. By mid-July, with neither Frank's nor Apo's health improving, their doctor recommended that they spend the remainder of the summer at the seashore. Consequently, they packed young George off to stay with Lizzie and his grandparents at Silver Spring, while Jim and Pres were dispatched to Fort Garland, New Mexico, where Andrew and Evy Alexander were now stationed. Frank secured a place at East Hampton on Long Island and reported that the sea air proved beneficial to the entire family except Apo, who was making a slow recovery.[51]

By September, Frank was back in St. Louis and ready to dive into yet another campaign, while Apo and the children remained at Silver Spring. The Democrats had held their state convention during his absence and, to his dismay, had turned to Silas Woodson, rather than Jim Rollins, as their gubernatorial choice on a fusion ticket. Blair told Rollins that he would go through as much of the schedule that the state committee had outlined for him as possible, "but I have been very unwell all summer & I am still an invalid and I may not be able to do much in that way."[52]

A concerned family sent Phil Lee and his fifteen-year-old son, Blair, home with Apo and the children in mid-October to check on Frank. Although the

50. EBL to SPL, May 30, June 5, 8, 9, 18, 1872, B-LP.
51. EBL to SPL, June 18, July 10, 11, 18, 20, 25, 1872, B-LP.
52. FB to Rollins, September 19, 1872, Rollins Papers; EBL to SPL, October 7, 9, 1872, B-LP.

latter, happy to have his family reunited, sounded cheerful in his letters, it soon became evident that his health was continuing to deteriorate. An anxious Rollins wrote him in early November as reports of his condition circulated throughout the state. After a frightening letter from Apo, his father urged Frank to come east to seek assistance from physicians in New York or Philadelphia. Lizzie wrote Phil that she was in a panic about her brother. If necessary, she volunteered to go to New York and nurse him if Apo could not accompany him east. The whole family remained anxious, she reported. Lizzie reiterated her assurances to Apo on November 8, saying that she had plenty of room for all of them at No. 4 if they brought Frank east.[53]

Ten days later Apo sent the news they had all been dreading:

> Frank has a stroke of paralysis. It had been coming on gradually for several days tho I had no idea what it was and [Dr.] Franklin did not intimate it to any of us tho he says he now anticipated it. The attack is not severe & the physicians say it seems to be held in check by the medicine. One arm the right one & leg are perfectly powerless. All we have to hope for is his grand constitution which may carry him thro without another attack.

She reported that Frank was "much depressed," although pleased to learn that Montgomery, for whom she had sent without asking him, was en route to St. Louis.[54]

Even in the midst of his illness, Frank's mind and energies remained devoted to politics. His senatorial term would expire in March. Although the Liberal Republican–Democratic ticket of Greeley and Brown had gone down to defeat nationally, the Democrats had elected Woodson governor in Missouri with a comfortable majority in both houses of the legislature. Frank had already begun gearing up for his reelection as the paralysis crept up on him. Two days before Apo's report of his collapse, he had written his father that he had just returned from Ste. Genevieve and anticipated leaving that night for northern Missouri with everything looking favorable for him. The stroke put an end to that campaigning. Gratz Brown told Rollins that Frank had been with him just the day before, and he had found him "looking so well and talking in his own free exultant brave way, confident & exultant even in

53. EBL to Blair Lee, October 13, 16, 1872, EBL to SPL, October 15, November 4, 1872, B-LP; Rollins to FB, November 3, 1872, FPB to FB, November 4, 1872, EBL to Apo, November 8, 1872, BLC.
54. Apo to SPL, November 18, 1872, B-LP.

the midst of disaster, and the shock I received at hearing of his casting down has not left me yet."[55]

Although Montgomery urged his brother to return east with him for treatment, Frank declined. Even though incapacitated, his mind was engrossed with his reelection campaign. Gratz Brown had warned Rollins, "[Frank's] enemies will make the most of [his illness], and his friends will have difficulty in sustaining him in the impending contest." Frank quickly found this to be true with even some of his old friends, like James Broadhead, angling for support in case Frank had to drop out of the race. Determined to fight it out, Frank worked hard on his therapy. Within a month, with the help of Turkish baths, he could stand on his feet and walk around his room. Since his arm had not similarly responded, he had Apo write his letters for him as he sought help from every quarter he could think of. He told Rollins and others that he fully expected to be in Jefferson City in January to lead the fight when the legislature reconvened.[56]

Summoning all his energy, Frank arrived in Jefferson City on January 4, 1873, accompanied by Bart Able and other supporters. Taking rooms at the Madison House, Frank entertained legislators in his suite. The *Missouri Democrat*'s correspondent reported, "While receiving guests he paces slowly backward and forward across the room, carrying one arm in a silken sling, and mildly emphasizing his talk with the other." He was too feeble to go to the capitol to address the Democratic caucus. One of his opponents, Lewis V. Bogy, a Southern sympathizer who had played no part in the war, told the caucus that Blair should retire for two years to regain his health and then be given Carl Schurz's seat when it became available in 1875. Frank's friends countered that Missouri needed someone of his national reputation in the Senate.

The caucus began voting on the eleventh with Blair receiving twenty-eight votes to twenty-nine for John S. Phelps, twenty-one for Bogy, and the others scattered. As the deadlock continued, "Blair became nervous, and talked in low tones and with a most serious face" with Bart Able and his other friends. Jo Shelby, Basil Duke, and other former Confederates were called in to lend

55. Parrish, *History of Missouri*, 281; FB to FPB, November 16, 1872, B-LP; Brown to Rollins, December 7, 1872, Rollins Papers.

56. Brown to Rollins, December 7, 1872, FB to Rollins, December 20, 1872, Rollins Papers; FB to FPB, December 17, 1872, FB to MB, December 18, 1872, B-LP. There are numerous letters in the Broadhead Papers, November–December 1872, indicating his interest in running for the Senate seat.

support, but with little change in results. On the ninth ballot the caucus turned to the newly elected governor, Silas Woodson, as a compromise; but the governor declined, and the Bogy forces moved adjournment until the following day. In the interim, Bogy's supporters played upon the legislators' fears about Frank's health. When Blair did not return to the caucus the next day, the tide slowly turned against him. On the seventeenth and final ballot, Bogy was nominated with sixty-four votes to Frank's forty-seven. The legislators then flocked to Bogy's suite at the opposite end of Madison House from Blair's while Frank sat "sadly dejected" in his rooms with only a few loyal friends. The defeat left Blair completely demoralized. He had literally driven himself beyond his physical capacity the past year, trying to serve the interests of his conservative constituency in the Senate, as he saw them, only to have his party desert him in his hour of need.[57]

In spite of his disability Frank returned to Washington in late January, taking his Senate seat on the twenty-seventh, where he was warmly greeted by his colleagues, to whom he was compelled to give his left hand as his right arm and hand were completely useless. Although seldom addressing his colleagues, he continued sporadic appearances on the floor until the session ended March 4. Soon afterward the family decided that he should receive treatment at the Clifton Springs Sanitarium near Clifton Springs, New York, under the care of a Dr. Foster. The sanitarium was conveniently close to their longtime friends the Martins, Evy Alexander's parents, at Willowbrook in the Finger Lake region so that Frank could go there on weekends while Apo and other family members could stay there as needed. Twenty-year-old Christine was with him most of the time, while Apo remained in St. Louis with the younger children. Andrew had married the previous October, even as Frank's illness progressed; he and Annie settled near his parents in St. Louis, where he continued in the metallurgy business. Jim had left Princeton to enter a local business, while Pres had begun his military training at West Point.

Frank maintained his interest in politics, writing to Rollins and others occasionally with his left hand, which he had trained to replace the poorly functioning right one. He reported that he could walk two or three miles a day "without a cane & without dragging my foot." In June, his parents and Lizzie's

---

57. *Missouri Democrat*, January 6, 7, 8, 12, 14, 1873. Unfortunately, Frank's physical setback exacerbated his financial plight. On December 27, he had to ask Phil Lee if he and Montgomery could forward five hundred dollars. They would be a major source of financial support during his ensuing convalescence (FB to SPL, December 27, 1872, B-LP).

son Blair arrived by train, having traveled in Simon Cameron's private car, for a visit; and Apo came for the summer when school was out, leaving the children at Silver Spring. The days must have seemed interminably long for Frank, used, as he was, to an active life; but he complained little.[58]

Summer dragged on into fall. Apo took the children back to St. Louis at the end of August. Christine stayed at Clifton Springs through the early fall and then traded places with her mother, caring for the younger children. It had to be galling to both Frank and Apo that they depended heavily on Phil and Montgomery for financial assistance, but there was no helping it. Apo talked of moving into a smaller house in St. Louis, hoping thereby to save money; but this did not prove practical.

At the end of October, relief arrived at the hands of Governor Woodson. He had found it necessary to remove the state commissioner of insurance for improper conduct in office, and he now offered the post to Frank at an annual salary of five thousand dollars. Blair gratefully accepted, as he could hire a deputy to do much of the work. While it meant that he would have to leave Clifton Springs, he convinced himself that he could continue his therapy successfully at home. To his critics who questioned the appointment, the governor simply replied that the Democratic Party owed Frank that much, and the state Senate confirmed the appointment in January by a nonpartisan vote of twenty-two to ten.[59]

Blair returned to St. Louis to enter upon his new duties. Tom Gantt and several other friends arranged the necessary funding for the one-hundred-thousand-dollar bond he required. Frank wrote his father that his son Jim had begun to study law and was working part-time in the insurance office "to enable him to buy clothes." C. B. Rollins, James's son, who saw Frank during this period, was shocked by the change. He later recalled, "Blair at this time, was a wreck of his former self. With crutch and cane, and an old negro body servant to aid him, he managed with difficulty to get about. Yet despite his condition, one arm and one leg literally in the grave, that unquenchable flame, ambition, the motive power of his life, still urged him to reach out after

58. *Missouri Republican,* January 21, 1873; *New York Times,* January 28, 1873; *CG,* 42:3:867, 2206; Mira Alexander to Preston Blair, April 23, 1873, BLC; Apo to FPB, May 30, 1873, FB to EBL, May 27, 30, June 7, 11, 17, 1873, B-LP; FB to Rollins, May 30, 1873, Rollins Papers; FB to Apo, June 17, 1873, BLPLC.

59. FPB to MB, August 25, 1873, FB to MB, October 16, 1873, BLC; FB to SPL, September 25, 1873, October 6, 1873, n.d. [but received October 28, 1873], Apo to FPB, October 9, 1873, B-LP; Apo to Apolline Hankey, September 26, 1873, BLPLC; *Missouri Statesman,* October 31, 1873, January 16, 1874.

the little baubles of this world, evoking my sympathy and admiration." The old Blair spirit remained even though his body was decimated.[60]

Frank planned to return to Clifton Springs for additional treatments once he was confirmed as insurance commissioner, if Montgomery and Lizzie could pick up the costs. His salary, plus some outside income that Apo had, covered their expenses in St. Louis, but the cost of the sanitarium was beyond him. The family agreed, facilitating the return to New York in early February 1874, where Apo and the children joined him for the summer as treatments continued. During this second sojourn at Clifton Springs, Frank made a long-postponed religious decision. He told a friend, who had encouraged him by sending some of Philip Brooks's books, that he was ready to profess Christ. "I have never been an unbeliever," he assured the friend, "but I have been so engrossed with other matters that I have not given myself a chance to think upon these all important subjects." With lots of time to ponder lately, he had determined not to put off the decision any longer and soon appeared at a local church to announce it publicly. In mid-September, Frank took a turn for the worse, and Apo summoned Montgomery. With little hope for recovery, Dr. Foster seemingly having given up, the family decided to take him back to St. Louis at the end of November.[61]

Apo sent the children to stay with Lizzie while she brought her now seriously ill husband home. Tom Gantt, who visited Frank in March 1875, reported to Montgomery, "He breathes, eats, and sleeps, but has, I am afraid, no more sense of the world around him than the chair in which he sits." Frank's brother-in-law and longtime associate Franklin Dick was shocked by his final visit to the home the following month when Blair failed to even recognize him. Apo undoubtedly suffered greatly through this period, concerned, as always, about their dependence on Frank's family. In May, she returned a bank draft to Lizzie with a note that she did not wish them to be "a pensioner on Mr. Lee (who has always been most kind) & the Judge [Montgomery]," although she could not refuse anything sent by his parents. Frank's salary as insurance commissioner remained sufficient for their needs at present. Lizzie

60. FB to MB, November 3, 1873, FB to FPB, December 17, 1873, January 16, 1874, BLC; FB to MB, January 10, 1874, FB to SPL, January 14, 1874, B-LP; C. B. Rollins, "Some Impressions of Frank P. Blair," 358.

61. FB to "Dear Major," April 26, 1874, BLPLC; *New York Times*, July 18, 1875; FB to MB, February 14, March 24, May 11, 1874, Andrew Blair to MB, April 15, 1874, MB to FB, June 22, 1874, MB to Minna Blair, September 13, 16, November 30, 1874, Apo to MB, November 22, 1874, Franklin Dick to MB, November 25, December 4, 1874, BLC; Andrew Blair to SPL, November 1, 1874, B-LP.

quickly replied that Preston and Eliza could not afford to help now, but that Frank's mother had asked her and Phil to help with fifty dollars a month "to get a good man nurse for Frank." With her father's health also failing, Lizzie did not wish to worry her parents by denying to Frank and Apo what little she could forward on their behalf.[62]

On July 5, Apo wrote her mother-in-law, "Frank continues very comfortable in spite of the heat which is intense. He walks around the rooms quite easily with Annie's [a servant] help as mine. We take him downstairs to sit in the parlor by the open window & look out at the back yard." The end came within a week. On July 9, 1875, Blair returned to his room following an afternoon carriage ride, which had become a daily ritual. Suddenly hit with a seizure of vertigo, he fell, striking his head on some of the furniture, knocking him unconscious. Apo quickly summoned the doctor, but Frank never regained consciousness and died that same evening, at age fifty-four.[63]

Tributes poured in from across the country as friend and foe alike eulogized the man with whom many of them might have disagreed. They stressed his courage, his war record, and his commitment to his principles. Although the family would have preferred a private funeral, it was not possible. St. Louis was draped in mourning with the ships in the harbor lowering their flags to half-mast. On the morning of the service, Frank lay in state at the home on Chestnut Street as hundreds passed by. Then, accompanied by a large entourage of officialdom and an escort of his old First Missouri Regiment, the casket was taken to the hearse for transfer to the First Congregational Church. Too weak to attend, Apo remained secluded at home. A vast crowd waited at the church, including General Sherman, Gratz Brown, and a variety of dignitaries, as well as many old friends. The pallbearers included those who had been closest to him throughout his career: Jim Rollins, Tom Gantt, Ben Farrar, Samuel Simmons, James O. Broadhead, Arden R. Smith, Giles Filley, and Gerald B. Allen. After a service filled with eulogies, the long train of carriages wended its way to Bellefontaine Cemetery at the western edge of the city, where Frank Blair was finally laid to rest.[64]

Blair's tragic final illness and death took a heavy toll on his Washington family. His sister, Lizzie, who had been devoted to him since their childhood, mourned openly. Frank's parting gift to her had been a request to his father

62. Gantt to MB, March 11, 1875, Apo to EBL, May 9, 1875, EBL to Apo, May 11, 1875, Dick to MB, August 7, 1875, BLC.
63. Apo to EB, July 5, 1875, B-LP; *St. Louis Globe-Democrat*, July 10, 1875.
64. *St. Louis Globe-Democrat*, July 12, 1875.

that the Silver Spring estate, originally intended for him, be willed instead to the Lees upon his parents' demise. In return, Preston stipulated in a codicil that the Lees should pay twenty thousand dollars to Frank's family within six months of Eliza's death, the money to be held in trust by Montgomery for Apo and her children. Montgomery, who had strongly promoted his younger brother's career from their early days in the St. Louis bar through all of his political ups and downs, wrote anguished notes to several friends in reply to their condolences. Frank's elderly parents had been quite active up until his death in spite of frail health, riding regularly into Washington from Silver Spring. Their healths failed rapidly thereafter, and, within two years, both were dead, Preston in October 1876 and Eliza in July 1877.[65]

Apo remained in St. Louis at the family home. She reported to her aunt Apolline in England in December 1876 that they lived frugally with help from Andrew, who eventually relocated to Philadelphia, where he continued his career as a metallurgist. Her son James lived at home, studying law, while earning twenty-five dollars a month as a clerk. He would eventually marry a cousin, Apolline Alexander, of Philadelphia and return to St. Louis, where he cut quite a social figure at the turn of the century before falling victim to charges of embezzlement at the expense of his Dick cousins. Preston had remained at West Point, graduating the previous June. While serving as an ROTC instructor at the University of Missouri, he would marry the daughter of a prominent Columbia banker and later turn to a legal career. George was still in high school in 1875, while Cary was in the lower grades and the youngest, William Alexander, at age two, would hardly remember his father. Within a year, Eveline, the next-to-youngest, who had never been well, died, adding to Apo's sorrows. Both George and William died in their early twenties. The oldest daughter, Christine, married a wealthy St. Louis manufacturer, Benjamin Graham, six years after her father's death.[66]

Apo gathered with her family and several thousand others at the northeastern corner of Forest Park in St. Louis on May 21, 1885, to watch Christine unveil a large bronze statue of Frank. Sculpted by Washington W. Gardner, it depicts Blair in characteristic pose with his right arm upraised delivering one of his stump speeches. Erected at a cost of ten thousand dollars, the funds

65. W. E. Smith, *Blair Family in Politics*, 2:462–65; E. B. Smith, *Francis Preston Blair*, 436–39; Cornish and Laas, *Lincoln's Lee*, 176.

66. Apo to Apolline Hankey, December 22, 1875, BLPLC; Blair genealogy charts, BLC and Blair House Archives. The story of James's scandal is detailed in George E. Vogle, *The Life and Death of James L. Blair: Original General Counsel of the Louisiana Purchase Exposition*.

had been raised by public solicitation over the past six years through the Blair Monument Association, headed by Peter Foy. Many of Frank's associates, including General Sherman, spoke of their memories of him that afternoon.[67]

Apo could reflect with pride on this recognition of her husband, even though she might still have pangs of regret at the political ambitions that had overwhelmed him and strained their marriage from time to time. She lived for another twenty-three years and watched her children make successful careers for themselves, although her son James was tainted by the scandal mentioned above at the turn of the century. Paralyzed by a stroke the last thirteen years of her life, she made her home in her declining years with the Grahams on Lindell Boulevard, from where she could look out across the street at Frank's statue in Forest Park, until her own death on September 5, 1908.[68]

67. *St. Louis Globe-Democrat*, May 17, 22, 1885; Koerner, *Memoirs*, 2:739–41. The records of the Blair Monument Association may be found in MHS.

68. *St. Louis Globe-Democrat*, September 9, 1908. In 1899, the State of Missouri honored Thomas Hart Benton and Blair by placing their statues in Statuary Hall in the nation's capitol (*Proceedings in Congress upon the Acceptance of the Statues of Thomas H. Benton and Francis P. Blair Presented by the State of Missouri; St. Louis Globe-Democrat*, February 3, 1899). In 1911, members of the Blair family donated a bust, sculpted by William Couper, to the Vicksburg National Military Park, where it stands on the site of Frank's attacks on Stockade Redan (interview with Terrence J. Winschel, November 3, 1995).

Bibliography

Manuscripts

Abstract of Election Returns, St. Louis County. 1852, 1854, 1856, 1858, 1860, 1862, 1870. Missouri State Archives, Jefferson City.

Affeld, C. E. Diary. Vicksburg National Military Park, Vicksburg, Miss.

Bates, Edward. Papers. Library of Congress.

Benton, Thomas Hart. Papers. Missouri Historical Society, St. Louis.

Blair Family Papers. Library of Congress.

Blair Family Papers. Missouri Historical Society, St. Louis.

Blair Family Papers. State Historical Society of Missouri, Columbia.

Blair-Lee Family Papers. Princeton University Libraries, Princeton, N.J.

Blair-Rives Papers. Library of Congress.

Blair Monument Association Papers. Missouri Historical Society, St. Louis.

Blow Family Papers. Missouri Historical Society, St. Louis.

Broadhead, James O. Papers. Missouri Historical Society, St. Louis.

Brown, Orlando. Papers. Filson Club, Louisville, Ky.

Cameron, Simon. Papers. Library of Congress.

Carr, William C. Papers. Missouri Historical Society, St. Louis.

Civil War Papers. Missouri Historical Society, St. Louis.

Dick, Franklin A. Papers. Library of Congress.

Donelson, Andrew Jackson. Papers. Library of Congress.

Doolittle, James R. Papers. Library of Congress.

Drake, Charles D. Papers. State Historical Society of Missouri, Columbia.

Eads, James B. Papers. Missouri Historical Society, St. Louis.

Eighth Missouri Regiment File. Vicksburg National Military Park, Vicksburg, Miss.

Francis, Owen. Diary. Vicksburg National Military Park, Vicksburg, Miss.

Gamble, Hamilton R. Papers. Missouri Historical Society, St. Louis.

Gardner, W. T. Memoir. Vicksburg National Military Park, Vicksburg, Miss.

Gross, Albion. Letters and journal. U.S. Army Military History Institute, Carlisle Barracks, Pa.

Hagaman Family Papers. Missouri Historical Society, St. Louis.

Hickenlooper, Andrew. Reminiscences. In the Papers of Andrew Hickenlooper and His Family, Mss. fH628, Cincinnati Historical Society, Cincinnati Museum Center. Typed copy in U.S. Army Military History Institute, Carlisle Barracks, Pa.

Johnson, Andrew. Papers. Library of Congress.

Leonard, Abiel. Papers. State Historical Society of Missouri, Columbia.

Lincoln, Abraham. Papers. Library of Congress.

Long, Breckinridge. Papers. Library of Congress.

Madison County, La., Notarial Record Book G. Tallaluh, La.

Magill, Ellen. Papers. Missouri Historical Society, St. Louis.

Marmaduke, M. M. Papers. State Historical Society of Missouri, Columbia.

Napton, William B. Papers. Missouri Historical Society, St. Louis.

Read, Benjamin M. Collection. State Records Center, Santa Fe, N.Mex.

Record Group 393, Part 1, New Mexico. National Archives.

Record of Wills in Woodford County, Kentucky, 1788–1851. Compiled by Annie Walker Burns, 1933. Filson Club, Louisville, Ky.

Reichhelm, Edward Paul. Papers. Library of Congress.

Reynolds, Thomas C. Papers. Missouri Historical Society, St. Louis.

Roberts, Cyrus Marion. Diary. U.S. Army Military History Institute, Carlisle Barracks, Pa.

Rollins, James S. Papers.

Rutgers College Papers. Missouri Historical Society, St. Louis.

Sappington, John. Papers. Missouri Historical Society, St. Louis.

Schofield, John M. Papers. Library of Congress.

Schurz, Carl. Papers. Library of Congress.

Schweitzer, Edward E. Diaries and correspondence. U.S. Army Military History Institute, Carlisle Barracks, Pa.

Sherman, William T. Papers. Library of Congress.

Sladen, Joseph. Diary. U.S. Army Military History Institute, Carlisle Barracks, Pa.

Smith, George R. Papers. Missouri Historical Society, St. Louis.

Snyder, John F. Collection. Missouri Historical Society, St. Louis.

St. Louis History Collection. Missouri Historical Society, St. Louis.

U.S. Bureau of the Census. St. Louis County, Mo., 1850, 1860, 1870. Microfilm copy, State Historical Society of Missouri, Columbia.

Van Buren, Martin. Papers. Library of Congress.

Woodford County, Kentucky, Marriage Records, 1788–1851. Compiled by Annie Walker Burns, 1932. Filson Club, Louisville, Ky.

Printed Government Documents

Biographical Directory of the American Congress, 1774–1989. Washington, D.C.: Government Printing Office, 1989.

Congressional Globe. 35th through 38th and 42nd Congresses. Washington, D.C.: Government Printing Office, 1857–1864, 1871–1872.

House Executive Documents No. 70. 30th Congress, 1st sess. Washington, D.C.: Government Printing Office, 1847.

Journal of the House of Representatives of the State of Missouri. 17th and 18th General Assemblies. Jefferson City: James Lusk, Public Printer, 1852–1856.

Journal of the Senate of the State of Missouri. 18th General Assembly. Jefferson City: James Lusk, Public Printer, 1855–1856.

Messages and Proclamations of the Governors of the State of Missouri. Ed. by Buel Leopard and Floyd C. Shoemaker. Vol. 3. Columbia: State Historical Society of Missouri, 1922.

Missouri Contested Election. 36th Congress, 1st sess. House Miscellaneous Documents No. 8. Washington, D.C.: Government Printing Office, 1860.

Proceedings in Congress upon the Acceptance of the Statues of Thomas H. Benton and Francis P. Blair Presented by the State of Missouri. Washington, D.C.: Government Printing Office, 1900.

Report of the Joint Committee on the Conduct of the War. 37th Congress, 3rd sess. Part 3. Washington, D.C.: Government Printing Office, 1863.

Report of the Special Committee in the Blair Investigation Case, April 23, 1864. 38th Congress, 1st sess. Washington, D.C.: Government Printing Office, 1864.

Testimony Taken by the Joint Select Committee to Inquire into the Condition of Affairs in the Late Insurrectionary States. Vol. 1, Majority Report and Minority Views. Washington, D.C.: Government Printing Office, 1872.

War of the Rebellion: A Compilation of the Official Records of the Union and Confederate Armies. 4 series. 128 vols. Washington, D.C.: Government Printing Office, 1881–1901.

Newspapers

Jefferson Inquirer (Jefferson City, Mo.)
Liberty (Mo.) Tribune
Memphis Daily Appeal
Missouri Examiner (Jefferson City, Mo.)
Missouri Statesman (Columbia)
New York Times
New York Tribune
Niles Register (Baltimore)
People's Tribune (Jefferson City, Mo.)
St. Joseph (Mo.) Gazette
St. Louis Daily Globe-Democrat
St. Louis Daily Missouri Democrat
St. Louis Daily Missouri Republican
St. Louis Daily Union
St. Louis Evening News
Washington Globe

City Directories

Edwards Annual Directory in the City of St. Louis for 1871. St. Louis: Southern
    Publishing, 1871.
Edwards Eleventh Annual Directory in the City of St. Louis for 1869. St. Louis:
    Richard Edwards, 1869.
Edwards Twelfth Annual Directory in the City of St. Louis for 1870. St. Louis:
    Richard Edwards, 1870.
Gould and Aldrich's Annual Directory of the City of St. Louis for 1872. St. Louis:
    Review Steam Press, 1872.
Gould's St. Louis City Directory for 1873. St. Louis: David B. Gould, 1873.
Gould's St. Louis Directory for 1874. St. Louis: David B. Gould, 1874.
Gould's St. Louis Directory for 1875. St. Louis: David B. Gould, 1875.
Green's St. Louis Directory for 1851. St. Louis: Charles and Hammond, 1850.
Kennedy's St. Louis Directory for the Year 1857. St. Louis: R. V. Kennedy, 1857.
Morrison's St. Louis Directory for 1852. St. Louis: Missouri Republican, 1852.
St. Louis Business Directory for 1853–1854. St. Louis: R. A. Lewis, 1853.
St. Louis Directory for the Years 1854–1855. St. Louis: Chambers and Knapp,
    1854.
St. Louis Directory 1859. St. Louis: R. V. Kennedy, 1859.
St. Louis Directory 1860. St. Louis: R. V. Kennedy, 1860.

Printed Primary Materials

Alexander, Eveline M. *Cavalry Wife: The Diary of Eveline M. Alexander, 1866–1867*. College Station: Texas A M University Press, 1977.

Anderson, Galusha. *A Border City during the Civil War.* Boston: Little, Brown, 1908.

Bates, Edward. *The Diary of Edward Bates, 1859–1866.* Ed. Howard K. Beale. Vol. 4 of the Annual Report of the American Historical Association for 1930. Washington, D.C.: Government Printing Office, 1933.

Bay, W. V. N. *Reminiscences of the Bench and Bar of Missouri.* St. Louis: F. H. Thomas, 1878.

Blaine, James G. *Twenty Years of Congress: From Lincoln to Garfield.* 2 vols. Norwich, Conn.: Henry Bill, 1884–1886.

Boernstein, Henry. *Memoirs of a Nobody: The Missouri Years of Henry Boernstein (1849–1866).* Ed. Steven Rowan. St. Louis: Missouri Historical Society, 1997.

Brooks, Noah. *Washington in Lincoln's Time.* New York: Century, 1895.

Byars, William Vincent, ed. *B. and M. Gratz, Merchants in Philadelphia, 1754–1798: Papers of Interest to Their Posterity and the Posterity of Their Associates.* Jefferson City, Mo.: Hugh Stephens Printing, 1916.

Byers, S. H. M. *With Fire and Sword.* New York: Neale Publishing, 1911.

Carter, Harvey L., and Norma L. Peterson, eds. "William S. Stewart Letters, January 13, 1861, to December 4, 1864." *Missouri Historical Review* 61 (January 1967): 187–228.

Chase, Salmon P. *Inside Lincoln's Cabinet: The Civil War Diaries of Salmon P. Chase.* Ed. David H. Donald. New York: Longmans, Green, 1954.

―――. *The Salmon P. Chase Papers.* Ed. John Niven. 3 vols. Kent, Ohio: Kent State University Press, 1993–1996.

Chittenden, Lucius E. *Personal Reminiscences, 1840–1890.* New York: Croscup, 1893.

Clay, Cassius Marcellus. *The Life of Cassius Marcellus Clay.* 2 vols. Cincinnati: J. F. Brennan, 1886.

Cooke, Philip St. George. *The Conquest of New Mexico and California: An Historical and Personal Narrative.* New York: G. P. Putnam's Sons, 1878.

Cox, Jacob D. *The March to the Sea, Franklin and Nashville.* New York: Charles Scribner's Sons, 1882.

Crittenden, H. H. *The Crittenden Memoirs.* New York: G. P. Putnam's Sons, 1936.

Cutts, James Madison. *The Conquest of California and New Mexico.* Philadelphia: Carey and Hart, 1847.

Dana, Charles A. *Recollections of the Civil War.* New York: D. Appleton, 1892.

Dickens, Charles. *American Notes and Pictures from Italy.* New York: P. F. Collier and Sons, n.d.

———. *The Letters of Charles Dickens.* Ed. Madeline House, Graham Storey, and Kathleen Tillotson. Pilgrim Edition. 8 vols. Oxford: Clarendon Press, 1965–1995.

Duke, Basil W. *Reminiscences of General Basil W. Duke, CSA.* Garden City, N.Y.: Doubleday, Page, 1911.

Eaton, John. *Grant, Lincoln and the Freedmen: Reminiscences of the Civil War.* New York: Longmans, Green, 1907.

Emory, William H. *Notes of a Military Reconnaissance from Fort Leavenworth in Missouri to San Diego in California.* Washington, D.C.: Wendell and Van Benthuysen, 1848.

Fremont, Jessie Benton. *The Letters of Jessie Benton Fremont.* Ed. Pamela Herr and Mary Lee Spence. Urbana: University of Illinois Press, 1993.

———. *The Story of the Guard: A Chronicle of the War.* Boston: Ticknor and Fields, 1863.

Gantt, T. T. *Frank Blair's Memory.* St. Louis: Correras Press, 1881.

Garrard, Lewis H. *Wah-To-Yah and the Taos Trail.* Ed. Ralph P. Bieber. Glendale, Calif.: Arthur H. Clark, 1938.

Gibson, George Rutledge. *Journal of a Soldier under Kearny and Doniphan, 1846–1847.* Ed. Ralph P. Bieber. Glendale, Calif.: Arthur H. Clark, 1935.

Glyndon, Howard. *Notable Men in "the House": A Series of Sketches of Prominent Men in the House of Representatives: Members of the Thirty-seventh Congress.* New York: Baker and Godwin, 1862.

Grant, Ulysses S. *The Papers of Ulysses S. Grant.* Ed. John Y. Simon. 18 vols. Carbondale: Southern Illinois University Press, 1967–1991.

———. *Personal Memoirs.* 2 vols. New York: Charles L. Webster, 1885.

Gratz, Rebecca. *Letters of Rebecca Gratz.* Ed. David Philipson. Philadelphia: Jewish Publication Society of Philadelphia, 1929.

Gresham, Matilda. *Life of Walter Quintin Gresham, 1832–1895.* Chicago: Rand McNally, 1919.

Grissom, Daniel. "Personal Recollections of Distinguished Missourians." *Missouri Historical Review* 20 (April 1926): 397–98.

Gurowski, Adam. *Diary.* 3 vols. Boston: Lee and Shepard, 1862.

Haney, M. L. *Pentecostal Possibilities.* Chicago: Christian Witness, 1906.

Hay, John. *Lincoln and the Civil War in the Diaries and Letters of John Hay.* Ed. Tyler Dennett. New York: Dodd, Mead, 1937.

Hazen, W. B. *A Narrative of Military Service*. Boston: Ticknor, 1885.

Hitchcock, Henry M. *Marching with Sherman*. Ed. M. A. deWolfe Howe. New Haven: Yale University Press, 1927.

How, James F. "Frank P. Blair in 1861." In *War Papers and Personal Reminiscences, 1861–1865*. St. Louis: Becktold, 1892.

Howard, Oliver Otis. *Autobiography*. 2 vols. New York: Baker and Taylor, 1907.

Hughes, John Taylor. *Doniphan's Expedition and the Conquest of New Mexico and California*. Ed. William E. Connelley. Kansas City, Mo.: Bryant and Douglas, 1907.

Hume, John F. *The Abolitionists, Together with Personal Memories of the Struggle for Human Rights*. New York: G. P. Putnam's Sons, 1905.

Irwin, Ray W., ed. "Missouri in Crisis: The Journal of Captain Albert Tracy, 1861." *Missouri Historical Review* 51 (October 1956): 8–21, (January 1957): 151–64, (April 1957): 270–83.

Jackson, Andrew. *Correspondence of Andrew Jackson*. Ed. John Spencer Bassett. 7 vols. Washington, D.C.: Carnegie Institution of Washington, 1926–1935.

Jackson, Oscar L. *The Colonel's Diary*. N.p., 1922.

Johnson, Andrew. *The Papers of Andrew Johnson*. Ed. Leroy Graf and others. 12 vols. Knoxville: University of Tennessee Press, 1967–1995.

Johnson, Charles P. "Personal Recollections of Some of Missouri's Eminent Statesmen and Lawyers." In *Proceedings of State Historical Society of Missouri*, 1903.

Johnson, Robert Underwood, and Clarence Clough Buel, eds. *Battles and Leaders of the Civil War*. 4 vols. New York: Century, 1884–1888.

Kellogg, J. J. *The Vicksburg Campaign and Reminiscences*. N.p., 1913.

Kendall, Amos. *Autobiography*. Ed. William Stickney. Boston: Lee and Shepard, 1872.

Knox, Thomas W. *Camp Fire and Cotton Field: Southern Adventure in Time of War*. New York: Blelock, 1865.

Koerner, Gustave. *Memoirs*. 2 vols. Cedar Rapids, Iowa: Torch Press, 1909.

Lamon, Ward. *Recollections of Abraham Lincoln, 1847–1865*. Chicago: A. C. McClurg, 1895.

Lawson, Rowena, transcriber. *Woodford County, Kentucky 1810–1840 Census*. Bowie, Md.: Heritage Books, 1987.

Lee, Elizabeth Blair. *Wartime Washington: The Civil War Letters of Elizabeth Blair Lee*. Ed. Virginia Jeans Laas. Urbana: University of Illinois Press, 1991.

Lincoln, Abraham. *The Collected Works of Abraham Lincoln*. Ed. Roy P. Basler. 9 vols. New Brunswick: Rutgers University Press, 1953–1955.

Logan, Mrs. John A. *Reminiscences of a Soldier's Wife.* New York: Charles Scribner's Sons, 1913.

Magoffin, Susan Shelby. *Down the Santa Fe Trail and into Mexico.* Ed. Stella Drum. New Haven: Yale University Press, 1926.

Martin, Edward W. *Behind the Scenes in Washington.* N.p.: Continental Publishing and National Publishing, 1873.

McClure, Alexander Kelly. *Abraham Lincoln and Men of War Times: Some Personal Recollections of War and Politics during the Lincoln Administration.* Philadelphia: Times Publishing, 1892.

McGhee, Lucy Kate Walker. *Historical Records of the Kentucky Blue Grass Region: Versailles (Woodford County).* Washington, D.C.: n.p., 1951.

Nichols, George Ward. *The Story of the Great March from the Diary of a Staff Officer.* New York: Harper and Brothers, 1865.

Osborn, Thomas W. *The Fiery Trail: A Union Officer's Account of Sherman's Last Campaigns.* Ed. Richard Harwell and Phillip N. Racine. Knoxville: University of Tennessee Press, 1986.

Peckham, James. *General Nathaniel Lyon and Missouri in 1861.* New York: American News, 1866.

Poore, Benjamin Perley. *Perley's Reminiscences of Sixty Years in the National Metropolis.* Philadelphia: Hubbard Brothers, 1886.

Porter, David Dixon. *Incidents and Anecdotes of the Civil War.* New York: D. Appleton, 1885.

Proceedings of the Liberal Republican Convention in Cincinnati, May 1st, 2d, and 3d, 1872. New York: Baker and Godwin, 1872.

Richardson, Albert D. *The Secret Service, the Field, the Dungeon, and the Escape.* Hartford: American Publishing, 1865.

Riddle, Albert Gallatin. *Recollections of War Times: Reminiscences of Men and Events in Washington, 1861–1865.* New York: G. P. Putnam's Sons, 1895.

Rollins, C. B. "Some Impressions of Frank P. Blair." *Missouri Historical Review* 24 (April 1930): 352–58.

Rowan, Steven, ed. *Germans for a Free Missouri: Translations from the St. Louis Radical Press, 1857–1862.* Columbia: University of Missouri Press, 1983.

Rusling, James F. *Men and Things I Saw in Civil War Days.* New York: Eaton and Mains, 1899.

Schofield, John M. *Forty-six Years in the Army.* New York: Century, 1897.

Schurz, Carl. *Reminiscences.* 3 vols. New York: McClure, 1907–1908.

Senour, Faunt L. *Major General William T. Sherman and His Campaigns.* Chicago: H. M. Sherwood, 1865.

Sherman, William T. *Memoirs*. With notes by Charles Royster. Library of America Edition. 2 vols. New York: Library Classics of the United States, 1990.

Smith, Walter George. *Life and Letters of Thomas Kilby Smith, Brevet Major General United States Volunteers, 1820–1887*. New York: G. P. Putnam's Sons, 1898.

Snead, Thomas L. *The Fight for Missouri from the Election of Lincoln to the Death of Lyon*. New York: Scribner's, 1886.

The Story of the Fifty-fifth Regiment, Illinois Volunteer Infantry in the Civil War, 1861–1865. Reprint, Huntington, W.Va.: Blue Acorn Press, 1993.

Tilden, Samuel J. *Letters and Literary Memorials of Samuel J. Tilden*. Ed. John Bigelow. 2 vols. New York: Harper and Brothers, 1908.

Townsend, E. D. *Anecdotes of the Civil War in the United States*. New York: D. Appleton, 1884.

Upson, Theodore F. *With Sherman to the Sea: The Civil War Letters, Diaries and Reminiscences of Theodore F. Upson*. Ed. Oscar Osburn Winther. Bloomington: Indiana University Press, 1958.

Ware, Eugene F. *The Lyon Campaign in Missouri, Being a History of the First Iowa Infantry*. Topeka: Crane, 1907.

Warmouth, Henry Clay. *War, Politics and Reconstruction*. New York: Macmillan, 1930.

Warren, Edward. *A Doctor's Experiences in Three Continents*. Baltimore: Cushing and Bailey, 1885.

Watterson, Henry. "The Humor and Tragedy of the Greeley Campaign." *Century Magazine* 85 (November 1912): 27–43.

Welles, Gideon. *The Diary of Gideon Welles*. Ed. Howard K. Beale. 3 vols. New York: W. W. Norton, 1960.

Willkie, Franc B. *Pen and Powder*. Boston: Ticknor, 1888.

Secondary Sources

Adamson, Hans Christian. *Rebellion in Missouri, 1861: Nathaniel Lyon and His Army of the West*. Philadelphia: Chilton, 1961.

Adler, Jeffrey S. "Yankee Colonizers and the Making of Antebellum St. Louis." *Gateway Heritage* 12 (winter 1992): 4–21.

Ambrose, Stephen E. *Halleck: Lincoln's Chief of Staff*. Baton Rouge: Louisiana State University Press, 1962.

Anders, Leslie. *The Eighteenth Missouri*. Indianapolis: Bobbs-Merrill, 1968.

Atlas of Bourbon, Clark, Fayette, Jessamine and Woodford Counties, Kentucky.
    Philadelphia: D. G. Beers, 1877.

Baker, Jean H. *Affairs of Party: The Political Culture of Northern Democrats in the*
    Mid-Nineteenth Century. Ithaca: Cornell University Press, 1983.

———. *The Politics of Continuity: Maryland Political Parties from 1858 to 1870.*
    Baltimore: Johns Hopkins University Press, 1973.

Barclay, Thomas S. *The Liberal Republican Movement in Missouri, 1865–1871.*
    Columbia: State Historical Society of Missouri, 1926.

Barrett, John G. *Sherman's March through the Carolinas.* Chapel Hill: University
    of North Carolina Press, 1956.

Bearss, Edwin C. *The Campaign for Vicksburg.* 3 vols. Dayton: Morningside
    Press, 1985–1986.

Belcher, Wyatt Winton. *The Economic Rivalry between St. Louis and Chicago,*
    1850–1880. New York: Columbia University Press, 1947.

Belden, Thomas Graham, and Marva Robins. *So Fell the Angels.* Boston: Little,
    Brown, 1956.

Bellamy, Donnie D. "The Persistency of Colonization in Missouri." *Missouri*
    Historical Review 81 (October 1977): 1–24.

———. "Slavery, Emancipation, and Racism in Missouri, 1850–1865." Ph.D.
    diss., University of Missouri, 1970.

Belz, Herman. *A New Birth of Freedom: The Republican Party and Freedmen's*
    Rights, 1861–1865. Westport, Conn.: Greenwood Press, 1976.

———. *Reconstructing the Union: Theory and Policy during the Civil War.* Ithaca:
    Cornell University Press, 1969.

Bent, Allen H. *The Bent Family in America.* Boston: D. Clapp and Son, 1900.

Berwanger, Eugene H. *The Frontier against Slavery: Western Anti-Negro Prejudice*
    and the Slavery Extension Controversy. Urbana: University of Illinois Press,
    1967.

Bloch, Maurice. *George Caleb Bingham: A Catalogue Raissone.* Berkeley and Los
    Angeles: University of California Press, 1967.

Blue, Frederick J. *Salmon P. Chase: A Life in Politics.* Kent: Kent State University
    Press, 1987.

Blum, Virgil C. "The Political and Military Activities of the German Element
    in St. Louis, 1859–1861." *Missouri Historical Review* 42 (January 1948):
    103–29.

Bradley, Harold C. "In Defense of John Cummings." *Missouri Historical Review*
    57 (October 1962): 1–15.

Cain, Marvin R. *Lincoln's Attorney General: Edward Bates of Missouri.* Columbia:
    University of Missouri Press, 1965.

Carman, Harry J., and Reinhard H. Luthin. *Lincoln and the Patronage*. New York: Columbia University Press, 1943.

Carpenter, John A. *Sword and Olive Branch: Oliver Otis Howard*. Pittsburgh: University of Pittsburgh Press, 1964.

Carter, Samuel, III. *The Final Fortress: The Campaign for Vicksburg, 1862–1863*. New York: St. Martin's Press, 1980.

———. *The Siege of Atlanta, 1864*. New York: St. Martin's Press, 1973.

Castel, Albert. *Decision in the West: The Atlanta Campaign of 1864*. Lawrence: University Press of Kansas, 1992.

Catton, Bruce. *Grant Moves South*. Boston: Little, Brown, 1960.

Chambers, William Nisbet. *Old Bullion Benton: Senator from the New West*. Boston: Little, Brown, 1956.

Cheetham, Francis T. "The First Term of the American Court in Taos, New Mexico." *New Mexico Historical Review* 1 (January 1926): 23–41.

Coleman, Charles H. *The Election of 1868: The Democratic Effort to Regain Control*. New York: Columbia University Press, 1933.

Cornish, Dudley Taylor, and Virginia Jeans Laas. *Lincoln's Lee: The Life of Samuel Phillips Lee, United States Navy, 1812–1897*. Lawrence: University Press of Kansas, 1986.

Covington, James W. "The Camp Jackson Affair." *Missouri Historical Review* 55 (April 1961): 197–212.

Cox, John H., and LaWanda Cox. "Andrew Johnson and His Ghost Writers: An Analysis of the Freedmen's Bureau and Civil Rights Veto Messages." *Mississippi Valley Historical Review* 48 (December 1961): 460–79.

Cox, LaWanda. *Lincoln and Black Freedom: A Study in Presidential Leadership*. Columbia: University of South Carolina Press, 1981.

Crittenden, Huston. "The Warrensburg Speech of Frank P. Blair." *Missouri Historical Review* 20 (October 1925): 101–4.

Croly, David G. *Seymour and Blair: Their Lives and Services*. New York: Richardson, 1868.

Crozier, Emmet. *Yankee Reporters, 1861–1865*. New York: Oxford University Press, 1956.

Culmer, Frederic A. "Abiel Leonard." *Missouri Historical Review* 28 (October 1933): 17–37.

Curry, Leonard P. *Blueprint for Modern America: Nonmilitary Legislation of the First Civil War Congress*. Nashville: Vanderbilt University Press, 1968.

Davis, Burke. *Sherman's March*. New York: Random House, 1980.

DeArmond, Fred. "Reconstruction in Missouri." *Missouri Historical Review* 41 (April 1967): 365–71.

Dell, Christopher. *Lincoln and the War Democrats*. Rutherford, N.J.: Fairleigh Dickinson University Press, 1975.

Donald, David Herbert. *Lincoln*. New York: Simon and Schuster, 1995.

Dorsey, Florence. *Road to the Sea: The Story of James B. Eads and the Mississippi*. New York: Rinehart, 1947.

Downey, Matthew T. "Horace Greeley and the Politicians: The Liberal Republican Convention of 1872." *Journal of Southern History* 53 (March 1967): 727–50.

Dunne, Gerald T. *The Missouri Supreme Court: From Dred Scott to Nancy Cruzan*. Columbia: University of Missouri Press, 1993.

Dwight, Margaret L. "Black Suffrage in Missouri, 1865–1877." Ph.D. diss., University of Missouri, 1978.

Engle, Stephen D. *Yankee Dutchman: The Life of Franz Sigel*. Fayetteville: University of Arkansas Press, 1993.

Ewing, Joseph H. *Sherman at War*. Dayton, Ohio: Morningside, 1992.

Faust, Albert Bernhardt. *The German Element in the United States*. 2 vols. Boston: Houghton Mifflin, 1909.

Foner, Eric. *Free Soil, Free Labor, Free Men: The Ideology of the Republican Party before the Civil War*. New York: Oxford University Press, 1970.

———. *Reconstruction: America's Unfinished Revolution, 1863–1877*. New York: Harper and Row, 1988.

Freehling, William W. *The Reinterpretation of American History: Slavery and the Civil War*. New York: Oxford University Press, 1994.

Fuess, Claude M. *Carl Schurz: Reformer*. New York: Dodd, Mead, 1932.

Gannon, Gerald. "The Harney-Price Agreement." *Civil War Times Illustrated* 23 (December 1984): 40–45.

George, Sister Mary Karl. *Zachariah Chandler: A Political Biography*. East Lansing: Michigan State University Press, 1969.

Giffen, Lawrence E., Sr. "The Strange Story of Major General Franz Sigel." *Missouri Historical Review* 84 (July 1990): 404–27.

Gillette, William. *Retreat from Reconstruction, 1869–1879*. Baton Rouge: Louisiana State University Press, 1979.

Glatthaar, Joseph T. *The March to the Sea and Beyond: Sherman's Troops in the Savannah and Carolinas Campaigns*. New York: New York University Press, 1985.

Goodrich, James W. "Robert Eaton Acock: The Gentleman from Polk." *Missouri Historical Review* 73 (April 1979): 281–306.

Grimsley, Mark. *The Hard Hand of War: Union Military Policy toward Southern Civilians, 1861–1865.* New York: Cambridge University Press, 1995.

Grinnell, George Bird. "Bent's Old Fort and Its Builders." *Kansas State Historical Society Collections* 15 (1919–1922): 28–88.

Harding, Samuel Bannister. *Life of George R. Smith: Founder of Sedalia, Missouri.* Sedalia: private printing, 1904.

Hart, Jim Allee. *A History of the "St. Louis Globe-Democrat."* Columbia: University of Missouri Press, 1961.

Hendrick, Burton J. *Lincoln's War Cabinet.* Boston: Little, Brown, 1946.

Herr, Pamela. *Jessie Benton Fremont: American Woman of the 19th Century.* New York: Franklin Watts, 1987.

Hollister, Wilfred R., and Harry Norman. *Five Famous Missourians.* Kansas City: Hudson-Kimberly Publishing, 1900.

Holt, Glen E. "The Shaping of St. Louis, 1763–1869." Ph.D. diss., University of Chicago, 1975.

Hubbell, John T., and James W. Geary, eds. *Biographical Dictionary of the Union: Northern Leaders of the Civil War.* Westport, Conn.: Greenwood Press, 1995.

Hughes, Nathaniel Cheairs, Jr. *Bentonville: The Final Battle of Sherman and Johnston.* Chapel Hill: University of North Carolina Press, 1996.

Hunt, Roger D., and Jack R. Brown. *Brevet Brigadier Generals in Blue.* Gaithersburg, Md.: Olde Soldier Books, 1990.

Ilisevich, Robert D. *Galusha A. Grow: The People's Candidate.* Pittsburgh: University of Pittsburgh Press, 1988.

Jennings, W. W. *Transylvania: Pioneer University of the West.* New York: Pageant Press, 1955.

Johannsen, Robert W. *Stephen A. Douglas.* New York: Oxford University Press, 1973.

Johnson, Allen, and Dumas Malone, eds. *The Dictionary of American Biography.* 20 vols. New York: Charles Scribner's Sons, 1928–1936.

Johnson, Edgar. *Charles Dickens: His Tragedy and Triumph.* 2 vols. New York: Simon and Schuster, 1952.

Jones, James P. *"Black Jack": John A. Logan and Southern Illinois in the Civil War Era.* Tallahassee: Florida State University Press, 1967.

Jones, Katherine M. *When Sherman Came: Southern Women and the "Great March."* Indianapolis: Bobbs-Merrill, 1964.

Jordan, David M. *Winfield Scott Hancock: A Soldier's Life.* Bloomington: Indiana University Press, 1988.

Katz, Irving. *August Belmont: A Political Biography.* New York: Columbia University Press, 1968.

Keleher, William A. *Turmoil in New Mexico, 1846–1868.* Santa Fe: Rydal Press, 1952.

Kelley, Brooks M. *Yale: A History.* New Haven: Yale University Press, 1974.

Kellner, George Helmuth. "The German Element on the Urban Frontier." Ph.D. diss., University of Missouri, 1973.

Kirkpatrick, Arthur Roy. "Missouri in the Early Months of the Civil War." *Missouri Historical Review* 55 (April 1961): 235–66.

Kohl, Martha. "Enforcing a Vision of Community: The Role of the Test Oath in Missouri's Reconstruction." *Civil War History* 40 (December 1994): 292–307.

Laas, Virginia Jeans. "Elizabeth Blair Lee: Union Counterpart of Mary Boykin Chesnut." *Journal of Southern History* 50 (August 1984): 385–406.

Laughlin, Sceva B. "Missouri Politics during the Civil War." *Missouri Historical Review* 23 (April 1929): 400–446; 23 (July 1929): 583–618; 24 (October 1929): 87–113; 24 (January 1930): 261–85.

Lavender, David. *Bent's Fort.* Garden City, N.Y.: Doubleday, 1954.

Leslie, Anita. *Lady Randolph Churchill: The Story of Jennie Jerome.* New York: Charles Scribner's Sons, 1969.

———. *The Remarkable Mr. Jerome.* New York: Henry Holt, 1954.

Lewis, Donna May. "The Bents and St. Vrains as Pioneers in the Trade of the Southwest." Master's thesis, University of California–Berkeley, 1924.

Lewis, Lloyd. *Sherman: Fighting Prophet.* New York: Harcourt, Brace, 1932.

Liddell Hart, B. H. *Sherman: Soldier-Realist-American.* New York: Dodd, Mead, 1929.

Long, David E. *The Jewel of Liberty: Abraham Lincoln's Re-election and the End of Slavery.* Mechanicsburg, Pa.: Stackpole Books, 1994.

Lucas, Marion Brunson. *Sherman and the Burning of Columbia.* College Station: Texas A & M University Press, 1976.

Luthin, Reinhard H. *The First Lincoln Campaign.* Cambridge: Harvard University Press, 1944.

———. "Organizing the Republican Party in the 'Border State' Regions: Edward Bates's Presidential Candidacy in 1860." *Missouri Historical Review* 38 (January 1944): 138–61.

March, David D. "Charles Daniel Drake of St. Louis." *The Bulletin (Missouri Historical Society)* 9 (April 1953): 291–310.

———. "The Life and Times of Charles Daniel Drake." Ph.D. diss., University of Missouri, 1949.

Marszalek, John F. "Lincoln's Special Session." *Civil War Times Illustrated* 10 (June 1971): 22–27.

———. *Sherman: A Soldier's Passion for Order.* New York: Free Press, 1992.

———. *Sherman's Other War: The General and the Civil War Press.* Memphis: Memphis State University Press, 1981.

Martin, Cornelia Williams. *The Old Home, 1817–1850.* 2 vols. Auburn, N.Y.: privately published, 1894.

Martin, Ralph G. *Jennie: The Life of Lady Randolph Churchill: The Romantic Years, 1854–1895.* Englewood Cliffs, N.J.: Prentice Hall, 1969.

Mary Loyola, Sister. "The American Occupation of New Mexico, 1821–1852." *New Mexico Historical Review* 14 (April 1939): 159–73.

McCabe, James D., Jr. *The Life and Public Services of Horatio Seymour, Together with a Complete and Authentic Life of Francis P. Blair, Jr.* New York: United States Publishing, 1868.

McClure, Clarence Henry. *Opposition in Missouri to Thomas Hart Benton.* Nashville: George Peabody College for Teachers, 1927.

McDermott, John Francis. *Bingham: River Portraitist.* Norman: University of Oklahoma Press, 1959.

McDonough, James Lee. *Chattanooga—A Death Grip on the Confederacy.* Knoxville: University of Tennessee Press, 1984.

———. *Schofield: Union General in the Civil War and Reconstruction.* Tallahassee: Florida State University Press, 1972.

McElroy, John. *The Struggle for Missouri.* Washington, D.C.: National Tribune, 1913.

McFeely, William S. *Grant: A Biography.* New York: W. W. Norton, 1981.

McKee, Howard I. "The 'Swamp Fox,' Meriwether Jeff Thompson." *Bulletin* 13 (January 1957): 118–34.

Mering, John V. "The Political Transition of James S. Rollins." *Missouri Historical Review* 53 (April 1959): 217–26.

———. *The Whig Party in Missouri.* Columbia: University of Missouri Press, 1967.

Merkel, Benjamin C. "The Anti-Slavery Movement in Missouri, 1819–1865." Ph.D. diss., Washington University, 1939.

———. "The Slavery Issue and the Political Decline of Thomas Hart Benton, 1846–1856." *Missouri Historical Review* 38 (July 1944): 388–407.

Miers, Earl Schenck, ed. *Lincoln Day by Day: A Chronology, 1809–1865.* 3 vols. Washington, D.C.: Lincoln Sesquicentennial Commission, 1960.

———. *The Web of Victory: Grant at Vicksburg.* New York: Alfred A. Knopf, 1955.

Military Order of the Loyal Legion of the United States. *In Memoriam: Samuel Simmons.* N.p., 1901.

Miller, Robert E. "Proud Confederate: Thomas Lowndes Snead of Missouri." *Missouri Historical Review* 79 (January 1985): 167–91.

Million, John W. *State Aid to Railways in Missouri.* Chicago: University of Chicago Press, 1896.

Mitchell, Stewart. *Horatio Seymour of New York.* Cambridge: Harvard University Press, 1938.

Morris, Lloyd. *Incredible New York.* New York: Random House, 1951.

Nevins, Allan. *The Emergence of Lincoln.* 2 vols. New York: Charles Scribner's Sons, 1950.

———. *Fremont: Pathmarker of the West.* New York: Appleton Century Croft, 1939.

———. *The War for the Union.* 4 vols. New York: Charles Scribner's Sons, 1959–1971.

Newton, Joseph Fort. *Lincoln and Herndon.* Cedar Rapids, Iowa: Torch Press, 1910.

Nicklason, Fred. "The Civil War Contracts Committee." *Civil War History* 17 (September 1971): 232–44.

Nicolay, John G., and John Hay. *Abraham Lincoln: A History.* 10 vols. New York: Century, 1890.

Niven, John. *Salmon P. Chase: A Biography.* New York: Oxford University Press, 1955.

Oates, Stephen B. *With Malice toward None: The Life of Abraham Lincoln.* New York: Harper and Row, 1977.

O'Flaherty, Daniel. *General Jo Shelby: Undefeated Rebel.* Chapel Hill: University of North Carolina Press, 1954.

Parrish, William E. *David Rice Atchison of Missouri: Border Politician.* Columbia: University of Missouri Press, 1961.

———. "Fremont in Missouri." *Civil War Times Illustrated* 17 (April 1978): 4–10, 40–45.

———. "General Nathaniel Lyon: A Portrait." *Missouri Historical Review* 49 (October 1954): 1–18.

———. *A History of Missouri: Volume III, 1860 to 1875.* Columbia: University of Missouri Press, 1973.

———. *Missouri under Radical Rule, 1865–1870.* Columbia: University of Missouri Press, 1965.

———. *Turbulent Partnership: Missouri and the Union, 1861–1865.* Columbia: University of Missouri Press, 1963.

Peter, Robert. *History of Fayette County, Kentucky.* Chicago: O. L. Baskin, 1882.

Peterson, Norma Lois. *Freedom and Franchise: The Political Career of B. Gratz Brown.* Columbia: University of Missouri Press, 1965.

Phillips, Christopher. *Damned Yankee: The Life of General Nathaniel Lyon.* Columbia: University of Missouri Press, 1990.

Primm, James Neal. *Lion of the Valley: St. Louis, Missouri.* Boulder: Pruett Publishing, 1981.

———. "Yankee Merchants in a Border City: A Look at St. Louis Businessmen in the 1850s." *Missouri Historical Review* 78 (July 1984): 375–86.

Railey, William E. *History of Woodford County (Kentucky).* Frankfort, Ky.: Roberts Printing, 1938.

Randall, James G. *Lincoln the President.* 3 vols. New York: Dodd, Mead, 1945–1953.

Randall, James G., and Richard N. Current. *Lincoln the President: Last Full Measure.* New York: Dodd, Mead, 1955.

Rawley, James A. *Race and Politics: "Bleeding Kansas" and the Coming of the Civil War.* Philadelphia: Lippincott, 1969.

Reavis, L. U. *The Life and Military Services of General William Selby Harney.* St. Louis: Bryan, Brand, 1878.

Riddleberger, Patrick. *George Washington Julian, Radical Republican: A Study in Nineteenth Century Politics and Reform.* Indianapolis: Indiana Historical Bureau, 1966.

Roed, William. "Secessionist Strength in Missouri." *Missouri Historical Review* 72 (July 1978): 412–23.

Rolle, Andrew. *John Charles Fremont: Character as Destiny.* Norman: University of Oklahoma Press, 1991.

Rombauer, Robert J. *The Union Cause in St. Louis in 1861.* St. Louis: Nixon-Jones Printing, 1909.

Ross, Earle Dudley. *The Liberal Republican Movement.* New York: Henry Holt, 1919.

Ryle, Walter Harrington. *Missouri: Union or Secession.* Nashville: George Peabody College for Teachers, 1931.

———. "Slavery and Party Realignment in Missouri in the State Election of 1856." *Missouri Historical Review* 39 (April 1945): 320–32.

Saalberg, Harvey. "The *Westliche Post* of St. Louis: A Daily Newspaper for German-Americans, 1857–1938." Ph.D. diss., University of Missouri, 1967.

Scharf, John Thomas. *History of St. Louis City and County.* 2 vols. Philadelphia: Louis H. Everts, 1883.

Schweiner, Lucy M. "The St. Louis Public Schools at the Outbreak of the Civil War." *Bulletin* 13 (October 1956): 11–22.

Shalhope, Robert E. *Sterling Price: Portrait of a Southerner.* Columbia: University of Missouri Press, 1971.

Sharkey, Robert P. *Money, Class, and Party.* Baltimore: Johns Hopkins University Press, 1959.

Silbey, Joel. *A Responsible Minority: The Democratic Party in the Civil War Era, 1860–1868.* New York: Norton, 1977.

Simpson, Brooks D. *Ulysses S. Grant and the Politics of War and Reconstruction, 1861–1868.* Chapel Hill: University of North Carolina Press, 1991.

Smith, Donnal V. *Chase and Civil War Politics.* Columbus: Ohio Historical Collections, 1931.

Smith, Elbert B. *Francis Preston Blair.* New York: Free Press, 1980.

———. *Magnificent Missourian: The Life of Thomas Hart Benton.* Philadelphia: Lippincott, 1958.

———. "Worthy of the Steel of Our Best." *Missouri Historical Review* 56 (July 1962): 315–18.

Smith, George Winston. "New England Business Interests in Missouri during the Civil War." *Missouri Historical Review* 41 (October 1946): 1–18.

Smith, William Benjamin. *James Sidney Rollins, Memoir.* New York: DeVinne Press, 1891.

Smith, William E. *The Francis Preston Blair Family in Politics.* 2 vols. New York: Macmillan, 1933.

Snider, William D. *Light on the Hill: A History of the University of North Carolina at Chapel Hill.* Chapel Hill: University of North Carolina Press, 1992.

Spencer, Donald S. *Louis Kossuth and Young America: A Study of Sectionalism and Foreign Policy, 1848–1852.* Columbia: University of Missouri Press, 1977.

Sproat, John. *"The Best Men": Liberal Reformers in the Gilded Age.* New York: Oxford University Press, 1968.

Stevens, Walter B. "Lincoln and Missouri." *Missouri Historical Review* 10 (January 1916): 63–119.

———, ed. *The Brown-Reynolds Duel: A Complete Documentary Chronicle of the Last Bloodshed under the Code between St. Louisans.* St. Louis: Franklin Club, 1911.

————. *St. Louis, the Fourth City.* 3 vols. St. Louis: S. J. Clark Publishing, 1909.

Summers, Mark W. *The Press Gang: Newspapers and Politics, 1865–1878.* Chapel Hill: University of North Carolina Press, 1994.

Tap, Bruce. "Reconstructing Emancipation's Martyr: John C. Fremont and the Joint Committee on the Conduct of the War." *Gateway Heritage* 14 (spring 1994): 36–53.

Tasher, Lucy Lucile. "The *Missouri Democrat* and the Civil War." *Missouri Historical Review* 31 (July 1937): 402–19.

Taylor, Joe Gray. *Louisiana Reconstructed, 1863–1877.* Baton Rouge: Louisiana State University Press, 1974.

Thomas, Benjamin. *Abraham Lincoln: A Biography.* New York: Alfred A. Knopf, 1952.

Thorp, Willard, ed. *The Lives of Eighteen from Princeton.* Princeton: Princeton University Press, 1946.

Thurman, A. L., Jr. "Ratification Speaking in Missouri in 1860." *Missouri Historical Review* 56 (July 1962): 365–79.

Trefousse, Hans L. *Benjamin Franklin Wade: Radical Republican from Ohio.* New York: Twayne, 1963.

————. *Carl Schurz: A Biography.* Knoxville: University of Tennessee Press, 1982.

————. "The Joint Committee on the Conduct of the War: A Reassessment." *Civil War History* 10 (March 1964): 5–19.

————. *The Radical Republicans.* New York: Alfred A. Knopf, 1969.

Trezevant, Daniel Heyward. *The Burning of Columbia, South Carolina: A Review of Northern Assertions and Southern Facts.* Columbia: South Carolinian Power Press, 1866.

Tunnell, Ted. *Crucible of Reconstruction: War, Radicalism and Race in Louisiana, 1862–1877.* Baton Rouge: Louisiana State University Press, 1984.

Turkoly-Jozik, Robert L. "Fremont and the Western Department." *Missouri Historical Review* 82 (July 1988): 363–85.

Twitchell, Ralph Emerson. *The History of the Military Occupation of the Territory of New Mexico from 1846 to 1851 by the Government of the United States.* Denver: Brooks-Smith, 1909.

Ulbricht, John H. "Frank P. Blair and Missouri Politics." Master's thesis, University of Missouri, 1936.

Van Ravenswaay, Charles. "Lafayette Park." *Bulletin* 14 (July 1958): 369–77.

————. "Years of Turmoil, Years of Growth: St. Louis in the 1850s." *Bulletin* 23 (July 1967): 303–24.

Vogle, George E. *The Life and Death of James L. Blair: Original General Counsel of the Louisiana Purchase Exposition*. St. Louis: n.p., 1904.

Volpe, Vernon L. "The Fremonts and Emancipation in Missouri." *Historian* 56 (winter 1994): 339–54.

Wallace, Doris Davis. "The Political Campaign of 1860 in Missouri." *Missouri Historical Review* 70 (January 1976): 162–83.

Warden, Robert Bruce. *An Account of the Private Life and Public Services of Salmon Portland Chase*. Cincinnati: Wilstack, Baldwin, 1874.

Warner, Ezra J. *Generals in Blue: Lives of the Union Military Commanders*. Baton Rouge: Louisiana State University Press, 1964.

Weigley, Russell F. *Quartermaster General of the Union Army: A Biography of M. C. Meigs*. New York: Columbia University Press, 1959.

Welcher, Frank J. *The Union Army, 1861–1865: Organization and Operations*. 2 vols. Bloomington: Indiana University Press, 1989–1993.

Wertenbaker, Thomas Jefferson. *Princeton: 1746–1896*. Princeton: Princeton University Press, 1946.

White, Horace. *The Life of Lyman Trumbull*. Boston: Houghton Mifflin, 1913.

Williams, T. Harry. *Lincoln and the Radicals*. Madison: University of Wisconsin Press, 1941.

Wilson, James Harrison. *The Life and Services of Brevet Brigadier-General Andrew Jonathan Alexander, United States Army*. New York: n.p., 1887.

Winschel, Terrence J. "The First Honor at Vicksburg: The 1st Battalion, 13th U.S. Infantry." *Civil War Regiments* 2 (1992): 1–16.

Wood, Forrest G. *Black Scare: The Racist Response to Emancipation and Reconstruction*. Berkeley and Los Angeles: University of California Press, 1970.

Wood, James Madison, Jr. "James Sidney Rollins of Missouri: A Political Biography." Ph.D. diss., Stanford University, 1951.

Woodward, Ashbel. *Life of General Nathaniel Lyon*. Hartford: Case, Lockwood, 1862.

Wurthman, Leonard B., Jr. "Frank Blair: Lincoln's Congressional Spokesman." *Missouri Historical Review* 64 (April 1970): 263–88.

———. "Frank Blair of Missouri: Jacksonian Orator of the Civil War Era." Ph.D. diss., University of Missouri, 1969.

Younger, Edward. *John A. Kasson: Politics and Diplomacy from Lincoln to McKinley*. Iowa City: Historical Society of Iowa, 1955.

Zornow, William Frank. *Lincoln and the Party Divided*. Norman: University of Oklahoma Press, 1954.

Index